Hammer and Rifle

MODERN WAR STUDIES

16.00

Hammer and Rifle
The Militarization of the
Soviet Union, 1926–1933

David R. Stone

 University Press of Kansas

Published by the University Press of Kansas (Lawrence, Kansas 66049), which was
organized by the Kansas Board of Regents and is operated and funded by Emporia
State University, Fort Hays State University, Kansas State University, Pittsburg State
University, the University of Kansas, and Wichita State University.

Library of Congress Cataloging-in-Publication Data

Stone, David R., 1968–
    Hammer and rifle : the militarization of the Soviet Union, 1926–1933 / David R. Stone.
        p. cm. — (Modern war studies)
    Includes bibliographical references and index.
    ISBN 0-7006-1037-5 (cloth : alk. paper)
    1. Soviet Union—Defenses.   2. Soviet Union—Armed Forces—Appropriations
and expenditures.   3. Civil-military relations—Soviet Union.   4. Soviet Union—
Politics and government—1917–1936.   I. Title.   II. Series.
UA770.S863 2000
355'.033047'09041—dc21   00-028314

British Library Cataloguing in Publication Data is available.

Printed in the United States of America
10 9 8 7 6 5 4 3 2 1

The paper used in this publication meets the minimum requirements of the American
National Standard for Permanence of Paper for Printed Library Materials Z39.48-1984.

Contents

Acknowledgments

It is my great pleasure to thank those who assisted me in this project. The personnel of the State Archive of the Russian Federation, Russian State Archive of the Economy, Russian Center for the Preservation and Study of Documents of Contemporary History, and Russian State Military Archive, especially Liudmila Dvoinikh, Vera Mikhaleva, and Nonna Tarkhova, were exceedingly helpful in my search for archival materials. The staff of the Russian State Library and State Public Historical Library were also unstinting with their assistance. Jeffrey Burds, Mary Habeck, and Lonia Vaintraub provided invaluable archival advice.

My Moscow research was supported by generous grants from the MacArthur and Smith-Richardson Foundations through Yale's International Security Studies. Ann Carter-Drier and Florence Thomas dealt with numerous crises with aplomb.

Many colleagues read this work in whole or in part, or provided valuable commentary in response to conference papers. They include Jeffrey Burds, Paul Bushkovitch, Julian Cooper, Jonathan Haslam, Paul Kennedy, Steven Main, Bruce Menning, Steven M. Miner, William Odom, Heather Ruland, Fernande Scheid, Jennifer Siegel, Mark Steinberg, Jeremi Suri, and an anonymous reviewer. Many more friends, Russian and Western, helped maintain my sanity during my Moscow research; I am deeply grateful to all of them.

I began this project before I met my wife, Kristin. Though I managed to start it without the benefit of her love and support, I do not think I could have finished it. It is dedicated to her.

Introduction

From 1926 to 1933, a vast transformation swept through the Soviet state, economy, and society, a transformation as stark in its changes and as far-reaching in its implications as the simultaneous and better-known revolutions shaking Soviet society. While collectivization changed the face of the Soviet countryside, and Joseph Stalin quashed dissent both within and without the Bolshevik party to turn it into a tool of his personal rule, a military-industrial revolution transformed the Soviet Union into an immensely powerful war machine. The militarization of the Soviet economy and political system, marked by increased control from the center, a substantial role for the military in making policy, and a large and growing defense industry, was an essential element of Stalin's revolution from above.

The story of the late 1920s and early 1930s is of the steady and inexorable destruction of every barrier to massive rearmament in the USSR. This destruction had multiple roots growing out of ideology, Soviet social tensions and the paranoid nature of Bolshevik politics, and finally Stalin's struggle to build a coalition and destroy his enemies. Bolshevik ideology perceived the world as an unremittingly hostile place, demanding constant vigilance as the price of survival. At the same time, Soviet military thinkers saw a ruthlessly centralized economy as the only means of successfully waging war. The growing technological complexity of warfare required the total organization of state and society, especially in a country as backward in its infrastructure and industrial development as Soviet Russia. These intellectual constructions, however, were based on foundations of social conflict and political strife that supported ever-greater defense spending and increasing military domination of the civilian economy.

In the mid-1920s, the Red Army suffered from paltry funding and commensurately low procurement of weaponry and equipment. Little touched by technical advances, it was still a World War I army centered around infantry, artillery, and cavalry. The economic infrastructure that supported it bore the scars of seven years

1

of war and revolution. Factory machinery had been so overused during the frantic days of the First World War that what was not obsolete was worn beyond service-ability. During the Russian civil war, hunger and unemployment had forced urban workers to return to their roots in the countryside simply to eat, depopulating Russia's cities, and the war's fluid fronts devastated factories as it swept over them. With the end of war, many of the factories that had churned out arms for the tsar lay idle, as their workers either abandoned the factories for lack of orders to fill or produced consumer goods to cover the shortfall left by scarce govern-ment contracts. The Bolsheviks running Soviet industry paid little attention to military production, and those planners responsible for preparing the Soviet economy for war were caught in a web of bureaucracy, leaving the USSR com-pletely unprepared for potential conflicts. The highest-ranking Bolsheviks had concerns other than building up the Red Army; sorting out their own political struggles and securing themselves against popular discontent took precedence over rearmament.[1]

All had changed by 1933. Military budgets were high and growing steadily, while great quantities of ordnance flowed into the Red Army's warehouses and armories. The Red Army's equipment was among the most advanced in the world, with its BT tank in particular representing the state of the art, much as the T-34 tank would in 1941. With research and development fortified by technical assis-tance and models purchased from the developed West, the Soviet military was the most modern in the world, at least as measured by the size and technological sophistication of its aviation and tank park. Military factories that had produced arms since the time of Peter the Great were now expanding, while new plants across the breadth of the Soviet Union pumped out shell casings, explosives, powder, and rifle cartridges. The Soviets had built a tank industry from scratch, and 4,000 tanks rolled out factory gates each year in Leningrad, Kharkov, and Moscow. Defense plant managers breathed easier, knowing that their plants would have first priority in the allocation of scarce raw materials, skilled labor, and rail transport, while their rank-and-file workers would no longer find that working in military industry meant a cut in pay. The USSR, thanks to the First Five-Year Plan, now produced the foundations of a modern war economy: steel, railroads, electricity, chemicals. A sizable bureaucracy within Soviet industry not only allocated peace-time defense orders among military plants and assured quality but also created detailed economic plans and industrial mobilization schedules for the war to come. The lines dividing military and civil sectors grew increasingly blurred. At the top, Joseph Stalin himself now kept close control over defense policy by participating in the regular meetings of the USSR's defense cabinet chaired by his closest henchman, Viacheslav Molotov.

In short, the USSR's military economy had been transformed beyond recogni-tion in less than a decade. This military-industrial revolution went beyond the industrialization of the First Five-Year Plan to change the Red Army itself and the political structures that governed the Soviet state. The system established during this period, giving military concerns priority in economic policy and ensuring that the Red Army would never want for funds, would last far beyond 1933. It continued in its essentials through the fall of the Soviet Union, but this military-industrial revolution exacted a terrible price for the power it gave the Soviet state. It bequeathed a bloated and inefficient defense sector to the Soviet economy that worsened Soviet stagnation and hinders economic reform in Russia today. This book describes that revolution.[2]

Bolshevik rhetoric was dominated by the conviction that war with the capitalist world was inevitable—sooner or later, an epic clash of social systems would occur. From the earliest days of Soviet power, the Bolshevik leadership believed that the outbreak of war was imminent. Lenin's Brest-Litovsk peace treaty with Germany in 1918 was not a permanent end to war but a desperate attempt to gain "breathing space" for the revolution. On 7 March 1918, Lenin told the party's Seventh Congress that "international imperialism, with its capital's entire might, with its highly organised military technique . . . could not under any circumstances, on any condition, live side by side with the Soviet Republic." Frantically trying to convince his own party that the only alternative to certain destruction was ratification of a peace agreement with Germany, however draconian the terms, Lenin explained that there was no way of knowing if the breathing space would last a week, two weeks, or more. Any chance to recover before the final struggle, however brief, was "the greatest good."[3]

Even in 1920, with civil war victory near, Lenin and the Bolsheviks could be certain only that their breathing space would be "longer and stronger" than hoped for in 1918, but "this is still no more than a breathing space." With the capitalist world arming itself, the USSR's task was preparing for the battle to come. As Lenin remarked in "'Left-Wing' Communism—An Infantile Disorder," the Russian Revolution had served as a beacon and inspiration to proletarians throughout the world and, as a result, had earned the enmity of bourgeois states. In June 1920, he said "world political developments are of necessity concentrated on a single focus, the struggle of the world bourgeoisie against the Soviet Russian Republic." By May 1921, Lenin could recognize that the immediate threat had receded and Soviet Russia could exploit divisions within the capitalist world, but he maintained that the ultimate danger still remained.[4]

The resolutions of the Bolshevik party's Fourteenth Conference declared in April 1925 that "bourgeois Europe is pregnant with new imperialist wars." As long as "two opposing social systems" existed in the world, there would always be a "constant threat of capitalist blockade, other forms of economic pressure, armed intervention, [and] restoration [of the capitalist system]." Until revolution had created other socialist states, the Soviet Union's security could never be guaranteed.[5] The same year, the Fourteenth Congress applauded the Central Committee's policy that had led the USSR to "receive new diplomatic recognition from a series of capitalist states, conclude with them a series of new trade agreements and concessions, increase the volume of its foreign trade, and strengthen its international position," but at the same time, it found that "the contradictions between these two social systems are not weakening, but growing." The very recovery the Soviet economy enjoyed made it more vulnerable to external pressure, and the political and social stabilization of Europe only increased bourgeois domination. The Locarno system, directing German expansionism east toward the Soviet Union, clearly displayed the West's unremitting hostility. The only reasonable policy, the congress concluded, "was to provide the USSR with economic independence, shielding the USSR from transformation into an appendage of the capitalist world economy, by means of a course towards the industrialization of the country, the development of the production of means of production, and the formation of reserves for economic maneuver."[6]

Stalin carried on Lenin's belief in the world bourgeoisie's unremitting hatred for the USSR. In 1925, he saw that the world's balance of power made temporary coexistence possible, though this respite was only for the short term. A year later, he argued that "to think that the capitalist world can look with indifference on our successes on the economic front, successes that revolutionize the working class of the whole world, is to succumb to an illusion."[7] Leon Trotsky and his sympathizers were no less adamant than Stalin about the danger of war with the capitalist world, though they might have agreed with him on little else. Committed to the need for world revolution to ensure the survival of socialism in the Soviet Union, they could hardly believe anything else. Trotsky declared in September 1927 that "a war of the imperialists against the Soviet Union is not only probable but inevitable."[8]

This universal Bolshevik belief in the inevitability of war with world capitalism occasionally crossed over into advocacy of revolutionary war: spreading socialism by force of arms. Richard Pipes finds a "monotony suggestive of sincerity" in Bolshevik insistence that revolution must eventually spread. Mikhail Tukhachevskii's failure to capture Warsaw in 1920, combined with Bolshevik shock that Polish workers and peasants would join their Polish bourgeois oppressors in a national struggle against the Russians, had disabused many within the party of revolutionary war's feasibility. Still, some military theorists harbored hopes that the bayonet would prove the most useful instrument in socialism's toolbox. Mikhail Frunze, for example, argued that, as a revolutionary ideology, Bolshevism could have only a fundamentally offensive military doctrine, that its doctrine "cannot *not* be active in the very highest degree." Though the balance of forces might often be against the Soviet army, it could find ways to even the odds by allying itself with the oppressed classes of the enemy state.[9]

The Great Depression only deepened Bolshevik conviction that the final crisis of capitalism was near. Even in the midst of domestic economic chaos, the capitalist West could turn its armies against the Soviet state in an attempt to save itself. Valerian Kuibyshev, chair of Vesenkha, the Soviet Ministry of Industry, wrote in *Izvestiia* in early 1930 that the imperialists are preparing for war with us. They are mobilizing against us all the forces they can use for this goal. From regular armies to fascist and police organizations, from the Roman pope to our village kulak, from the open White Guards abroad to the wreckers at home—everything has been mobilized by the imperialists everywhere, by all open and secret means, in order to rip up the building of socialism on one-sixth of the earth's surface, break the defense preparedness of the USSR and make their victory easier.

The Soviet Union had to take advantage of the breathing space it had been offered to prepare for this confrontation.[10] Such statements were not just for public consumption. Stalin wrote to Molotov in September 1930 that Poland was assembling an alliance of Baltic states for a war against the USSR: "as soon as they've put this bloc together, they'll start to fight." He thought the situation called for an expansion of the Soviet wartime army by forty to fifty divisions and the Soviet peacetime force from 640,000 to 700,000 men.[11]

This overarching worldview was an ideological conclusion supported by the concrete experience of hundreds of thousands of Bolsheviks who had fought in the Russian civil war and whose formative ordeal as party members was a desperate struggle for survival against domestic counterrevolution and foreign intervention. Their experience supported the intellectual consensus among military and economic thinkers that the next war would inevitably be total, eliminating the distinction between front and rear. All of society would be involved in the war effort, and only comprehensive state direction could achieve success. The logic was clear: the outside world was both a terrible threat to the Soviet state and a glowing opportunity, should the occasion arise, to spread the revolution by force. To emerge victorious from the next war, society and economy would have to be centrally directed to maximize the amount of resources that could be brought to bear. The extent of this consensus is difficult to overstate. No Bolshevik leader ever publicly questioned that the outside world was fundamentally hostile, nor that the state had to assume a comprehensive peacetime role by permeating industrial administration with a network of war planners. Differences might arise over how pressing any particular foreign threat was, or how precisely to implement state control over all defense preparations. Industrial managers and military officers would struggle bitterly over details of production and investment but not over those basic assumptions of Bolshevik foreign and security policy.

These ideological seeds fell on fertile social ground. Social tensions between technical experts from the old regime and upwardly mobile Bolshevik cadres combined with a political culture poisoned by denunciation and paranoia to speed the militarization of the Soviet economy. Constant purges and witch-hunts for saboteurs, wreckers, and spies created an atmosphere in which conservatism in economic planning or resistance to grandiose production schemes, from Moscow ministries down to the factory floor, was highly dangerous. Arrests of key industrial personnel disrupted production and thereby created more evidence that saboteurs must be at work, mandating further arrests. This vicious circle of purge, chaos, and purge made moderation in defense planning criminal.[12]

One might reasonably argue that all of Soviet industry suffered from this vicious infighting and the chaos it produced. The essential difference between military industry and other branches, however, was that the Red Army acted for defense factories as a taskmaster, customer, and patron of immense influence. When defense industry was disrupted by wrecking and its subsequent purges, the Soviet military could provide the material means and political lobbying to make things right. In Janos Kornai's classic formulation, firms in socialist economies are fundamentally constrained by resources (whereas capitalist firms are constrained by demand), and the political imperative of expansion creates "investment hunger." Essential decisions on the allocation of investment capital, or even the distribution of scarce physical inputs, are made administratively, not through a market. The conclusion is that investment flows to sectors most able to mobilize political support.[13] This phenomenon gave defense industry, unlike other sectors of the Soviet economy, an immensely powerful lobby in Moscow, ensuring a disproportionate share of scarce resources. Put another way, all Stalinist industry suffered from self-inflicted wounds; the Red Army had the power to guarantee that its favorite patient received the necessary medication.

The same cycle of purge, disruption, and remedial action plagued the top management of Soviet industry. The three men who in this period ran Vesenkha, the de facto Soviet ministry of industry, all came from the party-state's organs of discipline and control. Feliks Dzerzhinskii, founder of the Cheka secret police, assumed command of Vesenkha in 1924 and ran it until his death in 1926. His replacement, Valerian Kuibyshev, came to Vesenkha from Rabkrin, the Workers'-Peasants' Inspectorate devoted to ferreting out incompetence, inefficiency, and malfeasance.[14] Sergo Ordzhonikidze, Kuibyshev's successor at Rabkrin, did such a good job finding corruption and disorder in Kuibyshev's Vesenkha that he got Kuibyshev removed and took over Vesenkha himself, bringing a cohort of Rabkrin inspectors with him to run his new domain.

Within Vesenkha, those running military industry were just as vulnerable to suspicion. Petr Bogdanov, in charge of defense industry until 1925, was sent in disgrace to a post in the North Caucasus for his poor stewardship. He was replaced by Varlaam Avanesov, a protégé of Dzerzhinskii and a veteran Cheka operative. Avanesov was forced to retire due to poor health, but his successor, Aleksandr Tolokontsev, was driven from office under a cloud for permitting sabotage—"wrecking"—on his watch. Tolokontsev was eventually replaced by Ivan Pavlunovskii, another Cheka veteran who came to industry from Rabkrin along with his patron Ordzhonikidze.

The pattern is clear. In deciding who should run industry and remedy incompetent or criminal management, Stalin's Politburo turned to those who had uncovered that malfeasance: those trained and experienced in investigation, punishment, and terror. Industry's personnel had to be compelled to perform, especially the "bourgeois specialists," technicians and engineers inherited from the tsarist regime. Although this was a general phenomenon in Soviet industry, again, the Red Army's power as an institution and its leadership's close personal relationship with Stalin meant that defense industry would receive the funding, technology, and access to resources it needed to overcome the damage done by purges and arrests.

The nature of Stalinist politics generated still another impetus to rapid rearmament: the destruction of the one group advocating limits to military spending. When Stalin defeated the loosely organized Bolshevik Right led by Nikolai Bukharin, Aleksei Rykov, and Mikhail Tomskii, he removed not only his last competitors for power but also the last of the Bolshevik elites restraining Soviet defense spending in the name of balanced budgets and fiscal orthodoxy. Previous work on the Right has focused on Bukharin as its charismatic and prolific intellectual leader and on the peasant question as the key issue dividing the Right from Stalin and his followers. This study suggests a modified view of the Right: Rykov was as important as Bukharin, perhaps more, to the Right's political fortunes. The Red Army's unwavering support for Stalin in the political battles of the late 1920s came from the wrath People's Commissar for Military Affairs Kliment Voroshilov felt toward Rykov. Rykov, chair of the Soviet defense cabinet, the RZ STO, had to impose fiscal discipline by blocking Voroshilov's constantly growing budget requests. Voroshilov's resentments ensured that the Red Army remained reliably behind Stalin in his struggle for total power.

After social conflicts within Soviet defense industry boosted the capital flowing into rearmament, and the Red Army had solidified its position as a key element in Stalin's coalition, crisis abroad provided the catalyst that turned rapid growth in military spending into a full-blown war economy. The general Bolshevik fear of *eventual* war with the capitalist world did not mean that the Soviet government always saw conflict as *imminent.*[15] The 1931 crisis triggered by Japan's occupation of Manchuria, however, pushed Stalin and the rest of the Soviet leadership into a state of near panic. While frantically attempting to head off conflict with Japan in Siberia by diplomatic means, the Soviet Union simultaneously engaged in an equally desperate attempt to build up its defenses by rapidly scaling up armaments production to put its economy on a war footing. In the wake of the Manchurian crisis, Soviet defense production remained at a half-war, half-peace level. Military industry never scaled back once the crisis had passed, and it finally managed to accelerate *again* with the approach of World War II. The mobilized economy created by the Manchurian crisis solidified the militarization of the Soviet Union.

Describing this process as militarization requires some caution. *Militarism* as a term can be as pejorative and vague as *imperialism;* additionally, it smacks of waging the cold war over again. Judicious care in defining terms, however, allows militarization to serve as a useful conceptual tool encompassing a number of particular Soviet phenomena, and providing some comparative insight. Several thinkers exploring the nature of militarized societies have neglected the Soviet Union, distorting their attempts to generalize about the nature of militarization.[16] Such omissions are understandable; as Mark Von Hagen correctly reminds us, "the Soviet state . . . can by no means be reduced to a simple version of the garrison state; it was always much more than that."[17] But while Stalin's Soviet Union was indeed more than a garrison state, its military nature was fundamental.

Admittedly, the Soviet Union fits awkwardly at best into some understandings of militarization, in terms of both definition (what militarization means) and causation (how militarization comes about). Many authors use the terms *militarism* and *militarization* interchangeably, but under John Gillis's definition of militarism[18]—rule by military officers—the Soviet Union does not qualify. It was never governed by officers, though most of Stalin's inner circle did have civil war experience. The Soviet state demonstrated repeatedly, most spectacularly in 1937, that the military's high command could be used and disposed of at will. Throughout the USSR's history, the Soviet leadership was able to keep its military power firmly subjugated to political authority.

The earliest thinkers on militarism, writing before World War I fully demonstrated the industrial nature of modern warfare, exaggerated the importance of personnel policy at the expense of economics. Details of conscription, universal service, and military obligation crowded aside issues of industrial and organizational preparations for war. This made militarism an atavistic phenomenon, one antithetical to industrial society. Herbert Spencer explicitly contrasted the authoritarian, centralized, hierarchical "militant type of society" with the "fundamentally-unlike" enlightened, liberal, industrial society. In 1906, Otto Hintze focused on the progressive effects of universal military service in expanding the franchise and democratizing society. In both Prussia and Russia, he found, universal military service was leading to a convergence between military and industrial societies.[19] In addition to being sadly mistaken about societal progress and the opposition of military and industrial society, these models miss the vital economic dimension of militarization in general and its Soviet variant in particular.

Other criteria of militarization, appropriate to other societies, are simply inapplicable to the Soviet case. The military's usurpation of control over defense and foreign policy from elected representatives as carried out in Wilhelmine Germany lacks resonance in the USSR. Elected representatives had no authority to usurp.[20] Proposed causes of militarization are equally problematic. Crude attempts to blame militarization on press magnates selling newspapers or rapacious industrialists eager for arms sales, variants on the *Merchants of Death* thesis, are entirely out of place in a state without capitalists. William McNeill makes a much subtler argument for a "feedback loop" between economic interest groups and technological change in the origins of European military-industrial complexes, but his model is still dependent on voters pushing for increased public spending and industrialists eager for profits, two elements absent from Soviet society.[21]

Stalin's Soviet Union falls awkwardly between the two variants of militarism Volker Berghahn describes. The first, found in preindustrial and industrializing societies, revolves around an exclusive military caste and a pervasive military spirit in culture. While military phrases occupied a central place in Bolshevik political language and culture, Stalin's Soviet Union lacked a military caste. Bolsheviks moved easily and often between military and civil posts during the civil war, a phenomenon that continued into the interwar period. This fluidity is more characteristic of Berghahn's second variant of militarism, one applicable to industrialized, technologically sophisticated societies. Here, military and civilian elites exist in a kind of symbiosis, but in a structure that combines mass consumption and push-button warfare. While those characteristics might have been relevant to Leonid Brezhnev's USSR, they were alien to Stalin's.

As this study of the political dynamics of Stalinism will make clear, a definition of militarization that excludes Stalin's Soviet Union is necessarily incomplete, and a theory of causation inapplicable to the USSR needs modification. Fortunately, the Soviet Union epitomizes the understanding of militarization employed by the most recent scholarship. "Militarization is," in Gillis's words, "less a thing than a process," involving the organization of society for violence. This "pervasive economic, cultural, and psychological mobilization for war" has many aspects, but one of the most vital is the progressive breakdown of distinctions between military and civil spheres through a "comprehensive, managerial effort at national organization."[22] The ultimate result is a society organized for war and lacking clear boundaries between military and civil life.

The breakdown of distinctions between military and civil spheres can take many forms. One is the transfer of military culture and such values as hierarchy, obedience, and sacrifice to civilian life.[23] The briefest acquaintance with Stalinist political language finds it awash with campaigns, battles, and fronts—military phrases for civil life growing directly from the legacy of the civil war. Although Stalinism never glorified struggle in the same way Italian fascism or German Nazism did—armed struggle was a means to an end for the Bolsheviks, not an end in itself—the importance of militarized culture to understanding Stalinism is undeniable. Von Hagen's pathbreaking work on the cultural and social legacy of demobilized soldiers for the nascent Soviet state demonstrates the military themes of Soviet political culture clearly. This book serves as a complement to Von Hagen's discussion of "militarized socialism." Its attention focuses on the increasing military role in the Soviet economy and the importance of burgeoning defense spending to building and maintaining Stalin's political domination.

The decay of barriers between military and civilian spheres is amply displayed in Stalin's inner circle. This is not merely a matter of style or Stalin's affection for uniforms. Among the Stalinist elite, there was a shared assumption of the necessary and unbreakable link between industrialization and military power. As

Stalin solidified his own grasp on power, the military took an increasing role in Soviet industry, while economic administrators grew more and more amenable to military demands. This does not mean that the military high command always agreed with civilian authority on every issue, but in *this* period among *this* group on *these* issues of industrialization and rearmament, the consensus on economic development and military power as complementary goals was remarkably strong.[24]

In a larger context, what Soviet militarization seems to have in common with the processes at work in the interwar period in other militarized (albeit to a lesser degree) societies is the changing nature of warfare. The industrial requirements of modern war and the rapid pace of technological change affected the United States, Japan, Germany, France, the United Kingdom, and the Soviet Union. The lessons of World War I, that victory required comprehensive peacetime organization and planning, were the same for all. What distinguished the Soviet Union, far ahead of the pack in 1933 in the extent of its militarization, was not so much the presence of any particular factor but the absense of any effective checks on militarization. As outlined earlier, the social and political nature of Stalinism eliminated forces pushing against untrammeled militarization, allowing Bolshevik ideology, intellectual consensus on the need for military control over the civilian economy, genuine but exaggerated foreign threats, and military desires to produce the complete militarization of the Soviet economy.[25]

A history of Stalinism that does not incorporate its military side must be incomplete. Understanding the origins of the total claim the Bolsheviks made on Soviet society is just one example. This is not to refight the old battles of totalitarian and revisionist interpretations. I am not referring to total control over Soviet society, which Stalin did not have, but instead to his total *claim* on society. In the early 1920s, Soviet military theorists were already arguing for the complete merging of state and military spheres to wage and win modern war. Military theory and the Red Army's plans for the USSR dovetailed neatly with Bolshevism's already existing tendency to absorb all of society's institutions within the party-state. The particular phenomenon of the extreme centralization of economic management under Stalin is also incomprehensible without taking into account the assumption that centralized control was a military necessity.

This marks one of the signal differences between the Soviet Union and its tsarist predecessor. Russia's vulnerable frontiers, multiethnic population, and discontented peasantry always produced a large military establishment.[26] The Russian Empire, however, never displayed the same kind of urge to inject military control over industry in preparing for war, as witnessed by its performance in the First World War. Not only were the terrible demands of modern warfare not yet clear, but a difference in culture made the late Russian Empire's military planning very different from the Soviet Union's. To borrow George Yaney's phrase, Bolshevik military and economic planners displayed an "urge to mobilize," to end the chaos, randomness, and mess of Russian economy and society and impose a new order to make the economy a smoothly running mechanism for producing military hardware. The militarization of the Soviet Union was, as a result, far greater in degree and in kind than anything in tsarist Russia.[27] The dichotomy was so great that Soviet military-economic planners found only negative lessons to draw from tsarist Russia's experiences in World War I and turned to German, British, and American models to learn how to organize. In only one respect was Soviet militarization more restrained than its tsarist precursor: the interwar Soviet Union never entertained pretensions to a powerful, blue-water navy as the tsars had.

In the case of collectivization as well, the military side of the story is essential to understanding the political history of Stalinism. Scholars have long been aware of rumors of Red Army resistance to mass collectivization. Roger Reese's work on the social history of the Red Army has shown conclusively that at least the rank-and-file soldiers were alarmed and indignant at what was happening to their families in the countryside. Why, then, did the Red Army's high command not stand against Stalin with Nikolai Bukharin and the Bolshevik Right, a loose grouping of those supporting a moderate policy toward the Soviet peasantry? As Reese frames the issue, "why Bukharin did not ally himself with the generals is a question that cannot yet be answered with any certainty."[28]

The solution to Reese's puzzle, as suggested earlier, cannot be found without a thorough understanding of Soviet defense. The stumbling block in an alliance between the Right and the Red Army, this book suggests, was not Bukharin but his ally Aleksei Rykov, Soviet head of government as chair of the Council of People's Commissars. The nebulous Bolshevik Right was linked as much by a commitment to fiscal orthodoxy and balanced development as by a soft line toward the Soviet peasantry. As a result, Rykov, and Dzerzhinskii before him, defended balanced budgets through the late 1920s. This was incompatible with rapid military expansion. Rykov's repeated efforts to foil Kliment Voroshilov, the people's commissar for military affairs, in his pushes for higher spending on the Red Army led to considerable animosity. Rykov and Bukharin's conspicuous lack of experience on the fronts of the civil war only made matters worse, throwing their commitment to Soviet patriotism into question. As Stephen Cohen has noted, "the warfare themes of nascent Stalinism were central to the struggle between Bukharin and Stalin." To the Red Army's high command, Rykov represented opposition to building Soviet defenses, and there could be no question of allying with him and Bukharin against Stalin.[29]

This book traces the narrative of a revolution with its political and social dynamics. This military-industrial revolution was partly a result of Stalin's revolution from above and partly a motivation for it. Without the imperatives of the defense economy, industrialization would have come more slowly and aimed at different goals. But even members of the Red Army's high command were surprised by the profound ways that industrial growth could change the way they made war. Their appetite whetted by a taste of the goods that industrialization could produce, they pushed the Stalin revolution further. In perhaps the crowning irony of the entire story, Stalin's military-industrial revolution, intended to ensure the security of the Soviet socialist state, went so far in committing the Soviet Union to rapidly obsolete technology and draining resources from productive investment that it nearly brought about the destruction of the Soviet Union in World War II. Though the Soviet state managed to survive the war, so did its bloated defense sector. Soviet defense industry ultimately contributed to the failure of the socialist experiment. The Soviet Union's military burden worsened the economic stagnation of the Brezhnev era and made Mikhail Gorbachev's desperate attempts to repair the system doomed to failure.

1

Laying the Foundations of Rearmament

When the smoke cleared from the battles of the civil war, Vladimir Lenin and the Bolsheviks faced the long and painful task of building a socialist state and repairing a devastated economy. At the Tenth Party Congress in March 1921, Lenin accepted a truce with the peasantry by retreating from full confrontation and replacing the extremes of war communism with the mixed economy of the New Economic Policy (NEP) to let factories start working again and bring life back to the Soviet economy.[1] Although NEP ameliorated relations between the Bolshevik regime and the countryside, it created new problems for Soviet security policy. The Soviet state could not survive without some recovery of agriculture and private trade, but a policy of economic moderation and restraint implied that the Soviet economy would remain largely agrarian and hence dependent on technology and industrial goods from the hostile capitalist world.

When the Bolsheviks seized power, they assumed that their revolution would soon be followed by other revolutions abroad. Russia, the weak link in the capitalist chain, had broken first, but other states would soon follow as workers and soldiers tired of the burdens war had placed on them. To Bolshevik chagrin, the fall of the German and Austrian empires did not produce European revolution. On the contrary, as the nascent Soviet state fought and won a bitter and brutal civil war, capitalist regimes survived the end of World War I. Bourgeois Europe stabilized itself, repressing and accommodating working-class upheaval.[2] As the failure of revolution in the West became increasingly apparent, Bolshevik elites gradually accustomed themselves during the early 1920s to a new way of thinking: world revolution was not imminent. The German Social Democrats had made their peace with the German forces of order at the end of World War I, and the 1920 failure of the Soviet drive on Warsaw in the Russo-Polish war showed that nationalism trumped class solidarity for Polish workers and peasants. Realizing that it had to start coming to terms with the outside world, the Soviet Union began signing treaties with foreign powers in February 1921. Decisive disillusion finally came

13

with the ignominious failure of communist revolution in Germany in October 1923. The Soviets had to rethink their approach to the outside world.[3]

Paradoxically, the dawning realization that revolutionary Armageddon was far away made it more important for the Soviet state to build up its defenses and ensure its own security, both economic and military, for it would have to provide for its own survival for an indeterminately long period. Although Joseph Stalin coined the term "socialism in one country" in December 1924 to characterize the Soviet Union's path of autonomous development without world revolution, it was Nikolai Bukharin, the party's chief ideologist, who developed Stalin's phrase into a full-fledged theory. While asserting that ultimate salvation was not possible without world revolution, Bukharin emphasized that the Soviet Union's internal resources were more than adequate to build socialism. Stalin turned "socialism in one country" into a theme for Soviet proto-nationalism and a rallying cry against his and Bukharin's most dangerous political opponent: Leon Trotsky, the brilliant and charismatic founder of the Red Army.[4]

If, as Stalin and Bukharin were always careful to stress, safety was impossible until world revolution came, then the logical conclusion was that the Soviet Union had to defend itself. "Socialism in one country" therefore carried, as R. Craig Nation put it, "the positive goal of security through strength."[5] The viability of socialist development in the Soviet Union required the ability to resist military and economic threats. Armed intervention was always a possibility, so the Red Army would have to be on constant guard. Stalin held that complete security and the final achievement of communist utopia would have to await world revolution, but in the meantime, the Soviet state could be confident of its ability to defend itself, providing, of course, that suitable preparations were taken: "Uniting the might of our Red Army with the readiness of our workers and peasants to defend with their breasts the socialist fatherland—is all this enough to repel imperialist attacks and win for ourselves the necessary conditions for serious constructive work? It is enough."[6] In keeping with Stalin's position and the philosophy of "socialism in one country," the Fourteenth Party Congress in December 1925 declared that the Soviet Union must "change from a country importing machines and equipment into a country producing machines and equipment" so that the Soviet Union would not become "an appendage of the capitalist world economy." Voicing a theme that would be repeated in congresses and conferences to come, the Party Congress charged its Central Committee with "taking all measures for the strengthening of the defense readiness of the country and the might of the Red Army."[7]

MIKHAIL FRUNZE AND THE INTELLECTUAL BASIS FOR MILITARIZATION

The Red Army had demobilized at the end of the civil war to go on a peacetime footing for the first time; forged in war, it had no institutional memory of peace.

The most important task for the Soviet military, and for the USSR's military industry, was to use NEP's respite from struggle to impose order on the workings of Soviet defense. Administrative order not only answered a crying need for stability but also was cheaper than spending scarce rubles to modernize weaponry and factories. People's Commissar of Finance Grigorii Sokol'nikov struggled to stabilize the ruble and balance the budget, and little capital could be spared to ensure a decent living for the military's officers and men, let alone build new arms factories or rearm the Red Army. As Teddy Uldricks put it, under NEP, "wars or even an impressive defense establishment were simply too expensive."[8] During the mid- to late 1920s, the Red Army and military industry would be forced by financial constraints to build the intellectual and organizational framework for rearmament and the concomitant militarization of the Soviet economy without engaging in rearmament itself. Bitter disputes over the USSR's small defense budget, how best to organize defense production, and how to plan for future expansion laid the groundwork for the rearmament still to come. Planning rearmament was cheap; factories and arms themselves were expensive and would have to wait for better times.

Administrative reform in the Red Army under the leadership of Mikhail Frunze went hand in hand with the struggle of Stalin, Lev Kamenev, and Grigorii Zinov'ev against Trotsky to become Lenin's successor.[9] Destroying Trotsky politically required ousting him from his influential post at the head of Soviet Russia's war ministry, the People's Commissariat for Military and Naval Affairs (NKVM). A carefully orchestrated campaign, taking advantage of the undeniable chaos and disorganization plaguing the Red Army, accused Trotsky's deputy Efraim Sklianskii of incompetence and mismanagement. A Central Committee investigation charged Sklianskii and (by implication) Trotsky with the Red Army's sad state, forcing Sklianskii from office on 3 March 1924. Frunze, an ally of the Stalin-Kamenev-Zinov'ev triumvirate, took over as Trotsky's deputy, acting simultaneously as Chief of Staff and director of the military academy. Combined with Trotsky's lame-duck status, this situation made Frunze the real power in the Red Army. When Trotsky resigned in disgust as people's commissar on 15 January 1925, Frunze was his anointed successor and quickly began far-reaching reforms. Reducing political commissars' authority and increasing unit commanders' autonomy, Frunze's reforms also minimized the military's burden to the economy. By switching to a mixed system of regular units and territorial militia, the Red Army would cut costs without seriously damaging readiness.[10]

Frunze, despite not being a professional soldier, also provided the intellectual foundation for militarization. A Bolshevik since 1904 and a professional revolutionary, Frunze bolstered his party authority with that of a civil war hero. Although his pre–civil war military experience consisted solely of being the son of a medical corpsman, wartime necessity made Frunze an officer in the Red Army, and he found a natural talent for soldiering. Shining as an army and front commander in the Urals, Siberia, Central Asia, and the Crimea, Frunze became the commander of Soviet military forces in Ukraine at the end of the civil war. He was clearly marked for greater things, an opportunity that came when Trotsky lost his grip on the Red Army. Frunze, in addition to his administrative duties, wrote widely on military matters. His polemics against Trotsky centered on Red Army doctrine, but his most influential and lasting work concerned militarizing the Soviet state. His essay "Front and Rear in Future War," the introduction to P. P. Karatygin's *General Foundations of the Mobilization of Industry for the Needs of War,* was a manifesto that gave the explicit rationale for systematic and all-encompassing preparation for war, as well as concrete steps to achieve that.[11] Frunze's essay, together with the Karatygin book it introduced, was a blueprint for the Red Army's vision of the Soviet economy.

Frunze's essay became a classic of Soviet military thought, whereas Karatygin's book, advocating similar ideas, languished in obscurity. Not only the cult of personality around Frunze but also his explicitly Marxist approach made him the right person at the right time to crystallize new Soviet military thinking, revolutionary in both senses of the word. As Frunze saw it, old thinking about war had been doubly undermined: the Soviet Union was a new type of state that would employ new military technology. The Soviet Union itself, the first proletarian state, must have a qualitatively new military doctrine, for "the character of military doctrine accepted in the army of a given state is determined by . . . that social class which stands at the head of it." According to Frunze, "with the nature of our state power," not based on class exploitation, "overcoming these problems [of future war] will be easier than it would otherwise be." Those problems of future war represented the second way in which old military doctrine was obsolete. Improvements in technology had eliminated any distinction between front and rear; now, all society had to be an active part of the war effort. The increased demands of modern war made the militarization of rear areas essential to victory. In short, the task was "to strengthen general work on preparing the country for defense; to organize the country while still at peace to quickly, easily, and painlessly switch to military rails. The path to this goal lies in mastering in peacetime the difficult path to militarizing the work of the whole civil apparatus."[12]

In particular, Frunze advocated training officers in civil universities, not just military schools. Tractors could be designed to both plow fields and haul artillery. Preparing the state for war was conditional on close contact between military and civil authorities "by means of the introduction of army representatives into corresponding civil organs and institutions." Industrial managers must constantly bear in mind the applicability of their peacetime work to the needs of the army. Frunze's particular complaint was that although the importance of careful preparation for industrial mobilization was obvious, little had been accomplished. At least here, Frunze noted, "carrying out [mobilization planning] is made extraordinarily easier by the state character of the fundamental branches of our industry."[13]

Karatygin, whose book Frunze introduced, shared Frunze's belief in the centrality of economics to war but went further. Whereas Frunze argued that military policy must be determined by a state's class structure, Karatygin linked economics not just to policy but also to operations, tactics, and the nature of battle. In his view, for example, the positional stalemate on the western front in World War I resulted from the exhaustion of military stocks, owing to states' having improperly prepared for modern war. In sharp contrast to Frunze, however, Karatygin paid little attention to differences between capitalist and communist states. The demands of future war were so intractable and harsh that all states would be forced into identical policies, since World War I had shown conclusively that future war would demand total concentration of the resources of state and society. In short, "For the conduct of contemporary war it is necessary to have a powerful army, supplied with all the newest means of battle, provided with uninterrupted replenishment of combat equipment and manpower and relying on a steady, organized rear," a dictum that applied to *all* states, regardless of their class nature.[14]

Modern war, in Karatygin's view, would consume men and metal on an unimaginable scale, since "combat drains the army, the army drains the state." Faced with a terrible dilemma, no state could afford to stockpile all the arms and ammunition needed for war, but converting civil to military production would take months or even years and require careful and expensive preparation. Even providing factories with a full complement of the machinery, parts, and personnel needed for a rapid transfer to a fully mobilized, wartime economy would be beyond the reach of any state. Karatygin's solution was "military assimilation," or "the maximal convergence of civil industry with military via the development of those branches [of industry] which are equally necessary for peacetime and wartime," and employing military goods in peacetime. Industry should include a core of factories that would produce munitions even in peacetime, as well as a much larger group of factories prepared for instant conversion to a war footing.[15]

This in turn required, Karatygin argued, specific organizational measures. Industrial trusts would group factories together in order to share expertise and allocate raw materials rationally. Standardization of parts and technology and even the "scientific organization of labor" would ease the defense burden. Furthermore, World War I had shown the need for a single body, existing in peacetime, to coordinate all military preparation, one to which Karatygin went on to assign responsibility for "the conduct of all questions connected with the organization and expansion of military industry, with providing for the corresponding production, dividing assignments, control over work, rationing of materials." The most essential element of the whole process was planning—careful, comprehensive, painstaking, thorough planning of the entire process.[16]

The importance of Frunze's essay does not lie in its originality, nor even in his ability to implement the visions he described—he was people's commissar for only a short time. Instead, Frunze's "Front and Rear in Future War" crystallized a host of ideas circulating among the USSR's military thinkers on the importance of a militarized economy.[17] Michael Geyer described the essence of militarization in interwar Europe as eliminating the distinction between civil and military spheres through a "comprehensive, managerial effort at national organization."[18] No state in Europe would become as militarized in this sense as Stalin's Soviet Union, and Frunze's essay would provide the inspiration for the comprehensive integration of military concerns into society.

Soviet military writings were rife with the need for total organization of the civil economy. Mikhail Tukhachevskii, the Red Army's rising star, commissioned a secret report, *Future War,* that emphasized the political and economic capabilities of the Soviet Union's potential foes. Even Aleksandr Svechin, a non-Bolshevik and a veteran staff officer in the tsar's army, was entirely orthodox on the need for full integration between army and society and the economic nature of war. "War," he wrote in *Strategy,* "has economic causes, it is conducted on a certain economic base, it is a feverish economic process . . . and it leads to certain economic results." He continued:

> The military high command must have permanent liaisons with the civil authorities for the purpose of advising them on military requirements. And every higher civilian agency must have a department that represents military interests and makes preparations to get the agency on a war footing in order for it to meet the requirements made by a war. . . . The extensive militarization of all aspects of state and public activity is a law of modern war preparation.[19]

Abram Vol'pe's article on military industry in a 1928 history of the civil war commented that the disasters of World War I had shown that "it is necessary to work out a mobilization plan for industry in peacetime, and not only of industry, but of the entire economy." Boris Shaposhnikov (then Chief of Staff) explained in 1929 that "in our time there is no need to prove the necessity of economic preparation for war, of the creation of an *economic* war plan. That is now recognized everywhere." Frunze's ideas about the "necessity of full integration of military and economic planning and activities," that is, complete militarization, were ubiquitous. Writing in 1985, Michael Checinski found that "most of the Soviet military theoreticians and top commanders of the early 1920s shared Frunze's ideas, and in their writings are to be found the roots of current Soviet war-economic thinking, despite the many years that have elapsed and the many economic changes that have taken place."[20] Stalin's Soviet Union would come to match Frunze's and Karatygin's picture of the ideal militarized state.

MAKING DEFENSE POLICY

Even with Frunze's status, force of personality, and political connections, he could not institute the militarization of Soviet society alone. Within the Red Army, Frunze had to wield authority through its collective Revolutionary-Military Council, or Revvoensovet, a body made up of the Soviet Union's ambitious and headstrong high commanders.[21] More importantly, the Revvoensovet's authority, dominant within the Red Army, was limited outside it. Questions that were entirely military in nature, involving training, maneuvers, and approval of weapons systems, and any matters not impinging on the rest of the Soviet state and society were generally left to the Revvoensovet to decide. Any questions involving finance, industry, or education—that is, society at large—had to be decided in another forum. For defense industry in particular, the Revvoensovet could formulate proposals, lobby, and petition but could not make decisions alone. In effect, the Revvoensovet had a relatively free hand on strictly military questions but had only restricted authority outside that sphere.

Where the military met the state, two levels of authority determined policy. The Bolshevik party's Politburo was paramount. In theory, supreme power in the party lay in periodic congresses, which delegated that power to the party's Central Committee. In actual fact, the Politburo, technically only a subcommittee of the Central Committee, wielded true power.[22] During the 1920s and 1930s, power was centralized even further under Stalin, the party's general secretary. For most of this period, however, Stalin's power was immense but not absolute. Implementation of policy depended on working through the other members of the Politburo and Central Committee, all of whom held influential posts in the party and state.

In practice, the Politburo's decisions on defense were limited to the most important issues and top personnel moves. Although it remained the final arbiter of internecine disputes, the court of last resort, the Politburo's activities left a gap between the Revvoensovet's authority over internal military matters and its own pronouncements on key issues of high policy. During the civil war, the Council of Labor and Defense, or STO, had coordinated defense policy, but that role had rapidly fallen into abeyance. By the mid-1920s, defense matters were simply not discussed in meetings of the STO. That gap between the Revvoensovet and the Politburo, encompassing week-by-week decisions on defense and the economy, was covered by a series of defense cabinets varying over time in name and in precise makeup. During the period covered by this study, these defense cabinets were, in succession, Rykov's Commission (1925–1927, occasionally referred to as the Defense Commission), the Executive Session of the Council of Labor and Defense (1927–1930, referred to as the RZ STO), and the Defense Commission (1930 on).

These groups, despite their differences, had several things in common. Most importantly, they handled regular decisions on defense: budgets, production, mobilization plans, conscription. Second, they were primarily if not entirely state bodies; that is, their members held their seats not by virtue of a particular party position but from a specific government post, be it head of Gosplan (the State Planning Commission) or chair of Sovnarkom (the Council of People's Commissars). After ad hoc adjustments to its membership in April and June 1925, Rykov's Commission finally set its own membership at six, with Aleksei Rykov as chair of his namesake group. He earned the position by virtue of being the Soviet Union's head of government as chair of Sovnarkom. The deputy chair of Rykov's Commission was Lev Kamenev. The remaining four members were Frunze and Kliment Voroshilov, people's commissar and deputy people's commissar for military and naval affairs, respectively; Feliks Dzerzhinskii, chair of the OGPU secret police and of Vesenkha, the Soviet ministry of industry; and Grigorii Sokol'nikov, people's commissar of finance.[23]

More important than the political and administrative arrangements constraining Frunze's vision of a militarized society was the simple lack of money to pay for it. Sokol'nikov and his Commissariat of Finance, having stabilized the ruble after great effort, remained in the 1920s defenders of fiscal orthodoxy and budget austerity, with little cash to spare for the Red Army or anyone else. In 1924, for example, the Politburo approved a 1923–1924 overall defense budget of 329.2 million rubles (for a Soviet fiscal year running from 1 October to 30 September). Only about two-thirds of that, 248.2 million rubles, went directly to the Red Army—a paltry sum in relation to the tasks facing it. The navy received 30 million rubles, and an additional 91 million rubles went to industry.[24]

Commitment to fiscal rectitude was so strong that the Red Army's leadership found itself in the unenviable position of competing for funds with the USSR's own defense industry. In 1924, Gosplan's military sector argued that the Soviet Union's ability to arm its soldiers was so restricted by industrial inadequacy that the Red Army could hardly field a credible force in the event of war. Gosplan accordingly suggested slashing the peacetime army and directing funds instead to building up military industry. Frunze had to plead to Rykov and Stalin that cutting the peacetime Red Army below 600,000 men would cripple the USSR's defenses. Regardless of the state of the technology at the Red Army's disposal, Frunze argued, Poland, Romania, and the other states on the USSR's western border could field at least ninety-four division equivalents against the Soviet Union, and whatever industry could produce "will not make up for a disparity in the number of maneuverable combat units." The USSR's great advantage, population, was worthless unless young men could be funneled regularly through the Red Army's ranks for training, and even a peacetime army of 600,000 men trained only a third of the yearly cohort of 700,000 men available for service. For all Frunze's entreaties, money was so short that the peacetime Red Army was set on 1 October 1924 at 562,000 men.[25]

The same trade-off between the Red Army and military industry arose again in the second half of 1924 over the 1924–1925 budget. A bad harvest threw the Soviet economy into crisis, cutting Soviet grain exports from 2.7 million tons in 1923–1924 to almost nil in 1924–1925. More of the Soviet budget had to go toward agriculture, requiring decisive cuts in all other expenditures. Despite the crisis, the Revvoensovet proposed a 410 million–ruble budget for the army, navy, and procurement from industry, plus an additional 17 million in imports for military industry. A Politburo commission cut that 427 million rubles to 380 million rubles. The Revvoensovet protested, arguing that reorganization and reduced funds for military industry could trim the military's total budget to 410 million rubles, but any further cuts would either eliminate essential orders or decrease the number of peacetime divisions by a third. The Revvoensovet demanded no less than 410 million rubles, to no avail.[26]

The 1924–1925 budget dispute could not be resolved until a January 1925 Central Committee plenum served as a forum for deciding between competing budget proposals. By that time, government revenues had expanded, and the overall budget grew from 2,100 million to 2,280 million rubles, easing the crisis. At the plenum, Frunze portrayed the Soviet Union as in mortal danger—foreign states were preparing economic and military offensives against the USSR, and Poland would complete its war preparations by 1927. Anti-Soviet émigrés were planning an uprising in Transcaucasia. Despite this, the Red Army led a hand-to-mouth existence, cutting its overall numbers to 562,000 men with critically low stock-piles of equipment. As Frunze saw it, "all summer we practically lived without a Red Army." New wars would demand the most advanced military equipment, so the Red Army would need every ruble of a 405 million–ruble budget. After Frunze spoke, Stalin rose "in order to support comrade Frunze's suggestion in every way," condemning the "liquidating mood" that would turn the Red Army into a simple territorial militia. After Stalin's intervention, debate was closed, and Frunze's version of the budget was approved.[27]

Later in 1925, thanks to the USSR's improving finances, the 1925–1926 Red Army budget provoked less controversy. Grain exports had returned to a relatively healthy 2 million tons from the previous year's abysmal showing. The rapid NEP recovery allowed the Soviet state to boost its military budget to 600 million rubles, with an additional 5 million rubles in orders deferred to 1926–1927. This apparent one-year lull would not last long—disputes over the 1926–1927 budget would be as bitter as ever.[28]

Future budget battles and the further development of the Red Army would take place without Frunze. He died during surgery on 31 October 1925 under mysterious circumstances and was replaced as people's commissar for military affairs by Kliment Voroshilov, a dim-witted professional revolutionary and Bolshevik since 1903.[29] Although Voroshilov had some talent for political maneuvering and obsequious loyalty to Stalin, he was a political general whose administrative talents and military sophistication were far inferior to those of his fellow officers in the Revvoensovet. His talented subordinates might resent Voroshilov's preeminence, but their abilities compensated to some degree for his inadequacies, especially in the quest for more resources for the Red Army.[30] All the Red Army's commanders could agree that the military was starved for cash and equipment in a time of increasing danger.

Over the summer of 1926, the Red Army once again sounded the alarm of foreign invasion. In the debates over the 1924–1925 budget, Frunze had pointed to Polish preparations for war against the USSR, demonstrating the chief concerns of Soviet military planners. Through the 1920s, while the People's Commissariat of Foreign Affairs and the Comintern concentrated on the United Kingdom,

Germany, or China, the military's focus was squarely on Eastern Europe—the only place where hostile states could threaten the Soviet heartland. Diplomatic histories of the 1920s have seen Soviet-Polish relations as a sidebar to Soviet-German relations; that is, relations with Berlin determined Soviet attitudes toward Warsaw. Military documents reveal, however, that the Soviet concern in the mid- to late 1920s was always with a war against Poland and Romania.[31] This preoccupation was little affected by the vicissitudes of diplomatic dealings. Whatever the state of Europe, the USSR in the 1920s methodically planned in terms of war with Poland and Romania. By the end of the 1920s, China and Japan would increasingly become concerns, but for most of NEP, when the Red Army planned its next war, it expected to deal with a coalition of Eastern European states, perhaps with support from Britain or France.

At a meeting of Rykov's Commission held 29 July 1926 to discuss mobilization readiness and the Red Army's 1926–1927 budget, Voroshilov and Chief of Staff Mikhail Tukhachevskii combined to paint a frightening picture of the underfunded Soviet military. Despite their personal rivalry, Tukhachevskii and Voroshilov could cooperate to defend the Red Army. Voroshilov told Rykov's Commission that he had met privately with Dzerzhinskii, who died soon after their meeting, and been warned of an impending attack on the USSR. This intelligence led Tukhachevskii to evaluate the Red Army's preparedness. He found that the Locarno agreement had only unsettled Eastern Europe, where Poland, Romania, and the Baltic states were allying against the USSR. To make matters worse, Britain was not only supporting that coalition but also fomenting anti-Soviet activities in Afghanistan and Iran. Tukhachevskii asserted that the Soviet Union's western border states, its most likely adversaries, could draw on a pool of 6,710,000 men, of whom 4,290,000 had military training, allowing them to muster 111 rifle divisions, plus cavalry and aircraft. Given their reserves, those states could field an additional 150 rifle divisions with British assistance and production from the rapidly growing Polish military industry.[32]

This, weighed against the ninety-one rifle divisions and 3.17 million men the USSR could field, meant to Tukhachevskii that the Soviet Union could not prevail in an extended war. His solution was a strategy aiming at quick victory, a conclusion with profound implications for the allocation of resources. Scarce funds should not go to industrial investment, since by the time Soviet industry made its presence felt in any future war, sheer weight of numbers would tell against the USSR. Instead, because quick victory was essential, military spending had to create a Red Army able to go on the offensive at a moment's notice and "disrupt the deployment of forces" by its enemies. The poor state of Polish and Romanian railways would allow the Red Army to win a rapid victory before the enemy had completed mobilization.[33] Tukhachevskii buttressed his advocacy of preventive war by pointing out the sorry state of the Red Army's stockpiles. Nearly a third of soldiers mobilized would not have uniforms. There was a severe shortage of modern light machine guns, and the Red Army could count on repeating World War I's shell shortage almost as soon as the next war began. Even given a year to expand production, Soviet industry would not approach the level of production the Red Army would require. In short, the Soviet Union would be incapable of repelling serious attack in the autumn of 1926. Here, Tukhachevskii drew the opposite conclusion from that drawn by Svechin in *Strategy*. Svechin had suggested that the path to victory lay through attrition in a long, defensive struggle. Tukhachevskii saw that as leading to defeat and pushed instead for preemptive strikes to counteract the Soviet Union's material weakness. Rykov agreed with Tukhachevskii that the situation demanded quick action, and his commission resolved "to take a series of urgent measures for strengthening the defense potential of the USSR." In particular, the commission would consider advances on the next year's budget due to "the catastrophic position of mobilization stocks."[34]

Tukhachevskii was playing a game on several different levels, since the Red Army's ability to deliver a preemptive strike in 1926 and 1927 was highly questionable. Although he might have believed that Soviet security depended on quick victory, to strike while the Red Army's opponents were still mobilizing entailed an offensive spirit closely akin to the revolutionary warfare dear to Tukhachevskii. Furthermore, building up immediate military potential, rather than more general industrial capacity, meant that the Red Army's position in the always bitter fights over the budget would be strengthened—the Red Army needed funds and equipment *now*. The working group under Chutskaev that Rykov's Commission created to examine Tukhachevskii's proposals in September 1926 came to just that conclusion. It found that full preparations for mobilization, over and above 613 million rubles for the day-to-day expenses of running the Red Army, would cost 510 million rubles. Cutting mobilization expenses to the bone would reduce that to 460 million rubles, split between 287 million rubles for Red Army stockpiles and 173 million rubles for industrial mobilization.[35]

Opposition to Chutskaev's proposal to boost spending on military mobilization stocks came from the People's Commissariat of Finance, which refused to spend that much on defense. Even the 705 million rubles that Finance deigned to grant, with only 210 million rubles going to prepare for mobilization, would require major cuts in other areas of the Soviet budget. The contrast between what Soviet defense required and what the budget could withstand was stark:[36]

1926–1927 Defense Budget Recommendations (in Million Rubles)

	Chutskaev's Commission	Commissariat of Finance
Red Army current needs	613	495
Red Army stockpiles	287	155
Vesenkha defense expenditures	173	55
Total budget	1,073	705

Financial arguments outweighed military weakness. The Red Army received a healthy increase in its budget, but nothing like what it had hoped for. An 8 November report to Stalin from Rabkrin, the Workers'-Peasants' Inspectorate, endorsed a total budget of 707.673 million rubles, 123 million greater than the previous year, and on 11 November 1926, the Politburo voted "to confirm the general sum of outlays on the NKVM for the army and military industry in the range of 700 million rubles." The Politburo further decreed that the prices for military production were not to change from the previous year's.[37]

Despite the Politburo's ruling on a military budget of 700 million rubles, Tukhachevskii continued to lobby for higher military budgets by arguing that the Soviet Union needed the capacity to fight a preventive war via a preemptive strike. In a 26 December 1926 report to the RZ STO on the USSR's defenses, Tukhachevskii repeated the Red Army's belief that its probable foes on the western border had superior forces and the prospect of receiving aid from the capitalist powers. "The bloc's weak point," however, "is the vast expanse of its eastern border and its comparatively insignificant territorial depth." Given this, "in the event that we destroy in the first period of war even one of the bloc's links, the threat of defeat would be weakened."[38]

Despite Tukhachevskii's plea for the resources to wage preventive war, the 700 million–ruble budget would remain roughly the canonical figure for the 1926–1927 fiscal year, leaving the Red Army far less than it wished. On 7 January 1927, on the recommendation of the People's Commissariat of Finance, Sovnarkom approved a defense budget of 700 million rubles that included 53 million in grants to military industry. The Central Committee plenum meeting from 7 to 12 February 1927 referred to nearly identical budget targets. By comparison with the previous 1925–1926 fiscal year's outlays, the NKVM budget went from 602.48 million rubles to 692.534 million for 1926–1927. In addition, direct grants to Soviet industry from the state budget went from 167.2 million to 386.1 million rubles, and military industry's particular grants went from 27.3 million to 43.9 million rubles.[39]

THE PARLOUS STATE OF THE SOVIET DEFENSE INDUSTRY

The essence of Frunze's militarization was transforming the Soviet economy, but the limited military budgets of the early 1920s and the Red Army's insistence on protecting its own budget at the expense of military industry meant that the defense industry could hardly recover from the devastation of World War I and the civil war. With the completion of the Frunze reforms, however, the sad state of military industry and the need for radical change became increasingly obvious. Blame for the USSR's dilapidated defense industry initially centered on Petr Alekseevich Bogdanov, chair of Voenprom, the production association uniting the USSR's dozens of military factories. Bogdanov, a long-standing party member, had held several high-ranking economic posts, but despite this, his career fell apart in 1924 and 1925 thanks to the seemingly intractable problems of military industry.[40]

Bogdanov reported on Voenprom's continuing crisis to the Revvoensovet on 14 April 1924, revealing disorganization and bloated bureaucracy. Sensing continuing dissatisfaction with his performance, Bogdanov unsuccessfully offered his resignation to the Politburo on 16 February 1925. When he reported again on military industry on 31 March 1925, he could claim little improvement, and by May, as he later wrote, "it was communicated to me that the members of the Politburo by unofficial agreement had approved the need for my exit from military industry." Delaying his departure long enough to restructure Voenprom and prepare the 1925–1926 budget, Bogdanov tendered his resignation on 16 June 1925, and the Politburo replaced him temporarily with his deputy, Zharko.[41] Bogdanov's troubles did not end with his dismissal. Sent on a three-month trip abroad in July 1925 to acquaint himself with foreign technology, he returned to find his position as chair of the Russian Republic's Vesenkha under attack. In November 1925, the Politburo removed him from that job as well, sending him to the North Caucasus to serve under the local party secretary, the rapidly rising Anastas Mikoian.[42]

Bogdanov accompanied his resignation from Voenprom with a defense of his record. He argued that defense industry's apparent shortcomings were in fact the results of difficult circumstances and necessary, well-considered policy. Voenprom's first priority was, Bogdanov wrote, "such an organization for military industry that would provide the army and fleet with the most refined types of military technology with minimal outlay of government funds." That final qualification was the most important: strict cost accounting, hard budget constraints, layoffs, and plant closures had been absolutely necessary. Although these belt-tightening measures were painful—Voenprom's fifty-seven factories at the end of 1923 had been cut to thirty-eight by mid-1925, with three or four more closures to follow, and at least 8,000 workers had lost their jobs—Bogdanov simply had no choice. Only after cost-cutting could Voenprom shift its attention to other important matters: mobilization readiness, war planning, and research and development. Bogdanov's worst handicap, he claimed, was lack of money to replace worn equipment, provide liquidity, import materials and machinery, buy foreign patents, or hire and train more qualified workers.[43]

To the Soviet political and military leadership, Bogdanov's worst sins were the way military industry distributed military orders to factories and prepared for wartime mobilization. Vesenkha's Committee for Military Orders handled the first responsibility, "planning distribution of military orders among state industries, regulating mutual relations between the military and state industry and establishing conditions and prices for military products." The awkwardly named Committee for De- and Mobilization took up the second task, "revealing and calculating the maximal possibilities and suitability" of factories for military production to "assemble a mobilization plan for industry in correspondence with the demands of the NKVM in the event of war." Bogdanov chaired each organization, but they were crippled by the division between them. The Committee for Military Orders and the Committee for De- and Mobilization worked "completely independently, not connected between themselves," when they should naturally have coordinated their efforts. The best way to verify readiness for wartime production, of course, was judicious use of peacetime orders: forcing a factory to make shell casings in peacetime ensured some expertise in the event of war. Splitting wartime mobilization and peacetime production between two bodies made that quite difficult. To make matters worse, both committees were alike in that they lacked trained and qualified personnel, were terribly disorganized, jealously guarded their privileges, and expected imminent closure or reorganization.[44]

WHO RUNS MILITARY INDUSTRY: THE MILITARY OR INDUSTRY?

Although Bogdanov's dismissal revealed mismanagement and chaos inside military industry, Feliks Dzerzhinskii stubbornly resisted any outside interference, in particular from the Red Army, in his management of the Soviet economy. As chair of Vesenkha, the Supreme Council of the National Economy, Dzerzhinskii strove to keep military industry under his close, personal control. His insistence on running Soviet industry himself clashed directly with the Red Army's interests. Despite his ruthless conduct as founder of the Cheka, the Soviet secret police, Dzerzhinskii maintained a conciliatory and moderate attitude on questions of management and economics. He consistently restrained attacks on noncommunist specialists within Vesenkha, was a guardian of fiscal orthodoxy and balanced budgets, and pushed for modest military spending. More than anything else, Dzerzhinskii resented attempts to undermine his authority over the Soviet economy.

Dzerzhinskii wished to keep the military from intruding on his territory and dominating economic policy. That principle required two organizational strategies. First, Dzerzhinskii could not allow the formation of a military-industrial directorate *(upravlenie)*. An effective branch of Soviet industry devoted to solely military production would give too much weight to the Red Army and undermine Dzerzhinskii's authority. Second, industrial mobilization needed to be under the control of Vesenkha's Main Economic Directorate, not any military body. That would ensure that considerations of wartime mobilization were kept subordinate to the proper functioning of the Soviet economy as a whole.[45] Dzerzhinskii rejected schemes that would undercut his autonomy at Vesenkha by according economic power to the Red Army. His priority was the integration, not the separation, of military industry into the general industrial economy of the Soviet Union, while keeping ultimate control in his own hands. Systematically introducing military personnel into Vesenkha's hierarchy was unacceptable. Military industry, if granted the status of its own directorate, would be less under control and more easily used without regard to what Dzerzhinskii saw as the best interests of the Soviet economy.

Dzerzhinskii accordingly fought the creation of a military-industrial directorate, declaring in 1925 that he could not accept such a thing and "insisting" instead on a military section under Vesenkha's Main Economic Directorate. In August, S. I. Ventsov of the Red Army Staff sent a proposal to Rykov's Commission advocating a Military-Industrial Directorate for Vesenkha. Ventsov described Dzerzhinskii as holding a "dissenting opinion" on the whole question, to which Dzerzhinskii shot back that Rykov's Commission had no jurisdiction over the question. He contended instead that this was a Vesenkha internal matter and wholly under his purview: "*I* answer for Vesenkha."[46]

The military's proposed directorate, Dzerzhinskii held, "would mean . . . ripping the administration of military industry and military matters within industry from the entire apparatus [of Vesenkha] and creating an empty space with a fine-sounding name." Vesenkha should instead subordinate military industry to the Main Economic Directorate, whose resources it could then draw on.[47] The military's proposed Military-Industrial Directorate could then be wholly tied into Vesenkha's work.[48] The only room for maneuver Dzerzhinskii was willing to allow on the question of a Military-Industrial Directorate was if "questions of defense . . . stop being the affair of an inter-institutional commission and pass wholly to the responsibility of Vesenkha."[49]

In the wake of Bogdanov's disgrace, the Red Army had a quite different vision, diametrically opposed to Dzerzhinskii's, of how military industry should be run. The Red Army had already engineered the creation of a short-lived Inter-institutional Mobilization Commission to push military priorities in mobilization planning. Frunze, speaking for the Red Army, found Dzerzhinskii's resistance to a Military-Industrial Directorate unacceptable. The situation instead demanded "unified leadership" under the military-dominated Interinstitutional Mobilization Commission. Finally, Frunze insisted that the NKVM be accorded a greater role in economic planning, in particular through the inclusion of Red Army officers in military industry. The overall thrust of Frunze's remarks was clear: though he phrased his argument in terms of administrative efficiency, his proposal was to increase military authority over economic policy and over Vesenkha.[50]

The military's model for the defense industry had two key principles: all defense factories should be united under one directorate, and that directorate should be run by as high-ranking an official as possible. This would permit quick and efficient decisions.[51] Naturally, the Red Army's high command understood that centralization would give military industry more bureaucratic clout than if it were split among several industrial conglomerates. Likewise, the powerful leader of a powerful Military-Industrial Directorate would be in an ideal position to lobby for scarce resources. The Red Army therefore fought Dzerzhinskii's attempts to subordinate military industry to any intermediate body that would distance it from the heart of Vesenkha.[52]

The Politburo finally approved a Revvoensovet-Vesenkha compromise on 12 November 1925 in which the Red Army achieved almost everything it desired. Vesenkha would have a new Military-Industrial Directorate (the VPU) directly under Dzerzhinskii to handle military industry. Dzerzhinskii's price for agreeing to what he had opposed so insistently was the appointment of his close associate from the Cheka, Varlaam Aleksandrovich Avanesov, to head the new VPU. As a trusted protégé, Avanesov could be relied on to keep matters under strict control. The new directorate's collegium, besides including Avanesov and Samsonov from Vesenkha, had a spot reserved for the Red Army, one that Λ. I. Egorov eventually filled.[53]

Varlaam Avanesov was born Suren Karametovich Martirosian in 1884 in western Armenia, now part of Turkey. An Armenian nationalist early in life, he later abandoned nationalism and by 1903 had joined the Social Democrats while attending gymnasium in Stavropol in the North Caucasus. His revolutionary activities during the 1905 revolution made staying in Russia too dangerous. To escape the tsarist police and to receive treatment for tuberculosis, he left for Switzerland in 1907. The name from his false passport, Armenak Aleksandrovich Avanesianets, became his party identity in exile and the source of his later nom de guerre. Avanesov attended medical school while in Switzerland, but by 1913 he had returned to Russia and resumed revolutionary work. After the February Revolution, he served in the Moscow Soviet before heading to Petersburg as secretary for the Military-Revolutionary Committee, planning an armed uprising against the Provisional Government. After October 1917, Avanesov took a number of key posts in the Soviet government, distinguishing himself by a fanatic energy for work despite his recurrent bouts with tuberculosis. Sharing Kremlin quarters with Iakov Sverdlov and working as deputy in the All-Russian Central Executive Committee, he also ran the Armenian affairs branch of the Commissariat of Nationalities, chaired the Commissariat of State Control (forerunner of the Workers'-Peasants' Inspectorate), was deputy commissar of foreign trade, and briefly chaired the Executive Council of the STO. Most importantly for his subsequent career, Avanesov worked in the secret police under Dzerzhinskii.

In 1925, now an experienced troubleshooter, Avanesov followed Dzerzhinskii to Vesenkha, where he founded its internal inspectorate before moving on to the distressed Soviet defense industry. The collapse of his health would eventually prevent him from fixing military industry's problems, but the reforms he outlined were later characterized by Voroshilov as a great service to the Red Army. Although he would not serve long as director of military industry, his driving approach to his duties (and the fortunate fact that his poor health forced him to resign before the millstone of military industry dragged down his reputation) made Avanesov the model defense administrator against which all his successors were judged. Living longer than any of his comrades expected him to, he finally died of tuberculosis in March 1930.[54]

VPU VERSUS VOENPROM

The new Military-Industrial Directorate (or VPU) that Avanesov took over in November 1925 combined the functions of the older Committee for De- and Mobilization and the Committee on Military Orders. From the first committee, the VPU received the mandate to "assemble a mobilization plan for industry in accord with the demands of NKVM in time of war." From the second committee, the VPU inherited responsibility for "planning distribution of [peacetime] military orders among state industries, regulating relations between the military and state industry, and establishing conditions and prices for military products." The VPU, by combining the functions of the two earlier groups, would eliminate duplication of effort. In addition, Vesenkha's Presidium intended for the VPU to "assemble plans of military production and plans for technical reconstruction of present-day production," thus taking over the supervisory role that had earlier belonged to Voenprom, the trust uniting the USSR's military factories. In an important reservation, however, the VPU would *not* actually run military factories themselves. The VPU, despite being the Military-Industrial Directorate, was not directly administering the Soviet Union's defense plants, at least not yet. Voenprom, the production association handling day-to-day factory management, still held that responsibility. The last of the VPU's duties, in fact, would be breaking up the large and unwieldy Voenprom into smaller, more homogeneous, and more manageable trusts.[55]

The new VPU, with a better-qualified staff of 180, still showed the marks of its heritage in its internal organization. Run by Avanesov with two deputies and two assistants, the VPU was split into three main sections *(otdely)*. One, the descendant of the old Committee for De- and Mobilization, handled preparations for war. By the beginning of December 1925, the VPU was already starting work on expanding the network of mobilization organs and stockpiles of key materials. A second section, the remnant of the Committee on Military Orders, distributed peacetime military orders among factories and determined their financing, price, and technical specifications. The third section had been created specifically to handle splitting Voenprom into component trusts.[56]

The reorganized military industry that Avanesov took over was a sprawling group of disparate plants spread across the Soviet Union, with a core of thirty-five factories employing 80,141 people as of 1 May 1926. Three additional factories were mothballed but still nominally under Voenprom (including Barrikady, later famed as a center for artillery production and a Stalingrad battlefield). The plants still functioning ranged in size from old giants of Russian military industry such as the Izhevsk and Tula firearms works, with workforces of 13,597 and 12,434, respectively, down to the Leningrad Optical Glass Factory, with 226 workers. The Tula and Izhevsk factories also dominated military industry as measured by production—total orders at Tula came to 15.6 million rubles (9.8 million military) and at Izhevsk to 8.7 million rubles (4.4 million military). Those factories were closely followed by the Tula Cartridge Factory, with an 8.2 million–ruble program (5.1 million military), and the Lugansk Cartridge Factory, with 6.8 million rubles (all military). Although the division of Voenprom into trusts was not yet complete, the factories broke down quite naturally by production type. Seven artillery factories accounted for 22.9 percent of the total workforce, and four firearms factories accounted for another 35.7 percent of the total. Seven bullet, cartridge, and fuse plants had 21.1 percent of the workforce, with twelve powder and explosives factories making up 17.9 percent. The remainder, only 2.4 percent, was divided among five optics, experimental, and surgical instrument factories.[57]

Although military industry's most important customer was the Red Army, a significant proportion of the defense industry's production was civilian and would remain so through the end of the USSR—five of Voenprom's factories had no military orders at all. Military orders made up 67.5 percent of Voenprom's production program for 1925–1926, with the Red Army's Artillery Directorate dominating the list of customers. It took 58.1 percent of Voenprom's production, with the air force taking another 7.7 percent. Civilian production made up nearly a third of Voenprom's output: 32.7 percent of a total production program of 145,857,314 rubles. This represented a growth of 46.5 percent over the 1924–1925 program of 99.5 million rubles, 69.7 percent of which was military.[58]

Avanesov nominally took over at the VPU in December 1925 but was in fact not able to begin work until late spring 1926. Writing after his retirement, he said that he actually ran military industry only from April to July 1926, and one month of that was spent visiting factories. It was just this tour, ordered by Rykov's Commission on 20 May 1926, that convinced him of the true depth of the crisis he had inherited. Touring with Egorov and Kulik from the Red Army and Tamarin from Voenprom, Avanesov visited sixteen military plants from 23 May to 20 June 1926, and in his words, the state of military industry "in actuality turned out to be much worse than one could have imagined."[59]

What Avanesov found was so dire that it could not wait until the next meeting of Rykov's Commission. Dzerzhinskii called an emergency meeting in late June 1926 with Voroshilov and Iosif Unshlikht from the Red Army to hear Avanesov's findings and decide on remedial measures. Avanesov painted a grim picture of overstaffing, poor discipline, incompetence, insufficient planning, and inefficient use of resources. As industrial administrators themselves admitted in October 1926, Voenprom had been characterized by "unprecedentedly disgraceful selection of personnel and a chaotic organizational structure." Furthermore, "one can say directly that if the craftiest spy had been given the task of disorganizing Voenprom at its roots, then he could hardly have invented greater chaos and worse personnel than that which existed in Voenprom until the middle of the third quarter of this operational year."[60]

Dzerzhinskii's group quickly decided on a series of remedial measures, most of which concerned internal housekeeping: both military factories and Voenprom's central bureaucracy needed personnel cuts, along with the dismissal of Voenprom's old management and all "criminals, White guards, and unsuitable people." Dzerzhinskii's group also ordered that the cumbersome Voenprom—made up of thirty-nine factories—accelerate its split into smaller, more manageable production trusts and gave Voenprom's party collective, given to shrill protests over its lack of say in policy, "the necessary indications . . . on the impermissibility of interference in the administrative-managerial conduct of administration." All work norms and collective bargaining arrangements were to be recalculated and renegotiated, and Voroshilov and Unshlikht agreed to provide Voenprom with some stability by committing the Red Army to a three-year plan of long-range orders and a "hard order" for the coming 1926–1927 fiscal year. Although delaying a Politburo hearing on the matter, the group agreed to take Avanesov's report to Rykov's Commission for further discussion, while organizing an oversight board to implement the new policies.[61] When Avanesov repeated his findings to Rykov's Commission on 5 July 1926, it endorsed the conclusions Dzerzhinskii had already approved: Voenprom would be broken up, the labor unions were to assist, and Voenprom's staff was to be cut.[62]

The problems Avanesov found on his tour were all the more galling for being preventable, even taking into account the Bolshevik tendency to see all challenges as soluble by force of will. The most crippling difficulty Avanesov found was not physical but financial. Military industry was debilitated by a cash-flow crisis, a situation Avanesov described as "close to catastrophe." Enterprise treasuries were empty, wages (paid in cash) were in arrears, suppliers received no payments, and military industry's books were so bad that Avanesov could not even determine the scope of the problem. Wage payments had run 10 million rubles over budget, excess workers had not been laid off, consumer production languished unsold, bank credits dried up, and 12 million rubles of excess raw materials lay in warehouses. Nine factories had managed to amass 350,000 rubles in travel expenses alone.[63] An accurate financial picture was a prerequisite for resolving the cash crunch, but clear accounting was hard to achieve. Inventories proceeded slowly, and of the sixteen factories Avanesov had visited, only four kept accurate books. Three of those were months behind schedule. Poor bookkeeping drove the Red Army to distraction as well—the same rifle that cost 51.33 rubles at Izhevsk cost 69.89 when it came from Tula, and cartridges were no better. To add insult to injury, the day after Avanesov testified to the Defense Commission, Tamarin, chair of Voenprom, went to Voroshilov with hat in hand: he would not be able to make payroll on 10 July 1926 without help from the military.[64]

The financial problems resulting from the cash-flow crisis proved persistent. Avanesov's successor, Aleksandr Tolokontsev, would spend several months putting his financial house in order. In explaining to Stalin and other high party figures why progress was so slow, and at the same time appealing for support, Tolokontsev had to admit that sloppy accounting meant that military industry's financial statements "differ sharply from the factual position." The only solution he saw was continuing the stalled breakup of Voenprom.[65] As late as December 1926, Tolokontsev appealed to Stalin for intervention against the military for its refusal to pay a 7.5 million–ruble advance on an artillery order. The Red Army held that until industry's outstanding debts to the military from 1925–1926 were paid, it should not be obligated to advance further funds. Tolokontsev had quite another opinion on the legal merits of the matter, but more importantly, as he told Stalin, without the advance, he could not pay his employees.[66]

When Rykov's Commission heard Avanesov's devastating report on 5 July 1926, the immediate result was the decision to split Voenprom into five trusts, repeating the still unfinished task the VPU had been created to perform at the end of 1925. The trusts were to be ready to function by the 1926–1927 fiscal year.[67] Dzerzhinskii gave immediate orders to partition Voenprom into five new trusts: the Artillery-Shell *(Orudiino-snariadnyi),* later renamed the Artillery-Arsenal *(Orudiino-arsenal'nyi);* the Firearm–Machine Gun *(Ruzheino-pulemëtnyi);* the Fuse-Cartridge *(Trubochno-patronnyi),* later Cartridge-Fuse *(Patronno-trubochnyi);* the Military-Chemical *(Voenno-khimicheskii);* and the much smaller and less significant Military-Optical *(Voenno-opticheskii)* Trusts.[68] The split would not affect the physical plant, but even so, determining new administrative structures and sorting out assets and obligations would prove fiendishly difficult.

The Red Army did not help. Although Voroshilov had attended Avanesov's meeting with Dzerzhinskii in late June and endorsed the resultant conclusions, at least some in the Red Army believed that reorganization was only a cosmetic measure intended to cover up incompetence in Vesenkha. The NKVM's representative in Vesenkha asserted that military industry had "colossal potential strength," given competent management, and "there is no need at all to carry out any kind of fantastic experiment with military industry in the sense of breaking Voenprom up into trusts."[69] The final preparations for liquidating Voenprom were not complete by the start of the 1926–1927 fiscal year as ordered. The STO could finally proclaim the breakup complete on 15 December 1926.[70]

Over the summer and fall of 1926, illness and death brought in a new cast of characters to direct both Soviet industry as a whole and military industry in particular. Feliks Dzerzhinskii, hours after violently haranguing opposition to the party line at a plenary session of the party leadership, died of a heart attack on 20 July 1926. This triggered a series of personnel changes: Ian Rudzutak had already replaced Dzerzhinskii as people's commissar of transportation, but at the time of his death, Dzerzhinskii was still chair of both Vesenkha and the renamed OGPU secret police. Viacheslav Menzhinskii took over the OGPU, and Valerian Kuibyshev, head of Rabkrin, the Workers'-Peasants' Inspectorate, moved from investigating and overseeing the workings of industry to running the Soviet economy as the new chair of Vesenkha. Sergo Ordzhonikidze, a charismatic and volatile Georgian, transferred from the Caucasus to Moscow to replace Kuibyshev at Rabkrin.[71]

Shortly thereafter, only months into his term at the VPU, Avanesov's health failed, and in the fall of 1926, he had to pass his office to his deputy, Tolokontsev.[72]

Avanesov's forced resignation, not coincidentally, made him the only inter-war head of Soviet military industry who did *not* leave in disgrace, though his short tenure was not enough to do more than begin reorganizing Voenprom. It fell to Tolokontsev, with the cooperation of the Red Army's Aleksandr Egorov temporarily seconded to military industry, to restructure defense industry, assemble a plan of investment and expansion, and prepare industry for mobilization. In addition to putting Egorov in charge of mobilization, Tolokontsev assigned P. I. Sudakov to handle organizational and bureaucratic matters, while leaving actual peacetime production to V. S. Mikhailov, a holdover from the tsarist era.[73]

THE PROBLEM OF PLANNING

With the organizational structure of military industry somewhat stabilized by late 1926, the Red Army and Vesenkha could focus their attention on economic development and wartime mobilization. Instead of simply haggling over the yearly order of weapons, ammunition, and other ordnance, all parties had to focus on three fiendishly complex and closely interrelated issues: a long-range peacetime order plan, a capital investment plan for military industry, and a wartime economic mobilization plan. None of these could be entirely separated from the other two: an ambitious wartime mobilization plan depended on investment to build the necessary production capacity, but directing resources to investment would hurt peacetime production and procurement, leaving the Red Army less prepared for war and industry less experienced in munitions production. The necessary trade-offs were the subject of bitter, ongoing disputes, and only by early 1927 would an interim solution be found that all parties could reluctantly accept.

The comprehensive reorganization of military industry, although it heightened the Red Army's expectations, caused such disruption that things would get worse before they got better. Tamarin and Mikhailov made just that point in theses prepared in October 1926. Overstaffing and entrenched bureaucracies would take time to overcome—Voenprom was 10,000 employees over its plan, and central management had 844 employees instead of the 400 in its table of organization. Voenprom's output per unit of capital was significantly lower than that in other sections of industry. Even though Dzerzhinskii had advocated one-man management in factories, lack of clear hierarchies in Voenprom had left organization "a sheer orgy," with no effective record keeping or planning.[74]

Tamarin and Mikhailov did suggest that the Red Army was partly responsible for industry's woes. In particular, the NKVM had not committed itself to a long-range order schedule, so year-by-year orders were subject to constant change and often were not approved until well after the fiscal year had begun. For example, the 1923–1924 production program was initially set on 28 April 1922, but final approval for the first quarter of the year came on 25 September 1923, only five days before the start of the fiscal year. The full 1923–1924 program of 65.5 million rubles in orders was finally set on 25 February 1924, five months after the start of the fiscal year. The initial 1924–1925 order plan of 75.6 million rubles was set on 10 June 1924, but the final agreement on a much-altered 52.6 million–ruble program did not come until 20 December 1924. The next year was the same: an initial 1 June 1925 program was settled on 17 December 1925, nearly three months into the fiscal year, after six major changes.[75]

This instability meant that production shortfalls were chronic. As measured at the end of the fiscal year, military orders not actually produced (*nedodel)* had fallen slightly from 7.5 million rubles (15 percent of the total order) for the 1924–1925 program to 6 million rubles (7.5 percent of the total order) for the 1925–1926 program. When evaluated in terms of equipment actually approved for receipt by military inspectors, military industry's performance looked much worse. Non-delivery (*nedodacha)* had grown from 7.5 million rubles (15 percent of the total program) for 1924–1925 to 27.4 million rubles (30 percent of the total program) for 1925–1926. Although part of that shortfall could be explained by simple delays in delivery, some of it probably resulted from rejections by military inspectors on grounds of poor quality. Precise figures for underproduction and nondelivery were difficult to come by. When Tolokontsev reported to the Revvoensovet in March 1927, he had slightly different data on the production program, which had gone from 64 million in 1923–1924 to 52 million in 1924–1925 to 87 million in 1925–1926. His overall conclusion was nevertheless the same: "Such wavering [in the production program] is extraordinarily difficult for industry," so "underproduction grows with every passing year."[76]

Tolokontsev attempted to win a long-range order plan from the Politburo. Reporting in December 1926, he stressed the need for a stable relationship with the Red Army. While he conceded that military industry suffered from poor accounting, low productivity, high wages and low work norms, regular financial crises, nonexistent mobilization preparation, shoddy civil production, and unqualified personnel, he suggested that those problems were largely the Red Army's fault. His first four requests to the Politburo were to force the Revvoensovet to establish a firm order plan for the next two to three years, raise the prices it paid on loss-making military production, conclude firm contracts with military industry, and pay its debts to military industry regularly and promptly. Tolokontsev also asked for more control over personnel appointments and more integration of military production into civilian factories, but his focus was clearly on taming the Red Army and nailing down a production program.[77]

In response, Voroshilov and the Revvoensovet he chaired endorsed Tolokontsev's request for a long-range order plan, probably in the hope of expediting a long-range budget for the Red Army itself. If nothing else, the Revvoensovet saw definite improvement in military industry's performance under Tolokontsev and, despite some reservations, was willing to give him time to consolidate his achievements.[78] The Red Army had a five-year plan of industrial orders through 1930–1931 ready by February (see tables 1 and 2).[79]

This long-range order plan is strikingly conservative. It suggests, above all, that the Red Army's high command did not yet realize in 1927 the full extent of the bounties that industrialization could offer. In 1931, the actual procurement budget for one year would be substantially greater than the combined total of *five years* of spending as projected in 1927. The Red Army's 1927 order plan was basically static, with purchases of existing weapons systems holding steady, growing slowly, or even declining (cartridges, Nagant revolvers). Procurement grew somewhat for new types of production, but only to moderate levels (automatic rifles, Degtiarev light machine guns, tanks). Judging both by this order plan

Table 1. Spring 1927 Long-Range Plan of Peacetime Orders for Military Equipment

Type	1926–1927	1927–1928	1928–1929	1929–1930	1930–1931
Rifles	200,000	225,000	225,000	225,000	225,000
Nagant revolvers	16,000	16,000	15,000	10,000	10,000
Maxim medium machine guns	1,200	800	800	750	750
Maxim/Tokarev machine guns[1]	1,750	2,500	2,500	2,500	2,500
Degtiarev machine guns	100	2,500	3,000	7,000	9,000
Bullets (million)	400	400	400	375	375
Total firearms (million rubles)	43.915	48.246	49.196	52.052	54.247
76mm artillery (1902)	12	18	24	84	174
76mm hill artillery (1909)	20	20	20	20	20
76mm AA artillery (1914)	80	100	120	150	150
122mm howitzer (1910)	200	220	220	220	220
107mm field gun	30	30	30	30	30
152mm howitzer (1909)	30	30	30	30	30
Battalion artillery	—	10	50	100	100
Total artillery (million rubles)	13.424	16.595	18.526	20.446	22.496
Tanks	2	—	48	100	100
Ammunition (million rubles)	26.457	33.090	34.542	36.000	38.905
Grand total of nonchemical production of military industry (million rubles)	90.079	103.740	108.098	115.697	124.041
Military-chemical production of military industry (million rubles)	1.480	5.200	7.250	7.850	8.800
Military production of nonmilitary industry: 76mm short artillery (1913)	—	100	300	300	400
Total military production of nonmilitary industry (million rubles)	15.446	21.154	24.183	25.588	28.775
Grand total of planned orders for military equipment from military and civil industry (million rubles)	107.005	130.094	139.531	149.135	161.616

[1]Before the Degtiarev light machine gun proved its superiority, the Soviets planned to use a cut-down Maxim machine gun as their light machine gun.

Table 2. Prices of Military Equipment as Calculated from Order Plans

Equipment	Price (rubles)
Rifle	56.9
Nagant revolver	41–45.2
Maxim machine gun	2,007.5–1,990.67
1,000 bullets	61.625–61.68
76mm artillery (1902)	8,166.67–8,189.66
76mm hill artillery (1909)	10,100
76mm AA (1915)	15,375–15,353.83
122mm howitzer (1910)	17,300
107mm field gun	36,400
152mm howitzer (1909)	24,666.67
Tank	35,000

and by the summer 1927 five-year plan for the Red Army's own development (see chapter 2), the Revvoensovet did not expect a qualitative change in its forces and did not foresee the rapid growth in arms procurement that industrialization could produce. In the end, this shortsightedness would do no harm to the Red Army's ability to grow; this five-year order plan would soon be discarded and forgotten.

This long-range plan incorporated the 1926–1927 procurement order. For that particular order, a detailed breakdown among the various production trusts of military industry is available (see table 3). Equipment purchased in 1926–1927 went much more to stockpiles than to current needs; the Red Army calculated that 80.8 percent of the output of military industry, when transportation costs were included, built up mobilization stocks. The rest, less than a fifth of the order, went for immediate use.[80]

The precise 1926–1927 order is difficult to determine, as it varied greatly with fluctuating prices, differing definitions of military orders, and actual changes in the order. A Red Army evaluation from March 1927 broke it down not by producer, as in table 3, but by the Red Army directorate that placed the order. This included not only ordnance, for which the chief purchaser was the Artillery

Table 3. 1926–1927 Military Order for Industrial Production

Production Trust	Cost (rubles)
Firearm–Machine Gun	18,260,000
Cartridge-Fuse	34,268,608
Artillery-Arsenal	15,505,154
Military-Chemical	18,718,752
Military orders outside military industry	10,926,211
Total	97,678,725

Directorate, but also communications and electrical equipment for the Military-Technical Directorate; uniforms, greatcoats, tents, boots, and other supplies for the Military-Management *(voenno-khoziaistvennoe)* Directorate; planes and motors for the air force; and ships for the navy. It also included unfilled orders from 1925–1926 (see table 4).[81] In still another reckoning of military industry's order, the RZ STO in May 1927 confirmed military industry's production at an overall volume of 183.5 million rubles, of which 58.2 million was civilian in nature and 125.3 million was military. In June 1927, Director of Supply Dybenko calculated the total order of the entire Red Army, not limited to military industry, at 277.7 million rubles.[82]

MOBILIZING THE SOVIET ECONOMY

Although the Red Army's high command was obviously concerned with industry's yearly output, it was just as preoccupied with how industry would cope with the transition to full military production in the event of war. The Revvoensovet had never been happy in the mid-1920s with the performance of the Committee for De- and Mobilization. Its name illustrates the chief objection the military had to its work: it was created more to handle industrial demobilization after the civil war than to mobilize for any future war. After receiving its first mobilization order from the NKVM in 1923, the committee's plodding pace made the plans it drew up obsolete before their completion. A few halfhearted attempts at mobilization plans were evident failures, even within their limited scope. The committee's own personnel estimated that a full plan would take at least ten and possibly eighteen *years* to finish. In the opinion of Genrikh Iagoda of the OGPU, this "amounted to in fact a refusal to assemble such a plan at all." Poor communications between the committee and Voenprom meant that Voenprom drew up its own mobilization plans and the committee worked with obsolete data.[83]

Table 4. Military Orders to Industry for 1926–1927

Directorate	1926–1927 Orders (rubles)	Leftover from 1925–1926 (rubles)	Total (rubles)
Artillery (to military industry)	92,222,136	24,742,570	116,964,706
Artillery (to nonmilitary industry)	7,519, 628	1,277,343	8,796,971
Artillery total	99,741,764	26,019,913	125,761,677
Military-Technical	9,673,065	4,455,215	14,128,280
Military-Chemical	6,550,390	2,009,701	8,560,091
Air Force	22,484,575	—	22,484,575
Military-Management	87,286,281	4,106,197	91,392,478
Navy	25,597,000	1,514,095	27,111,095
Total	251,333,075	38,105,121	289,458,196

When the Committee on De- and Mobilization finally dissolved into the new VPU, Dzerzhinskii took the opportunity in March 1926 to endorse Avanesov's new "basic principles" for Vesenkha's mobilization work. These simple statements of economic defense policy established that industry must have a mobilization plan and that some entity must be entrusted with drawing one up, correcting it for continual industrial and military expansion, and shepherding it through governmental approval. Contrary to earlier efforts, the new mobilization plan would enlist local cooperation down to the factory level, correcting the excessively centralized efforts of the Committee on De- and Mobilization, with special mobilization cells in all Vesenkha's main directorates and in union republic Vesenkhas.[84]

These "basic principles," though quite elementary, serve as a guide to the priorities of Soviet economic policy makers and to the principles behind mobilization. World War I had shown the need for comprehensive preparation for war, and the delicate state of relations with the Soviet peasantry meant that mobilization had to be carried out with minimal disruption to the production of civilian goods.[85] Since post–civil war demobilization had closed many military shops in civilian factories, those factories would need "production cells" familiar with military manufacturing to serve as cadres, even if small production runs cost the factory money. To minimize disruption, assimilation of military and civilian goods was a priority. *Assimilation,* as Avanesov defined the term, meant making military goods standard for peacetime use: "development of those branches of industry which are identically needed both for peace and war and the maximal use in peacetime of military goods," with standard machinery and parts across all industry. Surrogates would replace scarce, expensive, or imported raw materials, and bottlenecks in the manufacture of military hardware would be found and eliminated. None of these ideas was especially original or insightful—Karatygin had alluded to them—but they were the natural and logical response to limited resources.[86]

The VPU thus took responsibility for economic mobilization. Acting as "the central leading organ conducting mobilization work and work on the fulfillment of military orders," it exercised direct jurisdiction over "all existing military trusts and individual factories of military significance." The VPU was charged with drawing up wartime organizational changes and combining disparate economic mobilization plans into a coherent whole. Its mandate ran far beyond Vesenkha, including union republic factories, remaining Soviet private industry, and even foreign concessions.[87]

The VPU's first mobilization plan in the summer of 1926 envisaged two separate production schedules. Plan A took into account *only* actually existing capacity in military industry. Completely supported, at least in theory, by supplies of parts and raw materials, plan A would go into effect immediately upon the outbreak of war. Plan R grouped together two types of capacity: existing excess production capacity above that needed for wartime demands, and capacity "in conditions not appropriate for mobilization plan A," either because that capacity was only planned and not actually built or because it was not reliably supplied with raw materials.[88]

The essence of plan A was what it would provide the Red Army during the first year of war, and Soviet practice characterized mobilization plans by the output the military would receive over that first year. In keeping with its rudimentary nature, plan A concentrated on the supply basics for a World War I army. As Tukhachevskii in 1926 described the Red Army's requirements to sustain war for one year, it would need (over and above that with which it began the war) 900,000 rifles, 10,000 medium and 8,000 light machine guns, 3,250 million cartridges, and 1,180 76mm artillery pieces and 5,350,000 shells for them, to list only a few. In 1928, by comparison, under industry's plan A, the Red Army could in theory expect 14 million shells (of all types), 1,450 million cartridges, and 700,000 rifles over one year—not nearly enough to meet its expected needs.[89] Despite all its faults, including being outdated at the time it was drawn up, plan A would serve as the basis for Soviet industrial readiness for several years and as the sole available option. Even in early 1929, as work went forward on completing plan S, the mobilization schedule that would replace plan A, the NKVM and Soviet industry were forced to recognize that in the event of war, their choice would be plan A or no plan at all.

The VPU's emphasis on making plan A as realistic as possible fell between two stools: based on nonexistent capacity, it was still inadequate. First, this "realistic" plan could only partially meet the Red Army's demand for supplies in the event of war: 77 percent of rifle demand, 50 percent of bullets, 90 percent of artillery, 38 percent of shells. The disparity would get worse, not better: by May 1927, Efimov reported that the Red Army's needs for a year of war had increased to 1 million rifles and 3,015 million bullets. Second, although it was, in principle, based only on actually available capacity, the plan did not fully take into account bottlenecks where limited supplies of imported raw materials such as rubber or saltpeter could disrupt production. Furthermore, despite stressing actually existing capacity, plan A depended on planned but not yet built industrial plants or even whole new types of domestic production. Through at least 1928, the Red Army believed that it lacked an acceptable mobilization plan.[90]

The military's complaints about inadequate industrial preparation were constant. Tukhachevskii found in mid-1926 that improving the disorder Avanesov had uncovered had to be the first priority—without that, no other progress was possible. Still, he expressed muted concern over the continuing absence of an industrial mobilization plan and the VPU's neglect of the problem.[91] Tukhachevskii's criticism was muted only because he took the VPU's optimistic assurances at face value. By September 1926, when the Red Army began to realize just how little ordnance Soviet industry could actually provide, its critiques became much harsher. Chutskaev of Rabkrin compared the Red Army's needs for mobilization and one year of war with the stockpiles it could expect by 1 October 1926 (see table 5). The results were ominous. Although the mobilized army of 3.2 million

Table 5. Red Army Requirements to Deploy and to Wage One Year of War Compared to Stockpiles

Equipment	Number Needed for Deployment	Additional Needed for Year of War	Number in Red Army's Stocks by 1 October 1926 (percent of number needed)
Rifles	1,015,363	427,500	1,467,774 (101.7)
Medium machine guns	27,458	5,480	22,296 (67.7)
Light machine guns	17,428	3,480	8,286 (39.6)
Cartridges	828,000,000	1,771,000,000	1,336,000,000 (51.4)
76mm artillery	4,027	490	3,733 (82.6)
122mm howitzers	1,264	65	1,138 (85.6)
76mm shells	2,588,710	11,134,000	4,841,690 (35.3)
122mm shells	438,902	2,000,000	691,000 (28.3)
Gas masks	3,500,000	3,500,000	91,000 (1.3)

men would have 101.7 percent of the rifles and 67.7 percent of the medium machine guns it needed in stock, other types of equipment would be considerably more scarce. There would be few light machine guns, bullets for only 100 days of war, and only two months' supply of 76mm artillery shells. With only about 1,000 rounds per gun, the Soviet army could hardly expect to do better than the tsarist army, which had started World War I with 1,200 rounds per gun and ran short after three or four months.[92] Chutskaev concluded that more spending was needed to boost the Red Army's stockpiles.

Egorov, who had come to the VPU from the Red Army, was even gloomier than Chutskaev when he discovered the shocking truth behind plan A's promises. As he revealed in November 1926, Vesenkha's plan A represented yearly production not from the outbreak of war but *from the end of the transition from peacetime to full wartime production.* This transition period for retooling to a war footing was expected to last thirteen months for rifle production, sixteen months for machine guns, and ten to fourteen months for artillery. For Vesenkha's purposes, the first year of war would not start until more than a year after hostilities began, much like a building's first floor might be one story above the ground. As a result, Egorov came up with still lower figures for the supplies the Red Army could rely on to fight a war. In the first year of fighting, the Red Army would have only 51.5 percent of the rifles it needed and 24.5 percent of the machine guns. The number of shells it could expect to receive varied by type but was in no case greater than 19.7 percent of its needs, and in most cases was under 10 percent. Matters would improve in the second year (under Vesenkha's assumptions, the first year), but shell production would still provide the Red Army with only 30 to 60 percent of its needs. The biggest problem was bottlenecks. Shell-manufacturing capacity went to waste, limited by low production of powder and fuses. Stocks of nonferrous metals were critically short. By Egorov's calculation, only 44 percent of the copper, 13 percent of the zinc, 8 percent of the lead, and none of the aluminum necessary for shell production would be available from stockpiles. The only salvation for the mobilization plan was more funding and stricter discipline.[93]

Such a dangerous situation persisted, in Egorov's view, only because Vesenkha's personnel did not take military work seriously. The VPU could not get Vesenkha's other main directorates to pay attention to its decrees on mobilization issues. Instead, "mobilization organs both in the center at Vesenkha and at the periphery do not take part in linking industrial construction, long-range development plans, and current industrial plans with the demands of defense." During a Vesenkha reorganization, both the staff and the VPU's Mobilization-Planning Section advocated a new, more powerful body to coordinate mobilization work, without success.[94]

Egorov had come to the VPU as a military liaison and warned the Revvoensovet in January 1927 about industry's mobilization plan: from the Red Army's point of view, there was no plan. The Revvoensovet responded to Egorov's concerns with a protest to Vesenkha that enumerated what the Red Army considered vital for smooth supply in wartime. Finally approved by the Revvoensovet on 5 March 1927, the proposal listed a series of errors in the ways Vesenkha and the VPU had planned for war, errors the Red Army would hammer on for years to come. Not so concerned with the VPU itself, the Red Army was appalled by the lack of power the VPU had within Vesenkha. The Revvoensovet wished to make the VPU a "central functional organ" of Vesenkha, which would give it control over mobilization work at all Vesenkha's main directorates and all the union republic Vesenkhas. In addition to the standard military demand that Vesenkha chair Valerian Kuibyshev devote more attention to defense, the Revvoensovet asked for the extension of mobilization organs down to the local level. Industry's long-range planning, in the Revvoensovet's opinion, was not sufficiently linked to defense needs.[95]

These general demands accompanied specific proposals to ensure steady supplies for the military. The hitch, as always, was that what the military deemed essential required Vesenkha to spend resources and energy on military priorities, not on its own. The Red Army wanted more stockpiles of strategic raw materials, but taking these away from current production only made industrial managers' jobs more difficult. Standardizing civil and military goods, *rationalizing* production (the Soviet term for finding efficiencies), and devising surrogates for scarce raw materials were all vital for the Red Army but headaches for Kuibyshev and his industrial managers.[96] The Revvoensovet resolved that it would take some responsibility for mobilization by assisting civil defense against chemical attack, and the Supply Directorate would provide technical advice on production. The Revvoensovet also promised to help in assimilating military and civilian goods. The Staff, along with the Supply Directorate, would help Vesenkha plan the strategic distribution of industry away from vulnerable areas. Perhaps most importantly, the Revvoensovet agreed to deliver its five-year order plans and projected mobilization demands to industry in full and on time.[97]

Vesenkha responded to the Red Army's demands with still another reorganization to reemphasize mobilization in its defense work. It had not resolved the thorny issue of how to maximize peacetime defense production while at the same time devoting resources to preparing for future wars, and Soviet defense planners would never truly perceive or deal with this problem. By not choosing between those two goals, the Soviet Union would eventually devote staggering resources to both of them. Vesenkha attempted to deal with the problem by reversing the unification of defense management brought about by the creation of the VPU. When Voenprom had been broken up into trusts, the VPU had taken over as sole authority for military industry, handling war planning, distribution of orders, and the day-to-day supervision of the production trusts. In late April 1927, however, Kuibyshev created a new Mobilization-Planning Directorate (MPU) within Vesenkha, expanding the VPU's Mobilization-Planning Sector into a full-fledged directorate to handle war preparations. The split in authority over military industry was restored, with the VPU handling current production and the MPU taking over industrial mobilization, but this time, there was a key difference. The MPU had clear precedence over the VPU, and its director, Aleksandr Mikhailovich Postnikov, confirmed by the Politburo on 30 April 1927, would dominate military industry for the next three years. Mobilization would now dominate concerns over peacetime production. Kuibyshev reported to the RZ STO on 7 May 1927 on the formation of the MPU and on Postnikov's appointment,[98] but it took some time for full understanding of the MPU's significance to sink in among military and industrial administrators. On 28 May 1927, the RZ STO directed Vesenkha to create a "special military planning division for the rapid development of a concrete mobilization plan," in effect, the already established MPU.[99] At the next meeting, the RZ STO recognized with satisfaction the creation of the MPU and Vesenkha's measures to strengthen the MPU's powers and authority.[100]

By April 1927, then, with Postnikov in place at the head of the newly formed MPU, the Red Army and the Soviet state had created the intellectual and administrative infrastructure of a militarized economy and society. With fiscal austerity preventing extensive investment in defense production, the Soviet Union instead established an organizational framework for militarization. The MPU, organizing the civilian economy to serve the demands of war, had taken clear precedence over the VPU, managing peacetime military production. Under Dzerzhinskii and Kuibyshev at Vesenkha, a series of administrators and managers had fine-tuned Frunze's vision of a society organized for war into a system to coordinate the Soviet Union's industrial resources and supply the Red Army in peace and in war. The only factor still missing was capital. The tight budgets of the mid-1920s meant that grand visions and comprehensive plans remained only on paper. For the present, the Red Army could not afford to rearm itself with the most modern weaponry, and Soviet industry could not afford to build the industrial capacity to meet the military's growing demands. Until more money could go to the needs of defense, that infrastructure would remain only a paper achievement.

2

Rumors of War

As the Soviet state's capacity for war grew, the NEP economy withered and died. By the late 1920s, with Soviet industry recovering to prewar levels of production, the changes began that would eventually become Stalin's "great turn," eliminating the private sector of the Soviet economy, subjugating the peasantry to the state (and, in the process, slaughtering millions), destroying the relative cultural pluralism of the NEP years, and imposing the iron law of Stalinist orthodoxy on the party. The Soviet economy was increasingly directed from above to serve the needs and whims of the state, as central control over investment and planning burgeoned. Inside the Bolshevik party itself, power became more concentrated in the hands of General Secretary Joseph Stalin, who expelled from power one by one all those who would not recognize his absolute supremacy.[1]

In Bolshevik theory, Stalin's revolution made the Soviet state far more formidable as a military power. Petit bourgeois peasants could be converted into true proletarians from property owners and class enemies.[2] Centralized control of the economy would make it a precise yet flexible instrument for producing the sinews of war. Quashing political dissent would render the Soviet polity united in defense of the socialist fatherland. That this logic was deeply flawed hardly matters; true Stalinists could not doubt that centralization and order were infinitely superior to the chaos of NEP. Frunze's and Karatygin's ideals of militarization through central control were incompatible with the pluralist NEP economy.

Seen in this context, the war scare of 1927 takes on profound significance. This event, a combination of foreign crises and domestic panic culminating in late spring and early summer of 1927, determines in large part our understanding of the fate of NEP. If the war scare were genuine, and Stalin along with the rest of the Politburo truly believed that war was imminent in the summer of 1927, then NEP died an accidental death. That is, even if foreign dangers were not real but only perceived, the Soviet state's need to defend itself meant that a relatively moderate peasant policy had to be replaced by rapid industrialization to guarantee the safety of the new socialist state from outside dangers. If, however, the war scare were a manipulated panic created to discredit Trotsky and any other opposition to Stalin's autocratic power, then the conclusion is that NEP was murdered. The war scare, in that case, would be only a cover story to mask a policy of relentless centralization, for NEP was incompatible with a Stalinist understanding of the needs of Soviet security.[3]

But intention and belief are fiendishly difficult to determine under any circumstances, let alone the secretive world of Soviet high politics. Fortunately, the twists and turns of Soviet defense policy provide an excellent means of establishing that the essence of the war scare was a political tool to attack Trotsky and solidify Stalin's support. As the previous chapter demonstrated, the militarization of the Soviet economy began long before the war scare, albeit with limited funds. The war scare therefore did not precede but followed increased attention to defense. Moreover, as argued later, it did not bring about significant changes in defense policy or dramatic increases in preparations for war, despite fevered rhetoric. At the war scare's height, the Red Army was still starved for capital, despite public warnings of an imminent attack on the Soviet Union. The war scare proved far more useful for arming Stalin against his enemies, leaving the Red Army and military industry with little new to show for all the fevered rhetoric of danger.

The true target of the war scare was not foreign aggressors but Leon Trotsky. This was evident to some. For example, Georgii Chicherin returned to Moscow from a trip abroad in the summer of 1927 and was stunned and puzzled by talk of imminent war. "Then," he told Louis Fischer in 1929, "a colleague enlightened me. He said 'Shh. We know that [this is ridiculous]. But we need this against Trotsky.'"[4]

The war scare was, in Alfred Meyer's words, "essentially a phony issue, manipulated by politicians in the course of a factional struggle in the ruling Communist party." Stalin himself seized upon the war scare to attack Trotsky and the opposition:

> What can one say after all this about our ill-fated Opposition, in connection with its new attack on the party in the face of the threat of a new war? What can one say about the fact that the Opposition found it appropriate at a time of war danger to strengthen its attacks on the party? . . . Can it be that the opposition is against the USSR's victory in the battles with the imperialists that threaten us, against increasing the USSR's defense readiness, against the strengthening of our rear? Or, perhaps, this is cowardice before new difficulties, desertion, desire to flee responsibility, covered by the chattering of leftist phrases.

As John Erickson observes, "this threat of war was conjured up at a time suspiciously convenient for the embarrassment of the Opposition . . . it was not undesirable to silence internal criticism with talk of external dangers, to transform the righteous indignation of Stalin's opponents into traitorous agitation."[5]

Fundamental continuity in defense policy through 1927 bears out that inter-pretation. The Red Army's concern over its ability to fight a war was as strong as it had been before the war scare; the financial support to do something meaningful about that was as weak as before the war scare. Before the war scare, the military had already started revamping its five-year development plan, and Vesenkha had begun a similar five-year plan for investment in military industry. In early 1927, before the war scare had hit its height, defense policy making was streamlined by replacing Rykov's Commission with the Executive Session of the STO (the RZ STO) as the USSR's defense cabinet. The climax of the war scare in April–May 1927, explored in more detail later, only slightly accelerated trends that had already existed long before. N. S. Simonov's argument that the war scare brought home to the Soviet leadership its military weakness is not tenable: as Avanesov's reforms of military industry indicate, consciousness of weakness and the resulting repairs had started years before.[6] The war scare did not change defense policy. Continuities between the periods before and after the war scare are striking; changes are relatively minor.

The first hints of the war scare (evident only in retrospect) came from Eastern Europe in 1926. Poland and Romania strengthened their ties, and after Pilsudski seized power in a 12 May 1926 coup, Soviet-Polish relations went quickly down-hill. In an attempt to forestall Polish influence over the Baltics and head off the possibility of Poland's exchanging a German corridor to East Prussia for compen-sation at Lithuanian expense, the USSR proposed nonaggression pacts to Estonia and Latvia on 21 May; when these were coolly received, it proposed a pact to Poland itself on 24 August. Failure of these initiatives and a similar one to Finland convinced the Soviets that Poland's aim was hegemony in the Baltic regardless of Soviet interests.[7]

Despite these unpleasant developments, Stalin did not see foreign war as a near-term danger. Addressing the Fifteenth Party Conference on 1 November 1926, Stalin held that "we live in capitalist encirclement. . . . The danger of military intervention exists and will continue to exist for a long time." There was, how-ever, no need to panic. "It's another question," he stressed, "whether the capitalists can venture a serious intervention against the republic of Soviets," for labor move-ments in the West would hinder any strike against the Soviet Union. In the long term, danger remained: "if the capitalist world isn't now in a position to start a military intervention against our country, that doesn't mean that it will never be in a position to do that."[8]

In December 1926, however, the *Manchester Guardian* broke the story of the Soviet military's collaboration with the Reichswehr.[9] Shortly afterward, at the January 1927 Moscow party conference, Nikolai Bukharin amplified remarks circulating in the Soviet press by warning of a British-led campaign against the Soviet Union. Despite this, Stalin, Rykov, and Deputy Foreign Minister Maksim

Litvinov played down the danger. Stalin repeated that there was no short-term threat: "we will not have war in the spring or fall of this year," for the capitalists were simply not ready for war. In short, Meyer finds that "the party leaders seem to have been in agreement on the absence of a genuine threat of war, with the exception of Bukharin and a group of his Comintern colleagues who seem to have taken the alleged danger they themselves had conjured up more seriously."[10]

That relative calm disappeared in late spring 1927, however, as a series of events produced hoarding and near hysteria among the Soviet public, which expected an immediate attack. On 6 April 1927, the Chinese government in Beijing raided the Soviet embassy, seizing diplomatic personnel, Chinese revolutionaries, and incriminating documents. The Soviets gingerly protested this action (suggesting a desire not to score points at Beijing's expense) and blamed the raid on the fact that "the Peking Cabinet has become the instrument of foreign imperialist circles" that "wish to provoke the USSR into a war." Soon after, Chiang Kai-shek's Kuomintang in southern China purged its communists, marking a double setback for Soviet policy.[11]

At the time of the China crisis, relations with Britain had been in a parlous state for some months. On 23 February 1927, Foreign Minister Austen Chamberlain had officially complained of Soviet anti-British propaganda, a complaint Litvinov rejected point by point and countered with accusations of British misdeeds. On 12 May, British authorities raided the offices of ARCOS, the Soviet trading company. The raid, for all its drama and the protests it provoked from the Soviets, turned up little evidence to implicate the Soviets in subversive activity, but Prime Minister Stanley Baldwin still severed relations with the USSR on 24 May 1927.[12]

Finally, on 7 June 1927, Soviet ambassador to Poland Petr Voikov was assassinated by a Russian émigré. The Politburo composed a protest note, ordered its publication, and arranged public demonstrations. Later in the month, the Politburo further ordered the publication of a warning on the danger of war and subversion, with practical instructions on improving readiness. A special "Defense Week" was declared, and Andrei Bubnov of the Red Army's Political Directorate was to pay special attention to mobilization and training, especially of the civilian population. *Pravda* published a call for "greater vigilance," and Stalin wrote an editorial at the end of July on "the real and actual *threat* of a new war in general, and of a new war against the USSR in particular."[13] The war scare had arrived.

STABILITY IN DEFENSE POLICY

Public demonstrations and calls for vigilance did not signal any policy changes. Defense industry's recovery had begun in 1925, and the 1927 innovations in Soviet defense came before the war scare, not after it. In a retrospective speech to the Fifteenth Congress of Soviets in December 1927, War Commissar Kliment

Voroshilov summarized the three chief positive changes resulting from the war scare: Vesenkha's renewed commitment to mobilization, Gosplan's increased attention to defense, and a new spirit in the Council of Labor and Defense (STO). Unfortunately, Voroshilov knew better. Vesenkha's renewed commitment to war preparedness predated the war scare, Gosplan's attention to defense was an entirely cosmetic reorganization, and the STO's new spirit was both cosmetic and predated the war scare. Voroshilov's self-congratulatory remarks in utter disregard of the truth provide further evidence of the political nature of the war scare: he used his speech to stress the acuity of Stalin's leadership.

In his December 1927 speech, Voroshilov first hailed Vesenkha's dedication to mobilization, referring to the creation of the VPU to handle peacetime production and the MPU to run mobilization. As discussed in the previous chapter, both organizations predated the triple crises of April and May 1927 (the VPU, 1925; the MPU, April 1927) and were the result of long-standing internal political pressures, not the exigencies of foreign policy. The only novelty in Vesenkha after the war scare was a newly formed group to execute existing policies more efficiently. In June 1927, the MPU's director Postnikov began chairing Vesenkha's new Standing Mobilization Conference. *Not* responsible for ongoing military production, this conference was a forum for managers of Vesenkha's directorates to coordinate mobilization and long-term investment in defense. The first meeting, for example, discussed the Soviet chemical industry and wartime production for Leningrad's machine-building factories; the third focused on specific grants to expand military plants. As a sign of how little the conference concerned itself with the day-to-day management of military industry, Aleksandr Tolokontsev, responsible for munitions production as director of the VPU, did not even attend until five meetings and one month had already passed. Postnikov's group vetted investment and construction plans, mobilization assignments, and Vesenkha's general defense work. The Standing Mobilization Conference, in effect, patched the split in defense policy created when the MPU was separated from the VPU; it did not represent a particularly new phenomenon.[14]

In his December 1927 speech on the positive results of the war scare, Voroshilov next hailed a new defense cell "in the bowels of Gosplan, which will be obliged to take the needs of defense into account in all economic planning." Voroshilov certainly knew better, since he himself had participated in discussions on reforming Gosplan's already existing Military Commission. Although Gosplan's Defense Sector was indeed created after the war scare, it only continued the operations of Gosplan's earlier Military Commission under a new name. Voroshilov's own investigation of Gosplan's defense responsibilities had recommended that its Military Commission continue to function until the new Defense Sector was up and running, since Gosplan had had a military section since at least 1923. The essential difference was that the new Defense Sector would not be under the control of Trotsky-supporter I. T. Smilga, suggesting again that the war scare had more to do with the Soviet Union's internal power struggles than its foreign enemies.[15]

In May 1927, Mikhail Vladimirskii offered to lead a Gosplan commission to handle war planning and military production. Although the Politburo briefly considered appointing Tukhachevskii to head Gosplan's new Defense Sector, it chose Vladimirskii instead. Ordered to share responsibility for planning the Soviet Union's defense with the Red Army Staff, Vladimirskii took office in July 1927.[16] Vladimirskii had a rather unlikely background for defense work. Born a priest's son in 1874, he received a medical education before being exiled from tsarist Russia. Returning from Paris after the February Revolution, Vladimirskii served both in the Central Committee and as chair of Ukraine's Gosplan. In December 1926, he returned to Moscow as deputy chair of the all-union Gosplan. In the Defense Sector, Vladimirskii's deputy, Konstantin Mekhonoshin, compensated for his lack of military experience. Mekhonoshin, another Old Bolshevik, had fought in the civil war and then served in the Red Army. He would take over the Defense Sector himself in April 1929.[17]

The third accomplishment Voroshilov hailed in December 1927 was that Sovnarkom's subcommittee, the Council for Labor and Defense (STO), was showing interest in security and thereby living up to all parts of its name: "Only since spring has the STO gotten back its third letter—*O* [for *oborony*, defense]." Voroshilov continued that after the civil war, "the STO little by little lost its third letter. We didn't have an STO, but an ST, i.e., a Council of Labor. If we had an STO, it was only in spelling and pronunciation."[18] Not only did Voroshilov spoil the joke by his pedantic insistence on explaining it, but he stole it from Frunze, who had made the same quip in a speech three years before.[19]

Voroshilov's digression on the letters of STO referred to the pre–war scare creation of a new defense cabinet in February 1927: the Executive Session of the Council for Labor and Defense, more handily referred to as the RZ STO. In effect, the RZ STO was a restructured Rykov's Commission, retaining Rykov as chair. Well before the war scare, Voroshilov made a secret report on the USSR's defenses to a plenary session of the Central Committee and Central Control Commission.[20] Immediately afterward, on 12 February 1927, the STO created a "Defense Commission"—later renamed the RZ STO—to serve as a defense cabinet. Six days later, the STO set the new group's roster, subsequently confirmed by the Politburo, of state officials directly involved in the USSR's defense: Aleksei Rykov, head of government and de facto prime minister as chair of Sovnarkom; Ian Rudzutak, deputy chair of Sovnarkom and commissar of transport; War Commissar Kliment Voroshilov; Andrei Bubnov, the Red Army's chief political officer and Voroshilov's deputy at the RZ STO; Valerian Kuibyshev, chair of Vesenkha and head of Soviet industry; Commissar of Finance Nikolai Briukhanov; Viacheslav Menzhinskii, chair of the OGPU, the secret police; Gosplan chair Gleb Krzhizhanovskii; Commissar of Trade Anastas Mikoian; and Aleksandr Tsiurupa, member of the Presidium of the Central Executive Committee. This group was given the right to make final decisions in the name of the STO with legally binding force and was to meet at least once a month.[21]

After three months' delay, the Defense Commission had its first meeting on 7 May 1927 as the rechristened RZ STO. There is no doubt that the organization was the same; the membership of the group was nearly identical, with only minor expansion. Menzhinskii's deputy Iagoda gained the right to stand in for him at meetings; Tolokontsev, director of the VPU, became a member; Vladimirskii of Gosplan and Tukhachevskii of the Red Army had advisory votes. The first meeting of the RZ STO created an apparat, and the Red Army's Semen Ventsov was made its secretary to manage paperwork. Rykov was chair of the RZ STO by virtue of his office, but Rudzutak occasionally took over those duties. Six days after the RZ STO's first meeting, the STO officially established its existence under that name and approved its new membership. By July, the Politburo had likewise approved the new setup, giving the RZ STO practical control over defense affairs while regularly reporting to the Politburo.[22]

So despite Voroshilov's December 1927 claims, the war scare had little impact on the organization of Soviet defense. Ian Berzin, the Red Army's head of military intelligence, had found at the start of 1927 that there was little immediate danger of war, and so no precipitous actions were necessary to prepare the USSR's defenses. Assessing the complicated European political situation and military preparations in the USSR's Western neighbors, Berzin concluded that "we do not see any immediate war preparations during 1927." The small chance of creating a united coalition in Western Europe against the USSR also made "military action in 1927 unlikely."[23]

Even at the height of the war scare, members of Stalin's inner circle were careful to match their calls for greater vigilance with measures to ensure that the economy's proper function was not disrupted. Valerian Kuibyshev, speaking to an audience of managers and economic bureaucrats immediately after the assassination of the Soviet ambassador to Poland, told them, "we must tie industry's development plans more closely to the defense readiness of the country." At the same time, however, he warned against letting military spending and production hurt economic performance. "It would, of course, be a mistake and dangerous if we . . . said to ourselves, well, we're living through a frightening time, we need to get rid of everything not relating directly to defense." That would disrupt planning, ruin cost-cutting, and generally set back the cause of industrialization.[24]

The host of military-economic plans debated in Vesenkha and the Red Army in 1927 produce a consistent impression: the war scare did not significantly boost defense spending or produce particular innovations in Soviet defense. First, these plans originated in 1926, and second, their continuities over 1927 are striking. Whether the plan was for investment in military industry, long-range procurement for the Red Army, or the functioning of the Soviet economy at war, the overriding constraint was limited resources. The need not to disturb the delicate balances of the Soviet economy was paramount, public warnings of imminent war notwithstanding. This further suggests that the war scare had domestic political aims, for there was no serious attempt to prepare the Soviet Union for war.[25]

The intricate bargaining to craft an investment plan for defense industry had begun in earnest on 5 October 1926, when the STO ordered the Red Army Staff and Vesenkha to create a five-year plan for military industry. Chief of Staff Tukhachevskii found that he could do little until the Red Army completed plans for its own development.[26] The military's slow response allowed Vesenkha to assemble its five-year investment plan without military input, working from an old 1925 war plan and thereby making its own wartime job much easier. By April 1927, Rukhimovich and Budnevich, working at Vesenkha, had finished an investment and construction plan for military industry. In order to determine the scale of investment required, they started from the Red Army's old mobilization order: the materiel the Red Army expected to need for one year of war. Even using an outdated mobilization plan, industry's ability to meet the Red Army's demands was poor and in some cases catastrophic. In over half the categories Rukhimovich and Budnevich examined, projected production was less than 50 percent, and occasionally only 10 to 15 percent, of the military's needs. The conclusion was simple: effective defense required substantial capital investment in Vesenkha's investment plan.[27]

For example, by 1 October 1927, yearly bullet capacity using three shifts would be 1,226 million, but wartime demand would be nearly twice that: 2,250 million. The Red Army would need 900,000 rifles from industry but could count on no more than 489,000; instead of 16,500 Maxim and 27,000 Degtiarev machine guns, it could expect only 6,500 Maxims. The situation was worse elsewhere: estimated production capacity for 76mm field guns (1902 model) was 60, whereas projected need was 1,450; for gas masks, the figures were 600,000 available versus over 7 million needed. In each case, Rukhimovich's plan projected the capital investment necessary to meet the army's needs (see table 6).[28]

Housing the additional workers required would cost 160 million rubles. This plan assumed slow growth in military procurement over five years:[29]

Five-Year Military Order Plan (1926–1927 prices, million rubles)

	1926–1927	1927–1928	1928–1929	1929–1930	1930–1931	Total
From military industry	91.6	108.9	115.3	123.5	132.8	572.1
From civil industry	13.4	21.2	24.2	25.6	28.8	115.2
Total order	107.0	130.1	139.5	149.1	161.6	687.3

Vesenkha's five-year plan for capital investment in military industry finally made it to the RZ STO four months behind schedule for the 28 May 1927 meeting. Ventsov, the RZ STO's secretary, requested preliminary reactions from both the Red Army and Gosplan to this 323.9 million–ruble Vesenkha draft. Gosplan found

Table 6. Projected Capital Investment

Equipment	Investment (million rubles)
Bullets and cartridges	41.3
Firearms	60.1
Fuses and detonators	47.5
Artillery—two variants	47.9 (variant: 41.9)
Powder	49.85
Optics	5.2
Explosives	34.3
Poison gas and gas masks	14.7
Shells	23.0
Total capital investment required	323.9

it basically acceptable, and Unshlikht likewise replied that the Red Army had no substantive objections. Revealing a split in military opinion, the Staff's reaction was far more negative and found that Vesenkha's plan failed to achieve even the Red Army's 1925 projected needs, irrespective of advances in military technology. Vesenkha expected to make 17 million shells, not the 24 million the Staff regarded as essential. Doing that alone would require an additional 60 million rubles of investment, bringing the grand total to 383 million.[30]

The RZ STO rejected Vesenkha's five-year plan and returned it for revisions, but not because (as the Staff held) the plan was inadequate to provide for military needs—quite the opposite. The RZ STO concluded instead that Vesenkha had not been conservative enough and had not taken sufficient care to ensure that military expansion would not hinder the development of the civil economy—a rather startling decision, given the supposed expectation of imminent war. On 28 May, the RZ STO ordered Vesenkha to produce a plan based on the "necessity of maximal coordination of military production with the expansion of civil industry."[31]

After Vesenkha's draft five-year plan for military industry had been rejected, Postnikov, director of the MPU, contributed his own five-year investment plan to the debate. On 16 June 1927, he and Grigor'ev presented a Vesenkha planning commission "with starting data for assembling a military variant of the industrial control figures for 1927/8 and for the introduction of corrections into the five-year plan for developing industry." The First Five-Year Plan, aimed at the rapid industrialization of the entire economy, was already under development. According to Postnikov, however, that plan did "not concern itself with military industry and likewise with the special military production of civil industry." He thus felt obligated as director of the MPU to take on that task himself. His plan, not coincidentally, required a great deal of investment capital to flow to the industries under his authority. He and Grigor'ev proposed a total defense investment program including military industry, civil industry, civil defense, and raw material stockpiles amounting to 893.972 million rubles, more than double Vesenkha's earlier proposal. For 1927–1928 alone, investment totaled 342.676 million rubles.[32] Postnikov either saw a five-year plan for military industry as a means of acquiring capital at the expense of other sectors of the economy or profoundly misunderstood the fiscal constraints on the Soviet state in the summer of 1927; his plan went nowhere.

Although two tries (Vesenkha's and Postnikov's) to create a five-year plan for military industry had foundered, Kuibyshev presented a third, less ambitious investment plan to the STO at the end of August 1927. Kuibyshev's attempt envisaged a trade-off involving the closure of some of the Soviet Union's least productive military factories, including a bullet factory in Podolsk and a powder factory in Shlisselburg, in return for 345 million rubles of major capital construction over three years at almost all the Soviet Union's remaining military factories. New building would double the rifle capacity of the Izhevsk and Tula armaments works; expand powder and explosives factories in Kazan, Tambov, and Samara; and create a new explosives plant in the Donbass. Kuibyshev included another 80 million rubles to house the expanded factories' workers. A significant step back from Postnikov's plan and only marginally more ambitious than Vesenkha's original plan (345 million over three years versus 323.9 million), Kuibyshev's variant focused on bullets, rifles, and shells, targeting a production capacity of 1 million rifles, 2,332 million bullets, 24 million shells, 1,350 76mm artillery pieces, and 520 122mm howitzers over a year of war. Its implicit picture of future war was conservative and much like the Red Army's own vision: it would equip itself to refight World War I.[33]

Despite Kuibyshev's efforts to satisfy the military, the Red Army Staff was still not impressed. Tukhachevskii saw this plan as only a slight improvement on Vesenkha's earlier one, with some added precision and a feeble attempt to take into account the Red Army's 1927 mobilization orders. It would, Tukhachevskii complained, only partially reach even Vesenkha's limited goals, let alone the Red Army's changing needs. By Vesenkha's own calculations, for example, yearly bullet capacity would reach 1,458 million by the end of 1927–1928. This would cover only 63 percent of Vesenkha's own goal of 2,332 million, and, as Tukhachevskii pointed out, the Red Army would require 3,000 million. Still, Tukhachevskii saw any plan at all as some improvement and could not object to increasing total investment (not including housing) from 36.9 million in 1926–1927 to 73 million in 1927–1928.[34] In fact, the direct grants to military industry turned out to be less lucrative than planned, amounting to 63.1 million rubles for 1927–1928, up from 52.6 million in the previous year.[35]

In the end, Kuibyshev's plan and the earlier attempts at long-range investment schedules for military industry were simply overtaken by the increasing speed of industrialization. Focus shifted away from long horizons, and Vesenkha's military planning concentrated instead on the short term, rarely aiming more than one year ahead. In a sense, the pace of developments had passed Vesenkha by. In August, while Kuibyshev was still engineering a five-year plan for military industry, the Standing Mobilization Conference had already approved investment and development for 1927–1928 for the Main Directorates of the chemical and machine-building industries. Both produced important military goods, and both went ahead with their own plans for eliminating bottlenecks and accumulating stockpiles, ignoring Vesenkha's efforts.[36] When the Main Directorate for Machine-Building cut defense investment unilaterally, provoking howls of protest from Postnikov at the MPU, it only underlined the fact that the slow progress of planning rendered all Vesenkha's attempts at a five-year plan for military industry unsuccessful.[37]

THE RED ARMY ATTEMPTS ITS OWN FIVE-YEAR PLAN

While Postnikov and Kuibyshev wrestled with a five-year plan for military industry, the Red Army was busy in the summer of 1927 assembling its own five-year plan.[38] For nearly a year, since well before the war scare, the Red Army Staff had been assembling a long-range development plan. In August 1926, Chief of Staff Tukhachevskii had promised a four-year plan for the fall, but it was not ready for the Revvoensovet's perusal until summer 1927. Tukhachevskii's original four-year plan was marked by striking traditionalism and conservatism. Bound by technological and budgetary constraints, Tukhachevskii foresaw a Red Army much like the armies that had fought World War I and the civil war, relying on a cadre force supplemented by reservists in wartime, based on infantry, heavy artillery, horse cavalry, and chemical weapons. Nikolai Efimov, Tukhachevskii's deputy for mobilization at the Staff, later remarked that "the Red Army's system of arms is fundamentally based on the inheritance of the 1914–1918 war"; modern technology had to wait on economic development.[39] Tukhachevskii linked his four-year plan to the mobilized strength of the Soviet Union's most likely wartime foes—its Western neighbors from Romania north to Finland. In this balance of forces, the Soviet Union was outclassed in the number of divisions it could field and in its technical arms, achieving rough parity only in artillery. Even Tukhachevskii's plan could only narrow the gap, not provide for Soviet supremacy.[40]

As a result, Tukhachevskii's four-year plan carefully husbanded resources and structured its goals to stretch limited budgets as far as possible. The air force was slated for maximum development, and the number of wartime divisions, border fortresses, tanks, and artillery pieces would grow. The shipbuilding program would be cut. Under these changes, in wartime, the Red Army would field ninety-two rifle divisions organized into twenty-nine corps under mobilization schedule 8, in effect from spring 1928 through spring 1930. From spring 1930 on, under schedule 10, that number would increase to 107 divisions in thirty-two corps. The air force would grow, though rather modestly by comparison with later plans: from 780 aircraft over 1926–1927 to 1,200 over 1927–1929 and 1,540 from 1929 on. Similarly moderate growth in artillery was expected; from 6,593 artillery pieces in 1926, the Red Army would have 8,405 by 1930, with the fastest growth in antiaircraft artillery. Tukhachevskii's planned growth in the Red Army's budget was just as modest as the increases he envisaged in the Red Army as a whole (see table 7).[41]

Table 7. Red Army Budget Projections (million rubles)

Fiscal Year	Tukhachevskii Projection	Percent Increase Over Previous Year	Gosplan's Projection	Percent Increase Over Previous Year
1927–1928	751.7	—	716.0	—
1928–1929	795.8	5.9	760.0	6.1
1929–1930	878.9	10.4	800.0	5.3
1930–1931	916.1	4.2	840.0	5.0
Total	3,342.5		3,116.0	

When the Revvoensovet met on 11 May 1927, it refused to endorse Tukhachevskii's development plan. It instead referred the draft, now envisioned as a five-year plan, to a subcommission that returned six weeks later on 22 June with a version basically acceptable to all branches of the Red Army.[42] When passed upward to the RZ STO for approval, however, the Red Army's five-year plan immediately ran into difficulties. The RZ STO sent it back for revision and resubmission in a week's time, but the plan would not be ready. The RZ STO took the stopgap measure of approving a 745 million–ruble 1927–1928 budget for the Red Army. A clue to the RZ STO's reasons for rejecting the Red Army's proposal comes from Voroshilov's declaration to the RZ STO that new military technology was a priority in the Red Army's long-range planning—something not at all evident from Tukhachevskii's original proposal. Voroshilov's defensive reaction suggests that the RZ STO desired more attention to technical advances than the Revvoensovet had been willing to allow and that the Red Army's commitment to technical innovation lagged behind that of its civilian overlords.[43]

The Revvoensovet approved a final five-year plan setting the outlines of military policy on 19 July 1927, despite the RZ STO's reservations. Contrary to Tukhachevskii's original plan for the Red Army to grow first to 652,000 and then to 700,000 men over five years,[44] the Red Army's peacetime strength would stay at 617,000 troops through the 1928–1929 fiscal year, then increase to 640,000 through 1930–1931. The Revvoensovet grudgingly accepted a five-year budget of 4,000 million rubles but noted that this was "minimal from the point of view of satisfying the army's development in peacetime and for mobilization preparation." The plan included a long-range order for basic munitions, more for industry's benefit than for the army's, allowing some stability in what industry would have to produce each year. What this long-range order did *not* discuss is more significant: it was silent on production and procurement of aircraft, artillery, and tanks, suggesting that those important questions remained unresolved.[45]

While the Red Army was putting together its development plan, it was (at the RZ STO's behest) still working on both a long-range plan of industrial orders and a projection of what it would need to fight for one year. On 28 May 1927, the RZ STO gave the Red Army one month to present the defense industry with plans the military and industry had been grinding out at length: the supplies and armaments needed for mobilization and one year of war, including "artillery, aviation, military-chemical and technical arms," along with a new five-year peacetime order plan breaking down what the Red Army would purchase in the absence of war and replacing the February 1927 plan.[46] The Red Army Staff did not rush to obey. With both halves of the assignment, the long-range order plan and the mobilization and war-year order, military planners displayed astonishing reserves of inertia. The Staff had only a preliminary and rough mobilization order ready by August 1927 for a Vesenkha feasibility study.[47] The mobilization order, delayed as it was, still outpaced the long-range order plan. As the Red Army's deputy supply director Garf explained, the primary stumbling block—delays in five-year orders from the Red Army's various branches—had been exacerbated by another problem. The Red Army's priorities and resources were changing too rapidly to permit a reasonably accurate five-year projection of needs, although Garf was still optimistic that the work would be complete by September 1927.[48]

That deadline fell by the wayside as well, and Deputy People's Commissar Unshlikht began futilely haranguing his subordinates over their missing order plans. The Red Navy proved particularly recalcitrant, as its leadership rejected the general consensus that the navy and shipbuilding would be a low priority in military development. Unshlikht insisted that "your announced objection to the orientation control figures for outlays on the navy" could not serve as an excuse for delay and demanded a final plan within two days.[49] Even by November, nothing had been accomplished. Ventsov, the RZ STO's secretary, wrote to Unshlikht six months after the original request for a mobilization order, and two months after the Staff had declared that it had all the information it needed, to ask why the RZ STO had still received nothing. Ventsov demanded that Unshlikht appear before him by 21 November to explain precisely when those long-range orders could be expected.[50] S. S. Kamenev, not Unshlikht, defended the Red Army's inglorious record of meeting deadlines. Given a constantly changing development plan and a budget always subject to revision, he argued, the Red Army could hardly be expected to plan effectively.[51] The Red Army finally obtained a de facto extension simply by not submitting any of its paperwork.

THE SOVIET ECONOMY AT WAR

It was only a small conceptual step from drawing up a schedule of wartime military production to preparing a more general plan for the entire wartime economy. All the Soviet literature on war stressed the interconnected nature of the economy, and efforts to create wartime plans for the economy as a whole, not just the defense industry, began in November 1927. As Chief of Staff Shaposhnikov saw the issue in May 1928, this plan, based on the "average normal variant of war," would project "control figures" *(kontrol'nye tsifry)* for the "first period of war" *(pervyi period voiny).* Instead of covering the details of production, these control figures would handle global measures such as aggregate production, capital investment, and changes in the labor force, all at a high level of abstraction. Shaposhnikov believed that such a plan would give broad guidelines for all sectors of the economy, not just military industry. Working from the demands of the armed forces, it would also "reveal the possible degree of satisfying these demands." The "plan for the first period of war," as this effort was termed, would also determine the required adjustments for wartime conditions. Finally, it would "reveal the sum total of measures which must be carried out in the Five-Year Plan and in peacetime control figures to provide for the uninterrupted work of the economy and complete satisfaction of the demands of defense," dictating the "paths of defense interests in peacetime construction."[52]

In November 1927, the RZ STO set up two commissions on wartime economic planning. The first, made up of first-rank officials such as Rykov, Mikoian, and Kuibyshev, would set the outlines of wartime economic policy; the second panel of second-rank administrators such as Unshlikht and Postnikov would work with Gosplan on planning methodology. Gosplan's job was to determine the wartime economy's needs for raw materials and labor, as well as the possibility of supplying them through domestic sources and imports, taking into account a possible wartime blockade. Working from the state of the economy in 1927–1928, Gosplan was given six months to determine the best possible structure for the wartime economy.[53]

Although the Red Army could hardly object to better war planning, the actual creation of wartime control figures reopened old, latent conflicts over what mobilization meant. A dispute over terminology, similar to the one Egorov had revealed in 1926 (see chapter 1), came to symbolize a deep division between army and industry over defense. A key term, the "first period of war," was decidedly ambivalent. To those on the economic side—factory managers and Vesenkha administrators—the term meant a stably running war economy *after* a transitional mobilization period following the outbreak of war. They thus assumed six months of mobilization and transition to a wartime economy; only then would the one year signified by the "first period of war" begin. War plans assumed that attacks would come in late spring or early summer to take advantage of good weather, so a six-month transition period would let the full-scale war fiscal year coincide with the normal Soviet fiscal year beginning in October. If war broke out in, say, April 1928, the "first period of war" would not begin until October 1928, by which time economic mobilization would be complete. This would, naturally, permit industry more time to retool; it also allowed a more gradual transition to the wartime economy.

Military officers found this interpretation of "first period of war" absurd. The Red Army could not spend a full campaigning season without any idea what supplies industry would provide. The difference was quite substantial. The agreed quantity of military supplies would be delivered either over twelve months from a standing start (the Red Army's interpretation) or over eighteen months, with the first six devoted to retooling (Vesenkha's interpretation). The corresponding requirements for investment and production capacity diverged sharply, for the Red Army's definition put a great deal more strain on Soviet industry. The RZ STO settled the dispute in Vesenkha's favor in February 1928 by letting calculations treat the second half of the 1927–1928 fiscal year (April to September 1928) as a transition period and the next 1928–1929 fiscal year as the one in which the full war economy would be at work. In effect, economic stability was more important than military necessity.[54]

Vesenkha assigned the MPU the job of determining the economy's wartime structure, and its initial suggestions were approved by the end of April 1928. Bemoaning the low level of preparation done to date and the "decay of the inherited physical plant in [defense] production of civil industry," Vesenkha's report stressed the factors outside its control that would limit its ability to prepare for war: loss of links with world markets, inadequate internal transportation, lack of the necessary raw material base in agriculture, and the limited production capacity of heavy industry.[55] Given these limitations, the MPU envisioned no fundamental changes in the wartime economy from the 1927–1928 benchmark year. The workforce in light industry,[56] especially textiles, would shrink, but in heavy industry it would grow by 170,000 workers, only 15.2 percent over its 1927–1928 base. Capital investment would fall by 8.8 percent but would shift from light industry to heavy and military industry. Wartime industrial production would *fall* from nearly 8,000 million rubles in 1927–1928 to 7,850 million rubles, 4,000 million in heavy and military industry and the remainder in light industry, with the 13.5 percent increase in heavy and military industry more than counterbalanced by a 14 percent fall in light industry. The mobilization assignment portion of this would total 2,200 million rubles, or nearly one-third of total output; production outside the mobilization assignment would itself fall by a third. Gross production of strictly military industry (the Artillery-Arsenal, Firearm–Machine Gun, Bullet-Fuse, Military-Chemical, and Aviation Trusts) would grow from 207.8 million rubles planned for 1927–1928 to 908 million rubles over eighteen months of war. If war were to begin halfway through 1927–1928, production would grow from 181 million in the second half of 1927–1928 to 327 million and 399 million in the first and second halves of 1928–1929, respectively. The most rapid increase would be in the trusts producing ammunition, not weapons: bullets, shells, explosives, and powder.[57] In keeping with the general concerns of the Soviet state and the military five-year plan, these figures are a remarkably conservative projection for the Soviet state at war. The "control figures" show little hint of notions of crash industrialization, instead emphasizing stability, gradual change, and minimal disturbance of the Soviet economy. The central concern was maintaining its delicate equilibrium and, in particular, not straining the internal truce with the peasantry. Although production of war materials would increase under wartime conditions, the changes foreseen were hardly drastic.[58]

Vesenkha's Presidium in April 1928 judged these proposals deeply flawed, not because of their conservatism but because of the subterfuges necessary to meet even those moderate targets. Total production was "extremely unsatisfactory," and the MPU had not paid enough attention to mobilization, surrogates for scarce raw materials, and general reduction of Soviet dependence on imports. Furthermore, although the shortfall in consumer goods would reach 2.5 billion rubles in the first year of war (a politically sensitive issue) and shortages of copper, zinc, lead, and other nonferrous metals would be acute, transport would still likely collapse under the strain of its wartime burdens. Despite all these defects, many of which were beyond the MPU's control, Kuibyshev approved these figures as a first approximation and passed them on to Gosplan for inclusion in the general wartime economic plan. For future policy, however, Kuibyshev and the presidium set a list of desired improvements. First was getting a firm mobilization order and long-term peacetime order out of the Red Army. This would aid planning, and it would also set a cap on the military's future demands. Although many of Kuibyshev's proposals were quite compatible with import-substituting industrialization—ending dependence on imports; finding surrogates for scarce raw materials; expanding machine building, metallurgy, and chemicals; training more technically skilled workers; shielding the defense workforce from conscription—other policies were harder to harmonize with rapid industrialization. Stockpiling raw materials and assimilating military and civil production would pull resources away from industrialization.[59]

Gosplan gave the RZ STO its final report on a wartime economic plan on 21 April 1928. Working from mobilization plan A and planning for eighteen months after the outbreak of a war beginning 1 April 1928, Gosplan concluded that the Soviet economy's prospects looked bleak. Dependence on imports was so great that relying solely on internal resources would mean "complete nonfulfillment of the demands of defense or work on an abnormally narrow base." Despite the heavy weight of defense production in wartime industrial plans, the absolute level of output was "far from corresponding not only to the demands of the People's Commissariat for Military Affairs, but to the minimal necessities to conduct a large war." As a result of "insignificant accounting of defense interests . . . in peacetime plans for industrial development," military industry suffered from insufficient investment, poor integration of civil and military production, no standardization, low productivity at the factories, and a neglect of mobilization work.[60]

The Red Army was even less impressed than Gosplan with projections of the Soviet wartime economy. Chief of Staff Shaposhnikov was particularly disturbed at how poorly those control figures fulfilled their fundamental task: putting weapons and ammunition in the hands of Soviet soldiers. Vesenkha's projected shell production amounted to only 13.5 million rounds, compared with the Red Army's demand for 24 million under the army's mobilization plan 8. Whereas in some respects Vesenkha's projected fulfillment of plan A was quite adequate (76mm, 107mm, and 122mm artillery pieces; light machine guns; and explosive charges for shells), in other cases, it was at a catastrophically low level. Less than two-thirds of plan A's rifles and a little over half its machine guns could be covered, and fuses would reach only 36 percent of the target level. Still worse, as Shaposhnikov pointed out, industry's mobilization plan A was outdated and inadequate—artillery capacity was too low.[61]

Shaposhnikov's reservations were not limited to ordnance: just as Gosplan surveyed the entire economy, Shaposhnikov found shortcomings in every sector. Metallurgy was weakly developed—not enough iron ore was being produced, and magnesium production was actually falling. There were not enough key chemicals such as sulfuric acid, chlorine, and saltpeter. Reserves of fuel were low, and Soviet transport could not support a war economy. It was therefore doubly important that the switch from peacetime to wartime production at Soviet factories be as rapid as possible: "lengthy delays in the transfer of particular branches of industry to military production are intolerable."[62]

This first attempt to map the roughest outlines of the Soviet Union's war economy demonstrated that a deep divide still separated the Red Army from Vesenkha over the most basic issues of mobilization and war planning. The fundamental difficulty, that there was not enough investment capital available to build the means with which to meet the Red Army's wartime demands, did not offer any simple solutions. The RZ STO could only ask Gosplan to summarize its work on the Soviet wartime economy in order to settle some basic questions, and after the dust had settled, it would eventually order the exercise to be repeated with the benefit of another year of experience.[63]

THE DRIVE FOR ECONOMY

Not only did the five-year development plans of the Red Army and Vesenkha, along with the "control figures for the first period of war," display a common conservatism and consciousness of fiscal and technological constraints, but concrete industrial plans and budgets displayed the strong stamp of stringent financial limits. This produced a constant urge to economize in any way possible. One way in which both the Red Army and Vesenkha hoped to do this was by employing dual technology—goods and parts with civil and military uses—which was easier to advocate than to implement. There was a key difference in approach, however, between army and industry. Whereas the Red Army stressed establishing military cells in civilian factories to expand its network of suppliers and hasten the transition to wartime production, Vesenkha aimed at producing civilian goods in military factories to reduce its peacetime burden of maintaining the excess capacity necessary for wartime.

Producing civilian goods in military factories appealed to both industrial managers and military planners. It is a universal characteristic of defense industry that more capacity is required in wartime than can be reasonably employed in peacetime. Keeping skilled workers and expensive equipment sitting idle is, however, terribly wasteful. Ideally, then, military factories employ their excess capacity producing goods for the civil market. Not only do consumer goods provide cash for the enterprise, but they also keep a workforce in existence for wartime. In the kopek-pinching atmosphere of the late 1920s, loading factories to capacity—*zagruzka*—was a Soviet priority. The phenomenon of civil production from defense factories existed, formally or informally, throughout the history of the Soviet state, but it became increasingly vital in the years around the end of NEP and the beginning of Stalin's revolution from above. In 1927, approximately one-third of military industry's production was civil, and that was no longer conducted on an ad hoc basis but had carefully planned distribution channels. The RZ STO directed Vesenkha to ensure that military factories were fully loaded with civilian assignments.[64]

In May 1927, the RZ STO stressed "the necessity of maximal coordination of military production with the expansion of civil industry and of planning for the maximal loading of military industry's production capacity in peacetime" in the creation of long-range plans.[65] In 1928, the RZ STO ordered Gosplan to load military industry with civilian orders, but it remained disturbed that military factories were still not running to full capacity. It then gave Vesenkha three months to draw up a five-year plan for civil production in defense industry through intensive orders to comparatively idle military plants. Concerned at the possibility of having the Red Army's own order crowded out, Voroshilov attempted to head off excessive civilian production at military factories. While leading a 1928 commission redrafting the Red Army's five-year development plan, he stressed building capacity through additional investment. The RZ STO's final verdict, however, took the opposite approach. It instructed Vesenkha to install civil production at military plants and assigned the auditors of Rabkrin, the Workers'-Peasants' Inspectorate, to find further cost reductions.[66]

By 1928, Soviet military factories produced a wide range of civilian goods and planned to introduce more. Some lines, such as hunting rifles, were hardly a switch from military goods; other bent-metal products were nearly as natural. Automobile, aircraft, and tractor parts were mainstays at defense plants. Others were more unusual. The Cartridge-Fuse Trust already made meat grinders, spark plugs, and samovars and hoped to add bicycles. The Firearm–Machine Gun Trust saw promise in sewing machines. The Military-Chemical Trust already had large civil markets for its explosives and industrial chemicals but could expand that into photographic film and artificial fibers. The only trust without civil production by late 1928 was Aviatrest (the Aviation Trust).[67]

Such a policy won peacetime revenue at the expense of skills in truly military production and could persist only as long as resources were so tight that the Red Army and military industry had no other choice. By 1930, with budgetary pressures easing, the Red Army Staff insisted that civil production in military factories was permissible only if the skills involved were directly applicable to defense work and if civil output did not interfere with mobilization. After peaking around 1929, civil production at military plants dropped off but never disappeared (see table 8). Through the fall of the Soviet Union, military industry would continue to account for a large proportion of consumer goods.[68]

Cutting costs was a high priority for the Standing Mobilization Conference, handling defense investment within Vesenkha. It judged where factory production could be most economically set up, prioritized projects, and explored alternative applications of investment capital. That even included cutting corners on workplace safety and the sturdiness of construction. On 13 July 1927, the conference resolved to explore "lowering outlays on work connected with labor safety at enterprises, proceeding from lowering the requirements of the People's Commissariat of Labor." It also agreed "to carry out new construction of a lighter type with smaller reserves of strength," but "within allowable bounds from the point of view of existing technology."[69]

On 19 May 1928, the conference issued a decree stressing economic expansion through rationalization. Although it included the usual exhortations for more assiduous labor, this particular directive incorporated concrete measures. To ensure that mobilization plan S was ready by 1 October 1929 as cheaply as possible, Vesenkha's main directorates and the union republic Vesenkhas were ordered to permit lighter construction and weaker strength reserves while simultaneously minimizing such nonproductive construction as worker housing. In addition, all possible rationalization of production and use of civil industry for military production were to be employed for further savings. Although the Standing Mobilization Conference paid lip service to developing surrogate raw materials, building stockpiles, duplicating production unique to a single factory, and bolstering anti-aircraft defense, its true emphasis was on building capacity without spending money. Postnikov and Tolokontsev concluded, "All work must be in the most decisive way subordinated to the principle of maximum economization."[70]

This concern for economy grew directly from the limited funds available for defense, despite the war scare and ostensible threat of attack. As a result, the annual fight over the Red Army's budget reflected acute financial constraints. All the time that planners thrashed out five-year plans of production and growth, they simul-

Table 8. Share of Civil Production in Output of Military Trusts (percent)

Fiscal Year	Artillery- Arsenal	Firearm– Machine Gun	Cartridge- Fuse	Military- Chemical	Total
1928–1929	38.4	40.7	45.7	34.2	40.7
1929–1930	40.6	52.3	53.0	48.7	48.8
Special Quarter	28.9	34.9	46.0	33.1	34.5
1931	31.1	31.0	38.8	40.0	35.2
1932 (plan)	9.5	24.4	29.1	34.2	23.2

taneously engaged in bitter debates over more immediate concerns: the budget
for 1927–1928. Inside Vesenkha, at least, determining military industry's investment budget for 1927–1928 was relatively painless. By late July 1927, two months
before the October start of the 1927–1928 fiscal year, the Standing Mobilization
Conference was close to the final budget figure. Postnikov and Tolokontsev
approved a 75.5 million–ruble investment plan for the VPU, the Military-Industrial
Directorate, to meet the demands of mobilization plan A. In the process of splitting
investment among the VPU's trusts, the total dropped slightly to 73 million rubles,
with the lion's share going to the Military-Chemical Trust. Housing added an
additional 12 million rubles, bringing the overall total to 85 million. This more
than doubled the previous year's investment of only 36.6 million for production
and 4.25 million for housing.[71] The RZ STO gave its approval for the VPU's
investment plan at the beginning of September 1927 and confirmed 85 million
rubles. Since the VPU carried some of the burden of providing its own capital,
budget negotiations were less bitter than over the Red Army's allocation. The VPU
received only 51.25 million rubles as a cash grant for investment, with the
remainder coming from profits, long-term loans and credits, and other sources.[72]
An RZ STO subcommission fixed an additional import quota in October 1927 at
20 million rubles—half on machinery and equipment and half on raw materials—
with 14 million rubles more for the NKVM.[73]

Setting the Red Army's 1927–1928 budget was more contentious. The Red
Army's five-year plan requested 807 million rubles, but the RZ STO cut that to
745 million. The Revvoensovet did not give up. In September 1927, an army
commission analyzed the budget. Finding no fat to trim, it accordingly brought
an 808 million–ruble budget back to the Revvoensovet. Voroshilov took that
budget to the RZ STO with an implicit request to reconsider its earlier decision.[74]
The RZ STO found that there simply was no room in the overall budget for the
Red Army's increased demands; as the People's Commissariat of Finance explained,
even the RZ STO's original proposal of 745 million rubles was too high. Gosplan
and Finance had allowed 800 million rubles for total defense spending in their
projections, which included OGPU forces and other miscellaneous measures. The
Red Army could get only 720 million rubles for 1927–1928, especially since both
Gosplan and Finance doubted that military industry could produce enough to
satisfy an 808 million–ruble budget. The RZ STO accepted this argument and
rejected the Revvoensovet's appeal. The figure of 745 million rubles had been
arrived at after careful consideration and would not be altered.[75]

Not discouraged by this setback, Voroshilov attempted to use his influence
with Stalin to rescue a higher budget for the NKVM. He pulled no punches, telling
Stalin that the budget was simply "insufficient" to meet even "minimal" needs of
the Red Army.[76] Voroshilov's begging won a special RZ STO commission to hear
his request. It returned a surprisingly anticlimactic conclusion. After negotiations,
the commission split the difference between the Red Army's 750 million–ruble
proposal and Finance's 736 million with a final budget of 743 million. The largest

share, 303 million rubles, would go for "technical supply," that is, weapons and equipment. The final figure, 743.915 million rubles, was finally approved by the RZ STO three months after the 1927–1928 fiscal year had already begun.[77] The budget actually implemented was slightly less than that, amounting to 742.4 million rubles. Even with the staggeringly low pay of Red Army soldiers, the majority of that went to salaries, provisions, construction, administrative expenses, pensions, and political and educational materials, totaling 51 percent of the budget. Procurement of industrial goods, as measured by purchase and maintenance of ordnance, chemical gear, engineering and communications equipment, and trucks and other motorized transportation, together with spending on the air force, came to only 30.7 percent, just over 226 million rubles.[78]

The Red Army's difficulties in getting a budget approved for 1927–1928, and the relatively low priority that budget gave to purchasing new equipment, exemplified Soviet military policy in the year of the war scare. Continuity outweighed innovation, and fiscal prudence took precedence over defense spending. The Bolshevik elites who deliberated over military budgets did not act especially concerned about immediate war. The Red Army and Soviet military industry benefited, to be sure, from the general economic recovery of NEP and the growing administrative capacity of the Soviet state. Still, there were limits to what the military could expect from the Politburo, the RZ STO, and Vesenkha, regardless of the war scare generated for public consumption. The Red Army and military industry continued to refine their organizational structure, but without the funds for substantial expansion. Only over the next two years, with the campaign against "wreckers," the defeat of Bukharin and the Bolshevik Right, Stalin's increasing monopoly on power, and the First Five-Year Plan, would limits on defense expansion finally dissolve, leaving nothing to hinder military dominance of economic policy.

3

The Hunt for Internal Enemies

In March 1928, the Soviet Union was shaken by revelations published in *Pravda* of a massive counterrevolutionary "wrecking" conspiracy in the Shakhty coal mines of the North Caucasus. Engineers and technicians trained before the revolution, the "bourgeois specialists," had embarked on a campaign of "wrecking," sabotage, and subversion, assisted by foreign nationals working in Soviet industry.[1] The Shakhty case, and the show trial of the involved "wreckers" that followed, served as many things: a pretext for intensified class war against the remnants of the bourgeois classes within the Soviet Union, a tool in the fight against the Right's opposition to Stalin, and even a means to mobilize the Soviet people against foreign threats. As a result of the antiwrecking campaign, military industry, like the rest of Soviet industry, suffered the loss of its most experienced engineers and technicians. Unlike the public harrowing of other branches of industry, however, defense industry suffered largely in silence from a hidden hunt for wreckers and saboteurs. As a result of its vital relationship to the survival of the Soviet state, for better or worse, it enjoyed the constant and concerned attention of Stalin and the rest of the Bolshevik elite.

The implication for military policy of the campaign unleashed by Shakhty was that any reservations about the speed of industrialization or the need for massive rearmament became immediately suspicious. This chapter covers a much greater chronological span than the remaining chapters of the book, for the developments after 1928 were always marked by the continuing legacy of the antiwrecking campaign. As Soviet policy makers ferreted out ostensible foreign agents and directed resources to repair the damage they had allegedly caused, moderation became criminal. The policy debates covered in the remaining chapters of this book were permeated and shaped by an atmosphere in which those who counseled restraining the speed of industrial development or the output of weaponry had been revealed as traitors. In the aftermath of the antiwrecking campaign in military industry, opposition to militarizing the Soviet economy was a dangerous and increasingly unpopular stand.

As the Soviet state industrialized its economy, its defense industry was shaken by a campaign against wreckers and saboteurs that would disrupt it for nearly five years. Beginning with internal disputes in late 1926, military industry was riven to its foundations by continuing attempts to root out class enemies and foreign agents responsible for sabotage and deliberate incompetence—in short, wrecking. Gleb Krzhizhanovskii, chair of Gosplan, told *Pravda*'s readers in February 1930 that the wreckers' ultimate goal had been ensuring the Soviet Union's defeat in the coming war of world capital against the USSR. Iosif Unshlikht, a Chekist and Red Army officer before becoming an economic administrator, explained in 1930 that the OGPU secret police had struggled against "counter-revolutionary organizations in industry [that] saw undermining the country's defense capability as one of the most important means to achieve their goal." Wreckers had derailed capital investment in military industry, sabotaged industry's preparations for war, disrupted production, and confused industry's attempts to meet military orders for defense material. Wreckers in individual factories had been "aided and in essence led by a counterrevolutionary organization" in the central military-industrial bureaucracy.[2]

The sheer unreality and fantastic nature of the Shakhty affair were magnified even more in this five-year internecine feud within military industry. Who could believe that dozens, hundreds, or even thousands of saboteurs could work undetected for years? As Sheila Fitzpatrick has written of the whole campaign:

> Obviously much (though not all) of this circumstantial evidence [implicating bourgeois specialists as wreckers in the service of foreign governments] was complete fabrication; and the mass arrests of "bourgeois" engineers following the Shakhty trial were highly counter-productive in terms of industrialization priorities. What then was the point of linking the foreign threat with the class struggle at home?[3]

How could the Bolsheviks, seeing themselves beset by enemies at home and abroad, arrest and execute their most qualified military-industrial specialists on such ludicrous charges?

Explanations for this seeming irrationality have split among three complementary theories, none of which fully untangles the case of military industry. The first interpretation holds that the campaign's primary motivation was sounding the alarm about foreign danger to provide Stalin with "graphic new evidence of imperialist enmity" to solidify his own position.[4] Another interpretation suggests that the antiwrecking campaign aimed to discredit the Right opposition. Sovnarkom chair Aleksei Rykov, *Pravda* editor Nikolai Bukharin, and trade union chief Mikhail Tomskii, the leadership of the loosely grouped Bolshevik Right, split from Stalin on a number of issues, but in particular on the need for a campaign against the bourgeois specialists as a group. Although Bukharin condemned individual cases of sabotage, Stalin was able to depict his resistance to blanket condemnations as weak and vacillating.[5] More recent scholarship has turned away from high politics to a third explanation: terrorizing nonparty engineers and specialists into acquiescing in Stalin's plans to transform the Soviet economy, or what Kendall Bailes has called "a general attack on the authority and sense of community of the Soviet technical intelligentsia." To achieve industrialization through class war, according to Hiroaki Kuromiya, "the Stalin group . . . employ[ed] violent purges to remove perceived institutional constraints on the class-war policy in general and rapid industrialization in particular."[6]

Although all these theories touch on essential ways in which the antiwrecking campaign was *used,* when measured against the case of military industry, they leave important questions of cause unanswered. The most obvious, perhaps, is cost: disrupting North Caucasus coal mines to achieve political goals is one thing, but throwing the Soviet Union's entire defense industry into disarray is quite another. The number of engineers and technicians arrested is difficult to determine but was probably in the range of 2,000 to 7,000.[7] The share from military industry is just as difficult to pin down, but Krzhizhanovskii wrote that those arrested in the defense industry included ten tsarist generals and nineteen tsarist colonels.[8] Each of several dozen military plants conducted extensive surveys to determine damage done by wreckers, and the central bureaucracy and production trust personnel were also hard hit. The number arrested could hardly have been less than several hundred, possibly more. The damage done was far out of proportion to the number of victims; those targeted were among the most capable administrators. For the Soviet Union to cripple its defense industry when it expected foreign war seems the height of folly—no political goal could be worth such a cost, particularly when there were so many other technicians and engineers in less important industries to be sacrificed for the same purpose.

Furthermore, wrecking in military industry was kept almost entirely out of the public eye—a fact inconsistent with an interpretation of wrecking as a way of sending a message. A few scattered references in *Pravda* were all that the Soviets read of defense industry arrests and executions. The contrast with Shakhty's publicity is striking. If the arrests in military industry were intended to dramatize foreign danger, why were they kept quiet? The same logic applies to explaining the antiwrecking campaign as a weapon against Bukharin or as an example for recalcitrant engineers *pour encourager les autres.* In all cases, logic requires publicity, not silence. Moreover, the expansion of military industry was still moving quite slowly at the time arrests began; there was no need to remove human impediments to industrial growth. The disruption caused by removing recalcitrant engineers was far worse than anything their presence might have created.

In short, understanding the antiwrecking campaign requires looking at the endogenous roots of conflict between Bolshevik administrators and nonparty specialists and taking seriously Soviet beliefs in the danger represented by class enemies. Accusations of wrecking in military industry did not result from directives from Moscow and did not appear ex nihilo after the Shakhty trial. They instead arose from workplace conflicts between Bolshevik administrators and the tsarist-era managers, engineers, and technicians who worked alongside them; conflict was horizontal, not vertical. Although state and military authorities later co-opted the antiwrecking campaign for their own purposes, it grew from real social tensions. To be sure, Bolshevik managers would never have turned against noncommunist specialists without believing that their actions would be met with approval, but their grievances were nonetheless real and local in origin. Military industry's Red administrators turned their everyday disputes with noncommunist specialists into ideological struggles and called in outside intervention from the party and state. As a result, bureaucratic strife turned violent. As early as 1926, communists within military industry were already accusing particular engineers and managers of "criminal" activities; two years later, those same engineers would be arrested and charged with wrecking with news of the Shakhty affair. As the campaign progressed, the Soviet government and the Red Army used it to impose discipline and order on the chaos within the Soviet defense industry. The means by which discipline was imposed, however, show just how seriously Soviet policy makers took their doctrines of class war, sacrificing security from foreign enemies to fight internal threats. The attack on wreckers was not just a means to the political end of discrediting the Right or eliminating opposition to crash industrialization, although it did serve that purpose. It was also a reflection of genuine Bolshevik belief in the reality of class enemies.

When Avanesov and Tolokontsev took over military industry (see chapter 1), expectations were high that old problems would be a thing of the past. Instead, difficulties remained and worsened as military procurement budgets and the consequent demands on military industry increased faster than industry's ability to meet them. Preexisting tensions intensified within the managerial elite, in particular between the old technically educated engineers (in the Soviet lexicon, specialists, or *spetsy*) and the newly promoted communist managers and administrators, many of whom lacked technical education. These tensions showed up first in the bureaucracy of the VPU's production trusts, far from the factory floor. Communist administrators, schooled by the civil war to think in terms of bitter class war, expressed prosaic concerns of promotion, policy, and bureaucratic politics through ideologically charged language.

Mundane fights over managerial policy became feuds between communists and "former *(byvshie)*" people, the engineers and technicians educated under the old regime. The highest-placed communist managers, Tolokontsev and the chairs of the production trusts, tended to side with experienced expert opinion over the generally more radical and less refined views of their Bolshevik subordinates. Under NEP, the needs of economic recovery demanded that engineers and specialists be permitted to work without hindrance. For example, in June 1926, Avanesov and Dzerzhinskii had agreed "to give the necessary instructions to military industry's party collective on the impermissibility of interference in the administrative-managerial conduct of the administration."[9] When Bolshevik managers were stymied by the refusal of their communist bosses to listen to their concerns and criticisms, they went out-side industry to call in the assistance of the Red Army, party authorities, Rabkrin, or the secret police. In this way, a horizontal workplace conflict over priorities and precedence festered over time, became linked to an ideological struggle when military industry's communists called in the assistance of the state and secret police, and finally resolved itself through state violence as it became criminal to disagree over managerial policy.

As early as 1926, the managers who would later be executed as wreckers were already being singled out for communist complaints. Grigorii Kulik (ironically, later accused of abetting wrecking in the Red Army's Artillery Directorate) went to military industry in December 1925 as a Red Army representative and took over responsibility for mobilization preparedness. His innovations, Kulik reported to the Revvoensovet, had been opposed by a "united group of specialists, who gathered in their hands the management of military industry and by a criminal policy from year to year led it to gradual disintegration." With Avanesov retired, Dzerzhinskii dead, and Tolokontsev now in charge, "the same small group of leaders of the former Voenprom who should sooner be in jail turned up in military industry's upper management, knowing how to get the trust of the Collegium." As Kulik described his predicament, "this clique of leaders of Voenprom, supported by some high-ranking party comrades from Voenprom management, justifiably saw me as a vehement enemy of their criminal policy and tried all measures possible to compromise me."[10]

The *same day* that Kulik reported to the Red Army's high command, a group of sixteen Bolsheviks from military industry's central bureaucracy sent a com-plaint of their own to Stalin, Ordzhonikidze, and Voroshilov. They described an intolerable situation within the VPU in which specialists' years of inactivity, concealed by a carefully constructed facade of assiduous labor, had been only temporarily interrupted by Avanesov's welcome arrival. When Avanesov's weak health forced him to step down, Tolokontsev took over and destroyed all that Avanesov had achieved. The same clique of "self-seeking specialists and philistine communists" had taken over once again, led by Vadim Mikhailov, Tolokontsev's assistant and the highest-ranking holdover from tsardom. Three years later, Mikhailov would be shot as the leader of a vast conspiracy of wreckers; in 1926, military industry's communists could only denounce him and hope that someone would listen. According to their complaint, Tolokontsev allowed Mikhailov to run the VPU himself and establish his own private ruling elite. The opinions of com-munists were routinely disregarded. Bad blood had grown to such an extent that "an excessively intrigue-filled situation has been established in the very depths of the VPU's apparatus among Tolokontsev, Sudakov [his deputy], and Mikhailov on one side and Egorov [Red Army representative] on the other." Acting "as good communists," the petitioners could not be silent.[11]

Responding to this discontent, the OGPU investigated the VPU. Genrikh Iagoda's November 1926 report stressed Mikhailov's efforts to place his noncommunist associates in posts of authority throughout military industry while at the same time impeding proper mobilization plans. "According to Mikhailov's calculations," Iagoda wrote, "the assembly of an industrial mobilization plan could only be finished in eighteen years [!], which meant in effect a refusal to put together such a plan at all." Since Tolokontsev was distracted by other duties and his deputy Sudakov was relatively inexperienced, Mikhailov's position as Tolokontsev's chief aide left him the de facto head of military industry. The situation deteriorated daily as the number of communists entering military industry fell while those already in place grew frustrated and quit. Iagoda suggested immediately firing Mikhailov and the other members of his group and imposing closer military control over the defense industry.[12]

The OGPU kept some specialists under surveillance through late 1927. During a debate over tank production at Leningrad's Bolshevik (ex-Obukhovskii) factory, the same accusations of criminal conduct reappeared. At Bolshevik, the plant's management had a choice between erecting a new building for tank production on factory grounds or finishing a partially completed structure at the "new place," which was physically distant from the old site. The factory director, Korolev, and his staff agreed on production at the new place, but two members of the commission deciding the issue disagreed. One of them, N. G. Vysochanskii, was in Leningrad to represent the Artillery-Arsenal Trust. Six months later, he was among the first specialists arrested for wrecking and shot.[13] The details of Vysochanskii's and his colleague Makarov's dissent are unimportant; more significant is the OGPU special section's belief that their policy would deliberately delay production. Furthermore, the OGPU feared that Vysochanskii would sabotage the factory's further development. Pronouncing relations between Vysochanskii at the trust and the Bolshevik factory "harmful," the OGPU believed that he and Makarov, once back in Moscow, would not ensure smooth production at Bolshevik.[14]

Tensions escalated over the winter of 1927–1928. Just before arrests began, the Cartridge-Fuse Trust's K. K. Lakhinskii, who made a habit of denouncing his coworkers, wrote to the Red Army's Mikhail Tukhachevskii to propose industrial reorganization. In an aside, however, Lakhinskii stressed the need for a purge of military industry: Tolokontsev, his deputy, Daniil Budnevich, and the "evil genius" of military industry Mikhailov had to be purged, along with the "White guard" ex-tsarist administrators "gathered and led by Mikhailov." Lakhinskii employed the Shakhty trial's language in a later denunciation to complain about the delays Mikhailov had caused, but his more telling comments concerned Mikhailov's personnel policy. Closely tied to tsarist-era engineers, Mikhailov gave work to his cronies but not to communists. Complaints to Tolokontsev had produced no results; instead, he had "unexpectedly called together all the representatives of the trusts' management and in Mikhailov's presence started berating them with foul language: 'How dare you not obey Mikhailov's orders?' and so forth." Ignoring the opinions of good communists had created "the most fertile ground for the counterrevolutionary activities of the Mikhailovites in military industry."[15]

On 25 March 1928, the OGPU finally arrested Vysochanskii after arresting a group of senior engineers and technicians from Vysochanskii's Artillery-Arsenal Trust. Head engineer Filippovskii, head mechanic Chizhevskii, senior engineer Sheiman, head of the Arsenal Subdivision Dykhov, and head of the Optics Subdivision Petrov were all rounded up for participating in a counterrevolutionary group led by disgruntled specialists. Mikhailov soon joined them in prison. This cabal, according to the OGPU, underestimated production capacity in their factories to receive more lucrative investment grants, while simultaneously directing those funds not to bottlenecks but to already developed manufacture. They delayed factory expansion, typically by "advancing a series of variants and organizing a lengthy debate over the superiority of this or that variant, and also consulting experts living outside Moscow." Filippovskii and Chizhevskii would later confess to deliberately disrupting tank production.[16]

These initial spring 1928 arrests of wreckers in military industry coincided closely with the much more widely publicized Shakhty affair—the OGPU's investigations must have run simultaneously. It is worth emphasizing, however, that when Shakhty made notions of wrecking and foreign conspiracy common currency among the Soviet people, the antiwrecking campaign in military industry had already begun. News of the Shakhty trial gave it additional impetus as workers and administrators learned from *Pravda* how pervasive wrecking was. After the arrest of the Mikhailov group, the antiwrecking campaign gained momentum and spread further.

The Artillery-Arsenal Trust's I. F. Sharskov reported to Voroshilov on the arrests, attacking not only the arrested engineers' excessive caution but, instructively, their personnel policy as well. Vysochanskii's clique "selected their own people for leadership positions in the trust's apparatus—it was very difficult for an engineer from outside to get in. Selection of engineers did not go according to qualifications, but in correspondence with some other type of conditions." The damage could be repaired, in Sharskov's view, only by appointing more communists to the trust. Sharskov was careful to establish for Voroshilov his long history of disagreements with the newly revealed wreckers. His reservations about new investment at Stalingrad's Barrikady artillery factory, hidden capacity at military factories, and proper employment of available investment capital had all, in his words, been proved correct. Despite this, Sharskov faced constant opposition from bourgeois specialists and even from Tolokontsev, a communist.[17]

As Sharskov's report shows, once Mikhailov was in prison, suspicion turned to the man who had defended him: Aleksandr Tolokontsev, director of the VPU. Lakhinskii, so fond of denunciations, wrote again to express his glee and the "sighs of relief" he heard once news of Mikhailov's arrest became public. With him gone, the time had come to realize that "the sabotage of VPU's apparat is inspired and supported by its director—Comrade Tolokontsev." When a commission under Ivan Pavlunovskii investigated wrecking in military industry, Tolokontsev tried to convince trust and factory directors not to cooperate—a maneuver intended, in

Lakhinskii's view, to prove Mikhailov innocent. Tolokontsev ordered that salaries be paid to the families of the arrested engineers and told the wife of one arrested man that he believed the charges to be groundless. In this, Lakhinskii felt, Tolokontsev showed his true colors: "And what do the Mensheviks and monarchists say? That the Bolsheviks invent every incident of wrecking, that the Bolsheviks, for no good reason, for nothing, abuse the engineers and intelligentsia. So what's the difference between Tolokontsev and the Mensheviks? Nothing."[18]

Beleaguered by the whispering campaign against him and by his evident negligence in allowing military industry to become riddled with wreckers and saboteurs, Tolokontsev was forced out of the VPU. On 28 March 1929, the Politburo replaced him with Mikhail Uryvaev. To salvage his reputation, Tolokontsev wrote a final testament on the progress military industry had made in its two and a half years under him, all the more necessary "in connection with the OGPU's information on the existence of a wrecking organization within military industry." He carefully laid out the low productivity and the 24 million rubles of late deliveries when he took office and the improvements made by the time of his dismissal: all late deliveries had been made up, the 1927–1928 production program 99.8 percent filled, costs cut, and profits increased—a substantial improvement over previous chronic shortfalls. Total production had more than doubled, and output per worker had improved steadily. In short, all was well except for the saboteurs infesting military industry and destroying the Soviet Union's defense readiness.[19]

Tolokontsev seemed to be explaining why Mikhailov had succeeded in deceiving him for so long and simultaneously why Mikhailov and the other wreckers could not be guilty:

> The conclusions of some quite respected comrades that old generals have lodged themselves in military industry are unjustified. In the GVPU apparat there are only a few. Even with such a high percentage of party members (39 percent) it was very difficult to identify the wreckers, since their leader, Mikhailov (leading the technical part of GVPU's Collegium), could seem completely Soviet in his outlook; he unreservedly delivered reports at a series of meetings, and at meetings of the party fraction he accepted constructive criticism for guidance and action. . . . He was among the first engineers and technicians rejecting the Shakhty wreckers and made a special declaration in the press.

Tolokontsev declared that he had no intention of resigning, in effect denying the charges against him. "I cannot *not* inform the Presidium of Vesenkha and the Politburo as well: that which incriminates me is a monstrous accusation, undeserved and reflecting very painfully on me."[20]

Tolokontsev's self-justification was insufficient to protect him from the party's Central Control Commission, although he was (at least temporarily) spared the death sentence Mikhailov received in July 1929. Tolokontsev was reminded of his mistakes, including "excessive trust" and insufficient watchfulness. In addition, the rosy reports he used to defend himself "gave an optimistic assessment of military industry, taking some accomplishments as indicators of overall health," and thereby concealed wrecking. He had refused to fire Mikhailov when ordered, defended Mikhailov instead of repairing damage, and declared to the Central Committee nine months after Mikhailov's arrest that it had been based on unreliable materials. Tolokontsev's predecessor, Petr Bogdanov, long since exiled to the North Caucasus, was reprimanded for "excessive trust in military industry's specialists, especially their leaders: the engineers Mikhailov, Dyman [sic] and others."[21] Tolokontsev's subordinates fared no better. Budnevich, ex-head of the Financial-Planning Directorate and Tolokontsev's temporary deputy, was strongly reprimanded and fired. The same fate awaited Khomytov, chair of the Military-Chemical Trust; Korolev, director of Bolshevik; and Chekmarov, director of the Motovilikhinskii factory. Bruno and Berezin, chairs of the Firearm–Machine Gun Trust and the Artillery-Arsenal Trust, respectively, would have been fired, except that they had already been removed by the time the Central Control Commission met to decide their fate.[22]

Tolokontsev did not remain long in limbo. The need for talented communist managers meant that everyone had to be employed, even those tainted by association with counterrevolutionaries. Even though his guilt in abetting wrecking was still beyond question, on 30 November 1929, he was appointed chair of the Association (ob"edinenie) of Medium Machine Building. He never returned to military industry, although Medium Machine Building would play an important role in subsequent Soviet tank development. His partial rehabilitation secured a similar pardon for Bogdanov, who would serve from December 1929 in the United States as head of the trading company Amtorg and de facto Soviet ambassador before diplomatic recognition in 1933.[23] They both would ultimately perish during the Great Purges.

Mikhailov and his fellow prisoners did not enjoy the same respite. On 15 July 1929, the Politburo agreed on the execution of the specialists leading the counterrevolutionary conspiracy. The OGPU was to present a list of those to be shot, but "the execution itself is to be delayed until a new Central Committee decision on the moment of execution." The Politburo finally decided on 21 October 1929 to accept the OGPU's recommendations and ratified the final list. The saboteurs were sentenced to be shot, and the Politburo approved a draft press release to announce it, published the next day in Pravda. V. S. Mikhailov, N. G. Vysochanskii, V. L. Dymman, V. N. Dekhanov, and N. V. Shul'ga, according to the press release, had all been tried, convicted, sentenced to death, and executed for a counterrevolutionary plot to cripple military industry. The release took pains to note that all had reached the rank of general in the tsarist army and that all but Shul'ga had a noble background.[24]

After the executions, the Politburo was still left with problems in the defense industry. Believing military production to be severely damaged, the Politburo undertook an overhaul of military industry from top to bottom. On 15 July 1929, the Politburo simultaneously issued two key decisions—one on the defense of the Soviet Union and the other on military industry (see chapter 5). The resolution on military industry set out its reason for being quite clearly: modern technology in warfare demanded vast output from industry, and Soviet military industry's shortcomings were the direct result of a lengthy campaign of wrecking. Industry had unfortunately evolved so that "all development of military industry and its preparation for war were based squarely on the caste of old tsarist-era specialists," and "when it was established that the majority of old specialists belonged to a counterrevolutionary organization, military industry found itself in a critical position." This was the result of "longstanding and systematic wrecking" from the factory floor to the central bureaucracy, made possible by the "absence of watchfulness" or even "minimal control" by military industry's party leadership, who left technical matters to specialists.[25]

According to the Politburo, the opportunity during 1928–1929 to correct the damage the wreckers had caused was lost due to both the chaos introduced by the wrecking itself and the "optimistic light" military industry had thrown on its own state of affairs, hiding the true extent of the damage. Immediate action was necessary. The Central Control Commission was brought in to establish who among military industry's leadership would be held responsible, and Rabkrin, along with the Orgburo (a committee responsible for certain personnel matters), was unleashed to conduct a comprehensive purge. Vesenkha was to send more technicians to military industry and assemble a plan to "liquidate the consequences of wrecking," paying particular attention to capital investment, precision tools and measuring instruments, and rationalization of production processes.[26]

MAKING SURVIVAL A CRIME

Finding true sabotage was quite difficult; even the accidents that Soviet industry suffered from during the First Five-Year Plan were not common enough to serve as useful pretexts for wrecking. Instead, investigatory commissions turned to a simpler task: the pursuit of sloppiness. Auditors condemned as wrecking the universal subterfuges Soviet factory managers, engineers, and bureaucrats employed to enable the economy to function. Managers and technicians underestimated their production capacity to preserve slack, some extra reserve with which to meet difficult production targets. Joseph Berliner, in fact, pointed to this "safety factor" as the first principle of Soviet management. Private stocks of machine tools and scarce raw materials were salted away and not recorded on inventories of mobilization stockpiles, in preparation for the black day when a new and unattainable production goal would be set. Petty corruption and reluctance to innovate were the natural tactics industrial managers employed to resist the constant pressure for results. The interests of factory management therefore ran directly counter to the interests of the state and the Red Army. No entreaties could persuade factory managers or shop foremen to accurately report how much they could in fact do; judicious use of terror might prove more effective.[27]

Close reading of actual confessions, once the fantastic tales of foreign spy networks and counterrevolutionary conspiracies are taken away, reveals not sabotage but merely the necessary maneuvers Soviet managers used to survive: substituting substandard materials or concealing stocks of desperately needed spare parts. What had been necessary to grease the wheels of the Soviet economic machine was now criminal. The Firearm–Machine Gun Trust's auditing commission found in July 1929 an example of what it termed sabotage by a counterrevolutionary conspiracy. This group had exacerbated production bottlenecks and underestimated capacity at its three key factories producing nearly all of the Soviet Union's rifles, pistols, and machine guns: the Tula, Izhevsk, and Kovrov works.[28]

The Tula armaments plant, producing arms since the time of Peter the Great, is a particularly good example of the criminalization of necessity that the OGPU and Rabkrin relied on to make their cases. Iagoda and Molochnikov from the OGPU reported to Voroshilov, Unshlikht, and Ordzhonikidze about Tula on 15 October 1929. According to their investigation, the conspiracy's leaders—technical director Boris Kanevskii, head engineer Boris Uspenskii, director of the metal laboratory N. P. Skvortsov, and director of the Scientific-Technical Bureau Ia. I. Kanevskii—had confessed to sabotaging the manufacture of Degtiarev machine guns by allowing the use of substandard, low-quality steel for vital parts.[29]

In Skvortsov's 1 October confession, he claimed that another conspirator permitted the use of iron with excessive amounts of phosphorous. With the full knowledge of Boris Kanevskii, the substandard steel produced from substandard iron was distributed to other factories; Tula's personnel figured that the Izhevsk plant would be blamed when the faulty parts eventually failed. Other confessions confirmed Skvortsov's allegations while adding more managers to the conspiracy, including its ringleader, Pavel Tret'iakov, director of the Machine Gun Division. Kanevskii told his OGPU interrogator that "you only need to be correct on paper—something like 'there's no suitable steel—Izhevsk will be blamed,' or 'if the military inspector takes the machine gun, that means everything's OK.'" Not only was substandard steel used with the knowledge and cooperation of Cherepanov, the Red Army's quality inspector, but this subterfuge had gone on since 1921. Head engineer Uspenskii's confession expanded the wrecking's scope to rifles and revolvers while denouncing more technicians.[30]

What seems clear is that there was a kind of conspiracy in Tula, though hardly a counterrevolutionary one. Although consistency of detail—the precise nature of the wrecking and its 1921 start—might have been imposed by OGPU interrogators, much of the remainder of the confessions has a core of plausibility. Soviet factories always had trouble finding enough high-quality metal. Managers faced terrible temptation to avoid falling below plan by cutting corners on quality control, and even the military representatives checking production must have faced that same pressure to keep quiet about minor violations of standards. Kanevskii's phrase "if the military inspector takes the machine gun, that means everything's OK" has the feel of authenticity. Modest efforts by technicians to meet high production targets through benign shortcuts became, in the hands of the OGPU, a counter-revolutionary wrecking cell.

In late 1929, the expanding arrests hit Aviatrest, heart of the USSR's over-whelmingly military aviation industry. Here the OGPU unearthed the same curious blend of foreign spies and humdrum Soviet factory life evident at Tula. In December 1929, Prokof'ev, head of the OGPU's Economic Directorate, reported to Rykov on the arrest of fourteen engineers and specialists. All but two had con-fessed to extensive sabotage, but in a chilling aside, Prokof'ev assured Rykov that this stubbornness would pose no difficulty; after all, one of the recalcitrant engi-neers had been in custody only one day. Active since 1921, the wreckers had worked at all major factories and even within the Red Army's air force to mis-direct research, rush planes into production without blueprints, allow capital investment without spending controls, and even import aircraft engines of parti-cularly low quality. Rykov took the matter to the Politburo in January, resulting in a comprehensive purge of Soviet aviation.[31]

In the confessions sent to Rykov, fantastic tales of émigré capitalist spymasters were combined with more plausible stories of drinking and complaining about the government or cutting corners on materials. In Prokof'ev's view, the engi-neers' class determined their conduct, and he took pains to establish links between their crimes and earlier wrecking. Veterans of prerevolutionary factories, Aviatrest's engineers considered themselves aristocracy and resented their drop in status in the new social order. Using drinking bouts as a cover for their scheming, the saboteurs toasted the solidarity of engineers and waxed nostalgic about past glories and the new world to come after counterrevolution. At the same time, senior engi-neers within the trust's central management strove to sustain an illusion of professionalism—one recalled how they "vigilantly followed the flow of produc-tion to keep it on track. . . . We warned, we predicted, we talked, we wrote, we directed attention." But their real goals were different: Makarovskii himself explained that "engineers weren't at the factory to work. No, they visit the fac-tory to get their share of rations, meet each other, talk over the latest news, specu-late on the continued existence of the Bolsheviks." The OGPU had trouble reconciling the widespread conspiracy it had uncovered with a disturbing lack of damage to Aviatrest's physical plant, so Makarovskii obligingly confessed that engineers had prepared for the restoration of capitalism by

keeping an eye on the upkeep of the machinery, the upkeep of the building, when possible hauling into the factory materials and machine tools (it's all the same which precise things you bring in), any kind of valuables, just as long as they're valuable. The owner is coming back and he'll say thank you, not just in words, but fortified with substantial material rewards.[32]

Just as in the Firearm-Machine Gun Trust, Aviatrest's engineers were in fact guilty of nothing more than sloppiness, cutting corners, or at worst petty corruption. In the tense atmosphere of Stalin's industrialization, they could be arrested for creating crises or equally for trying to correct them. After all, the OGPU noted that one wrecking tactic was to criticize harshly and excessively. Those who tried to dodge trouble by cooking the books also embroiled themselves in wrecking. As I. M. Kostkin recounted, "so there wouldn't be any direct evidence of wrecking, Kutovyi told those of us working in the bureau doing the accounts on fulfilling the production program to do them in such a way that there wouldn't be any formal indications of bad work at the factory and none of the members of the group would suffer." Engineers admitted to turning a blind eye to shoddy quality control on routine processes on occasion and to understating production capacity to obtain extra machinery and investment capital. New planes were rushed into production, cutting corners on design parameters and shortening aerodynamic testing to meet a plan deadline, just as new factory shops were built without waiting for blueprints and plans. In the only admission the engineers made that shared the twin virtues of plausibility and criminality, they confessed to selling excess materials for cash and to padding the books on projects, overstating expenditures in order to pocket the difference.[33]

Wreckers were also accused of planning the industrial workforce's mass demoralization in the event of war. Krzhizhanovskii told *Pravda*'s readers that wreckers would trigger fires and explosions to enable Poland to seize Ukraine. The director of Chemical Factory 15 in Chapaevsk charged that wreckers planned to create panic once war began. A report on Barrikady came to similar conclusions: counterrevolutionaries would disrupt the huge Stalingrad factory and "weaken the country's defense readiness through demoralization in a period of possible military intervention." This demoralization had already begun; in addition to unplanned growth, the factory's workers had been ground down by "repeated changes of the production program" and increases in the factory's load of civilian production. Fearful of enemy air attack in the event of war, the Soviets also saw wrecking in civil defense. Management at the Shlisselburg factory sought to avoid unpleasantness by pointing out in advance that their location in the immediate neighborhood of Lake Ladoga, the Neva River, and an old fortress made concealment rather difficult.[34]

LIQUIDATING WRECKING

By 1930, the campaign's focus shifted from criminalizing what engineers and managers did for survival to repairing damage and de-emphasizing arrests. Instead of searching out saboteurs, the Central Committee directed military industry to now "liquidate the consequences of wrecking." Although liquidation had been part of Vesenkha's mission since July 1929, before 1930, it played only a small role in the overall campaign. In 1930, the Red Army seized upon liquidation as a means of promoting its own interests. Military industry had been plagued since the civil war with chronically late production, poor mobilization readiness, and slow, misdirected, and inefficient capital investment. The new "liquidation of wrecking" attacked precisely those shortcomings that had driven the party and the Red Army to distraction. The campaign against the internal class enemy became a campaign for military readiness and rearmament, taken up and wholeheartedly adopted by the Red Army to solve its chronic problems with Soviet industry.[35]

This liquidation campaign was aimed at haphazard plans for industrial mobilization, a particular irritant for the Red Army. To cite one instructive example, assignments had been distributed for artillery pieces but not for the shells those pieces fired. A common error by industrial planners, occurring as one mobilization plan gave way to another, was removing an assignment from one factory but never transferring it to another. Even updating plans to account for new needs and new capabilities could disrupt production: Factory 8 in Mytishchi outside Moscow had its assignment under mobilization plan S-30 changed five times. The Morozov factory in Shlisselburg had by May 1930 received its fourth assignment in a year. Industrial mobilization plans generally ignored transportation and made little effort to minimize unnecessary and expensive rail transport between factories. New construction and new capital investment were late, disordered, incomplete, constantly changing, and often unrelated to the demands of the mobilization plan. Given the speed and scale of the industrialization program the Soviets hoped to achieve and the rigid administrative system within which managers worked, such chaos was quite natural. To the Soviet elite, however, these problems were conscious sabotage by hostile forces and had to be repaired before disaster struck.[36]

As a result, a new Politburo decision on 25 February 1930, supported by the OGPU and the military, emphasized liquidating wrecking. Its verdict was harsh: industrial managers had been dilatory or even obstructionist in tracking down wreckers. The Politburo accordingly created crash technical education courses for communist directors. To increase technical competence, Sovnarkom was to establish the forced dispatch of engineers to military factories, and all institutions educating technicians were to supply the VPU's demands first, regardless of other agreements. In addition, plans, drawings, blueprints, and stockpiles were to be checked and inventoried. All of Vesenkha's ancillary people's commissariats were instructed to improve their performance, with Labor supplying better technicians and Foreign Trade speeding the import of machinery.[37]

Sverdlov Chemical Factory 80 is an example of the two approaches of military industry's antiwrecking campaign: first, arrests of specialists, and, second, a mass movement to eliminate defects in factory work. By December 1929, it had become clear to factory managers that the factory's technical director, Gaevich, and chief mechanic Markov were delaying new production. Gaevich would have attracted attention earlier but for the unfortunate fact that he had originated "a series of ingenious innovations in production" that diverted suspicion from him. After they were arrested, along with the factory's head of basic production, commercial director, and chief accountant, the OGPU, Rabkrin, and a Central Committee delegation began putting the factory back into shape. With new organization and better planning, bragged factory director Ketura, the factory improved quality, rationalized production, and pushed through new capital investment.[38]

Liquidating wrecking was not done exclusively through investigating commissions; a thorough six-week purge in March and April 1930 winnowed the bureaucrats of the GVPU itself. The GVPU could not be trusted to run its own purge, so the OGPU's Economic Directorate guaranteed vigorous self-criticism.[39] In the GVPU's Production-Technical Section, which collected and disseminated technical data on armaments manufacture, engineers and managers alike lamented their failure to go beyond minimum requirements, following the "path of least resistance" by serving only as a technical library rather than promoting innovations. Dmitiev, an obstetrician *(akusher)* serving as an engineer for bullet, cartridge, and fuse production, bewailed the division's lack of competence to challenge the GVPU's trusts on any substantive question. His lack of relevant qualifications was typical; Bartenev, the senior engineer for artillery and tanks, had no technical production experience.[40] In principle, responsibility for planning new production and industrial plant fell under the GVPU's Scientific-Technical Council. The council was supposed to evaluate blueprints for new or expanded factories before work went forward; instead, the council was overwhelmed by the volume and complexity of its tasks. Adams, chair of the council, remarked that "we have factories which are already built and working, and only now the plan comes in." His subordinate, Korzun, admitted that the council could only file away the blueprints it received.[41]

The Red Army used the opportunity created by the liquidation campaign to advance its own interests: timely delivery of high-quality equipment and a high degree of mobilization readiness. Ieronim Uborevich, the Red Army's armaments director, ordered his quality-control inspectors to ensure complete liquidation of wrecking by working closely with factory management. The inspectors were to be unbending on technical conditions and quality control.[42] Uborevich and his Armaments Directorate missed no chance to push liquidation and thereby urge better production from military industry. Working through Unshlikht, who had formerly served in the Red Army as deputy people's commissar responsible for industrial relations, Uborevich forced military concerns onto Vesenkha's agenda. His report to Unshlikht on Vesenkha's flagrant violation of the Politburo's 25 February 1930 decree to eliminate wrecking said little that had not been said before—it was a litany of shoddy construction, uncoordinated production, and delays in import orders and military contracts. In short, Uborevich amply illustrated the systemic problems plaguing Soviet military industry—or all of Soviet industry, for that matter—on a daily basis. It was not Uborevich's place to concede that industry's problems were inherent in rapid industrialization; his role was to hammer on the point that shortfalls were the result of sabotage and were therefore correctable.[43]

Industrial administrators could do little in response. Six months after the Politburo's February 1930 liquidation decree, a Vesenkha report found only isolated progress. Given the ephemeral enemy that industry was fighting, little else could have been expected. The essential difficulty the military industry confronted was not any concrete person or policy but the system itself. When carelessness or petty corruption was tolerated or even encouraged by the economic environment in which engineers and managers functioned, the party and state had to harangue industrial employees to be careful and honest and threaten draconian discipline otherwise. Harsh penalties for failure and excessive centralization ensured that lack of initiative was the norm. As a result, Vesenkha had nothing to show after six months of liquidating wrecking. It had expanded its network of educational institutions as a long-term solution to the lack of communist technicians, but Vesenkha objected vigorously to dispatching officers and soldiers into the defense industry, and the directors of civil factories vehemently protested moving any of their engineers to military plants. In all other areas, Vesenkha reported profound concern, vigorous effort, frequent meetings, the best of intentions, and few concrete results. As a result, despite purges and the removal of "unsuitable" elements, the MPU could only conduct more investigations to continue the Sisyphean task of eliminating chaotic and haphazard practices from Soviet industry.[44]

MASS PARTICIPATION

The measures the Soviets chose to battle wrecking defy understanding unless one accepts that the rhetoric about class warfare and class enemies was taken seriously. The primary dispute between communists and specialists inside the defense industry was over mundane questions of bureaucratic power and privilege, but Soviet policies to liquidate wrecking make no sense unless Stalin's Politburo understood class enemy to mean precisely that, not as simply a cynical device to divide and rule. A key plank of the Soviet fight against wrecking was to *reduce* secrecy, *widen* access to secret materials, and *expand* the use of foreign technical expertise, while simultaneously involving substantially more workers from the bench in factory administration. Despite all the rhetoric of capitalist war and foreign espionage, including the specific claim that the Shakhty espionage was the work of Polish intelligence, wrecking was seen primarily as coming from the internal class enemy, the bourgeois specialist: this is borne out by the fact that foreign engineers would be called in to repair the damage the wreckers had caused. As the Bolsheviks understood it, specialists had used their claims to exclusive knowledge of the technical intricacies of engineering and production to conceal their activities from both communist managers and line workers. Whereas the long-term solution was a new cohort of communist technical specialists, in the short run, the bourgeois specialist could not be replaced. The solution was *kontrol'*[45] via worker oversight and reduction of the amount of material shielded by secrecy.

The first efforts in this direction came from a May 1929 joint order of Vesenkha, the Red Army, and the Soviet Union's trade unions calling on worker organizations to involve themselves more closely in oversight. Shortly afterward, the Central Committee's key July 1929 decree on defense complained that communist directors had not exercised "even minimal control over the work of specialists." As a direct result, "under the pretext of military secrecy (excessive classification of documents) communists and non-party workers had in fact been removed from active participation in organizing and rationalizing production." The Politburo ordered the NKVM, the OGPU, and Vesenkha to reexamine their regulations on secrecy to *ease* restrictions, allowing greater worker *kontrol'*.[46] The RZ STO declared on 14 March 1930 that the "most rapid liquidation of wrecking" demanded the involvement of workers' groups, particularly to fight slow production and poor quality. At Factory 15, in response, plant managers dutifully approved the measures suggested from on high for eliminating wrecking and stressed the need to keep the wider public better informed on defense matters. Shop-floor party organizers were to add this to their list of duties, providing production plans to the workers and minimizing secrecy.[47]

The military played the same theme, although its repetitiveness suggested that not all were dancing to the correct tune. In March 1930, Voroshilov complained to Pavlunovskii that "the non-party and communist workers are in fact cut off from participation in the organization and rationalization of production" as a result of excessive secrecy, but the Politburo had thankfully ordered "a rapid declassification where possible." The sole remaining obstacle was "the inertia of the old and the ossified in the economic bureaucracy." In June 1930, Uborevich saw nonparticipation of the "broad working mass" as the chief reason that the aftereffects of wrecking still plagued military industry. Industrial officials concurred: Smilga complained that "excessive secrecy of production processes" had crippled the defense industry by eliminating "worker innovation, production meetings, shock work, socialist competition, and mass control." Muklevich, speaking at the 1930 Sixteenth Party Congress, complained that in industry, "under the cover of secrecy, often nothing at all is done." In November 1930, Unshlikht declared that both central administrators and factory directors continually failed to involve the "broad working mass" in eliminating wrecking.[48] The reasons for this failure are not difficult to understand; although wrecking supposedly worked through excessive secrecy, one can easily imagine uneasy technicians fearing a charge of wrecking grounded on excessive declassification. Reducing secrecy thus had little success.

More startling than worker *kontrol'* and increased declassification of secret materials (considering that wreckers were ostensibly agents of foreign intelligence) was that the campaign to liquidate wrecking was inextricably linked to *increasing* foreign technical assistance and employment of foreign specialists. Once again, the most dangerous foe was not the external enemy but the internal class alien. Taking exclusive knowledge from the unreliable bourgeois specialists was the most important priority; the authority and knowledge of that specialist could be replaced by worker collectives, foreign technical experts, or newly trained Red specialists, but it must absolutely be replaced. As the Politburo expressed in its July 1929 decision, heavy reliance on bourgeois specialists had put the defense industry in an exceedingly vulnerable position.

Despite the Bolshevik line that wreckers were agents of foreign intelligence, the Politburo ordered Vesenkha to speed the elimination of wrecking by increasing the use of foreign assistance. When worker *kontrol'* and declassification failed to produce the hoped-for results and military industry's performance remained stagnant, the Politburo was forced to experiment with new measures to break the stranglehold of wrecking on military production. The Central Committee in January 1930 ordered the Revvoensovet to use German, Italian, and American assistance in eliminating wrecking and in designing and producing new, more technically sophisticated arms. Little over a month later, the Politburo followed with detailed instructions to Vesenkha to expand significantly foreign technical assistance. Eliminating dependence on the internal class enemy was more important than keeping foreigners away from sensitive military production. As late as November 1930, despite substantial reliance on foreign technology and a slower pace of arrests, internal commissions on liquidating wrecking found an inadequate use of technical assistance in military industry. In particular, foreign specialists and imported machinery were applied to military production of secondary importance or even civil production.[49]

BACKLASH

Backlash against mass arrests within military industry began almost as soon as the campaign itself but grew to significant strength only after the industry had been thoroughly disrupted. Only a few short months after the Shakhty affair, the Politburo was already trying to rein in the persecution of bourgeois specialists. It ordered the secret police to take high-ranking technical intelligentsia into custody only "with the maximum amount of care, more than has been shown thus far, permitting the arrest of only hardened counterrevolutionaries, wreckers, and spies."[50] Despite the dangers in defending saboteurs and counterrevolutionaries, some managers were brave enough to defend their personnel. Budniak, the deputy director of Aviatrest, complained to Voroshilov upon his exit from the trust that working conditions had become intolerable. Proud of the Soviet aviation industry's accomplishments, Budniak nevertheless had to admit that Soviet design still lagged far behind that of the West. By far the best policy for the aviation industry was to purchase models abroad, with license to produce them in the USSR. Unfortunately:

> Comrade Menzhinskii [head of the OGPU] would call that criminal, and counterrevolutionary to boot, and if he were not sufficiently informed about what in fact is going on, he'd be right. But the members of the government

should know that the conditions for a similar type of design work abroad are completely different, not at all comparable with ours. First, this or that piece of bad luck in the production of new models abroad does not qualify as a crime. Second, while working on prototypes the designer has a range of various models and aids and freedom of action in carrying out the kind of expenditures that he thinks are necessary. In our situation the designer must be sure in advance that his motor or airplane will be 100 percent beyond reproach and will go into serial production after the construction of a prototype. Only in that case can he begin designing a new model without risk to himself.

Moreover, aircraft designers were denied travel abroad and could not stay abreast of technology: "In order to think up something new, you have to first see that which already exists. We don't give them that opportunity."[51]

By 1931, so many of the Soviet Union's key technicians in the defense industry had been arrested and imprisoned or executed that the pendulum of terror began to swing back. Sergo Ordzhonikidze, replacing Kuibyshev as head of Vesenkha, proved to be a friend to the bourgeois specialists, making industrialization a higher priority than class warfare. Ironically, Ordzhonikidze had not previously been a great defender of the rights of specialists. In September 1929, he told the Moscow Oblast Party Conference that although a "significant collection" of the bourgeois specialists was loyal to the Soviet state, there were, to "a sufficient degree, all kinds of scum *(vsiakoi svolochi)*." In fact, the specialists who believed that their influence could wean the Bolsheviks away from extremism and toward a more moderate system were, in his view, *"the most dangerous, the most harmful for us."* In his campaign to oust Kuibyshev from Vesenkha, in fact, Ordzhonikidze had criticized Kuibyshev's soft line on wrecking.[52]

Ordzhonikidze was in temperament no more moderate than his fellow Bolsheviks. But when he reached Vesenkha, the situation demanded an end to antiwrecking campaigns: industry was already short of technical personnel, and arrests made a bad situation drastically worse. Even by early 1929, Mikhail Uryvaev, then director of the GVPU, reported "serious difficulties" in finding enough engineers and technical workers. By May 1930, the Shlisselburg factory complained of drastic shortages of technical personnel, being seven engineers and six technicians short in an already small technical staff. It had had no technical leadership at all for three and a half months and no head engineer for five. In the same month, a joint Vesenkha and OGPU circular ordered that liquidation of wrecking be treated as shock work, that all engineering and technical resources be tapped, and that even "engineer-wreckers condemned by organs of the OGPU should be employed." Although OGPU permission was required and the wreckers worked under guard, it was a first step in returning supposed saboteurs to the factory floor.[53]

In April 1931, Iagoda, director of the OGPU, suggested using rehabilitated wreckers under close supervision in industry once more, and the Politburo approved. By September, Ordzhonikidze had established a list of engineers to be released from custody not for production, but at least for research and development. In October, more engineers were released in conjunction with the construction of a blooming mill at the Izhorskii Works, closely linked to military production. Even Voroshilov was won over by the results rehabilitated engineers produced. Writing to Ordzhonikidze about Aviation Factory 39, he exclaimed that "the wreckers not only worked like devils, but created a large group of our engines." He suggested that they be awarded medals.[54]

The rehabilitation of these engineers and specialists took place not because the last traces of wrecking had been eliminated from Soviet industry, but precisely because traces still remained. No matter how many engineers the OGPU arrested, the same structural constraints slowed production innovations, forced managers to conceal supplies, and undercut quality control. Rabkrin reported in 1931 on the mixed results of efforts to cleanse Soviet industry of the pernicious results of wrecking. Concentrating on military industry, electrical power, transportation, and food processing, Rabkrin concluded that although a "significant share" of wrecking had been brought to light and expunged, "those sections of industry most seriously damaged by wrecking have to this date still (particularly in military industry) as a rule not recovered and are a very palpable brake on fulfilling the 1931 plan." Audits of military factories found industry's mobilization readiness "in the very same state it was under the wreckers," for not one factory had a complete mobilization plan. Furthermore, as a result of "contradictory directives from the Mobilization-Planning Sector of Vesenkha, factories and associations do not know which mobilization plan (MV-10 or S-30) to consider active and which one to use for planning work."[55]

The ailments Rabkrin uncovered were a depressingly familiar litany of the ills to which Soviet industry was vulnerable. No factory completely revealed its hidden capacity, and new capacity was far behind schedule. Quality control, especially in bullet manufacture, showed little sign of improvement. The same bottlenecks that wreckers had supposedly engineered still persisted years later, especially in factories' ancillary repair shops and on-site production of precision measuring instruments. Lastly, thanks to disorganized transportation, stacks of completed shells surrounded arms factories, easy targets for saboteurs.[56]

The end of the campaign against wrecking temporarily halted the use of mass terror against engineers and specialists but could do nothing to resolve Soviet industry's chronic problems. The antiwrecking campaign only ensured that the next time a crisis came, Red specialists would take the place of tsarist engineers. Policy conflicts and disputes over scarce promotions would no longer take shape along a communist versus noncommunist divide. In this way, the antiwrecking campaign served as a dress rehearsal for the Great Purges, creating within Soviet industry the rituals of denunciation, the practice of hunting internal enemies, and the resolution of policy disputes and personal conflicts through state terror. Mark Beissinger commented on the Great Purges of the late 1930s that the "absurdity of the purges lay not in the fact that [confusion and conflict] did not exist, for they were inevitable and all-pervasive characteristics of bureaucratic organization, but rather that normal organizational resistance and bureaucratic confusion were defined as crimes against the state."[57] But this was not an innovation of the Great Purges; it had been enshrined in the antiwrecking campaigns ten years earlier. The Great Purges would have been impossible without the example set by the hunt for wreckers.

This, however, was not the most persistent legacy of the antiwrecking campaign. Within military industry, finding traitors in every factory and directorate meant that resisting the Red Army's demands for more rapid rearmament would grow increasingly difficult. In the formative years of the Soviet defense economy, the bargaining strength of industrial managers was always undermined by the suspicion of treason surrounding any position opposed to the military. In the increasingly bitter debates over the militarization of the Soviet economy, managers were always weakened by the specter of wrecking that haunted Soviet industry. The system created under those conditions of military dominance would persist through the fall of the Soviet Union.

4

The Shift Toward Radical Rearmament

The campaign against wrecking began in 1928 and disrupted Soviet industry for years to come. Despite the ongoing chaos around them, military officers and industrial managers still had to hammer out yearly plans and long-term blueprints for the Soviet defense economy. As a result of the antiwrecking campaign, however, the Red Army's high command grew convinced that industry's continuing difficulties were the result of deliberate sabotage, and so were easily correctable. The military's desire for more arms hence grew far more quickly than industry or the Soviet budget's ability to sustain massive rearmament.

Military dreams clashed with economic realities in the meetings of the RZ STO. As the Soviet Union's defense cabinet, it had to arbitrate between the Red Army's continuing demands for more production and better preparation for war and the Soviet economy's chronic shortage of capital and capacity. Over the course of 1928, however, the political balance and economic constraints that kept military ambitions in check broke down. What the war scare had not achieved, namely, a shift to rapid rearmament, the increasing radicalization of Soviet politics would. The Red Army's high command grew increasingly bitter over the restrictions that Aleksei Rykov, chair of the RZ STO, imposed on military spending. In an atmosphere poisoned by revelations of espionage, after all, conservatism in military planning was now revealed to be base treason. At the same time, Stalin's strengthening grip on political power weakened Rykov's ability to constrain military spending. As a result, ongoing debates over military budgets, order plans, investment in the defense industry, and the Red Army's modernization moved toward more radical solutions, approaching the military's vision of the total militarization of society. The Red Army took increasing advantage of technology to modernize itself and prepare for the next war.

HOW FAST SHOULD THE RED ARMY GROW?

The RZ STO, where the struggle over military policy took place in debates over plans and orders, was the arena for this institutional competition between the Revvoensovet and Vesenkha over the development of the Soviet economy. As part of a continuing struggle to nail down a five-year plan for the Red Army, the RZ STO renewed its request in February 1928 to the Revvoensovet to supply two orders for Soviet industry: the first was a contingency plan to cover the Red Army's needs through mobilization and one year of war, and the second was a long-range procurement projection over five years of peaceful development. Military planners feared being limited by any growth projection they put on paper, so the Red Army was as slow as ever to deliver its data to Vesenkha and Gosplan. Postnikov at the MPU had to resort to threats to speed the process. He told Unshlikht that delays in submitting orders or even technical drawings and specifications for newly developed weaponry would delay long-range planning and, worse, hinder delivery of the Red Army's current orders. Delays persisted nevertheless. The RZ STO could not debate a complete military development plan until 23 April 1928, a year after Tukhachevskii first brought his four-year plan to the Revvoensovet.[1]

The debates over this military five-year plan brought to the surface the latent tensions over the extent of Soviet rearmament. When the RZ STO finally had a military mobilization order and five-year development plan to discuss, it decided that the issue was too complex to be settled at a single meeting. Following typical Soviet bureaucratic practice, in April 1928, the RZ STO referred the entire question to a subcommittee under Voroshilov. The instructions given to Voroshilov's commission attempted to strike a careful balance between military interests in maximal production and civil interests in minimal defense spending by stressing the need for economy and efficiency. In the commission's three tasks—the military's industrial order for mobilization and a year of war, a military five-year plan, and an intermediate three-year plan—its members were instructed to carefully match defense needs to the Soviet economy's "real possibilities," avoiding unnecessary capital investment. Expenditure on the Red Navy was "to proceed from the need for the most rational use of resources expended on strengthening defense potential," with the unspoken message that naval forces would be a low priority.[2]

A personnel shake-up in the midst of the commission's sessions altered the Red Army's representation at the meetings but did little to change the fundamental issues at stake. During April 1928, Chief of Staff Tukhachevskii became embroiled in a bitter dispute over just how powerful the Staff should be in running the Red Army. Tukhachevskii pushed for an all-powerful Staff to control all preparations for war, but his own ambition and arrogance prevented the rest of the Red Army's high command from trusting him in such a post. He resigned as Chief of Staff in May and became instead commander of the Leningrad Military District. Boris Shaposhnikov, a veteran of the tsarist General Staff who had successfully switched his allegiance to Soviet power, became the new Chief of Staff. Shaposhnikov was much less personally ambitious than Tukhachevskii, but both men shared with the rest of the high command a common commitment to boosting the resources available to the Red Army. Shaposhnikov's replacement of Tukhachevskii had no effect on the deliberations of Voroshilov's commission.[3]

The commission's preliminary agenda showed just how fundamental Voroshilov and his fellow participants believed their deliberations to be. The first meeting would cover the Red Army's most basic questions: its size, degree of mechanization, and projected budgets. The next three would discuss wartime burdens on industry, including existing stockpiles of war materiel, their rate of use, and industry's ability to replace losses. The final one would produce recommendations on the future of the Red Army: in addition to numerical strength and budgets, these would include a mobilization order, stockpile plan, and development schedule for military industry.[4]

In contrast to the relatively conservative charge the commission had been given, the participants took an optimistic and ambitious approach to planning the future of the Red Army. Their focus on technologically advanced rearmament was especially striking in comparison to the limited four-year plan Tukhachevskii had presented to the Revvoensovet just a year before. Nikolai Efimov, head of the Red Army Staff's Organization-Mobilization Directorate, opened the commission's deliberations on 30 April 1928 by setting the "basic task" of the armed forces' five-year plan as "strengthening technical resources through the air force, artillery, and tanks." He emphasized the "maximum possible further development" of airpower, reaching 2,000 active, 500 second-line, and 1,800 reserve aircraft by the end of the five-year plan. The high command would have a special fire and breakthrough reserve made up of heavy artillery and mortar units and nearly 1,000 tanks. Growth would be less dramatic in other branches: the wartime Red Army would expand by seven rifle divisions, and cavalry, chemical, and communications units would be strengthened. The Red Navy would fare worst, limited to a secondary role as a submarine and "mosquito" (torpedo boat) fleet. Efimov also presented a budget plan, structured with its most dramatic increases in the first two years of the plan to allow for early accumulation of stockpiles. In all, munitions stockpiles accounted for 30.2 percent, or 1,646.5 million rubles, of Efimov's 5,450 million–ruble five-year budget.[5]

Expanding on Efimov's proposal, Voroshilov's commission added 250 million rubles to his budget—50 million yearly—to build up mobilization stocks (see table 9). Vladimirskii, the head of Gosplan's Defense Sector, gave the commission his own budget projections, assuming outlays of 5,000 million rubles over five years. The 700 million–ruble gulf between the two plans was largely illusory; optimistic assumptions about cost reductions in industrial production rendered the two proposals not very far apart.[6] This suggestion of consensus over military budgets would make Voroshilov and the Red Army's high command that much more furious when the budget deal collapsed later in 1928. Despite the careful balance

Table 9. Comparison of Efimov's and Voroshilov Commission's Budget Projections (million rubles)

Fiscal Year	Efimov Proposal	Percent growth over Previous Year	Commission Proposal (after additional 250 million rubles)	Percent Growth over Previous Year
1927–1928	742.5	17		
1928–1929	919.3	23.8	969.3	30.5
1929–1930	1,045.0	13.6	1,095.0	13.0
1930–1931	1,123.6	7.5	1,173.6	7.1
1931–1932	1,164.1	3.6	1,214.1	3.5
1932–1933	1,198.0	2.9	1,248.0	2.8
Total	5,450.0		5,700.0	

in Voroshilov's commission between military and civilian interests, it did not take into account those who pushed most strongly for fiscal restraint and low military spending: Aleksei Rykov, any representative of the People's Commissariat of Finance, or a Gosplan representative from outside its Defense Sector. When Rykov eventually rejected the Red Army's budget, Voroshilov's sense of betrayal was palpable.

All that lay ahead; at the time, the commission's deliberations were dominated by an optimistic spirit that industrial obstacles to increased production and faster rearmament could be overcome with concerted effort. The third and fourth meetings of Voroshilov's group turned to industrial questions: how to expand military industry to cover the Red Army's needs for one year of war. The target for 1932–1933, the end of the five-year plan, was the capacity to produce 6,000 million cartridges and 66 million shells over one year of war. Cartridge capacity was currently 3,000 million but could increase rapidly given substitutes for scarce nonferrous metals. Shell capacity, Tolokontsev and Postnikov reported, was already 14 million and would reach 24 million by October 1929. In short, the five-year goals would require significant investment but were not out of reach. As a halfway step, the commission proposed a two- to three-year goal of a 3,200 million cartridge capacity and a 45 million shell capacity. Aviation production targets appeared similarly achievable. Five new factories, three for airframes and two for motors, were necessary to meet the Red Army's wartime needs. Still, the overall program was within reach, along with the three-year intermediate capacity target of 4,000 aircraft and 4,000 motors, increasing to 6,865 aircraft and 7,295 motors by the end of the five-year plan. Although the commission's final report would omit precise numeric targets, it did include Efimov's formulation that the Soviet air force needed "maximum possible development" and a commitment to five new factories.[7]

Tanks, trucks, artillery pieces, and firearms were all discussed in the same hopeful spirit that the Red Army's needs were not impossible to meet. Even though the Red Army's mobilization demands might greatly exceed current capacity, capital investment could make them easily achievable by the end of the 1932–1933 fiscal year if the Red Army would deliver models and technical drawings to industry on time. Voroshilov's commission found that no extraordinary measures were required to meet the mobilization order for 955 tanks two to three years in the future or the five-year target of 1,500 tanks. Completing the Stalingrad tractor factory and expanding existing factories, especially Leningrad's Bolshevik, would suffice. The nearly 17,000 1.5-ton trucks the Red Army would need could not be produced by the Moscow automobile factory alone, so an additional one would be required, and perhaps the expansion of the Kharkov motorcycle plant. The commission's final report repeated these conclusions while increasing the intermediate tank mobilization order by 100, to 1,055. Even without wartime mobilization to full production, the Red Army's peacetime tank force was projected to hit 1,075 by the end of the five-year plan. For artillery and firearms, the commission projected a three-year mobilization target for yearly production of 62,500 machine guns and a five-year mobilization target of 73,550, split among light, medium, heavy, and aviation models. This, along with a five-year peacetime order totaling nearly 100,000 machine guns, would be based on expanded production at the Tula and Kovrov firearms plants. The artillery mobilization target was 7,171 pieces of all calibers, and after the five-year plan, artillery would reach a peacetime strength of 11,743 pieces. None of these goals appeared far out of reach.[8]

In wrapping up its work, Voroshilov's commission produced two separate but closely linked decisions: one a contingency plan specifying the Red Army's industrial orders for mobilization and a year of war, and the other detailing the Red Army's five-year development. Their conclusions were naturally interconnected and reflected the Red Army's goal of matching any potential foe in numerical strength and surpassing it in technology. This meant, in particular, "maximal possible development of the air force" and "strengthening of means of suppression by fire," namely, artillery and tanks. Consequences of that assumption included the immediate stockpiling of military equipment. That, in turn, required rapid increases in military spending over the next two or three years (see table 10).[9] If Voroshilov's proposals were accepted, military spending would shoot up for 1928–1929 and grow more slowly thereafter, amounting to 5,700 million rubles over five years. The commission's report repeated its earlier conclusion that "no sharp disparity is found" between Gosplan and military budget projections. Expanding bottlenecks and introducing new production (battalion artillery, mortars, automatic rifles, antiaircraft systems) would, in the commission's estimate, cost at least 2,960 million rubles.[10]

The RZ STO's final ruling on the Red Army's development plan took place on 30 July 1928. In its decree, the RZ STO declined to go as far as Voroshilov recommended. In two separate decisions on mobilization orders and the Red Army's five-year plan, it only partially endorsed the commission's conclusions. The RZ STO refused to boost the wartime Red Army to 3.266 million men, holding at 3 million men by the end of 1930–1931. It further stipulated industrial tar-

Table 10. Voroshilov Commission's Final Budget Projections

Fiscal Year	Overall State Budget (Gosplan Projection) (million rubles)	Year-on-Year Increase (percent)	NKVM Budget (million rubles)	Year-on-Year Increase (percent)	Weight of NKVM Budget (percent)
1927–1928	4,854.4	11.0	742.4	17	17.7
1928–1929	4,163.0	11.0	969.3	30.5	23.2
1929–1930	4,540.0	8.0	1,095.0	13	24.1
1930–1931	4,909.4	8.1	1,178.6	7.1	23.9
1931–1932	5,310.4	8.2	1,214.1	3.5	22.8
1932–1933	5,761.1	8.2	1,248.0	2.8	21.7
Total	24,674.2		5,700.0		23.1

gets for the Red Army's mobilization and war-year orders, but only for three years in the future, not the five years that Voroshilov's commission had proposed (see table 11). The Red Army had the job of assembling a formal order for this list, and Gosplan's responsibility was to ensure the development of industry to reach those goals.[11] Three weeks later, another RZ STO decree expanded on the earlier decision by adding a mobilization target of 4,360 aircraft for a year of war but still refused to commit to a five-year program. In this second decree, Valerian Kuibyshev managed to carve out a larger role for Vesenkha in defense planning at the expense of Gosplan. Vesenkha would join the Red Army in determining the deadlines for creating mobilization capacity and would have an equal voice with Gosplan in drawing up a three-year development plan for military industry.[12]

The RZ STO accompanied these broader directives with more specific ones to implement the proposals of Voroshilov's commission. Five new aviation and two truck plants were approved. The Soviet tank industry, still in its infancy, was allowed more flexibility in determining its needs, including the option of converting the Stalingrad tractor factory to tank production. As Voroshilov's commission recommended, machine gun manufacture, an older and better-established type of production, would have to settle for the expansion of existing factories, not the creation of new ones. The RZ STO also stressed the need for further research and

Table 11. Wartime Military Requirements from Industry

5,000 million cartridges
45 million artillery shells
62,000 machine guns
2,100 76mm artillery pieces of all types
760 122mm howitzers
190 152mm howitzers
200 107mm guns
138 heavy artillery (non-naval)
1,055 tanks

development, including new workshops for rapidly advancing tank and aircraft design. Accepting that the Soviet Union's output of nonferrous metals could not cover military needs, the RZ STO insisted on better research into surrogate materials. The same measures were needed for powder; either nitric acid production would increase or surrogates would take its place.[13]

THE 1928 BUDGET CRISIS

If Voroshilov and the other members of the Red Army's high command felt that their budget and development plans were secure in the wake of the RZ STO's qualified endorsement, an autumn political crisis soon gave them a rude awakening. The RZ STO would reject the Red Army's budget, a reversal that produced fury in the Red Army's leadership just as the political struggle between Stalin and the Bolshevik Right led by Bukharin, Rykov, and Tomskii reached its height. By the summer of 1928, the contradictions between the twin goals of industrialization and civil peace with the peasantry had become even clearer. The more industry expanded, consuming its own output, the fewer goods would be available for peasants, who would have correspondingly less incentive to market (rather than consume themselves) the grain they grew. The Bolshevik leadership constantly feared an interruption in the flow of grain, and inflation could only exacerbate the situation. In E. H. Carr's words, "the grain collection crisis, while it had not led the party leaders to reduce the rate of industrialization, prompted a search in the spring and summer of 1928 for ways of maintaining the existing level of capital investment in industry without provoking further clashes with the peasantry." One obvious option for maintaining investment was cutting the military budget.[14]

In April and May 1928, the Red Army Staff and its Financial-Planning Directorate had drawn up a preliminary budget for 1928–1929 incorporating a 24 percent increase over the previous year to 920 million rubles.[15] A newly formed Financial-Planning Commission under Iosif Unshlikht met at least four times over that summer to determine the military's precise demands and took a moderate, nonconfrontational approach to industrial concerns about its ability to produce. The first meeting tentatively agreed to cut the Red Army's order for MS-1 tanks from 175 to 108 and scaled back light machine guns to what Vesenkha's representatives claimed they could manage. The second and third meetings did the same for medium machine guns, experimental automatic rifles, and aircraft, not pressing industry for more than it was willing to give.[16] Despite this solicitude for industrial concerns, the outcome was a budget slightly higher than the 920 million rubles projected in the spring. Although the Red Army's ideal budget would have come to 1,094 million rubles, a 47 percent increase in nominal terms over the previous year, the Red Army's Financial-Planning Commission was more restrained in the figures it gave the Revvoensovet for its request to the RZ STO. The Revvoensovet's draft proposal set its optimal budget request at 965 million but included an alternative minimum proposal of 865 million rubles. The final version the Rev-voensovet approved for submission to the RZ STO left the Red Army a safety margin by boosting its minimum figure by 35 million rubles, making its optimal and minimal proposals 965.7 million and 900 million rubles, respectively.[17]

Financial and political crisis made the military's proposals worthless. The RZ STO disregarded the Revvoensovet's request for 965 million rubles and in August 1928 set the control figures for the NKVM's budget at 890 million. This was painful enough, but to make matters worse, financial constraints triggered in part by twin crises in the supply of bread and iron pushed for still more belt-tightening. At the same time, Bukharin raised the political stakes in the Right's struggle against Stalinism by bringing his criticism of rapid (and, to his mind, unsustainable) industrialization into the open. On 22 September 1928, he published "Notes of an Economist" in *Pravda* and warned that "it is not possible to build 'present-day' factories with 'future bricks.'"[18] On 22 October, with the political tension more palpable, the RZ STO reopened discussion of the defense budget to reveal a sharp division between the hawks in the Red Army and Gosplan's Defense Sector on one side and the doves in Gosplan itself and the Commissariat of Finance on the other side. In debating the Red Army's budget, Gosplan's Defense Sector proposed only a minor reduction to 880 million rubles, Finance suggested 862 million, and Gosplan 839 million (see table 12). The RZ STO declared that the Defense Sector's figures, the starting point for budgetary calculations, were "maximal" and "subject to further reduction." Further cuts were expected.[19]

Voroshilov had felt confident enough in his budget's prospects to leave Moscow for a vacation in Sochi. Someone then had to break the news of how the Red Army's budget had suffered at the hands of the RZ STO. The first notice came from Ernest Appoga, the RZ STO's secretary. Telling Voroshilov that he was "sorry to disturb your vacation with this unpleasantness," Appoga sketched the budget process and the competing proposals. Trying to find something to say in

Table 12. Competing NKVM, Gosplan, and Finance Budget Proposals for 1928–1929 (million rubles)

	1927–1928 Outlays	NKVM	Defense Sector of Gosplan	Finance	Gosplan
NKVM	742.4	890	880	862	839
OGPU	49.386	57	55	55.4	
Medical Directorate	21.338	26	26	23.7	
Convoy troops	7.71	9	9	9.1	
Civil industry	91.502	120.2	120.2	100	
Military industry	51	110	100	80	
Transport	90	104	104	80	
Trade	.478	14.8	13	7.5	
Post and telegraph	3.75	3.4	3.4	3.48	
Total	1,057.564	1,334.4	1,310.6	1,221.58	

defense of Aleksei Rykov, Appoga noted that "Aleksei Ivanovich does consider it necessary even to add ten million to military industry." Litunovskii, one of Voroshilov's subordinates, also kept him well informed on Unshlikht's efforts to defend the military budget against cuts by the RZ STO.[20] Even with the news Voroshilov got from the military, it was left to Ordzhonikidze, a personal friend, to justify why the defense budget had been cut. "Everything's coming to a close with the budget figures," Ordzhonikidze explained:

> The budget's been increased . . . but there are so many demands from all sides that there's no way to balance things. We're cutting everything—it falls equally on you too, but please don't curse me. . . . You won't like this but don't think they're cutting you with a sharp knife here. We're talking about trifles—10–15–20 million.[21]

Sitting in Sochi, Voroshilov could only stew in isolation. Writing to Ordzhonikidze on 9 November, he complained, "my vacation's gone straight to hell. That I already know for sure. My heart aches, I've stopped sleeping." Voroshilov blamed the fiasco largely on one man: Aleksei Rykov, chair of the RZ STO and one of the leaders of the Right in its opposition to Stalin. Voroshilov poured out his anger and frustration:

> You can cut the budget as you like. You can even cut the military budget in half, but you should look the truth straight in the eye—we're half unarmed. The entire world is armed to the teeth *against us.* We've communicated this to the worker and peasant masses loudly enough (maybe more than enough), and they hope that we, in this twelfth year of Soviet power, will do something about it, and what do we do? We hope for good luck *(avos'),* Russian luck—for defense, that's our ace in the hole. I don't doubt for a second that someday Rykov will announce that "Kliment Efremovich [Voroshilov] is the one responsible for defense," and wash his hands of the matter, and forget his own helpful work preparing the Red Army.
>
>   Cut the budget, you know better, you're the boss. But I'll ask the Politburo to relieve me from responsibility for the army's preparedness.[22]

Voroshilov apologized to Ordzhonikidze for his rant and closed his letter, "I shake your hand, your K."

Despite Voroshilov's fury, an RZ STO commission found room for still more cuts, slicing an additional 50 million rubles from the NKVM's budget, reducing it to 840 million rubles, which was just over Gosplan's proposal, the smallest of all. Voroshilov had already been reduced to panic and near hysteria; the rest of the Red Army's high command followed. At a Central Committee plenum at the end of November 1928, Unshlikht pleaded for a restoration of desperately needed funds by painting an apocalyptic picture of the world outside and the crippled Red Army that would have to face it. England agitated for a Polish-Ukrainian union, press campaigns in France and Finland stirred up hate, and conservative governments in Sweden and Latvia strove for new alliances against the USSR. The Red Army was weaker than its neighbors in numbers of troops, divisions, tanks, machine guns, and bombers, and in the event of war, the situation would deteriorate further as the factories of France, England, and Czechoslovakia sent their production against the USSR. In short:

> The international situation dictates the necessity not to lengthen but to shorten the wait until the Red Army and the country are militarily prepared. Regardless of the tense economic and financial situation, we must find the means which will guarantee the complete and total fulfillment of our military program.

Budget cuts would mean, Unshlikht claimed, scaling down the accumulation of vital stockpiles, ending improvements in the Red Army's living conditions, losing an entire construction season, and slashing military production by 20 percent. Not only would the Red Army suffer, but defense preparations in industry, transportation, and trade would lapse as well. The naval program would be indefinitely delayed, and the overall result would be "an undoubted reduction in the combat readiness of the Red Army."[23]

The November Central Committee plenum retreated somewhat from fiscal conservatism by agreeing to invest 1,650 million rubles in industry for 1928–1929, an increase of 320 million over the previous year. This did not help the Red Army. Although this decision "marked the substantial defeat of the Right Wing," it was too late for Unshlikht's appeal or Voroshilov's rage to win more funds for the Red Army budget. The RZ STO soon confirmed the specific items of the military's funding for 1928–1929. Unshlikht was, however, given the cold comfort of an additional 10 million rubles to spend, and the final 1928–1929 budget came in at 850.7 million rubles, with procurement and upkeep of ordnance, chemicals, automobiles, and aircraft taking up 263.6 million rubles, or 31 percent of the budget.[24]

Contrary to Unshlikht's and Voroshilov's fears, the Soviet Union was not attacked by an imperialist coalition, and the Red Army's readiness was not tested. The long-term political effects of the budget crisis were nevertheless cataclysmic. Voroshilov's tirade did not blame the party leadership collectively for the cuts forced on the military but singled out Aleksei Rykov as the one person most responsible for undercutting the Red Army and Soviet defenses. In 1928, the fight between Stalin's faction and the loosely organized Right had heated up over whether to take a hard or soft line against the peasantry and the greater question of the pace of revolutionary transformation. In July 1928, Bukharin had told Lev Kamenev that Voroshilov and Ordzhonikidze were potential supporters of the Right, although Voroshilov had not voted with the Right and Ordzhonikidze denounced Stalin only in private. Rykov's actions in cutting the Red Army's budget ensured, however, that defense-minded elites like Voroshilov and Ordzhonikidze saw the Right as dangerous to their institutional position and the Soviet Union's defenses. When "the backstage fight came to a climax" with the January–February plenum of the party's leadership, Bukharin and the rightists had been fatally weakened. Tainted by the revelation in Trotsky's *Biulleten' oppozitsii* that they had conspired with Zinov'ev and Kamenev against Stalin and tarred with defeatism due to Rykov's overseeing cuts in the military budget, Bukharin, Rykov, and their associates were crushingly defeated, never to pose a threat to Stalin again. Voroshilov and Ordzhonikidze did not waver from their commitment to Stalin.[25]

While power struggles at the top played themselves out in the Politburo and the Central Committee, the inexorable bureaucratic march of economic war plans and investment plans for military industry continued unabated as the political environment changed. Anticipating Stalin's victory, military planning increased step-by-step its commitment to substantive rearmament and to the militarization of the Soviet economy. Despite two failures in 1927 to assemble a coherent long-range plan for military industry, Vesenkha's planners tried once again in the summer of 1928 to impose some kind of order on the hand-to-mouth patterns of investment in military industry by hammering out a five-year plan for military industry.

The first obstacle to an investment plan was Vesenkha's fractious bureaucracy. Aleksandr Postnikov from Vesenkha's Mobilization-Planning Directorate (MPU) sought to expand his role in planning industrial mobilization by taking over long-range investment as well. On 26 July 1928, he gave the Main Military-Industrial Directorate (GVPU), a slightly renamed Military-Industrial Directorate (VPU), one month to present rough figures on production capacity, investment, and workforce for a five-year plan. Daniil Budnevich, the GVPU's temporary director, replied that it made little sense to start such a time-consuming task until the RZ STO had confirmed the Red Army's orders and the assignment had been passed through proper channels, namely, the Standing Mobilization Conference.[26] This reference to proper channels incensed Postnikov, for he saw himself as having the authority to give orders in defense matters to any of Vesenkha's main directorates, but especially the directorate grouping military factories. As he fired back, the GVPU was "obviously insufficiently clear on its role in Vesenkha's organizational structure and the USSR's defense system." The GVPU, in Postnikov's interpretation, was only one production directorate among the many under his jurisdiction for matters of defense. Postnikov's own MPU was the sole body in Vesenkha responsible for mobilization and so had extraordinary powers in defense planning. In a dark allusion to the mass arrests of wreckers within the GVPU, Postnikov questioned why the GVPU, among all the directorates and union republics, found it so difficult to complete its work on time.[27]

In August 1928, Kuibyshev and Postnikov presented their latest five-year plan for military industry, this time linking it explicitly to the First Five-Year Plan for the entire economy now under development. They declared that "one of the central tasks of the Five-Year Plan" was the "maximum combination of the interests of the country's industrialization with strengthening the Union's defense capability and increasing industry's mobilization readiness." Kuibyshev, Postnikov, and the personnel of Vesenkha had managed to create a five-year plan for capital investment in defense while working under the assumption that construction of new defense plants should be kept to a minimum and civil industry employed to the maximum possible extent. This plan was far more ambitious than Kuibyshev's previous 345 million–ruble plan for military industry, and even doubled Postnikov's 894 million–ruble plan (see chapter 2). Postnikov's initial drafts had projected the investment of 1,843.2 million rubles over five years, with 833.3 million going to specifically military production and an additional 1,099.9 million to more generalized production necessary for defense needs. Further review had found, Postnikov reported, that much of the general investment could be subsumed in the overall First Five-Year Plan and need not be included in the defense investment plan. While leaving specifically military investment intact at 833.3 million rubles, general investment could be reduced to 312.7 million rubles, for an overall program of 1,146 million rubles. Slightly over half that, 650 million rubles, would go directly to military trusts and factories, and the rest would be split among metallurgical and metalworking plants (171 million), chemical plants (260 million), and others. When 360 million rubles of mobilization stockpiles and 40 million rubles of civil defense, research, and storage expenses were included, the grand total came to 1,546.7 million rubles.[28]

First and foremost, this five-year plan for military industry served Postnikov and Kuibyshev as a means of obtaining capital for Vesenkha by appealing to defense needs. It further provided them with more arguments for rapid industrial expansion in the ongoing race with Gosplan to see who could produce the most ambitious plans. Postnikov and Kuibyshev found that as defense needs became clearer, they would "unconditionally introduce substantive changes in both the direction of development and pace of growth for individual branches of industry." In particular, defense would accelerate the development of heavy industry. By the end of the First Five-Year Plan, the production of heavy (group A) industry was expected to reach 9,029.7 million rubles, but in the event of war, the Red Army would require 7,000 million rubles of production from heavy industry, putting a "colossal strain" on the Soviet economy. The shock this would produce was a direct result of an "insufficient development rate of group A industry, first and foremost the metal and chemical industries." The logical conclusion was to speed the growth of heavy industry.[29] For Kuibyshev and Postnikov, defense needs mandated the expansion of branches of industry far removed from tanks and artillery. Metallurgy's poor state meant that the most serious wartime shortage would be high-quality or special steel, with iron alloys with tungsten or manganese also in short supply. Nonferrous metallurgy was little better. The only options were substituting substandard alternatives, stockpiling, or expanding capacity even more quickly. Chemistry likewise needed more investment; the lack of technical knowledge made it "one of the worst defense bottlenecks," and "its development will determine to a significant degree the growth of the USSR's defense potential." Postnikov had become a crusader for defense within Vesenkha.[30]

The draft plan that Kuibyshev and Postnikov assembled still lacked details for its most important sector, military industry, because Tolokontsev's GVPU had not completed its own planning. In the fall of 1928, Tolokontsev begged Postnikov for additional time on his five-year plan while blaming Postnikov and the MPU for giving him a vague assignment. On 14 December, Tolokontsev again implored Voroshilov and Shaposhnikov to provide him with a five-year order plan—without it, he claimed, he had no way of completing the five-year plan for military industry. His efforts got him little credit with Postnikov, still stinging from the earlier difficulties. On 20 December and once more on 16 February 1929, Postnikov lambasted Tolokontsev for his ongoing failure to produce a five-year plan despite numerous warnings. Tolokontsev got his reprimand for dereliction of duty in a decision of the Standing Mobilization Conference, which noted "the impermissible attitude of several directorates towards defense as expressed . . . in the nonproduction of specific defense portions of the five-year plan despite the fact that all directives relating to this were made in a timely and complete fashion." Postnikov continued to badger Tolokontsev through March.[31]

Tolokontsev, directing munitions production, could scarcely be accused of neglecting the importance of defense. But that was not true of the directors of the Chemical, Machine-Building, Ferrous Metallurgy, and Nonferrous Metallurgy Directorates, whose "impermissible attitude," according to the Postnikov-led Standing Mobilization Conference, consisted of "insufficiently comprehensive account of defense needs in the five-year plan." The whole purpose of the conference's March 1929 reprimand was to speed the completion of the subplans, without which the overall military industry five-year plan would be entirely fictional.[32] Despairing of receiving defense plans from Vesenkha's directorates, Postnikov instead established rough guidelines for defense spending: 1,190 million rubles over five years. Investment would account for 800 million of that (615 million in military industry, the rest for defense production in civil industry); building up stockpiles in preparation for mobilization, another 350 million; and civil defense and other expenditures, 40 million. Imported machinery and raw materials made up 275 million of the 1,190 million–ruble plan. Although not up to the high standards set by Kuibyshev and Postnikov's more than 1,500 million–ruble plan, this still moved toward a major expansion of the Soviet defense economy.[33]

NEW MOBILIZATION PLANS

The same economic changes that mandated new investment plans for military industry required new contingency plans for industrial mobilization in the event of war. Over mid- to late 1928, Soviet industry reworked its mobilization plans in light of both newly created production capacity and rapid advances in military technology. The old plan A had been largely obsolete when drawn up; its replacement, mobilization plan S, would correct those faults. In July 1928, Postnikov warned directorates and trusts throughout Vesenkha that replacement of 1927's mobilization plan would soon begin, and by October, development was well under way. The RZ STO was ready by December to give final approval to a mobilization plan projecting wartime output of 970,000 rifles, 2,530 million cartridges, and 23.5 million shells, compared with earlier plan A targets of roughly 1,450 million cartridges and 14 million shells.[34]

Vesenkha's redesign of its mobilization planning put the Red Army in an awkward position. Although Soviet officers certainly approved of more effective mobilization planning, they were outraged by the RZ STO's decision to implement the capital investment underpinning plan S from January 1929 through April 1930, suggesting that the wartime supply included in the plan could not actually be counted on until that new capacity came on-line in 1930. Vesenkha's preoccupation with future goals had left such mundane work as enterprise-level mobilization plans and careful calculation of existing capacity lagging far behind. Other measures vital to the military, such as duplicating defense production unique to vulnerable Leningrad, had been ignored. To compensate for the absence of a workable mobilization plan from industry, the Staff wanted a detailed statement of monthly wartime production so the Red Army could work out a mobilization plan on its own.[35]

In February 1929, Voroshilov expressed the military's disgust with plan S in a memorandum for the RZ STO enumerating the faults in industrial planning. Not only would the Red Army have to wait until 1 April 1930 before the production capacity assumed in plan S became operational, but for some key goods such as powder and ammonia, the target date was six months later, 1 October 1930. To make matters worse, since plan S could not be counted on until then, in the meantime, the Red Army would have to go to war with the antiquated, slipshod mobilization plan A—in effect, without any plan at all. Voroshilov, in no position to issue orders to Kuibyshev, Postnikov, or anyone else in the defense industry, instead asked the RZ STO to exert pressure on Vesenkha and advance all deadlines for plan S to 1 April 1930.[36]

Although the RZ STO was reluctant to change Vesenkha's deadlines for completing the investment and construction for mobilization plan S, exhortation and admonition were cheap, and the RZ STO laid them on with a trowel. On three separate occasions in the spring of 1929, the RZ STO passed resolutions declaring plan S deadlines both imperative and immutable. The repetition suggests that the RZ STO feared they were neither. On 6 March, Vesenkha received a whole series of intermediate targets to ensure that the final deadline remained sacrosanct, and on 13 May, the RZ STO formed a commission to ensure that wrecking would not delay the completion of plan S. On 31 May, the RZ STO warned again that the plan S deadlines were "not subject to change," but it at least agreed that military industry would have priority over civil industry in the allocation of skilled workers and technicians.[37]

The natural counterpart to a mobilization plan for military industry was a broader plan for the entire Soviet economy at war. The first attempt in late 1927 and early 1928 to create a comprehensive economic plan for the "first period of war" had produced some beneficial results, so at the end of 1928, the RZ STO ordered another iteration of the process to take into account a year's worth of economic development. Rudzutak's September 1928 directives for an economic war plan followed the same pattern as the previous year's, basing targets on the mobilization assignment for 1928–1929 and allowing a six-month transition period before the "established" or "settled-in" (ustanovivshiisia) war-year. The goal was for a Gosplan-assembled plan to be ready by 1 April 1929 in the event of war in the summer. Just as in the previous year, the MPU was called on to prepare industry's control figures, not for a detailed production schedule but to indicate roughly the "volume and direction" of production for whole branches of industry, which would then take those figures and use them in their own planning.[38] In December 1928, the RZ STO gave further directions for assembling this new wartime economic plan, one that, like its predecessor, would run from the midpoint of the 1928–1929 fiscal year through the entirety of the next, 1929–1930.[39] After review by Rudzutak, the RZ STO specified that the target would be mobilization assignment S, to be achieved under the assumption of lengthy war and full blockade. This meant, in effect, serious capital investment in metallurgy to maintain adequate supply to munitions production.[40]

If Rudzutak had hoped that the eight-month advance notice he had given Gosplan would suffice to derive the final control figures on time, he was deeply mistaken. At the end of March 1929, Vesenkha and the People's Commissariats of Trade, Transport, Labor, and Finance were given a retroactive extension of two months on the deadlines that had expired at the beginning of March. Their rough figures were now to be in by the first of May, with a fully detailed plan by June. Rabkrin was called in to investigate the slow pace of work to uncover who was responsible.[41] Whatever it found, by this point, the twin disruptions of the campaign against wrecking and the quickening pace of industrialization made any coherent plan impossible—the priority, instead, was staying abreast of the rapid sequence of events.

REARMAMENT ON A SHOESTRING

Mobilization plans and economic war plans required great exertion from the planners and bureaucrats in the Red Army, Vesenkha, and Gosplan, but they were at least cheap. Planning could go on at full speed in the absence of mass infusions of capital. The construction and investment to bring those plans to fruition, in contrast, would require massive inflows of capital, something in terribly short supply in the USSR in the late 1920s. The Soviet military-economic hierarchy was put in the exquisitely difficult position of squaring the circle: modernizing and expanding the Red Army and military industry under a constant and terrible shortage of funds. To bridge this gap between ends and means, the Red Army and industry alike tried desperately to find ways of expanding on the cheap. While trying to cover the yawning gap between what the Red Army needed to fight a war and the limited amount Soviet industry could provide, Rabkrin declared that "the Soviet Union's economy will not allow us in the near future to solve this problem via colossal investment in building new military factories." Instead, "the only real way out of this situation" lay in intense and efficient exploitation of resources already at hand: "use at maximal intensity of existing factories."[42] Of course, such rhetoric about the need to find savings and economies was constant from the 1920s to the end of the Soviet Union, but the calls never sounded as clearly and the constraints of limited resources never bit as deeply as they did during the late 1920s.

One key to economizing on investment was to ferret out every last bit of production capacity in existing plants. Factory managers naturally found it in their interest to underreport both their ability to produce and their stocks of raw materials. In addition to reducing the tasks assigned to them, this provided a ready reserve in the event of hard times and harder production targets. Conversely, the Red Army saw that hidden capacity as vital to preparing for war. Given the concurrent campaign against wreckers and saboteurs, the Red Army's logic was clear: those managers who determined how much military equipment industry could produce were now revealed as agents of counterrevolution and foreign intelligence. Lakhinskii, director of the Cartridge-Fuse Trust's mobilization section, told Voroshilov and Ordzhonikidze that Tolokontsev himself, director of the VPU, had assigned the Cartridge-Fuse Trust a mobilization target of 2,325 million cartridges and over 13 million fuses. Upon the trust's reply that it could do more and its request for an increased assignment of 3,625 million cartridges and nearly 21 million fuses, Tolokontsev adamantly refused to approve such a change.[43]

The campaign to uncover hidden capacity was led by Rabkrin's Military-Naval Inspectorate under Ivan Pavlunovskii, a veteran of the Cheka. It was a perfect match of predator and prey: Rabkrin's mandate was to expose malfeasance and incompetence, and given the environment that encouraged managerial subterfuge, Pavlunovskii could hardly fail. His Military-Naval Inspectorate accordingly found systemic underestimation of production capacity, meaning that industry could produce more, with less investment, than the military and Vesenkha had calculated. The most widespread abuse was that managers ignored the greater sacrifices they could demand from men and machines in the event of war. A Rabkrin report found that "contemporary factory work norms in peacetime are transferred in wartime to work in three shifts over 320 days of the year without account of the possibility of intensified strain on equipment, extreme use of space, and development of mea-

sures directed to the maximum output of arms and combat supply." The amount
of floor space devoted to a particular piece of machinery could, for example, go
from 15 to 20 square meters to 4.5 square meters, just as in World War I. Although
machines were used in peacetime at a pace that would wear them out in twenty-
five years, such niceties could be disposed of in wartime. As a result, the Tula
armaments factory's estimated yearly capacity of 400,000 rifles could reach
525,000 to 600,000; the Izhevsk armaments factory was the same. The quality
and durability of military production could also be sacrificed to the exigencies of
war. As Aleksandr Svechin saw the issue, "in wartime there is no sense in producing expensive powder with a shelf life of 15 years if it will be expended in
several months."[44]

The Red Army's Staff was overjoyed with Pavlunovskii's conclusion that
military industry had systematically reduced its projections of what it could supply
the Red Army. A Staff report pointed out that, if anything, Pavlunovskii could
have gone further in his conclusions. First of all, concealing capacity was not
unique to directors of military factories—*all* industry could apply the same
intensive methods in wartime and so reveal hidden reserves. Stalingrad's Red
October metallurgical plant, for example, not technically under the purview of
military industry, had a wartime assignment of 350,000 76mm shells but a production capacity of over 1 million. The Staff therefore appealed to the RZ STO
and the Politburo for a full recalculation throughout Vesenkha, with auditing to
ensure compliance.[45]

Second, the Staff went beyond Rabkrin to stress cooperation in production.
That is, by contracting out the assembly of parts and subsystems to other enterprises, factories with wartime assignments could distribute their production burden
and thereby increase capacity. In retrospect, this seems quite obvious, but it ran
counter to the Russian tradition of giant, self-contained factories with shops and
branches added over hundreds of years (in some cases). Factory directors avoided
subcontracting chiefly because it would put their careers and even their lives into
the hands of other, perhaps unreliable managers far away. They preferred to keep
as much of the production process under their own control as possible. This was
a constant irritation to the Staff, which noted that the Tula firearms factory could
increase its rifle capacity from 600,000 to 1 million and more than double its
machine gun capacity through cooperative production with the State Sewing-
Machine Trust; compared with building a new factory, this would save nearly 60
million rubles.[46]

MODERNIZING WEAPONRY

Despite the pervasive influence of tight money on the development of the Red
Army during the late 1920s, the military and party elite, including Stalin, Voroshilov,
and their circle, agreed on the importance of modernizing the Soviet armed forces

within the bounds of low budgets. Although boosting military aviation and mechanizing the Red Army through the addition of tanks and motorized transport were clearly important, modernization had to begin more prosaically with artillery and firearms. On the last day of December 1928, after Voroshilov remarked to Stalin that he had new information to discuss about the possibilities offered by German technical assistance, Stalin replied that he was quite willing to discuss any German proposals, but that was not the point. "The point now," Stalin told Voroshilov, "is that our artillery is insufficient, is scandalously insufficient."[47]

The Red Army's problem with its artillery was quite similar to that confronting all Western armies after World War I and was closely linked to the pace of technological change. Rifles and pistols of older design and, to a lesser degree, machine guns had reached a design plateau, with few major improvements in available technology after the war. The tendency through World War II was to replace rifles with short-range weapons producing a greater volume of fire, but the older rifles were still quite serviceable. Indeed, the Red Army's chief rifle through World War II, the 7.62mm Mosin-Nagant, was designed in 1891 (but modernized in 1930). Tanks were, by contrast, such a rapidly developing technology that World War I designs were good for nothing but the museum or the scrap heap. Artillery fell in the middle. Artillery design progressed, but not so quickly that old pieces were useless. The solution was modernization, that is, the retooling and reworking of existing artillery pieces by a series of comparatively minor changes that, together with improved shells, would dramatically increase the effectiveness of the system by improved range, accuracy, and rate of fire.[48]

On 23 January 1929, the Revvoensovet approved a Staff plan for modernizing artillery and armor and for speeding the design and production of new models. It simultaneously condemned both the Red Army's own Artillery Directorate and military industry for inaction. The armor plan would not survive continuing technological innovation and political maneuvering, but the artillery modernization program would be one of the interwar NKVM's greatest successes, improving military effectiveness at low cost. The plan envisaged changes in the Red Army's entire artillery park. The old workhorse 76mm divisional field gun, a 1902 design, had a new design largely complete by January 1929. The 1915 76mm antiaircraft gun had its barrel lengthened to fifty to fifty-five times its caliber, increasing its ceiling to 6,000 to 6,500 meters. The heavier pieces of artillery, including the 122mm (1910 design), 152mm (1909), and 203mm howitzers and the 152mm Schneider siege gun, would all have new shells, and the 203mm howitzer would also have a new carriage. The 107mm field gun (1910) had its range increased to 13.9 kilometers by a new shell and, with a lengthened barrel, could expect to reach 16 kilometers.[49]

Despite the Red Army's emphasis on heavy and howitzer artillery, a second, later strand of the Revvoensovet's program was small artillery pieces for lower-level infantry units to provide antitank fire and immediate fire support against fortified positions, in contrast to heavier pieces intended for attachment to regimental-size and larger units.[50] The shape of this new type of "battalion artillery" was largely unclear in early 1929: a howitzer employing plunging fire and suitable for suppressing machine gun emplacements would be completely unsuitable for antitank fire, and vice versa. The Revvoensovet on 13 February 1929 decided to cover both options by ordering a hundred 45mm guns and twenty 60mm howitzers, although such a small production run would, as the Revvoensovet subsequently discovered, be excessively expensive and interfere with 76mm regimental gun production.[51]

Even once modernization began, the actual upgrades of older models took several years to achieve, as repair and retooling had to be shoehorned in around the Red Army's steadily growing orders for artillery. In January 1930, the Red Army's armaments director, Ieronim Uborevich, complained to the Revvoensovet that although the Red Army's rifle modernization was complete, artillery pieces were moving quite slowly due to the "intensively slow tempo of work in industry." In June, seeing no progress despite repeated complaints, the Revvoensovet condemned Vesenkha's work on artillery modernization as "criminal" and asked for RZ STO intervention, as well as a Rabkrin investigation to determine who was responsible for the glacial pace of innovation in artillery design.[52]

Modernization dragged on through the First Five-Year Plan; in July 1931, the Revvoensovet still complained about its slow pace.[53] Even by 1933, although much of the Red Army's artillery park had been converted to more modern types, it was still not complete. Efimov, deputy director of armaments, reported to the Revvoensovet that nearly 300,000 of the Red Army's 2.4 million rifles had been modernized, as had the entire stock of machine guns. Artillery had taken longer: thirty divisions had received battalion-level 37mm antitank guns, and forty-five divisions had battalion-level 76mm pieces. Fifty-four divisions had new 1927-model 76mm regimental artillery to supplement the 1902 field pieces that had been the backbone of Soviet artillery. The process of "howitzerization," initiated in 1928, had doubled the overall number of howitzers in the Red Army. Thirty-three divisions had modernized guns, and seventy-eight had modernized howitzers. Corps artillery had increased greatly in strength, going from 400 to 700 107mm guns and 400 to 900 152mm guns. Efimov expected that full modernization of corps artillery would be complete sometime during 1933. Despite long delays and the slow pace of renewing the Soviet artillery park, the modernization program had significantly increased the Red Army's firepower at a relatively limited cost.[54]

Another reform almost as far reaching as artillery modernization, and also dating to the late 1920s, aimed at increasing the firepower of Soviet infantry. In contrast to the World War I Russian army with rapid-fire weapons largely limited to heavier, mounted medium machine guns, the Soviet army in the late 1920s moved toward increasing the prevalence and mobility of rapid-fire weapons in its ranks by introducing tens of thousands of light machine guns and automatic rifles. This emphasis on putting automatic fire at the disposal of the individual soldier began the trend that would lead to the Red Army's World War II machine pistols, the PPD and PPSh, but in the 1920s and 1930s, it would express itself through the Degtiarev light machine gun.

The Red Army's initial experiments with light machine guns in 1923 employed reworked and lightened Maxim medium machine guns in two variants designed by I. N. Kolesnikov and F. V. Tokarev. The matter grew increasingly urgent as the Soviet air force's expansion demanded commensurate expansion in machine guns; the Red Army was, however, dependent on foreign sources, a clearly intolerable position.[55] Those experiments of the mid-1920s were brought to an abrupt halt by the design and approval of Vasilii Degtiarev's 7.62mm light machine gun, a design of such simplicity and effectiveness that it remained the basic automatic weapon of the infantry unit through 1944.[56]

The clear worth of Degtiarev's design, minor problems notwithstanding, did not preempt further design work on closely allied types of production. The distinction between a light machine gun and an automatic rifle, both tactically and technically, is rather subtle, and industrial managers saw little point in wasting their scarce resources simply to increase the variety of weapons available to the Soviet military. Postnikov, in particular, appealed to Voroshilov in 1928 to end development of an automatic rifle in order to turn designers' talents to other work. The Construction Bureau of the Kovrov machine gun factory continued to build an automatic rifle when the role of such a weapon and its advantages over the Degtiarev were unclear. Voroshilov agreed with Postnikov's argument but did not want to stifle the creativity of weapons designers in any way.[57]

Despite the suitability of the Degtiarev as the basic light machine gun for the Soviet army and its easy adaptability to tank and aircraft turrets (but not to firing through propellers), nagging technical problems persisted. The Revvoensovet requested that the Firearm–Machine Gun Trust further simplify the design and make the magazines easier to change, but its chief complaint was that the machine gun's parts were not interchangeable. That is, a skilled armorer had to finish each new Degtiarev individually to ensure that it functioned properly. Expensive in peacetime, this was disastrous in war. Heavy wear and tear on all equipment would require constant replacement of worn parts with spares and easy cannibalization of weapons. Without interchangeable parts, the whole repair process became much more complicated and required more skills from the military's supply arm.[58]

During the course of 1929, as the problem was not corrected, the Red Army grew increasingly restless over military industry's continuing failure to standardize the Degtiarev. In July, noting the Firearm–Machine Gun Trust's sloth, the Revvoensovet resolved to ask the RZ STO for legal redress "for the non-fulfillment of a responsibility they [the trust] took upon themselves in a matter having great significance for the Red Army's combat effectiveness." For all their blustering, Voroshilov, Unshlikht, and the Red Army's other high commanders could do little; they needed the machine guns, interchangeable parts or not. When Vesenkha representatives promised in September and Uryvaev, director of the GVPU, repeated in November that fully interchangeable parts would not be achieved until 1 April 1930, all the Revvoensovet could do was declare that it would accept no more than 4,250 machine guns with "individually adjusted spare parts."[59]

The real problem with the Degtiarev, besides the matter of interchangeable parts, was getting industry to agree to produce them in the amounts and on the schedule the Red Army wanted. On 8 August 1927, the Revvoensovet had authorized supply director Pavel Dybenko to place an order for 2,500 to 3,000 of the new machine guns.[60] Over 1927–1928, the military accordingly requested 2,500 Degtiarevs, but industrial representatives, claiming an inability to reach that target, accepted an order for only 1,900 and still fell 100 short by the end of the 1927–1928 fiscal year, taking an extra three months to fill the order. For 1928–1929, the Red Army boosted its order to 12,900, but after negotiations, Vesenkha accepted less than half that order, 6,000 Degtiarevs.[61] As a result of continuing friction over the issue, the Revvoensovet in January 1929 ordered Unshlikht and Tolokontsev to negotiate an agreement ensuring full compliance with the Red Army's orders and a possible increase in production. The day after the Revvoensovet's directive, Unshlikht and others from the NKVM met with industrial representatives and achieved an increase in the Red Army's order of 1,000 with an additional 500 for the OGPU, making a grand total of 7,500.[62] In August 1929, as the end of the 1928–1929 fiscal year approached, the Red Army found once again that placing an order was no guarantee of actually receiving the goods on time. Even the 1927–1928 order was not fully covered, and of the 5,000 infantry machine guns ordered by the Red Army and the OGPU, only 2,450 had been delivered, still without interchangeable parts. With more specialized versions of the Degtiarev adapted for use on tanks or in aircraft turrets, fulfillment was even worse. Only 667 of the 2,000 aviation Degtiarevs had been delivered by August, and only 40 of the 500 tank Degtiarevs.[63] Final resolution of the problem had to wait until the demands on industry were matched by the capital to meet them. On 30 November 1929, the RZ STO obliged Vesenkha to deliver the NKVM's order for Degtiarev machine guns in full. Uryvaev, then director of the GVPU, had to complete the current year's order of 15,000 machine guns, and he was also ordered to expand production for the next year more than 2.5 times to 40,000. That expansion would clearly require matching expansion of the Kovrov machine gun factory, now called Instrument Factory 2. After ordering Uryvaev to determine what investment would be required, the RZ STO on 5 February issued 5.5 million rubles to the plant, including 3 million for housing, 1.5 million for electricity, and 1 million for purchasing the needed machinery and equipment.[64]

A further modernization of the Soviet armed forces was the introduction of tanks, but this advance would prove much more difficult to implement in the late 1920s than either adding more machine guns or modernizing Soviet artillery. The first Soviet tanks had been trophies of the civil war, British or French tanks seized from

White and interventionist forces, so the fledgling Soviet tank industry started with the repair of these trophies at the Red Sormovo plant. The natural next step was dismantling and reverse-engineering captured French Renault light tanks to copy them and build new ones: from 1920 to 1922, Red Sormovo produced fourteen "Russian Reno" light tanks. A true domestic tank industry, however limited, had to wait until the design and manufacture of the T-18 (known after minor design changes as the MS-1) at Leningrad's Bolshevik. The first T-18, sharing the high silhouette, small turret, and short length of its Renault ancestor, rolled out the gates of Bolshevik in November 1927.[65]

The Soviet tank program remained extremely modest in its early stages. In October 1927, even before the first T-18 was complete, the Revvoensovet and the VPU negotiated a two-year initial program of only 108 tanks: 23 in 1927–1928 and 85 in 1928–1929.[66] The military was not satisfied with such a restricted and restrictive plan, however, and by May 1928, it had established its demand for T-18/MS-1 infantry escort tanks as well as the projected T-12 medium tanks and Lilliput (T-17) machine gun–carrying tankettes.

Five-Year Peacetime Military Order for Tanks (May 1928)

	1928–1929	1929–1930	1930–1931	1931–1932	1932–1933	Total	Wartime Demand
T-18	175	300	350	350	400	1,575	650
T-12	—	5	30	75	110	220	110
Lilliput	—	140	350	500	650	1,640	740
Total	175	445	730	825	1,160	3,435	1,500

Industry could not promise to meet this order; the best guess as to what could actually be produced over the five-year period was substantially lower, at least in the early years of the plan.[67]

Industry's Actual Projected Tank Production

	1928–1929	1929–1930	1930–1931	1931–1932	1932–1933	Total
T-18	90	100	200	350	450	1,190
T-12	2	18	45	100	100	265
Lilliput	0	0	10	300	650	960
Total	92	118	255	750	1,200	2,415

These rather grandiose plans were matched by an astoundingly small collection of actual tanks. By the end of 1928, a Red Army inventory revealed that only three of the new T-18 tanks had even made it to military inspection. The rest of the tank force consisted of a motley collection of museum pieces. Even the Kazan tank school established by the vaunted collaboration with the German Reichswehr had only one tank, six automobiles, three trucks, and three tractors in December 1928.[68] The Manchurian crisis of 1931 would eventually make the Soviet Union the world's foremost tank power, but production delays and limited financing meant that the 1920s were a bleak time for Soviet tank troops.

Modernization made the Red Army better prepared to fight the USSR's next war, but what Voroshilov, Unshlikht, Shaposhnikov, Tukhachevskii, and their fellow officers truly required was industrialization to enable the Soviet economy to produce the accoutrements of modern war and the budget to buy them. Their convictions, increasingly shared by Stalin and the Politburo, grew over 1927 and 1928 to give added impetus to Vesenkha's and Gosplan's race to draw up increasingly ambitious industrialization plans. The First Five-Year Plan, informed by the military's growing demands for modern equipment and drawn up in an atmosphere permeated with fear of foreign saboteurs, would finally turn the corner to rearming the Soviet military.

5

1929 and the Creation
of the First Five-Year Plan

"Has he any relations outside of his ex-wife and children?"

"A sister . . . that hasn't been on speaking terms with him for—it must be four or five years now. . . . He gave an interview to one of the papers saying he didn't think the Russian Five-Year Plan was necessarily doomed to failure."

—Dashiell Hammett, *The Thin Man*

The year 1929 brought a great turn for Soviet defense. In quick succession, the creation and approval of the First Five-Year Plan produced a fundamental acceleration of Soviet rearmament, shaped by the perception that Soviet military industry was riddled with saboteurs and foreign agents. That new policy triggered reorganizations of the Red Army that altered the future of Soviet military policy. Everything began from the First Five-Year Plan, a subject that presents a bewildering maze of contradictions. There is little consensus among historians on the degree to which the plan achieved its goals, and still less on how the Soviet Union hit the targets it did manage. Soviet figures show that by 1932, industrial production was twice the 1928 level, and by 1940, it was 6.5 times the 1928 level.[1] Physical indicators, less subject to distortion and manipulation, are less impressive but still show substantial growth.[2]

Production of Key Industrial Goods

	1927–1928	1932 Actual	1932 Goal	1940
Steel (million tons)	4.0	5.9	10.4	18.3
Coal (million tons)	35.4	64.3	75.0	140.5
Electricity (billion kilowatt hours)	5.05	13.4	22.0	48.6

Although the First Five-Year Plan fell well short of its lofty goals, it laid the foundations for even more rapid industrial growth in the Second Five-Year Plan. Despite constant upheaval and low levels of available investment capital, both human and financial, the Soviet Union achieved high rates of industrial growth—but how?

One interpretation holds that Stalin's industrialization was achieved simply and brutally by "holding down private consumption levels lower than anybody could have believed possible"—a strategy for capital accumulation made possible by the Soviet police state. Something like this approach was implicit in Evgenii Preobrazhenskii's theory of "primitive socialist accumulation," squeezing capital from the peasantry that made up the bulk of the Soviet population.[3] The problem is that the Soviet urban population was too small to be a source of investment capital, and the double blows of dekulakization and collectivization so damaged the Soviet countryside that agriculture drained resources instead of providing them.[4] But if the peasantry did not pay for industrialization, how was it done?[5]

Another explanation points to collectivization as an engine for industrial growth through the extraction of human capital, not investment capital. Terror and famine in the Soviet countryside drove millions of peasants to the cities to become the USSR's new industrial workforce. By 1932–1933, 45 to 60 percent of industrial workers had come to factory work in 1926 or later, and from 1928 to 1937, the number of industrial workers in the Soviet Union grew from 3,124,000 to 7,921,000. This movement of labor from the country to the cities was matched by the mobilization of women into the industrial workforce in unprecedented numbers. Between 1928 and 1940, women's role in the Soviet workforce skyrocketed in both absolute and relative terms, growing from 2.795 million, or 24 percent of the industrial workforce, to 13.19 million, or 39 percent, by 1940.[6]

The defense industry is a poor case for explaining general economic growth; the defense sector received first priority in capital, skilled labor, and scarce raw materials and so was hardly typical. The case of military industry, however, is powerful in exploring the no less contentious issue of motive: *why* did the Soviet Union launch itself on a terribly disruptive and costly course to forced industrialization? No Bolshevik ever doubted the need to industrialize—Bolsheviks were Marxists, not populists, and saw their social base in the industrial working class—but nothing mandated that industrialization must occur so rapidly. Alexander Erlich asks rhetorically, "What was the reason for this bizarre zigzag course? What were the motives which made the Soviet leadership embark upon a policy about the dangers of which there had seemed to be practical unanimity?" Holland Hunter echoes Erlich's conundrum: although economists can demonstrate the fantastic nature of the industrial targets named in the First Five-Year Plan, they "cannot answer the question 'Why were overambitious targets pressed for and accepted?'" High targets might mobilize human resources, but this can only partly explain the speed demanded. Moshe Lewin even suggests that such questions are unanswerable:

"the reason why scholars keep returning to the same question is that the state of the sources does not yet allow for definitive answers. We do not know enough, from internal sources, about the state of mind of the leaders, their arguments and considerations, held in private or among themselves in secret meetings."[7]

New sources, however, make some conclusions possible. One vital motivation pushing the Soviet Union toward rapid industrial growth was the imperative of building its military power. At one level, the tone, spirit, and language of Stalinism in the late 1920s and early 1930s were undeniably military; rhetoric was dominated by "fronts," "attacks," and "shock brigades."[8] At the level of concrete questions of politics and economics, the type of industries favored by the First Five-Year Plan, the central role of the Red Army in both defeating political opponents of rapid industrial expansion and pushing radical plan variants, and the vigorous and consistent public declarations by Stalin and other Bolsheviks that the danger of imperialist attack made rapid economic growth necessary all lead to the conclusion that rearmament was a central element in Soviet industrialization.

Much scholarly literature recognizes the evident militarization of Stalinist society and accords military motivations some role in Soviet industrialization, although Soviet secrecy has made a detailed narrative difficult to establish. Other scholars explicitly deny that defense played any role in the First Five-Year Plan by motivating rapid industrial growth. Naum Jasny holds that "industrialization was not simply the principal initial aim of the Drive; it was the only aim. Contrary to official and semiofficial assertions, 'defense' was not a problem at the birth of the Great Industrialization Drive." Considerations of national security entered Soviet calculations, in Jasny's view, only by about 1934. Lewis Siegelbaum's account of the end of NEP and the shift to radical industrialization makes no mention of defense or security.[9]

Adam Ulam argues that the voluminous declarations by Stalin and his cohorts on the importance of industrialization for defense were merely motivational tools. The First Five-Year Plan assumed peace and economic stability: "there is little doubt that the regime would not have embarked on a campaign which debilitated Russia economically for several years . . . if it had seen a serious threat of imminent war." Alexander Erlich agrees: if the Soviet Union had truly feared war, it would not have disrupted its economy to achieve future gains. Erlich concedes, however, that "considerations of preparedness have played an important role in the discussion [over the pace of industrialization] from the very beginning, with all participants without exception making more or less generous allowance for them." Erlich quotes a speech by Preobrazhenskii:

Each of us knows full well that we must build socialism, are building it and shall build it. We should know, however, that we won't be given much time to build. We should expect a drive of rich peasantry united with the world capital which will start an economic as well as a military-political offensive. . . . We are building socialism in a situation of a breathing spell between two battles.

But Erlich dismisses such reasoning as "distinctly secondary." If Soviet leaders feared foreign attack—difficult as it is, in retrospect, to find a state willing to undertake and capable of such an effort—crash industrialization for defense's sake would be "suicide prompted by fear of death." From 1929 to 1932, armaments plants would not yet be producing munitions, and the USSR would face foreign enemies while crippled by internal chaos.[10]

These arguments that industrialization had nothing to do with defense not only belie repeated and emphatic public declarations to the contrary by Bolshevik leaders but also are unconvincing. Although the Bolsheviks' public and private statements were often at odds, this was not the case with defense policy. Furthermore, Soviet policy makers certainly did not expect that industrialization would render them more vulnerable by throwing their economy into chaos. On the contrary, central planning was partly intended to rescue the socialist economy from the disruptive business cycles that regularly shook the capitalist world. Bolshevik theorists were also adamant that the Soviet Union's unique economic structure would make it better suited for modern war, particularly when planning was fully instituted.

In addition, whereas many of industrialization's military benefits, such as the creation of an aviation or tank industry, would take years to come to fruition, the general modernization of the Soviet economy and the particular expansion of the Soviet Union's capacity to manufacture ammunition would pay more immediate dividends. At the time that the First Five-Year Plan was drawn up, the Soviet army was still based on a World War I model and used World War I weapons, entirely divorced from the technological dreams of Soviet military theorists. Many of the Red Army's officers had lived through the shell shortage that had crippled the tsar's armies and felt no desire to repeat the experience. Expanding the production of metals, chemicals, and machine tools could only improve the USSR's readiness.

This does not mean, of course, that the Red Army's high command was entirely satisfied with every aspect of Stalinist industrialization. Although recognizing the payoff from industrialization, Voroshilov, Tukhachevskii, Shaposhnikov, and the rest of the military leadership had reservations about particular policy priorities. Soviet military planners continually complained that with pride of place given to iron and steel, equally crucial nonferrous metallurgy got short shrift. Here, Stalin's fascination with metal, including the nom de guerre he chose for himself, altered industrial policy in a manner actively prejudicial to military readiness.[11] Chronic complaints about low budgets aside, the Red Army's leadership had specific objections to the direction in which the First Five-Year Plan seemed to be headed, at least in the earliest years of its planning. Pugachev, writing in 1927 for the Staff, argued that the key factor for "the economic and even political stability of the USSR in wartime is the maintenance of the bond with the peasantry." A good rule of thumb, in his view, was that the level of goods provided to the peasantry in wartime should not drop below peacetime 1927–1928 levels, a view implying a greater concentration on consumer goods.[12]

Minor differences in emphasis between the Red Army's leadership and the economic bureaucrats who assembled the five-year plans should not obscure fundamental truths: industrialization would dramatically increase Soviet military might, soldiers and civilians were well aware of that fact, and although increasing military power was not the only goal of industrialization, it was one of the most important ones. Industrialization drove rearmament; rearmament drove industrialization. Hunter, for example, includes defense as one of several causes of the thirst for rapid industrialization. The speed of economic recovery over the 1920s led Soviet planners to refuse to accept slower growth once prewar production levels had been reached. This coincided neatly with the Bolshevik penchant for radical measures and the need to bolster the Soviet Union's defenses. As Stalin asked the Central Committee in November 1928, "Can't we get along without such strain? Is it really impossible to go at a slower pace, in a calmer state?" The answer, of course, was that a slower pace was impossible. The capitalist world kept moving ahead, and "it's impossible to maintain the independence of our country, not having a sufficient industrial base for defense."[13]

Other scholars have made military power the sole motivation for rapid industrialization. Perhaps the clearest presentation of this interpretation is David Glantz's evaluation of Stalin's revolution:

> By the late 1920s it was apparent to Soviet leaders that unless they undertook drastic measures to industrialize the Soviet economy, their ill-equipped military establishment would continue to lag significantly behind those of the other major European nations. . . . It was clear to all political and military leaders that a massive and expensive modernization program was necessary to transform the army into a modern force. It was equally clear that to finance such a program and build a new industrial base would require massive extraction of fresh financial and manpower resources from the population at large. This could only be done by unleashing a new social revolution against the landed peasant class, which would destroy older institutions and free peasant labor to work in the industrial sector.

In Glantz's view, the First Five-Year Plan was a vehicle for carrying out these changes, and the social upheavals of Stalinism followed logically from this fundamental decision to modernize the Red Army. Richard Pipes suggests the same in passing in discussing Nazi Germany's four-year plans, which were "directly borrowed from Communist practices and intended for the same end, namely rapid rearmament."[14]

Although the desire for military power was essential to the push for rapid industrialization, it was only part of the truly overarching motive: regime security. This security included military power as measured in tanks, planes, and shells, but it went far beyond that. Lenin had told the Fourth Comintern Congress that heavy industry was essential to maintain Soviet economic independence: "We know that without the rescue of heavy industry, without its recovery we will not be able to build any type of industry at all, and without that we will simply perish as an independent country."[15] The danger he described was not just the possibility of another intervention, although that could not be excluded, but also the prospect of becoming an economic colony of the capitalist world. Stalin and his cohorts believed that their regime could not sustain itself indefinitely on a semicapitalist peasant base: a proletarian state demanded an industrial proletariat. Similarly, the Soviet Union could not remain independent while relying on the West for machine tools and technology. Only a policy directed in the long run toward autarky could protect the USSR from economic blackmail and foreign domination. Although there were many objective economic reasons that pushed the USSR toward economic autarky,[16] Stalin and the Bolshevik party consistently portrayed an end to dependence on the capitalist world as a central plank of their policy.

Moreover, the Bolsheviks were conscious of their identity as a proletarian party. Industrialization therefore served the goals of regime security by both providing protection from foreign domination and creating the industrial working class, the foundation of a Marxist-Leninist state. Speaking on a tour of iron and steel plants in southern Russia, Valerian Kuibyshev remarked in 1927 that "we must strengthen industry not only to build a future paradise and a future kingdom of the workers, but also so that the whole organism of our country should be capable of rebuffing our enemies."[17] Soviet conceptions of security cut across borders, as the campaigns against wrecking in military industry amply demonstrated. Enemies were as much a presence inside the Soviet Union as abroad, and protecting the socialist state required the promotion of progressive classes and the liquidation of class enemies at home as much as it required tanks and aircraft. Such policies as relocating industrial plants in the Urals or Central Asia not only made the Soviet economy more secure from attack but also widened and deepened the presence of industrial workers in formerly backward areas.

Finally, narrow military considerations—whether the Soviet Union could put a modern army in the field to defend or spread the revolution—were integral to these broader notions of security and the need for industrialization. The only Bolsheviks who saw contradictions among a strong military, burgeoning heavy industry, and a strong state were Bukharin and the Right, and by the end of 1928, their ability to force budget cuts on the Soviet military was rapidly decaying. Stalin and those through whom he ruled, a group of civil war veterans "difficult to characterize as either purely civilian or strictly military,"[18] simply saw no need for a trade-off between guns and butter. A strong military would require industrialization, which was worthwhile as an end in itself—there was no need to choose between the two.

This thinking was already evident by 1927; the Staff, responding to early Gosplan proposals for a five-year plan, pushed for faster industrial growth. "In this," the report stated, "the interests of defense and general economic development completely coincide, for they are identically directed to the strengthening of those types of production which are the most important and largest contributors to war." Vladimir Bazarov, a nonparty Gosplan economist, made the point explicit in 1928:

> With regard to all those areas of industrialization which are supposed to serve "civilian" needs in peacetime, considerations of defense capability and the national economy as a whole coincide: the strengthening and increase of the economic power of the USSR is at the same time the strengthening of its defense capability.

Subsequent Soviet historiography has largely continued this line that industrialization and rearmament were inseparable and complementary. The emphasis, however, has been on military might as a spin-off of development rather than a goal, and on the role of fascism in provoking Soviet rearmament, even though rearmament began long before Hitler came to power. One official history of World War II authoritatively pronounces:

> In the course of fulfilling the First and Second Five-Year Plans the pace of development of defense industry significantly increased. The country's industrialization and the development of heavy industry were the necessary economic and technical base for the creation of large quantities of high-quality arms and military technology.[19]

With all the reasons Soviet policy makers saw to develop the Soviet economy, Soviet industrialization was overdetermined, to borrow a term from the social sciences. The regime wanted military and economic security and considered industrialization a means to that end, a way of creating the class that would be the backbone of its support, as well as an end in itself. The need to build up an industry that could support a modern military was not the only factor pushing for rapid industrialization, but it was central to and inseparable from the myriad factors pushing in that direction. Retracing the tortuous path the First Five-Year Plan took to completion shows that the Red Army's leadership, though disagreeing on points of detail with the overarching Stalinist line, provided pivotal support for the general consensus on the need for rapid industrialization.

THE ORIGINS OF THE FIRST FIVE-YEAR PLAN

The concept of a five-year industrialization plan had existed since at least the winter of 1925–1926, when Gosplan explored a structure for economic development that would both be comprehensive and extend over time. Proposals drawn up for Gosplan by economist S. G. Strumilin in March 1927 satisfied no one and were subject to biting criticism from two directions. The People's Commissariats of Finance and Agriculture attacked the plans for sacrificing peasant interests to the urban worker, and economist N. D. Kondrat'ev at Gosplan found that the plans lacked internal consistency. In contrast to this line (roughly identifiable with Bukharin and the Right), Valerian Kuibyshev and his Vesenkha planners articulated what became the Stalinist line. Speaking to the Fourth Congress of Soviets in April 1927, Kuibyshev declared that Gosplan's conceptions were marred by "methodological errors" and excessive pessimism. The inherent superiority of socialism could achieve productivity gains far beyond what Gosplan believed possible. The plan would have to be revised to include more ambitious goals, ones befitting a socialist economy and state. By spring 1927, the pattern of subsequent years was already set: extremism in planning was no vice; moderation in planning was no virtue.[20]

The Red Army fully shared Kuibyshev's dissatisfaction with Gosplan's draft and his demands for rapid industrialization, insisting that future plans needed to shift investment toward heavy industry and away from consumer goods. In Gosplan's draft, according to the Red Army's official response, "the projected development of industry does not provide for the needs of defense." In particular, the military advocated boosting investment in group I and II heavy industries at the expense of "excessive" investment in the consumer goods of group III.[21] Emphasis would instead fall on fuel and chemicals, with "maximum" development of machine tools and motors. Investment in nonferrous metallurgy, though "intensive" in Gosplan's draft, was still insufficient.[22] Gosplan also, in military eyes, said little about the defense industry and bungled what it did say. Gosplan's data did not take into account either the current state of military industry or its long-term prospects. Gosplan ignored not only the need for an estimated 383 million rubles worth of new and expanded factories required for military industry but also the need to import and stockpile raw materials, build housing for defense workers, and provide military factories with civil orders in peacetime.[23]

The Red Army's advocacy for heavy industry coincided closely with Kuibyshev's, but its high command was understandably far more preoccupied than Kuibyshev by Gosplan's attempts to finance industrialization by cutting the military budget. Tight fiscal policy was integral to Gosplan's vision of economic development in early 1927, but the Red Army was unwilling to see its funding lag behind that of other sectors of the economy. Gosplan's draft, while permitting yearly increases in the overall defense budget (including the OGPU and other defense-related expenses, in addition to the strictly military budget), slowed that growth over the five-year plan. Gosplan's total defense budget came to less than what the Red Army figured it required for only its own needs, let alone the other components of the defense budget. Gosplan's five-year budget fell 13 percent below the Red Army's estimates for the same period (see table 13).[24]

To make matters worse, the Red Army would have to shoulder part of the burden of investment in military industry and strategic railroads, further reducing its available funds. Under Gosplan's five-year plan, spending on the military would grow more slowly than on any other sector of the state budget, forcing the Red

Table 13. July 1927 Gosplan and Red Army Defense Budget Projections for 1926–1927 through 1930–1931 (million rubles)

Fiscal Year	Gosplan: Total Defense	Red Army: Total Defense	Red Army: Red Army Budget	Red Army: Procurement
1926–1927	699.2	699.4	634.5	245.5
1927–1928	742.0	849.3	765.2	352.3
1928–1929	779.0	892.3	809.9	388.2
1929–1930	819.0	959.2	874.9	459.9
1930–1931	861.0	1,004.8	915.5	488.9
Total	3,900.2	4,405.0	4,000.0	1,934.8

Army to protest that the worsening international situation made larger defense budgets a necessity. Current budget outlays were so low that they would "hinder the Red Army's optimal expansion in wartime," and Gosplan's budget would only exacerbate the problem. The five-year, 4,000 million–ruble budget that the NKVM had assembled concentrated on two key goals: building up stockpiles of equipment for mobilization (1,013.7 million rubles of the budget) and equipping the Red Army with the most up-to-date technology. "Up to the present time we have based ourselves on supplies and designs of the tsarist army," concluded the military's response, and the rapid rearmament of Western Europe meant that Gosplan's budget would leave the Soviet Union at a grave disadvantage.[25]

The Red Army's response was, in short, categorically opposed to Gosplan's conservative five-year plan, for "the extent of budgetary outlays projected by Gosplan is completely unsatisfactory and the NKVM's budget is minimal." Unlike Gosplan's budget, which would increase military spending more slowly than spending in any other sector, the military's proposal increased defense spending at the same rate as the general budget: 66 to 67 percent over five years. Although this defense burden would be difficult for the economy to bear, "in view of the sharp deterioration of the international situation, we insist on the complete fulfillment of this sum and must categorically state that the People's Commissariat for Military Affairs has included only minimal needs." There was a certain minimum level of funding consistent with the country's defense, but Gosplan "does not provide for the needs of defense and so does not carry out the directive of the Fourth Congress of Soviets,"[26] which had ordered Sovnarkom "to strengthen the provision of the Red Army with technological means in correspondence with the contemporary demands of defense." The Fourth Congress also demanded "that the defense of the Soviet Union be provided for materially with the necessary collection of mobilization stockpiles in all branches and types of supply" and that "the defense preparedness of the state must not in any way lag behind the general economic growth of the country."[27] In the Red Army's view, Gosplan's five-year plan neglected military needs and thus violated these fundamental directives.

The effort the Red Army put into demolishing Gosplan's early, conservative variant of the five-year plan did not go to waste, becoming part of the Stalinist consensus that more rapid industrialization was absolutely necessary. Although the military budget would remain a painful issue, the Red Army's insistence on boosting the weight of heavy industry in investment and expansion plans at the expense of light and consumer industries fit perfectly with the spirit of the time. Gosplan had clearly misjudged the political winds. Its March 1927 five-year plan quickly disappeared, and its conceptions were abandoned in favor of more rapid industrial growth, led by pressure from Kuibyshev at Vesenkha, who had been presiding over the production of his own plans for the Soviet economy all this time. The Revvoensovet, finding Gosplan's proposals politically dead, could temporarily remove the whole question of the five-year plan from its agenda.[28]

Once the political correlation of forces was clear by the summer of 1927, Gosplan and Vesenkha began an exchange of five-year plans, each more ambitious than its predecessor. Vesenkha had been assembling its own plan since September 1926 to supplement or supplant Gosplan's efforts. In June 1927, it released a five-year plan running from 1927–1928 through 1931–1932. Capital investment was higher than in Gosplan's program, and total growth in industrial production was marginally higher as well: 82.5 percent.[29] This Vesenkha draft was obsolete before it was finished, however, too cautious to be an acceptable plan. In the second half of 1927, Vesenkha's ideas increasingly diverged from Gosplan's more conservative approach: "Vesenkha was now openly prepared to go much further and faster in its proposals than the earlier . . . drafts . . . far outstrip[ping] those current in Gosplan." In September 1927, a Vesenkha commission under Kuibyshev and his deputy, Mezhlauk, began meeting to produce still another variant; Gosplan was simultaneously developing a revised version of its own proposals. By 1 November 1927, Vesenkha's presidium had approved a five-year plan aiming at 107 percent growth in industrial production, and Gosplan conceded that industrial growth could go more quickly than it had previously allowed.[30]

The nascent First Five-Year Plan was the center of attention at the Fifteenth Party Congress in December 1927, although the congress would produce no final verdict on its precise shape. The congress still showed some solicitude toward peasant opinion and endorsed the bond between the city and the countryside, but its resolutions on industrial policy clearly showed the growing radicalism of Soviet planning. Gosplan chair Krzhizhanovskii conceded that his earlier variants had lacked necessary input from the USSR's union republics and even central institutions; now, however, Gosplan was working with full information, and the earlier, conservative variants had long since been superseded. The congress's final resolutions put heavy industry, the production of means of production, at the forefront of the five-year plan, while still holding that the plan should not merely maintain but actually improve the Soviet standard of living.[31]

Gosplan's economic planners were increasingly preoccupied with problems of defense. By November 1927, Gosplan's Defense Sector was already soliciting Postnikov at the MPU for defense data, arguing that proper reflection of defense interests in the five-year plan "depends in the strongest degree on the Defense

Sector of Gosplan having data and materials on this question."[32] At the Fifteenth Party Congress itself, Gosplan chair Krzhizhanovskii reported to the delegates on the state of economic planning and told them of the three fundamental tasks of the five-year plan. The first, of course, was industrialization through electrification and planning. The second was the socialization *(obobshchestvlenie)* of the entire economy, both production and distribution, to improve the Soviet worker's living standard and cultural level. Third, in Krzhizhanovskii's view, "taking into account the international situation, we want to provide for our military might, the defense of our country, to strengthen it with all the resources at our disposal." The final resolutions returned to this theme:

> Bearing in mind the possibility of military attack from the capitalist states on the socialist state, we must in working out the Five-Year Plan devote maximum attention to the fastest development of those branches of the national economy as a whole and industry in particular on which the chief burden will fall in providing for the defense of the country and the economic stability of the country in wartime.[33]

The chief spokesman for the military side of the Five-Year Plan at the congress was, as one would expect, Voroshilov. Unexpectedly, however, Voroshilov was generally satisfied with the new importance defense had assumed. Industrialization and military strength were closely linked, and Voroshilov did not call for major alterations in party policy. As discussed in connection with the war scare (see chapter 2), he hailed the creation of the RZ STO, the Mobilization-Planning Directorate (MPU), and Gosplan's Defense Sector as important steps toward preparing the Soviet Union for the inevitable capitalist onslaught. Then, however, his speech changed into a justification of the status quo in military industry and an endorsement of precisely those goals that the final five-year plan encompassed. Voroshilov told the delegates that the Soviet Union's current capacity was adequate for defense: "*In the event of imperialist attack on us, we can construct the defense of the state on our existing domestic industrial base.*"[34]

When Voroshilov did draw attention to military industry's needs, he called not for more investment but for more efficient use of resources already available through cutting costs, improving quality, loading military factories with additional civilian orders, and rationalizing production. These actions would not drain vital capital away from the priority areas of the Five-Year Plan. Those priorities, as Voroshilov saw them, coincided precisely with the priorities of the eventual final version of the First Five-Year Plan: metallurgy, chemistry, automobiles, tractors, and aviation. In short, he had completely accepted the party line and fully endorsed the Stalinist variant of industrialization.[35]

Thus, over the course of 1927, the Red Army had assisted in the steady radicalization of Soviet economic planning. From the initial Gosplan drafts criticized by the Right as too ambitious and by Vesenkha as too conservative, a new consensus endorsing rapid industrial expansion had emerged. At the Fifteenth

Party Congress, Voroshilov had publicly put the weight of the military behind industrialization in its Vesenkha variant, and Gosplan had been forced to accept crash industrialization. According to Carr and Davies, "from the controversies of 1927 . . . Vesenkha had emerged as the author of a five-year plan considerably more ambitious than any of the Gosplan drafts." With quicker industrialization tempos winning a conditional victory after the Fifteenth Congress, Sovnarkom directed Gosplan to draw up a new five-year plan, with a final draft to be ready 1 February 1929.[36] The RZ STO, in turn, ordered Gosplan to include defense in its new plan variants. In particular, in issuing directives on the planning process for union republics, People's Commissariats, the Red Army, and military industry, Gosplan was to methodically introduce defense considerations, assisted by Revvoensovet data. Vesenkha itself was soon doing its own calculations of the defense requirements for the proposed five-year plans.[37]

As defense grew in relative importance, resistance to higher plan targets rapidly collapsed. The Shakhty trial made the opinions of the bourgeois specialists opposed to higher plan targets inherently suspicious, and those who harbored doubts about the viability of the various five-year plans were one by one driven from their posts: Kondrat'ev, who had earlier found that the Five-Year Plan's "particular tasks in their extreme expression come into collision with each other," was expelled from the People's Commissariat of Finance. Vesenkha's spring 1928 draft five-year plan for the 1927–1928 through 1931–1932 period projected growth in industrial production of 140 percent, reaching 150 percent in group A, heavy industry. Vesenkha's nonparty economists complained without success that the targets were too high and tried to do too much, but this time, Gosplan's bourgeois specialists acceded to the new targets without a struggle.[38]

The final hope for a plan based on a more limited rate of industrial growth and on calculation instead of exhortation came in the late summer and fall of 1928. Bukharin and the Bolshevik Right, identified with opposition to rapid industrialization at the expense of the peasantry, managed to get a conciliatory resolution through the Central Committee at its 4–12 July 1928 plenary meeting. The rightist resolution expressed concern over the danger of a split between the city and the countryside and reaffirmed that the basis of Soviet agriculture would be the "productivity of the individual poor and middle peasant economy," aided through the growth of voluntary cooperative organizations and amply provided with industrial goods. In addition, the plenum rejected any "unlawful searches and any type of violation of revolutionary legality" in grain collection.[39]

At Vesenkha, Kuibyshev responded to this momentary wavering in the steady shift toward hard-line agricultural policy and crash industrialization by producing an August 1928 draft for a five-year plan that was *less* ambitious than previous ones, projecting industrial growth of just over 120 percent for the five years 1928–1929 through 1932–1933.[40] Kuibyshev would quickly rectify this error once the Right was decisively defeated, but in the autumn of 1928, Bukharin was not yet beaten. Bukharin's critiques, as expressed in September's "Notes of an Economist," were not especially insightful or original—he simply pointed out that rapid industrial expansion in the midst of an agricultural crisis made no sense, and that the pace of growth that Vesenkha and Gosplan advocated would create terrible economic strains and shortages, not least in construction materials.[41]

The decisive showdown between Bukharin's Right and Stalin came in late 1928 and early 1929. During the autumn, Stalin undercut Bukharin's influence over the Soviet press. The Stalinist rank and file in the Moscow party organization subjected Uglanov, a key Bukharin supporter at the top of the Moscow party, to increasingly heated criticism. Uglanov's power was broken by the end of October, and he was formally ousted at the end of November. Rightists in the Moscow organization were quickly purged. Although the differences between Stalin and Bukharin were partly papered over for the November Central Committee plenum, the Right's power was clearly fading quickly. By December, rightists had been purged from the Comintern's foreign parties, and Tomskii's influence as chair of the Central Trade Union Council had been undermined. Bukharin was finally forced to quit his jobs as editor of *Pravda* and political secretary of the Comintern.[42]

With the Right clearly headed for total defeat, Kuibyshev at Vesenkha had a free hand to institute more radical policies. The November plenum of Vesenkha's Standing Planning Conference called for overall industrial growth of 134.6 percent—150.2 percent for group A heavy industry—based on a total capital investment of 10,200 million rubles. This proposal, quite close to Vesenkha's April draft, was rejected by Vesenkha's presidium as too limited and moderate. In December, a second try proved more acceptable. Running from 1928–1929 to 1932–1933, this plan envisaged general industrial production growing by 167 to 168 percent and group A production by 221 percent, with corresponding increases in industrial investment. In March and April 1929, Rykov attempted to hold the line on overall spending at a joint meeting of Sovnarkom and the STO, but without success. The final figures approved for the Sixteenth Party Congress were even more ambitious than Vesenkha's December 1928 plan, projecting five-year growth in industrial production of 180 percent.[43]

As the First Five-Year Plan approached completion in a cycle of steadily growing industrial production targets, the RZ STO mandated the completion of a military section for the plan, almost as an afterthought. On 4 February 1929, the RZ STO issued directives for defense planning, decreeing that the "Five-Year Plan of development for the national economy in the part concerning defense measures" would proceed in three stages. The first step, covering roughly the first two years of the plan, 1928–1929 and 1929–1930, would build enough capacity to meet industry's 1928 wartime mobilization plan S, projecting production of roughly 2,500 million cartridges and 24 million shells. The second stage, to be complete by the end of the 1930–1931 fiscal year, would aim for the targets the RZ STO set on 30 July 1928, namely, the ability to produce over one year of war 5,000 million cartridges, 45 million shells, 62,000 machine guns, 2,100 76mm artillery pieces, 760 122mm howitzers, 190 152mm howitzers, 200 107mm guns, and 1,055 tanks.

The third stage, for the last two years of the Five-Year Plan, 1931–1932 and 1932–1933, was less defined. Giving no concrete assignments, the RZ STO specified only that those two years must provide for "further development of the technical might of the armed forces and the increase of the general defense readiness of the country, on the basis of the achievements of the previous two stages." Final drafting of the Five-Year Plan's defense section was left to Gosplan and the NKVM, but this task would never come to fruition, for the First Five-Year Plan would never have a fully drawn defense counterpart.[44]

Konstantin Mekhonoshin, deputy director of Gosplan's Defense Sector, took advantage of this new assignment to draft a defense five-year plan to score points in Gosplan's continuing rivalry with Vesenkha and the MPU over who would run defense planning. He demanded complete information on Vesenkha's defense activities, allowing Vesenkha twelve days to assemble the data but only four to report on how defense had been reflected in industry's long-term plans. The quick deadline, as well as the fact that Mekhonoshin was careful to send copies of his request to the RZ STO and the Red Army, suggests that he was hoping for Vesenkha's failure rather than its success. That would demonstrate Vesenkha's inability to handle defense work and increase Gosplan's influence.[45]

Vesenkha's Standing Mobilization Conference did manage to find something to tell Mekhonoshin. On 19 March, it decided that Postnikov's MPU would take the lead both in distributing the new directives to Vesenkha's other directorates and in getting the directorates covering civil industry to take their defense responsibilities seriously. Several managers had taken "insufficiently exhaustive account of the needs of defense" in their planning, and the Main Directorate of Machine Building, along with many others, had submitted no defense plans at all. Allowing two weeks to collect information from laggards, Postnikov would have until 15 April to process it and present the results to the conference. The conference could, however, make some preliminary decisions on the scale of defense spending required. As discussed in chapter 4, 800 million rubles would go toward construction and investment, 612 million of that to the GVPU alone. Another 350 million would stockpile raw materials, and 40 million would cover antiair defense and other miscellaneous expenses, totaling 1,190 million in total defense spending on industry. Nearly a quarter of that, 275 million rubles, would be spent on imports.[46]

THE RED ARMY WINS ITS SHARE

Despite recognizing that industrialization would render the Soviet Union far more powerful militarily, high-ranking officers in the Red Army were not entirely satisfied with the First Five-Year Plan's priorities. In part because the plan emphasized investing in industry as rapidly as possible, temporarily reducing resources available to the military, and in part because it concentrated on iron, steel, and coal, some officers voiced reservations. Speaking at the March–April joint session of the STO and Sovnarkom, Bogodepov briefly mentioned the subject of defense. According to him, the plan was built around "cleanly budgetary motives," without reference to military considerations. "We set down here," he continued, "figures that in all probability do not cover that program which the military is obliged to bring into being over the Five-Year Plan. . . . our projection . . . is quite modest." Furthermore, Bogodepov argued, taking into account the behavior of the USSR's neighbors, "who very much love to fish with cruisers in the Far East," the military budget might need special discussion.[47]

Chief of Staff Shaposhnikov had similar reservations about the Five-Year Plan, but for different reasons. His verdict on the plan was that "the projected development of individual branches [of the economy] does not sufficiently provide for the needs of defense"; Gosplan's projections were based on "peacetime demand through the end of the Five-Year Plan, but not for that situation which may arise in the event of war." Shaposhnikov's concern was less the military budget per se, and more the plan's neglect of machine-tool production and especially nonferrous metallurgy. Gosplan had made no provision for the necessary reserves of these metals. For the key industrial metals—copper, lead, zinc, tin, aluminum, and nickel,[48] —"by the end of the Five-Year Plan only the demand for zinc will be covered in full. . . . Non-ferrous metals remain the tightest bottleneck in industry." At Gosplan, Mekhonoshin had to concede Shaposhnikov's point that a shortage of nonferrous metals would remain throughout the Five-Year Plan. Production of nonferrous metals matched the demands of the Soviet economy in neither peace nor war. Indeed, the RZ STO found in June 1929 that to cover wartime needs, the USSR would require a stockpile of 16,000 tons of copper, 28,000 tons of zinc, 29,000 tons of lead, 1,900 tons of tin, 2,300 tons of nickel, and 9,000 tons of aluminum.[49]

More narrowly, Shaposhnikov concluded that military industry's planning was woefully absent. Repeated efforts had still not produced a special five-year plan for military industry. When Postnikov promised the Staff that a plan would be ready by April, he could offer no details. At best, Postnikov could promise only that the military plan would reflect in general terms the overall Five-Year Plan. Mekhonoshin agreed that the military and civil plans would "basically correspond." The Red Army could not help hoping for more. Mekhonoshin tried to reassure Voroshilov that the First Five-Year Plan, though not as focused on military production as he might have hoped, still had much to offer. As he told Voroshilov, the Soviet Union's economy would deliver in wartime "a colossal collection of ammunition, weapons, equipment, food and forage." The plan would, in short, "increase the country's defense readiness," while its "basic lines" corresponded to just what the defense of the state demanded.[50]

Mekhonoshin's promises of great potential notwithstanding, he could not hide that a wartime economic plan was only in development "in the bowels of Gosplan," just like the five-year plan for the peacetime development of military industry. As Mekhonoshin explained in April 1929, those plans were entirely dependent on more general plans for industrial development. Until "the fundamental lines of the reconstruction of the most important branches of industry have been established," there could be no military plans. Still, Mekhonoshin told Voroshilov that Gosplan had worked from the assumption that defense expenditure would be held steady at "approximately the level of 1928–1929." To the Red Army's high command, that was not enough for all it wanted to achieve.[51]

When the Sixteenth Party Conference opened on 23 April 1929 to discuss and approve the First Five-Year Plan, Gosplan chair Krzhizhanovskii was forced to concede the Red Army's claim that the military had not received sufficient attention. "I strongly agree," Krzhizhanovskii told the delegates, "with the military's indication that in our plan the needs of the military are not sufficiently developed." If need be, he allowed, the resources devoted to the military could be increased. In contrast to the 1927 Fifteenth Party Congress, where Voroshilov had gotten little for the Red Army and pronounced himself satisfied, at the Sixteenth Conference, the military got a great deal and asked for more. From the Red Army, Unshlikht echoed Krzhizhanovskii's point and followed the same line that the Staff had taken in previous months. "The task before us," he said, "is to structure the Five-Year Plan of development of the national economy in such a way that we can use the results we achieve in certain branches of the national economy for the 100 percent satisfaction of the needs of the Red Army." Quibbles over the military budget and military plans could not, however, be allowed to disrupt the triumphal progress of the First Five-Year Plan, which was duly approved on 23 April 1929 by Sovnarkom and the Sixteenth Party Conference.[52]

Since the First Five-Year Plan lacked a defense section, slapdash and piecemeal efforts quickly began to extend it to the Red Army and military industry. Given the Red Army's continuing misgivings over some aspects of the First Five-Year Plan, particularly its lack of precision with regard to military matters, the RZ STO agreed on 8 April 1929 (even before the Sixteenth Party Congress) that defense needed rethinking. It ordered Gosplan to work out a new series of measures with the cooperation of, among others, Unshlikht and Shaposhnikov from the Red Army, Postnikov from the MPU, and Pavlunovskii from Rabkrin. First to fruition was an RZ STO decree on 16 April 1929 endorsing a new artillery order to replace the previous one from 23 August 1928 and obliging Vesenkha to meet the Red Army's long-term orders in full within three years for artillery and four to five years for shells and ammunition. Part of this would include the ongoing "howitzerization" of the Red Army's artillery park and the strengthening of heavy artillery as well. All these measures were to be incorporated in the upcoming 1929–1930 budget.[53] To set that 1929–1930 budget and the budget for the rest of the First Five-Year Plan, Gosplan staffers met with Shaposhnikov, Postnikov, Pavlunovskii, and others on 29 April 1929. They managed to establish only that there was a yawning gap between the Red Army's request for 1,032 million rubles for 1929–1930 and 5,828 million rubles over the entire five-year span and Gosplan's counteroffer of 900 million for 1929–1930 and 4,880 million for the entire Five-Year Plan.[54] Only intervention from the Politburo in the form of two key July decrees on defense would ultimately resolve that conflict.

The next item on the RZ STO's defense agenda was refining the Red Army's mobilization order. The RZ STO's 4 February decision had left the defense plan's final goal undefined, but its new 27 May 1929 decree added a new set of targets, extending those the RZ STO had set in July 1928 to specify exactly what capacity industry would be expected to build by the end of 1932–1933. In the event of war, the Red Army would field an army of 3.5 million men, and Soviet industry would deliver a substantial collection of material over the first year of war (see table 14).[55]

Three months after the First Five-Year Plan was officially approved, the Politburo finally introduced major changes in military policy to match it. On 15 July 1929, the Politburo issued two major policy statements, "On the State of Defense" and "On Military Industry," to guide development during the First Five-Year Plan. Soviet historiography has always recognized these decrees' importance, though they were never published in full.[56] Examined from archival sources, however, these directives reveal their true significance—they were as central to the Soviet military as the First Five-Year Plan was to the Soviet economy. The Politburo's two decisions are as pivotal for subsequent Soviet military development as any before or since; their importance can hardly be overstated.

"On the State of Defense" first commented approvingly on the results of the Politburo's last major defense decision from May 1927. The positive results of that decree had produced an army that was "completely reliable" politically and equipped with military technology on a level commensurate with the state's resources. The low state of the Soviet Union's technological resources meant, however, that the Politburo could not be completely satisfied with the Red Army, despite the organizational achievements of the 1920s. The Politburo's decree accordingly emphasized technology and supply. The Soviet Union would build a technologically sophisticated Red Army but limit its overall size to emphasize quality over quantity. The Red Army would grow by the end of the Five-Year

Table 14. Projected Production Capacity of Military Industry over the First Five-Year Plan (FFYP)

Equipment	Two to three Years into FFYP	End of FFYP
Cartridges	5,000 million	6,000 million
Shells	45 million	84 million
Machine guns	62,000	—
76mm artillery pieces	2,100	2,064
122mm howitzers	760	1,289
152mm howitzers	190	500
107mm guns	200	260
Heavy and siege artillery	138	228
Tanks	1,055	1,500
Planes	—	6,865

Plan to 643,700 troops and increase the weight of technical arms, especially armor and aviation. The Politburo declared that the Red Army should seek to match its likely enemies in troop strength, while maintaining superiority in two of three key technologies: aircraft, artillery, and tanks.[57]

Not only was the Soviet army's technical base far weaker than that of bourgeois armies, but as a result of industrial shortfalls, prospects of maintaining supply to the army in wartime were poor. Stockpiles of equipment to carry the mobilized army through the first period of industrial mobilization were similarly inadequate. In general, the Politburo found, industry's preparation was "completely unsatisfactory," for "to date there are no plans for industry's mobilization for servicing war." Existing plans took too long to reach full production and made no provision for necessary labor, especially skilled workers and engineers. Although some work toward raising the overall technical level of Soviet industry had taken place, the pace of new prototypes was "impermissibly slow," as was their introduction to mass production, delaying final use by the Red Army for years.[58]

The Politburo determined that full resolution of this problem required linking two five-year plans: the First Five-Year Plan for the Soviet economy and a new five-year plan for the military to "create a modern military-technical base for defense." The Politburo accordingly ordered the Red Army to speed the modernization of its artillery park, by both refurbishing older field pieces and introducing newer, more specialized artillery. For this, and to upgrade Soviet tanks and chemical warfare capabilities, the Politburo decreed "general use of foreign technical assistance and aid, and also acquisition of the most vital prototype models." The Soviet air force would benefit from the same treatment, especially in aircraft engines, the chief obstacle to further advances. Vesenkha was told to increase its spending on research and development.[59]

The Politburo also increased the size of the fully mobilized Red Army, enlarging it by the end of the Five-Year Plan from 2.6 million to 3 million men, with 2,000 peacetime aircraft to be expanded by 500 upon the outbreak of war and an additional reserve of 1,000. Tanks would similarly expand: by spring 1933, the Red Army was to have 1,500 active tanks, another 1,500 to 2,000 ready for immediate wartime use, and a reserve of 1,500 to 2,000 more. The current mobilization plan for the Red Army was based on an artillery force of 6,015 pieces; this would more than double to 12,802. The number of standard field guns would actually decline, compensated by a larger increase in howitzers, heavy artillery, and smaller guns. The only branch of service to suffer would be the Red Navy, its budget cut from 284 to 200 million rubles.[60]

Although the Politburo focused on the technical side of the Red Army, it also paid some attention to discipline and morale. It ordered improvements in the oppressively poor living conditions for soldiers, especially through additional housing. Since the Red Army would dramatically expand its numbers in wartime, bringing in a flood of peasants potentially hostile to Soviet power, maintaining reliable officers was extremely important. Difficulties were rife in the peacetime officer corps, including "kulak mood, anti-Semitism, distorted disciplinary practices . . . bureaucratism, decayed living conditions, and collectivism"; these were worsened by intra-army factions, including manifestations of "Belorusskii-Tolmachevskii"[61] tendencies. Although the Politburo's decision reaffirmed one-man command, and therefore a secondary role for political officers, the ideological dangers noted above left little choice but for political officers to play an active role in maintaining discipline.[62]

On the same day that the Politburo issued "On the State of Defense," it issued the equally significant decree "On Military Industry." It was largely based on a June RZ STO resolution concerning reform and the guilt of those who had kept "insufficient watchfulness over wrecking."[63] "On Military Industry" began by asserting the incontrovertible fact that Frunze had observed five years before: modern war would place unprecedented burdens on industry, both in war and in peace. In wartime, Soviet military plants would bear the burden of supplying the Red Army until the rest of industry could mobilize; in peacetime, they would stay abreast of technical advances in weaponry and assist civil industry's mobilization. Although the inherent superiority of the Soviet system should, the Politburo asserted, make the USSR better able to prepare for war than bourgeois states, wrecking had led to entirely unsatisfactory industrial performance.[64]

Despite the clear progress Soviet military industry had made through 1929, it had fallen short of expectations raised by the immense amounts of capital invested since the mid-1920s. The Politburo's catalog of problems in the defense industry displayed profound dissatisfaction. The eighteen months Soviet industry claimed it would need to fully mobilize would mean either critical shortages of munitions in wartime or the peacetime accumulation of hugely expensive stockpiles of equipment. Sloppy calculation of capacity and investment produced disproportions: not enough nitric acid was produced for powder and explosives, not enough powder was produced to charge shells, artillery manufacture lacked high-quality steel, and industry agreed to wartime production schedules without the electric power required to run factories at the necessary pace. Some military factories had been taken out of military production altogether, and factories introducing new production, especially of such complicated systems as tanks, spent years unsuccessfully trying to develop mass production. Even successful prototypes could spend three to four years in the transition to mass production and become obsolete by the time they reached the Red Army.

In addition to enumerating military industry's systemic deficiencies, the Politburo singled out individual factories for especially egregious failures: Motovilikhinskii and Bolshevik had spent two years on tank production without success. Antiaircraft artillery pieces consumed more man-hours and effort than they should. Industry had established neither facilities for wartime repair of damaged equipment nor internal production of precision instruments. Scarce foreign currency went to imported machine tools, while existing factory machinery rusted from disuse. Red Putilovets and Motovilikhinskii each had over 1,000 machine tools sitting idle; military industry as a whole had nearly 10,000. Plants employed outdated technical processes, and some goods lacked interchangeable parts. This defect was worsened by industry's chronic failure to produce enough spare parts to keep military equipment in working order. Late deliveries and insufficient development of civil production led to financial difficulties.[65]

As the discussion of wrecking in chapter 3 showed, military industry's problems were the inevitable result of managers and workers attempting to deal with too many demands too fast, but the Politburo could not accept such an explanation. Its July 1929 defense decrees pointed in another direction, blaming engineers and technical specialists for their rational responses to the environment in which they found themselves. "All development of military industry and its preparation for war," the Politburo declared, "was wholly based on the caste of old tsarist-era specialists. . . . when it was established that the majority of old specialists belonged to a counterrevolutionary organization, military industry found itself in a critical position in relation to technical leadership." This was the result of "longstanding and systematic wrecking of the work of military industry (including the VPU, trusts, and factories) by a large-scale counterrevolutionary organization," abetted by "the absence of watchfulness on the part of the party leadership of military industry, starting with the leading members of Voenprom and the VPU and ending with the factories." The party leadership of military industry, charged with maintaining a close watch on the activities of bourgeois engineers and technicians, instead displayed "inordinate trust in specialists, especially in their bosses (engineers Mikhailov and Vysochanskii), and the absence of even minimal control over the work of specialists." Red directors limited themselves to administrative affairs, accepting their own ignorance of technical matters. Even classifying sensitive information was turned into a means of wrecking: "under the pretext of military secrecy, through excessive classification of documents Communist and non-party workers were in fact removed from active participation in rationalizing production."[66]

None of this had been apparent from military industry's rosy reports. In fact, "the real state of military industry, uncovered by the joint work of Rabkrin and the OGPU, turned out not to correspond in any way with the optimistic light thrown on the system of military industry in evaluation reports to the Central Committee and the Government from the leadership of military industry." Despite a series of achievements, far greater results should have come from the capital and attention devoted to military industry. Much of the disarray in defense industry was supposed to have been corrected by capital investment over the 1928–1929 fiscal year, but wrecking spoiled even this.[67]

A desperate situation required desperate measures, most importantly a vast purge at all levels of industrial administration down to individual factories, a purge linked to other policy measures. The Central Control Commission, working with the Orgburo and a special purge commission, was to expel unreliable technical specialists and administrators from military industry and replace them with politically vetted communists. Vesenkha was ordered to assemble a policy, ostensibly to root out wrecking, but also to find possible savings in capital investment, power generation, and production procedures. All matters related to defense assumed a higher priority: more research and development, quicker production of new models, financial aid to cash-strapped military enterprises, and lower prices on military materials. To ensure that military factories were prepared for maximum wartime production, they were to be kept working at full capacity on civilian goods "to maximum bounds." Lastly, the Politburo ordered Vesenkha and the NKVM to harmonize their relations and procedures to eliminate unnecessary friction.[68]

Freed from the restraints on industrialization imposed by Bukharin, Rykov, and the Right, the Politburo moved quickly to implement its defense decrees by speeding the expansion of industries vital for defense and pushing the already lofty targets from the First Five-Year Plan still higher. It called for "the acceleration . . . of the pace of development for those sectors having defense significance," especially nonferrous metallurgy, chemicals, and machine building.[69] Accordingly, on 25 July 1929, the Politburo approved new programs for shipbuilding and engineering in Leningrad. On 2 August, the STO decreed a "fundamental revision" in the nonferrous metals plan. The Politburo on 29 August did the same for the chemical industry, citing its importance as "a terrible weapon of destruction and annihilation in forthcoming imperialist wars" and mandating that it free itself from dependence on imports by 1931–1932. The expansion was more general as well: speaking to Vesenkha's presidium on 14 August 1929, Kuibyshev called for a general 28 percent increase in production targets. The fuel industry's targets for 1932–1933 went from 22 to 26 to 40 million tons by October 1929; iron and steel targets for 1932–1933 grew from 10 to 12 to 16 million tons by December.[70]

THE RED ARMY REORGANIZES IN RESPONSE

The Politburo's directives triggered several months of far-reaching reforms in the Red Army. On 17 and 18 July 1929, immediately after the Politburo's decisions, Voroshilov presided over an unusual two-day meeting of the Revvoensovet. First on the agenda was Voroshilov's own presentation to his highest-ranking officers of the new policy, which the Red Army resolved to "take as exact and unwavering leadership . . . on the state and tasks of the construction of the USSR's defenses." More concretely, the Revvoensovet assigned the Staff to redo the military's five-year development plan (approved only one year before), the Financial-Planning Directorate to develop a new budget, and the rest of the Red Army to determine a new course.[71] It would take months, but the Red Army eventually redesigned its central bureaucracy to emphasize new technologies; created an Armaments Directorate to replace the old, sprawling Supply Directorate; and added a new Motorization and Mechanization Directorate to handle tanks and transport.

On 15 July, the same day the Politburo issued its key decisions on defense, Avgust Ivanovich Kork, only a little over a month after becoming the Red Army's supply director, argued to Voroshilov that his directorate required substantial reform. Kork's reform initiative happily coincided with the Politburo's mandate for far-reaching defense reform. Kork himself, however, may have been as interested in securing a transfer out of the Supply Directorate as in improving administrative efficiency or increasing his authority. As a successful combat officer during the civil war, Kork questioned his suitability for administrative office. When the possibility of Kork's transfer to the Red Army's Moscow bureaucracy had first arisen, he had protested to Voroshilov that "the duties of supply director are especially difficult for a person working exclusively in field command, and I personally feel myself completely unprepared." Kork accepted his appointment to the Supply Directorate reluctantly and quickly requested a new structure.[72]

As Kork described his duties to Voroshilov, the Supply Directorate managed not only the supply of weapons, ammunition, and communications and engineering equipment but also more mundane tasks. The Supply Directorate's Military-Management Directorate also handled uniforms, boots, tents, caps, blankets, and other military goods. Kork was additionally responsible for military construction, including bases, barracks, and border fortifications. The vast majority of the personnel under his direction had nothing to do with supply at all—nearly two-thirds of the Supply Directorate handled the Red Army's publications. Under Kork's proposal, a new Armaments Directorate would emerge leaner and more effective once subsidiary concerns were taken away. The Military-Management and Military-Construction Directorates would be split off, leaving the Armaments Directorate with three more focused subdirectorates: Artillery, Military-Chemical, and Military-Technical (handling communications and engineering equipment).[73]

Kork had several reasons for preferring his newer structure to the traditional centralized structure. First, the time and energy of the supply director and his staff were wasted on the tedious and undemanding tasks of delivering boots and newspapers, not in lobbying industry for more and better weapons. Splitting the Supply Directorate would allow a clearer focus on developing military technology. At all levels of command below the military districts (army, corps, division), the folly of a single directorate for all types of supply had been recognized and separate offices established; Kork believed that the process should continue in the military districts and within the People's Commissariat itself. Kork also appealed to the superiority of German methods. As he told Voroshilov:

The German army in the thoughtfulness and expediency of its organization, unarguably, can be considered a model. Of course, this does not mean that we could borrow everything in organizational matters from the German Reichswehr. However, there are branches of work where we still have muddle and to eliminate imperfections in our organization it would be useful to look at how similar questions have been solved in the German army.

While he was in Germany, Kork had noticed how the Germans had concentrated armaments alone under one institution, believing it "excessive" to have quarter-master services and construction together with ordnance in a single organization.[74]

Although Kork did not succeed on his first attempt, he would return to his reform plans when the establishment of a special center for the development of Soviet armor showed that reform was indeed possible. His proposal went before the Revvoensovet, but neither Voroshilov nor the rest of the Red Army's high command was enthusiastic. His plan went nowhere. On 3 November 1929, however, the Revvoensovet established the Motorization and Mechanization Directorate (UMM), charged with supplying the Red Army with "all types of transport and combat vehicles on mechanical drive," as well as conducting research and development on armored vehicles. Furthermore, the UMM's charter gave it the mandate to participate in developing plans and programs for relevant sectors of industry. Innokentii Khalepskii, formerly head of the Supply Directorate's Military-Technical branch, took over the new position.[75] This prodded Kork to try again at shaking up the Supply Directorate.

In his renewed appeal in November, Kork returned to the theme of foreign examples, this time alluding not only to good examples but also to bad. Whereas advanced states like Germany all had tightly focused armaments directorates, it was only the Soviet Union's border states, receiving most of their equipment from abroad, that continued to have supply directorates. Additionally, the Red Army's organization had not kept pace with the rapidly advancing military technology and the Soviet Union's own military-industrial potential, leading to incessant problems. Kork naturally refused to believe that these problems could be attributed to the "personal qualities of the management personnel of the Supply Director-ate," instead suggesting that many of the Supply Directorate's functions were superfluous and only distractions from more important tasks. Welcoming the creation of the UMM and plaintively asking for it to be subordinated to his Supply Directorate, Kork noted that since military finance had already been removed from his purview, his only role with regard to the Military-Management and Military-Construction Directorates had been passing financial information back and forth.[76]

The Supply Directorate did need reform. It was so overburdened with personnel that Kork's projected reform could cut its personnel from 1,841 to just under 400. The greatest savings resulted from detaching the Red Army's printing division with its 1,141 employees. Since nearly two-thirds of the Supply Directorate's workforce busied themselves with publications, not with the design or produc-tion of machine guns or shells, pruning was desperately needed.[77] Finally seeing the merit in Kork's proposals, the Revvoensovet dissolved the Supply Directorate on 18 November 1929 and replaced it with a new Armaments Directorate to create "the best and most rapid solution of the problem of the RKKA's technical rearma-ment, the basic task of the armed forces' Five-Year Plan of construction." The armaments director would be responsible for all artillery (which included firearms) and chemical and technical equipment. Although aircraft, tanks, and automobiles would be the responsibility of the air force and the UMM, the armaments director would handle the weapons to be mounted on tanks and planes. As Kork had outlined, the new directorate was built on the three divisions of the old Supply Directorate: Artillery, Military-Chemical, and Military-Technical. Uniforms, kit, construction, and finance were all removed from the purview of the armaments director.[78]

Kork's arguments were key to the Revvoensovet's decision, but Voroshilov and the rest of the Red Army's high command were also responding to wrecking within the Supply Directorate, especially in its subordinate Artillery Directorate. An investigation conducted by Ivan Pavlunovskii of Rabkrin's Military-Naval Inspectorate had found extensive wrecking in the development, manufacture, and procurement of artillery, firearms, and ammunition. Worse, military personnel, including previous supply director Dybenko and artillery director Kulik, had been implicated in loose oversight, if not actual sabotage. Kulik, ironically, had earlier blown the whistle on wrecking in military industry while serving as military liaison. That earlier service did not help him now. The Politburo's official endorsement of the Red Army's reorganization, given in January 1930, mentioned the importance of cleaning out the Artillery Directorate.[79]

Although the Armaments Directorate was Kork's idea, Ieronim Uborevich would run it. The same decision that created the Armaments Directorate ordered Kork to switch posts with Uborevich, commander of the Moscow Military District. N. A. Efimov, formerly head of the Staff's powerful Organization-Mobilization Directorate, was appointed Uborevich's deputy. As part of his new post, Uborevich quickly became a member of the important bodies formulating defense policy, the Revvoensovet and the RZ STO.[80] Uborevich was a Lithuanian—his last name was originally Uboriavichius and was consistently misspelled by Russians as "Ubarevich."[81] He had enlisted in the tsarist army in 1915 and, upon finishing artillery school, rose to become a battery commander. Joining the Bolshevik party in 1917, he fought on multiple fronts during the civil war and eventually became an army commander. He even served as war minister of the short-lived Far Eastern Republic. His rise in the Red Army was quite rapid. He became commander of the North Caucasus Military District in 1925, joined the Revvoensovet in October 1926, took command of the Moscow Military District in November 1928, and finally became the first armaments director. Uborevich became a candidate member of the Politburo in July 1930, a position he maintained until his execution in the Great Purges. He served as armaments director for a little over a year, until he was named commander of the Belorussian Military District on 11 July 1930. The circumstances of this transfer are cloudy; there seems to be no indication of dissatisfaction among military circles or the Soviet government with his work as armaments director. This switch likely had more to do with putting Tukhachevskii in the armaments director's office than removing Uborevich from it.[82]

Slightly built, wearing spectacles, Uborevich was not an imposing figure. As Uborevich told the story, he had first met Sergo Ordzhonikidze, later to direct

Soviet industry, during the civil war. Ordzhonikidze had burst into Uborevich's headquarters and asked him, "Is the commander here?" When Uborevich replied affirmatively, the intruder instructed, "Well, go and tell him Ordzhonikidze's arrived!" Despite his unprepossessing appearance, Uborevich had built an impressive reputation on the battlefields of the civil war. Marshal Zhukov termed him one of the most totally *military* officers he had ever encountered, an "extraordinary" leader. This military bearing had a darker side: as Zhukov put it, "his strictness was feared, though he was never rude or abrupt."[83] Like Tukhachevskii, his successor as armaments director, Uborevich had a reputation for arrogance, harshness, and intolerance for fools. This link between Uborevich and Tukhachevskii was no coincidence. The post of armaments director demanded a personality eager to impose its will on recalcitrant factory directors and industrial bureaucrats. The director's work on mobilization readiness demanded, above all, attention to detail and rejection of imprecision at any level of planning. From the other side, the difficult job ensured that any officer holding it would acquire a reputation for harshness and impatience if he did not have one already.

In the feverish rush to implement the Politburo's summer 1929 defense directives, Kuibyshev made yet another doomed attempt to put together a five-year plan for military industry that would be limited enough for industry, ambitious enough for the Red Army, and farsighted enough to match future advances in production capacity and military technology. In October, he told his subordinates at Vesenkha that although industrialization had created the preconditions necessary for building up the USSR's defenses, this had been hamstrung by the absence of a five-year plan for the defense industry. Kuibyshev declared that such a plan—one that would cover not only production but also labor, fuel, electric power, finance, and research—would be the "combat mission" of all industry. He enunciated principles for this plan that were nothing new—they had guided Soviet military-economic planning (to be sure, more in the breach than in the observance) since the mid-1920s. Kuibyshev prescribed the maximum employment of civil industry through dual-use production, cooperation with military factories, and peacetime production of small runs of wartime assignments. Vesenkha would economize wherever possible, end dependence on foreign materials, and emphasize production in safe geographical zones—all policies impossible to disagree with.[84] Kuibyshev created a network of working groups under a special commission of representatives from throughout Vesenkha as well as Gosplan and the Red Army. A dozen working groups specialized in individual types of production, from firearms to bullets to automobiles and tanks. Another half dozen groups were added later, each charged with writing a plan for its own branch of industry for the MPU to gather and collate into a grand, overarching plan for military industry. These groups worked toward guaranteeing that the Red Army's three-year order plan would be met by 1 October 1931 and its five-year order plan by 1 October 1933.[85]

This attempt at a five-year plan for military industry was no more successful than its predecessors. Despite the Politburo's pronouncement and Kuibyshev's good intentions, technology still advanced too quickly, industry expanded too rapidly, and the Red Army's demands grew too fast to make it possible to schedule military production five years in the future. Six months later, Voroshilov was still ordering Uborevich, his armaments director, and Shaposhnikov, his Chief of Staff, to maintain "the most active participation" in military industry's ongoing efforts at a five-year plan. Uborevich duly reported back that he and other officers had been consulting with their opposite numbers from Vesenkha and that work was still moving forward.[86] The rapidly accelerating arms orders from the Red Army, together with the feverish pace of Stalinist industrialization, rendered a long-range plan for military industry vaguely ridiculous, and the whole project quietly dropped from sight.

In October, at roughly the same time that Kuibyshev was ordering a new five-year plan for military industry, work restarted on the defense budget for the 1929–1930 fiscal year—subject to some recalculation, thanks to the Politburo's summer decrees. For the Red Army, however, the First Five-Year Plan's stress on future capacity meant that its particular share of the total budget would still not match its full hopes; beating Rykov had not yet gotten the Red Army all the budget it desired. The final budget was substantially less than the Staff's request for 1,109,695,000 rubles or the 1,106,780,000 rubles the Financial-Planning Commission approved.[87] In two October meetings, the RZ STO set the outlines of the budget, stipulating that the total Red Army budget would amount to just under 1,000 million rubles. Furthermore, grants for capital investment in military industry would total an additional 160 million rubles. Gosplan and Vesenkha were left to determine the final details.[88]

In December, the RZ STO approved final budget figures for 1929–1930, two months after the fiscal year had already begun. The NKVM's budget would be 995 million rubles, and OGPU troops would receive an additional 66.85 million. Defense spending for transportation came to even more, 93 million rubles. Other people's commissariats and miscellaneous defense measures accounted for another 71 million rubles. Military industry alone would receive a grant of 128 million rubles for capital investment, amounting to a total defense budget of 1,354 million rubles. The import plan came to slightly over 104 million rubles, 62.8 million of which went for military industry (44.3 million for machinery and equipment, 18.5 million for materials). Although the military budget would not be all that the Red Army had wished for, 995 million for the NKVM was still a 17 percent increase (in nominal terms) over 1928–1929's 850 million. Even that 995 million rubles was later boosted to 1,046 million, for a 23 percent increase.[89]

The 128 million–ruble grant for military industry represented less than half its total projected investment. Within military industry proper, total investment would amount to 280.1 million rubles, of which 196 million would go directly to expanding production capacity. The remainder would build housing, expand production of consumer goods, or collect raw material stockpiles. Why, then, did the defense budget mention only 128 million rubles of investment? First, military investment stretched over five quarters, from 1 October 1929 to 1 January 1931, so the total grant to military industry would amount to 160 million rubles, with only 128 million awarded during the 1929–1930 fiscal year. This still, however, left a shortfall of 120.1 million rubles, for which industrial planners scrambled to find other sources. The defense budget specified only direct grants to military industry, and the remainder was military industry's to supply—a 20 million–ruble loan to fund housing construction and 100.1 million from "internal means," that is, profits from earlier production, miscellaneous loans, grants, and credits. In addition, civil industry had to spend 100 million rubles on investment in defense production and on mobilization stockpiles.[90]

The year that had opened with the approval of the First Five-Year Plan and continued with the Politburo's key decisions on defense fittingly closed with Stalin's fiftieth birthday celebration. This event coincided with the beginnings of total collectivization of the Soviet countryside and marked the start of Stalin's cult of personality. Hailed as "the Lenin of today," Stalin retroactively became a great military commander. Voroshilov's article "Stalin and the Red Army," later republished as a pamphlet, celebrated Stalin's civil war career, accentuating the positive and eliminating the negative to create a work of historical fiction.[91] Stalin's role in military policy had, through early 1929, been limited. Partly because his institutional responsibilities had not placed him in regular contact with military policy, and partly because he had his trusted lackey Voroshilov in place at the head of the Red Army, Stalin did not have much reason to intervene regularly in military and defense affairs, playing instead more of a balancing role. But with Rykov and the Right in general rapidly losing influence, the door opened for the military to expand its demands for resources, with Stalin's Politburo increasingly amenable to listening to those claims. Even though the Red Army might not have achieved all that it had hoped to from the budget approved at the end of 1929, given the promising hints signaled by the First Five-Year Plan and the Politburo's July decision, its resource problems were slowly being resolved. Over the next few years, the resources devoted to the military, Stalin's personal involvement in defense affairs, and the militarization of the Soviet economic system would all grow from these beginnings in the year of the great turn.

6

The Red Army Consolidates Its Victory

Over 1930 and 1931, with the West's economic crisis deepening, Stalin and the Soviet leadership could take no comfort in the travails of the capitalist world. It might seem that with the world economy on the verge of collapse, no Western power could spare the resources to join a new interventionist coalition, but this was not the conclusion the Soviets drew. Instead, the Great Depression only strengthened the Soviets' understanding of the outside world as rife with potential military threats. In their view, economic crisis intensified class struggle in the West, making foreign war to eliminate the world's lone socialist state increasingly attractive to harried political and economic elites. Lenin had argued in *Imperialism* that the struggle for resources among the capitalist states would lead to inter-imperialist wars. And though this was rarely stated openly, some Bolsheviks could not help thinking about the chance of revolutionary war upon the collapse of Western society. After all, the First World War had brought the Bolsheviks to power and shaken Western Europe. Concretely, the demands of industrialization made the Soviet Union temporarily more dependent on imported goods, and the fall in worldwide commodity prices cut Soviet revenues from grain and raw material exports. In 1930, France imposed trade sanctions on the Soviet Union in response to what it saw as Soviet "dumping" on world markets. Soviet oscillation between the eventual certainty of war and the imminent danger of war was shifting toward immediate danger, so increased attention to defense was the logical response.[1]

The Sixteenth Party Congress, meeting in Moscow from 26 June to 13 July 1930, came to precisely this conclusion. In the run-up to the congress, Konstantin Mekhonoshin, chair of Gosplan's Defense Sector, wrote in *Izvestiia* of the need to focus "the whole attention of industrial and planning agencies, party and trade-union agencies," on specialized metallurgy and precision machine building to improve military performance. S. I. Ventsov followed with an *Izvestiia* article the day the congress opened, complaining of the defense industry's lag behind general economic growth.[2] The congress itself found in the world outside

> further and strengthened disturbance of capitalism's partial stabilization, growth in the danger of new imperialist wars, worsening of the position of the working and laboring masses in the entire capitalist world, fascistization of bourgeois-democratic states and transformation of social democracy into a direct means of pressure on the working class.

This accompanied *"an intensification of the contradictions between the USSR and the surrounding capitalist world."* The implacable hostility of world capital toward the USSR, the congress concluded, would lead to "attempts to organize an economic blockade, a struggle against Soviet exports, a campaign by churchmen, a frenzied slanderous campaign in the bourgeois and social-democrat press, [and] strengthened preparations for war against the USSR."[3]

This view of the outside world coincided neatly with Stalin's need to continue his vilification of Bukharin, Rykov, and the rest of the defeated Right opposition. The congress's final resolution linked Bukharin with Western social democracy as advocates of the now clearly mistaken doctrine of "organized capitalism," Stalin's earlier support for those ideas notwithstanding. Not only was Bukharin espousing the cause of the kulak, but his views on the capitalist system were objectively wrong, for the world economic crisis had "shattered with all clarity the social-democratic theory of 'organized capitalism' taken up by the Right opportunists." By taking this social-democratic line, Bukharin and his cohorts acted as "open apologists for capitalist stabilization."[4] Regardless of the justice of these accusations, they clearly show that Stalin and the Soviet leadership were unwilling to abandon domestic and international confrontation in the face of global economic crisis.

This Bolshevik worldview, nicely fortified by Stalin's domestic political priorities, led directly to the conclusion that the world in depression was much more dangerous, and several policies logically followed. The Comintern, due to the perceived links between the Bukharinist Right and social democracy abroad, was to intensify its campaign against "social fascists," that is, foreign social-democratic parties. Domestically, the congress "underline[d] the full significance of Bolshevik tempos for the country's socialist industrialization to provide for the USSR's *economic independence,* strengthen the defense readiness of the proletarian state, and resist any attempts at intervention by international imperialism." The party, along with "the full strength of the working class and the poor and middle peasant mass," had to "strengthen the defense readiness of the USSR, the power and combat potential of the Red Army, Fleet and Air Force."[5] Economic crisis abroad would provide no breathing space for the Soviet state; the Great Depression turned scarce resources to even greater defense spending.

DEFENSE INDUSTRY IN TURMOIL

After the First Five-Year Plan was approved in April 1929 and the Politburo's July 1929 decree gave added impetus to rearmament, the next two years saw the Red Army consolidate the victory it had won and the priority it had achieved in economic policy. Its budget to support itself and cover industrial procurement increased steadily, and the technology it could rely on benefited from growing imports of Western weaponry triggered by the antiwrecking campaign. Industry, in contrast, was politically weakened and shaken by repeated reorganizations and the replacement of civilian personnel by former military officers in prominent management positions. Less able to resist military pressure, especially since Rykov's ability to restrain military spending was declining in direct proportion to his ebbing political influence, Vesenkha could not stave off the Red Army's growing peacetime demands and ambitious wartime mobilization plans.

At the end of 1929, a major reorganization disrupted Soviet military industry. Vesenkha as a whole underwent a substantial administrative shake-up, and the defense sector in particular attempted once again to resolve its perennial tension between the competing goals of producing military goods in peacetime and preparing for wartime mobilization. These reforms and reorganizations would ultimately connect the Red Army even more tightly to the Soviet industrial economy. The two chief bodies running military industry—the Mobilization-Planning Directorate (MPU) handling war preparation and mobilization, and the Main Military-Industrial Directorate (GVPU) administering production trusts and peacetime manufacture—had a tense enough relationship under normal circumstances. The GVPU worked much like any other directorate in Vesenkha devoted to more pacific aims: chemicals or nonferrous metallurgy or machine building. Its management tried to keep production assignments small and available capital and capacity large. Through its trusts—the Firearm–Machine Gun Trust, the Artillery-Arsenal Trust, the Cartridge-Fuse Trust, and the Military-Chemical Trust, together with Aviatrest handling military aviation—it was responsible for most of the USSR's peacetime military production.

The MPU was responsible for mobilizing all Soviet industry, not just military plants, and its focus was always on the war to come. Tension arose from the increasingly obvious importance of mobilizing civilian industry to wage war successfully. Why did military industry deserve its own directorate when the proper policy course was to rely on converting civilian industry to military use once war began? The very existence of the MPU was based on the realization that the entire economy had to be integrated into the Soviet war effort—it had, after all, once been a subsection of the VPU that had grown to overshadow its parent in significance and power. This widening consensus on the need to restructure the defense industry grew further in the wake of the Politburo's July 1929 defense decrees and the Red Army's own internal reforms. Moreover, the Soviet management toolbox had only a limited selection of instruments, so reorganization often seemed the only remedial measure available. War preparation had been divided between peacetime production and wartime mobilization since 1927; the only obvious alternative was uniting it again. What resulted was reorganization for its own sake.

On 5 December 1929, a Central Committee resolution "on the reorganization of the administration of industry" put the individual enterprise at the center of economic life, while significantly downgrading the role of the syndicates and directorates that had previously played such an important role in running the Soviet economy. Rabkrin, the Workers'-Peasants' Inspectorate, had pushed for this Central Committee decree, for it perceived that the elimination of regionally based directorates would destroy a possible base for localist sympathies and return power to the center. Now individual enterprises would be the center of *khozraschet,* strict cost accounting of profit and loss, and the trusts that grouped enterprises together would lose operational control and concentrate instead on "technical direction, rationalization, and reconstruction." New centralized associations *(ob"edineniia)* would take over the trusts' previous planning and supply functions. In essence, then, the reform was meant to decentralize operations down to the factories and centralize planning up to the associations. As Savitskii's summary of the reform emphatically told the Red Army's high command, the Central Committee decision did *not* touch upon military industry. An additional RZ STO decision would have to apply the general reform to the defense sector.[6]

Before the Central Committee's decree, Vesenkha had already begun exploring the reorganization of military industry. In early December 1929, a Vesenkha commission began work ostensibly on military industry's civil production, but it quickly expanded its mandate to more fundamental questions about organization. The commission's chair, Sharskov (GVPU), and its secretary, Rakhmanin (MPU), suggested reorganizing the GVPU into three trusts—an artillery trust with responsibility for artillery, firearms, cartridges, fuses, and shells; a military-chemical trust to cover powder, explosives, and poison gas; and an aviation trust. The artillery trust would have a cell inside it suitable for conversion during wartime into an independent trust for shell and ammunition production. Each of these projected trusts would include a strong, independent research and development center—a central point of Sharskov's and Rakhmanin's recommendations.[7]

At the end of December 1929, drawing on Sharskov's proposals, Valerian Kuibyshev bemoaned to the Central Committee his own Vesenkha's failure to handle military production properly and proposed a series of reforms. His explanation for industry's chronic underproduction, underutilization of capacity, and fictional mobilization plans had two parts: lazy leadership and poor organization. Not only did the work of the "weak and little-qualified mobilization apparatus" have a "bureaucratic character," but it was also plagued by the "noncorrespondence of the organization of defense work to the organization of military production's management," the old tension between mobilization planning and peacetime production. Kuibyshev pointed out that in wartime, the GVPU's military factories would account for only 28 percent of the Red Army's needs under mobilization plan S. The majority of munitions would come from civil factories. Since the First Five-Year Plan concentrated on developing civil industry, the relative weight of military factories in wartime production would drop even further over time. Kuibyshev argued that the very existence of the GVPU led to an inordinate focus on military industry at the expense of civil industry. Military factories earned the lion's share of attention in mobilization readiness, while civil industry's military production, despite its importance, was left "orphaned."[8]

Kuibyshev's recommendations, though fortified with clichéd appeals for greater vigilance by managers and more active worker participation, included a core of proposals intended to cut down the GVPU's power and the defense industry's importance by subordinating more defense production to civil control. By specializing military industry in "combat supply," namely, firearms, cartridges, artillery pieces, and fuses, Kuibyshev would strip away the Military-Chemical Trust *(Voenkhim)* and attach it to Vesenkha's Chemical Association, its civilian competitor for raw materials. Aviatrest would become independent, and military factories that had long since stopped producing munitions (Krasnogvardeets, Kiev arsenal, Moscow Droboliteinyi factory, and the Sestroretskii factory) would join civil industry. The remaining military factories would become an association *(ob"edinenie)* functioning under strict *khozraschet* cost accounting. Military affairs in Vesenkha would become the responsibility of a single center with a network extending throughout Soviet industry. Although Kuibyshev did not specify what that center would be, it seems evident that he had in mind the MPU.[9]

Gosplan's Gleb Krzhizhanovskii and Konstantin Mekhonoshin went even further than Kuibyshev in proposing the diffusion of military industry into the civil economy. They agreed with his proposal to separate Aviatrest and the Military-Chemical Trust from the GVPU, leaving a new association for military industry in its place. They rejected, however, any centralization of military affairs under the MPU. "Completely obsolete and incapable of carrying out the tasks before it," the MPU should be abolished. Reviving Dzerzhinskii's old concept of putting defense planning entirely under the control of civil authority, they proposed that overall coordination be assigned to Vesenkha's Planning-Technical Directorate, which would have a mobilization sector staffed by a "strong cadre of production engineers and economists, not only military workers, who on the whole make up the MPU." Preparation for mobilization, including the distribution of orders among factories, would be the responsibility of each individual association. Gosplan's Defense Sector was growing increasingly marginalized by the MPU's strength and influence over the defense economy, so Mekhonoshin in particular had every reason to want the MPU cut down to size.[10]

Dissolving the MPU altogether was too radical a step for the Politburo to approve, so it endorsed Kuibyshev's more moderate variant, strengthening the MPU. Both the Politburo's 15 January 1930 decision and the RZ STO's equivalent decree of 21 January reaffirmed a central role for the MPU. Without specifying that the MPU would have control over day-to-day production, both decrees gave the MPU jurisdiction over capital investment and construction as "an operational-planning organ in all defense branches of industry," along with its more traditional powers over war planning and mobilization preparation. As the MPU expanded, it was only a matter of time before the GVPU withered away.[11]

The GVPU did not last long. On 25 January 1930, the Politburo instructed Voroshilov and Kuibyshev to find a new structure for Vesenkha's mobilization work. Five days later, the RZ STO duly ordered that the GVPU be broken up within ten days, with its decision endorsed by the Politburo. The RZ STO closely followed Kuibyshev's recommendations for "demilitarizing" much of defense production by linking it tightly to civil industry. The Military-Chemical Trust was transferred to the All-Union Association of the Chemical Industry to "unite technical leadership of all military-chemical production, linking plans for military-chemical development with the development of the fundamental raw material base, and providing for maximal use of basic capital in peacetime." Soviet aviation had matured enough to split off from military industry and became an independent trust subordinated directly to Vesenkha's Presidium. The remaining "metal" trusts—the Firearm–Machine Gun, Artillery-Arsenal, and Cartridge-Fuse Trusts—became an association of military factories, working under *khozraschet*.[12]

This arrangement of three trusts in the new association was short-lived, for the factories controlled their own operations. The trusts themselves had become a largely superfluous intermediary between factory and association, adding a layer of bureaucracy without appreciably increasing efficiency. Of course, rendering the trusts superfluous had been a central aim of the December 1929 reform. One of the new association's three trusts, the Firearm–Machine Gun Trust, consisted essentially of three factories: the Tula and Izhevsk firearms factories and the Kovrov machine gun factory (later Instrument Factory 2). This was not enough to make an additional layer of bureaucracy useful. In March, Vesenkha therefore decided that "leaving the trusts in the structure of the Association as independent units . . . creates a narrow field of activity for the trusts." It suggested a revision of the earlier decision: eliminate the old trusts entirely and replace them with two associations: the Ordnance–Firearm–Machine Gun and Bullet-Fuse-Detonator Associations.[13]

If Kuibyshev had thought that moving sections of military industry to the civilian economy would improve his bargaining position in disputes over defense, he was sorely mistaken. One important constituency had been ignored in Vesenkha's continuing deliberations on reorganization: the Red Army. The Red Army's high command was quite perturbed at its exclusion. At the start of industrial reorganization in December 1929, Chief of Staff Boris Shaposhnikov joked to Voroshilov that relations between the Staff and military industry were "as hostile as that between Poland and Russia."[14] Armaments director Ieronim Uborevich complained to Voroshilov in March that "without getting into the essence of the reform," which he believed mistaken anyway, "I consider it completely impermissible to carry out this kind of reorganization without discussion in the Revvoensovet or the RZ STO." He got his wish, at least formally. At the end of March, the RZ STO *did* discuss reorganizing military industry, but it granted Vesenkha permission to implement the reorganization of three trusts into two associations, despite Uborevich's objections.[15]

Within a week, the Politburo confirmed the RZ STO's decision and the new associations' dual subordination: in most matters, to Vesenkha's Presidium, and in matters of mobilization, to the MPU. It also appointed Venetskii director of the new Bullet-Fuse-Detonator Association and Mikhail Uryvaev director of the new Ordnance–Firearm–Machine Gun Association, with Daniil Budniak as his deputy.[16] Postnikov temporarily maintained his position at the MPU, despite the upheaval around him, but his position was looking unsound. While criticizing the MPU's work on mobilization, the Politburo had instructed the Central Committee's secretariat to explore replacing the top management at the MPU. By February 1930, the now-repentant Trotskyite Ivan Smilga was Postnikov's deputy at the MPU. Iosif Unshlikht also moved from the Red Army to Vesenkha, seemingly without any reprimand or aspersion cast in his direction, to serve as Kuibyshev's deputy for military industry. His new assignment was coordinating peacetime production and mobilization readiness, and the Politburo approved his transfer on 30 May 1930.[17]

The Red Army's high command took advantage of the defense industry's temporary disruption with a startling though short-lived attempt to run military production itself and thereby avoid any need for interminable and frustrating negotiations with Vesenkha over military priorities. By cutting off military aviation from the rest of Soviet industry, Voroshilov naively hoped to be able to dictate its development. In July 1930, Voroshilov wrote to Stalin to ask approval for a military takeover of the Soviet aviation industry, which already had the Red Army as practically its sole customer. He specifically requested the transfer of the All-Union Association of the Aviation Industry (VAO) to Red Army control. Voroshilov offered Stalin two rather irrelevant arguments for moving the aviation industry to military authority. First, aviation was a separate branch of industry that could be easily removed from Vesenkha. Second, "all the air fleet (both military and civil) is united in NKVM; the transfer of the aviation industry will create a unified center of Soviet aviation in both production and use." The real essence of Voroshilov's argument lay elsewhere: the Soviet aviation industry was developing far too slowly and needed the "special order" that only permanent military control could give. Although this switch would disrupt the usual channels by which the aviation industry was supplied with high-quality metals, machine tools, and labor, Voroshilov saw this as an advantage. He reminded Stalin that the move would require Vesenkha to take special care to supply aviation's needs after its removal from Vesenkha's jurisdiction.[18]

On 20 July 1930, the Politburo approved the transfer of the Soviet aviation industry from Vesenkha to the NKVM, the People's Commissariat for Military and Naval Affairs, but it stipulated that "the foundation of military aviation must be a developed network of civil aviation." The VAO, a new association that had existed only since 13 February 1930, was now under military control. As was standard practice, the decision reached in a central party organ was confirmed and implemented via a branch of state authority; Sovnarkom repeated the same decision eight days later. Aviation's two chief research and design institutes, the Scientific Aviation-Motor Institute (NAMI) and the Central Aero-Hydrodynamic Institute (TsAGI), remained behind in Vesenkha.[19]

The VAO's new dual nature—part industry, part army—quickly created new tensions. Its revised charter, approved by the Revvoensovet, established that "all production enterprises of the USSR's aviation industry have been united" in order for the VAO to supply the Red Air Force and civil aviation. Although an integral part of the military, the VAO acted as an "independent economic unit on the basis of *khozraschet* in accord with NKVM's planned assignments."[20] Such a grafting of an entire industry onto the Red Army proved disastrous. The Red Army found that having a branch of military industry directly under its control solved no existing problems but created some new ones. Its high command soon decided that the whole experiment had been ill conceived, and on 15 February 1931, the Revvoensovet agreed to petition for the VAO to be removed from its purview and given back to Vesenkha. The Politburo quickly approved the request.[21]

FROM SOLDIER TO WORKER

This period, with the defense industry disrupted by internal reorganization produced by continuing military dissatisfaction with industrial performance, also marks the high point of large-scale employment of military manpower in the defense industry. Although the military served as a filter through which a substantial number of the Soviet Union's young men passed, it took surprisingly long for military industry to begin tapping this manpower for its labor needs. Mobilization expertise was another matter: Red Army officers were routinely assigned to the mobilization sections of trusts, factories, or people's commissariats. Graduates of military-technical academies were likewise assigned work as engineers and technicians within industry, but military attempts to fill the yawning deficit of skilled industrial workers were apparently rare during most of the 1920s.

Demobilizing soldiers into civilian industry, as well as more general military assistance to industrialization, finally became more commonplace by 1929 and 1930. It was not unknown before; as early as April 1921, the STO had ordered the discharge of 3,000 men from the Red Army to work in defense factories.[22] The Soviet industrialization drive's constantly expanding demand for labor strengthened the links between the military and the Soviet economy. Since many of the new Soviet working class were peasants, veterans' experience with discipline and the rudiments of technology made them stand out in their suitability for industrial employment. An army regiment worked on the railroad to Magnitogorsk in 1929, and nearly 1,000 veterans followed them in 1930.[23] One source claims that a single Red Army regiment sent hundreds of skilled technicians to Nadezhdinsk, Magnitogorsk, and other industrial cities in the Urals. The military supported industrialization through propaganda and ritual acts as well, including things as simple as joining ostensibly voluntary *subbotniki,* Saturdays devoted to community labor. Other military units subscribed to loans for industrial construction, engaged in socialist competitions with industrial plants and building sites, or collected scrap and surplus metal. One Soviet newspaper told of a Cheliabinsk rifle regiment that over a period of three months collected over twenty-five tons of ferrous and nearly twelve tons of nonferrous metal, many times overfulfilling its plan.[24]

The Red Army's central bureaucracy also detached its own technically skilled personnel to industry. In December 1929, the Military-Management Directorate alone had prepared a list of twenty-one engineers and technicians for release from the Red Army to industry. As Nikolai Kuibyshev told the director of the GVPU in March 1930, the Red Army had sent over 100 of its officers and men to military industry in December 1929 and January 1930. Unshlikht had been deputy people's commissar for military affairs before moving over to industry, but he was not alone. Officers as high-ranking as corps commander K. A. Neiman, who would later run the Soviet tank industry, left military careers to join industry.[25]

The Soviet tank industry was for all practical purposes nonexistent before 1927, and its struggle to cope with rapid expansion by recruiting new labor illustrates both how the Red Army sought to provide workers for industry and how industry could resist even helpful interference from the military. Tank factory managers, like all Soviet industrial managers, constantly complained of a shortage of skilled labor to excuse their failure to meet production targets. Innokentii Khalepskii, director of the UMM, the Red Army's Motorization and Mechanization Directorate, attempted to alleviate this shortage using discharged soldiers. Along with Bokis, head of his technical staff, Khalepskii suggested in August 1930 that military district commanders and armored, motorized, and railroad unit officers canvass their units for soldiers due for discharge and possessing some skill in mechanics or metalworking. The Ural district party committee similarly prepared veterans for industrial employment. Those soldiers would then obtain work at one of the Soviet Union's industrial giants: Bolshevik, Izhorsk works, Stalingrad tractor factory, Motovilikhinskii machine-building, Kharkov locomotive factory, and Moscow's Automobile Factory 2. These factories had in common their direct connection to the Soviet Union's nascent tank industry and were scheduled for either final tank production or (as in the case of Izhorsk) assembly of key components. Once the lists of volunteers had been compiled, they would be forwarded by the UMM to the factories concerned, although many units skipped this intermediate step and sent their lists directly to the factories, avoiding the UMM's mediation.[26]

Rank-and-file soldiers responded enthusiastically, and the UMM received a flood of responses. Not surprisingly, the opportunity for guaranteed work in one of the Soviet Union's urban centers (Bolshevik and Izhorsk in Leningrad, Automobile Factory 2 in Moscow) proved exceedingly attractive to soldiers who had gotten a taste of life outside their villages. The reactions of factory directors to this unrequested assistance were more mixed. Much to Khalepskii's chagrin, and to the soldiers' as well, industry was not as keen to hire Red Army veterans as they were to be hired. The management at some factories was indeed desperate to find new workers—the Kharkov locomotive factory placed orders for over 100 workers of varying specialties—but others were not so excited.[27]

Ivanov, director of Moscow's Automobile Factory 2, wrote in a fit of pique that he had never asked the Red Army for any assistance in recruiting workers. His factory had been inundated by a flood of petitions for work, and still worse, "people have been drifting in, referring to an order from the army, and insisting on being hired and provided with living quarters. This is to inform you that our factory does not need the workers you are sending, and does not arrange for apartments. We request that you stop sending workers to auto factory 2." At the UMM, Bokis was not outdone in indignation. He expressed his surprise that Ivanov was turning away skilled workers, given that Ivanov consistently relied on his shortage of skilled workers to explain continuing failures in tank production. Red Army veterans deserved better treatment, Bokis believed, and he asked that Ivanov at least assist them in finding work elsewhere. He declared that "in the future the UMM will absolutely not accept references to insufficiency of work force as a real reason for delays in filling orders." The UMM issued corresponding orders that no further discharged soldiers or petitions for work be sent to Automobile Factory 2.[28]

Even factory directors wishing to bring in new workers found their room to maneuver extremely limited; soldiers had to be turned away from the Kharkov plant, which had requested over 100 workers, simply because there was no place for them to live. Similar problems developed at Stalingrad and Izhorsk.[29] The military's well-intentioned efforts to meet labor demand could have only a limited effect in the absence of other necessary measures. As Stalin's industrialization inflated the need for workers faster than it provided the housing stock to shelter them, there was little individual factory managers could do except to hope for allocations of capital and materials sufficient to build apartments for the workers without whom they could not meet production targets. In rapidly growing Soviet cities, underdeveloped infrastructure could not support the new rush of migrants from the countryside. Ivanov's open hostility to Red Army veterans, however, stemmed from other sources: he likely did wish (as Bokis insinuated) to maintain a labor shortage as a ready-made excuse for production difficulties. And he probably wanted to defend his autonomy in hiring from outside interference, standing on principle even when he might have wished to find skilled workers.

On the other side, Khalepskii and Bokis probably had ulterior motives in sending veterans to military factories: to deny factory managers the excuse of insufficient labor. If this was the case, enterprising industrial managers did not take long to devise suitable counterarguments. In August 1930, Unshlikht, who only three months before had been haranguing industrial managers while serving in the Red Army, argued that it was the Red Army's fault that Leningrad's Red Putilovets factory could not complete an order for 76mm field guns. Tukhachevskii, then commander of the Leningrad Military District, had broken his promise to supply the factory with forty-five machinists from his troops and another seventy from Leningrad's naval garrison. Unshlikht concluded that "the Red Army had only itself to blame for the shortfall in the artillery program."[30]

BUDGET BATTLES RESUME

The Red Army's one setback in 1930 was a temporary rebuff to its constantly growing budget requests. On 1 March 1930, the RZ STO set the Soviet military's preliminary budget for the 1930–1931 fiscal year at 1,017 million rubles. As experience suggested, that would be only a starting point for further debate, and a particularly modest one at that. The first step in revising that projection upward was the Red Army's own estimate of its needs. In June, Voroshilov and his fellow officers in the Revvoensovet set their preliminary 1930–1931 budget at 1,906 million rubles for procurement and ongoing expenses, an 87 percent increase over the RZ STO's figure. They evidently felt that their opponent, Aleksei Rykov, though still in place as chair of the RZ STO, was in no position to hinder them. This preliminary figure could become final only after the RZ STO set cost reductions for ongoing production of military goods; the Revvoensovet modestly suggested 35 to 40 percent.[31]

The Revvoensovet had judged the political winds well. On 20 June, the RZ STO created a subcommittee to examine the Red Army's order program and obliged Vesenkha to ensure complete fulfillment of the order regardless of the final scale of the program. GVPU director Mikhail Uryvaev proposed a 20 percent cut in costs for continuing production, but the RZ STO rejected that decisively and stipulated instead a 30 to 35 percent cut from 1929–1930 costs "in both all associations of military industry and all associations of civilian industry."[32] Rykov, however, soon reasserted his opposition to high military spending. On 28 July, his budget subcommittee rejected the 965 million–ruble procurement portion of the overall military budget for 1930–1931. The NKVM's procurement spending was cut to 700 million rubles, but as partial compensation, Vesenkha had to cut prices on continuing production by 30 percent. Rykov gave two reasons for denying the Red Army the budget it had previously agreed on with industry: it had not exhausted the 625 million rubles (increased from an initial 477 million rubles) allotted for the previous year, and the 30 percent reduction in production costs would produce a significant budget windfall for the military.[33]

Rykov's lowered procurement budget was so horrifying to armaments director Uborevich that the Revvoensovet immediately appealed to the Politburo to override Rykov's decision and restore a higher budget. First, Uborevich argued, equipment that the Red Army had not purchased as intended the year before would have to be bought in 1930–1931. That implied increasing the procurement budget, not cutting it as Rykov had proposed. Second, although a 30 percent cost reduction was welcome, much of the NKVM's budget went for wholly new types of production to which cost reductions could not apply. Uborevich estimated that the savings would amount to only 5 percent of the overall procurement budget. In sum, making do on Rykov's budget would be "completely impossible." Since the "worthless" increase of 75 million rubles over the previous year would endanger both current production and the accumulation of mobilization stockpiles, Uborevich had to "categorically object."[34]

Rykov's budget commission relented slightly and permitted an additional 50 million rubles, funds that went directly to Red Army aviation. When the Red Army appealed for more, the RZ STO largely rejected the Revvoensovet's pleas on 30 July and granted only that slight increase from 700 to 750 million. The RZ STO ordered the Red Army to accept the assigned budget, maintain a cash reserve from that budget to provide for unforeseen expenses, and present a complete order program.[35] Even after the RZ STO's decision, Uborevich continued to protest that this budget would put the Red Army in an extremely difficult position. The extra 50 million rubles might salvage the aviation budget, but the light tank program would have to be cut nearly in half, from 665 to 338 tanks. The medium tank order would drop from 300 to 200 tanks, and the artillery order would fall by almost a quarter, from 1,294 to 975 pieces. Uborevich's protests earned him nothing. On 10 August, the RZ STO reconfirmed 750 million rubles in new orders for 1930–1931, specifying the Red Army's cash reserve as 25 million rubles. The Red Army's only comfort was that Uborevich could serve on a commission to establish final prices for military equipment to incorporate the 30 percent discount in continuing production.[36]

On 13 August 1930, the same day that Smilga complained to Uborevich that he was still waiting for the military's order plan, the Revvoensovet finally approved its 1930–1931 order list. This new order, despite the RZ STO's repeated insistence on a budget of 750 million rubles, totaled instead 793 million rubles—43 million over budget, even without the mandatory cash reserve (see table 15). The Politburo itself was finally forced to step in a month later to arbitrate the dispute, rebuffing the Revvoensovet and settling on the RZ STO's 750 million–ruble procurement budget for 1930–1931.[37]

Bukharin, Rykov, and the Bolshevik Right had been defeated. How could Rykov's RZ STO now reject the Red Army's budget? It was Voroshilov's misfortune to test Rykov's resolve, and the Politburo's forbearance, in the midst of fiscal crisis. The temporary rebuff Voroshilov and the Revvoensovet received did not mark any turn back toward the Right: quite the opposite. The sheer speed of

Table 15. Competing Procurement Budgets for 1930–1931 (million rubles)

Entity	Original Red Army Request	Rykov's Budget Commission	Revvoensovet 13 August 1930
Artillery Directorate	410.65	261.65	330
Motorization and Mechanization Dir.	107.87	68.87	84.8
Air force	150	145 (originally 95)	145
Other	287.48	274.48	233.2
All procurement	956	750 (originally 700)	793

industrial expansion and investment played havoc with Soviet finance, creating an inflationary crisis in the summer of 1930 as new rubles streamed from Soviet printing presses. Metallic money, hoarded as a store of value, disappeared from circulation. With the economy overheating, it was a poor time for Voroshilov to push for bigger defense budgets. Still, this was not a permanent setback for the Red Army, and it was only a temporary reprieve for Rykov. Once the fiscal crisis eased in the fall of 1930, the Red Army would have a second chance to win the budget it wanted.[38]

The Red Army's second chance at improving its budget allotment came at the end of the 1929–1930 fiscal year with a shift in the Soviet official calendar. By a Politburo decree of 20 September 1930, from January 1931 onward, Soviet institutions would base their calculations on a fiscal year coinciding with the calendar year instead of the previous fiscal year running from 1 October through 30 September. To cover the gap in the shifting Soviet financial calendar, the period from October to December 1930 was made a "special quarter." This switch caught the Red Army's high command by surprise. As late as mid-September, the RZ STO and the Politburo itself were still approving budgets and orders for the military for the forthcoming 1930–1931 fiscal year.[39] At the end of September, all these calculations were thrown into disorder by the switch to a new fiscal year. Arguing that Lenin had established the October-to-September fiscal year to coincide with the agricultural cycle—an anachronism no longer necessary, given the USSR's socialized agriculture—the Politburo decreed a new 1 January–to–31 December fiscal year and ordered Sovnarkom to come up with an economic plan for the special quarter to run until 31 December 1930. The corresponding Sovnarkom and Ispolkom decree was published the same day. The best explanation for such a bizarre, sudden change in industrial policy seems to be that the quarter represented three months for industrial development to catch up after the summer's crisis.[40]

The RZ STO, meeting the same day as the Politburo's decree, had to scramble to redo its defense plans for the quarter and the year. It named a commission to examine budget projections and also demanded a new military procurement order by 26 September to be reconciled with financial limits by 27 September. All institutions that calculated special defense control figures were ordered to present new sets to Gosplan's Defense Sector by 25 September, which would compile and return them to the RZ STO by 29 September. With only ten days remaining until the start of the special quarter, the RZ STO unnecessarily added that delay was intolerable.[41] Because figuring a quarter was not much simpler than figuring a year, Soviet defense institutions had, in effect, ten days to rethink their yearly plans. This had its natural effect on ongoing projects: N. A. Efimov, directed by the Revvoensovet to work on specializing artillery factories, was forced to report to Uborevich and Smilga that his work had been unavoidably delayed by the need to redo the defense control figures. Unshlikht had ordered a halt to all studies on specialization until the new control figures were complete, and Efimov could not get MPU representatives to come to his meetings or to send him the necessary industrial data.[42]

The Red Army's high command did get something in return for its frantic efforts to redo defense plans and budgets: an opportunity to reverse the budget cuts Rykov had imposed. When the RZ STO met on 30 September, the last day of the fiscal year, it was able to approve a military procurement order for the special quarter of 242 million rubles. At an annualized rate of 968 million rubles, this would have exceeded the Revvoensovet's most aggressive requests for a 1930–1931 procurement budget, and it finally gave the Red Army something close to its ideal budget. With fiscal crisis easing, the RZ STO further loosened the budgetary restraints it had imposed: Vesenkha was ordered to lower its costs on new orders by 30 percent and on unfinished production from 1929–1930 by 10 percent. The next day, the RZ STO organized a commission with jurisdiction over outlays for the defense industry and its import plan. The Revvoensovet, seeing an opportunity in this change of heart, instructed all the Red Army's central directorates and provisioning directorates to press for "industry's complete liquidation of its debts to the People's Commissariat for Military and Naval Affairs."[43]

Making a virtue of necessity, Vesenkha and the RZ STO took advantage of the opportunity provided by the fevered preparation for the special quarter to call for greater attention to defense. The RZ STO ordered that all institutions, starting from 1931, include both quarterly and yearly defense goals and expenditures in their plans. Vesenkha, for its part, ordered that 1931 be "a decisive year in the strengthening and sharp expansion of the mobilization readiness of the USSR's entire economy." Striving to push its own personnel to greater efforts, Vesenkha ordered the MPU to distribute mobilization assignments and assemble a set of defense control figures by 20 October. It also told defense factories to make maximal use of their idle capacity, made the assembly of defense control figures shock work, and solicited worker and trade union participation. While the spirit was commendable, the results were limited. Exhortation to greater effort quickly reached a point of diminishing returns; factory directors had been urged to make better use of their idle capacity as many times as workers had been called on to exert greater efforts for defense preparedness. One more call to arms had little effect.[44]

On 5 October 1930, the RZ STO set figures for military industry's capital investment during the special quarter. General spending, including technical assistance, liquidation of debt, and mobilization stocks, amounted to 116.305 million rubles for military industry's three associations: Artillery–Firearm–Machine Gun, Cartridge-Fuse-Detonator, and Military-Chemical. An additional 37 million went to aviation. Of that overall 153.305 million, 108 million went to capital investment: 84 million for military industry, and 24 million for aviation. The RZ STO subcommission preparing the investment targets had proposed investment of 46.512 million rubles in civil industry's military production, but that was omitted from the final decision. Vesenkha received some assistance in its military burden; it had to find less of that investment—only 29 percent—from internal sources.[45]

Setting those investment targets did not end the allocation of funds for defense construction during the special quarter. On 11 December, the RZ STO assigned 6.1 million rubles for military-chemical production and 3 million for military aviation from Sovnarkom's reserve fund, all intended for capital investment over the special quarter. In accord with this, the STO gave a similar order to the People's Commissariat of Finance to grant an additional 7.1 million rubles for special-quarter investment in the defense industry.[46]

In addition to a generous budget in the special quarter, the Red Army could now produce a new 1931 budget to replace its outdated one for 1930–1931, this time with a calmer economic situation and Rykov's position at the RZ STO steadily eroding. On 26 October, the Revvoensovet sent the RZ STO its new budget target for 1931: 2,026.1 million rubles, slightly over half of which, 1,016.3 million, would be in industrial orders. The RZ STO requested reactions from Vesenkha and the People's Commissariat of Finance on the feasibility of such a budget.[47] Despite his years of service in the Red Army, Unshlikht had lost all solidarity with his old military companions and wholeheartedly defended Vesenkha's interests once he was transferred there to serve as Kuibyshev's deputy for military industry. He found the Red Army's proposed budget completely impossible for Vesenkha to bear. What he had received was in fact not an order for 1,016 million rubles but one totaling 1,085.6 million. At the prices established by a commission led by Pavlunovskii, Unshlikht argued, that order amounted instead to 1,118.1 million rubles. Expressed in 1929–1930 prices, that would come to approximately 1,400 million rubles, marking an increase of 790 million rubles over the actual 1929–1930 order of 610 million rubles. That is, industry was being asked to increase military production by 129 percent from one year to the next. Unshlikht asserted that Vesenkha could accept an order of no more than 1,057 million rubles (using Pavlunovskii's prices), but only under great strain.[48]

Unshlikht's plea for mercy was effective in winning some relief for Vesenkha. The Politburo appointed a commission to review the Red Army's request, and by November, the military's procurement order had been cut by a little over 10 percent, from 1,016 million to 890 million rubles. Artillery, firearms, and ammunition fell from 404 million to 338 million, tanks and automobiles from 92 million to 80 million, and aviation from 184 million to 173 million. Although this was smaller than the Red Army would have preferred, the 1931 order would at least, once complete, ensure that the army was fully equipped for deployment in the event of war.[49] The overall military budget likewise fell about 10 percent. Instead of the military's requested 2,026.1 million rubles, the budget came in at 1,810 million. This 10 percent cut should in no sense be seen as a defeat for the Red Army. Its final budget for 1931 was, after all, 82 percent higher in nominal terms than the 995 million–ruble initial budget for 1929–1930, and was even a 73 percent increase over the 1,046 million–ruble final budget for 1929–1930.[50]

NEW MOBILIZATION PLANS

At the same time that the military budget and the Red Army's yearly procurement were growing substantially, military planners boosted the size and scope of the mobilization plans that would govern what industry produced and what the military received in the event of war. Mobilization plan S gave way to S-30, which was in turn supplanted by "variant number 10." Each plan demanded more from Vesenkha and matched more closely what the Red Army saw as its just due for fighting the next war, especially since the Politburo's July 1929 decree had endorsed a new priority for defense. Rabkrin's auditors and inspectors played a vital role in pushing for more ambitious and comprehensive mobilization plans. Sergo Ordzhonikidze, head of Rabkrin, had set his sights on Vesenkha. Ivan Pavlunovskii, director of Rabkrin's Military-Naval Inspectorate, dutifully followed his patron's lead by ferreting out the waste and incompetence omnipresent in Vesenkha's mobilization planning. The result was further militarization of Vesenkha and the Soviet economy.

At the end of 1929, the Red Army, Rabkrin, and Vesenkha itself all joined in harshly criticizing Vesenkha's mobilization plan S. Postnikov at the MPU was among the first to denounce his own mobilization plan, hoping to preempt military criticism and set the terms of the debate over how to repair or replace it. He freely admitted that much of the production capacity on which plan S relied was theoretical at best, but he argued that by the spring of 1930, plan S would be fully functional. The successor to plan S, mobilization plan P, could not be complete by its 1 October 1930 deadline; it would require another six months before being ready by 1 April 1931. In the meantime, Postnikov suggested, Vesenkha could use an interim plan to cover the gap. This interim S-30 mobilization plan would improve on plan S by including newly built capacity, allowing the Red Army to take quick advantage of industrial expansion. Ironically, Postnikov's ostensibly temporary plan S-30 would become the central economic mobilization plan. Industrial capacity and military appetites were expanding too quickly, and plan P simply faded away.[51]

Despite Postnikov's enthusiasm for S-30, there was little in it to excite the Red Army. The yawning gap between the Red Army's wartime requirements and what Vesenkha planned to produce, whether under plan S or S-30, was as large as ever. Just as at the beginning of Soviet mobilization planning, Vesenkha maintained its commitment to treating the first six months of war as a transition period and starting the actual function of its mobilization plans only after a half year of combat. Even with eighteen months to produce a year's worth of military equipment, plans S and S-30 fell far short of the Red Army's demands. Plan S-30 improved rifle output to 1,120,000 from the 970,000 in plan S, but the Red Army's wartime order was 1,275,000. Critical output of ammunition not only came in far below military needs but also showed little improvement from plan S to S-30. Shell assignments held steady at 23 million versus the military requirement of 41 million. Cartridge production in the event of war went from 2,530 million to 2,800 million, but the Red Army would need 4,735 million. Plan S-30 would deliver 520 122mm howitzers and 870 76mm field guns and regimental artillery pieces, but the Red Army required 1,145 and 1,286, respectively.[52]

If Postnikov intended to preempt criticism, he failed miserably. The Red Army Staff and Rabkrin's Pavlunovskii both stepped in to pillory Postnikov's mismanagement of the MPU and to demand improvements. The Red Army Staff was particularly irritated by how the MPU moved the goalposts: each time a deadline approached that Postnikov feared he would not meet, he devised a new goal with a new deadline further in the future. After numerous promises in 1929 to fix plan S by ensuring adequate supplies of raw materials for its wartime program, Postnikov dropped that plan with an audible thud and promised instead that plan S-30 was the mobilization plan the Red Army had been waiting for. The Red Army could grudgingly agree that S-30 promised more output (with the notable exceptions of gas masks, poison gas, and explosives) and was more closely linked to actually existing production capacity. Nevertheless, the Red Army did not expect S-30 to be ready until October 1930 at the earliest, threatening the military's mobilization should war break out in the spring of 1930.[53] The Revvoensovet's official reaction to Postnikov's proposal in December 1929 was that "even the obsolete, minimal, and unsatisfactory mobilization plan S is unconditionally unrealistic." The Revvoensovet held that "just as one year ago, we do not have a mobilization plan." Since "in the event of war industry would have to mobilize itself spontaneously, without a plan," the Revvoensovet demanded that the RZ STO take timely measures to get a mobilization plan by spring 1930 and, in a veiled threat to Postnikov and the MPU, to determine who in particular should run war preparations to achieve that end.[54]

Postnikov's most vigorous critic was not the Red Army Staff but Pavlunovskii and Rabkrin's Military-Naval Inspectorate. Within a year, head of Rabkrin Sergo Ordzhonikidze would seize Vesenkha from Valerian Kuibyshev, and his subordinate, Pavlunovskii, would accompany Ordzhonikidze to take over military industry. In preparation for Ordzhonikidze's later move, Pavlunovskii made his assault with an eye toward discrediting Vesenkha's leadership, but he easily found irrefutable evidence to substantiate his claim that "Vesenkha's work on the assembly of a mobilization plan for wartime is to date an obvious, complete failure." The "two documents called mobilization plans [S and S-30]" showed few results from the hundreds of millions of rubles spent on military industry. Under plan S, Soviet industry would produce 10.5 million shells over the first twelve months of war; under plan S-30, 11 million. But in 1915, Russian industry had managed 11 million shells, and the antiquated Soviet plan A had promised 8 million to 10 million shells in 1926. Where, Pavlunovskii asked, were the fruits of the 600 million rubles invested in defense industry from 1925 to 1929?[55]

Stagnation was not the worst problem, Pavlunovskii argued. The devil of mobilization is in the details, and the MPU had let those details slide. Pavlunovskii found that factory after factory had wartime orders that came to only a fraction of what those factories could easily manage in peacetime. The projected time to switch factories from peace to war footing was little better than guesswork. The Red Army's Artillery Directorate had the task of assembling shell components into finished rounds, but the MPU had made no arrangements to deliver those components to Red Army warehouses. "In practice," Pavlunovskii found, "the MPU and the Artillery Directorate are cut off from each other by the Great Wall of China." Wartime rifle cartridge production needed to reach 4,000 million, but the USSR's supply of nickel and acceptable surrogates was good for only 1,000 million. Nitric acid, essential for explosives production, was entirely dependent on Chilean guano. Pavlunovskii blamed Postnikov and the MPU for the fact that "in the event of war . . . industry would have to mobilize chaotically, without plans." Postnikov had been at the MPU for three years without exercising leadership. "At best," Pavlunovskii wrote, "the MPU is a bureaucratic chancellery for mobilization paperwork. This chancellery directed its basic work towards receiving the military's orders and mechanically distributing those orders to the corresponding trusts." This, combined with the terrible state of relations with the Red Army's Artillery Directorate, made top-to-bottom reorganization of the MPU an absolute necessity.[56]

As a result of the Red Army's and Rabkrin's catalog of problems in mobilization planning, on 30 December, the RZ STO declared Vesenkha's work on preparing for war "completely unsatisfactory" and ordered "radical" measures to ensure the workability of plan S in the "shortest possible time."[57] The Red Army quickly seized this opening to take control of Postnikov's suggested plan S-30 and modify it decisively in the military's favor. Immediately after the new year, a group under Chief of Staff Boris Shaposhnikov met to review S-30 and expand its scope. Going through the plan's major categories, Shaposhnikov, along with Postnikov, Pavlunovskii, Martinovich, Ventsov, Efimov, and others—a near-complete gathering of the chief policy makers for military industry—found that in every case production targets could be increased. As an indicator of just how much authority the Red Army now had to dictate to industry, Shaposhnikov finally disposed of industry's old method of reckoning its wartime production after six months of war had already elapsed. Shaposhnikov's commission made all its decisions based on production from the first month of war.[58] Shaposhnikov had wasted no time before revising S-30; the Politburo took another two weeks to make its own pronouncements. Relying heavily on Rabkrin's attack on the MPU, the Politburo ordered the Central Committee's secretariat to explore firing the top people at the MPU. Echoing Rabkrin's lament over the 600 million rubles invested in military industry without result, the Politburo's decree repeated Pavlunovskii's complaints about the supply of nitric acid and saltpeter. Six days later the RZ STO issued a nearly identical decree that allowed Vesenkha only until 1 July 1930 to complete its mobilization plans.[59]

As soon as the Red Army seized Postnikov's interim plan S-30, despite its flaws, as the basis for industrial mobilization, that plan became increasingly irrelevant. The political balance of forces was shifting steadily toward the Red Army, which could get increasingly ambitious editions of its mobilization plans imposed on industry. Gradually disillusioned with Vesenkha's continuing excuses, the Red Army's high command became convinced that S-30, like its earlier cousins, was a mirage. If Vesenkha and the MPU were left to run their own mobilization, the military could never count on an accurate and reliable plan. In a subtle but significant shift, planning began to proceed less from industry's plans—what industry believed it could produce—and more from the military's own mobilization variants: numbers 8 and 10. This meant that economic war planning worked not from industry according to its ability, but to the Red Army according to its needs. The MPU would simply have to cope as best it could.

Chief of Staff Shaposhnikov made his dissatisfaction with the progress of S-30 known early on. By 2 March 1930, he was complaining that Vesenkha had shut out the Staff from developing the plan, and later in March, he noted that the MPU was still not close to meeting the Red Army's requirements, especially in artillery. Small-caliber artillery was particularly bad, and in general, there had been no effort to specialize artillery production among the various factories, leading to wasteful duplication of effort. Even within industry, the MPU and the GVPU could not agree on what artillery capacity their factories in fact had. The MPU, making mobilization plans, was significantly more optimistic than the GVPU, responsible for actually building the artillery pieces. To take one egregious example, whereas the GVPU expected that the Barrikady factory in Stalingrad could manage five 107mm artillery pieces over one year, the MPU expected forty 152mm and eighty 107mm guns. By the summer, Shaposhnikov found that the worst bottleneck in preparing the USSR for war was "working through economic mobilization questions."[60]

Anticipating as early as March 1930 that the MPU and Vesenkha would not be able to complete the production capacity required for S-30 as ordered, the RZ STO directed the Red Army, Vesenkha, and all economic people's commissariats to accelerate work on S-30 while starting on the *next* industrial mobilization plan, variant number 10, with an implicit completion date of 1 October 1930. The RZ STO's judgment that S-30 would be late turned out to be absolutely correct. On

20 July, the RZ STO ordered Vesenkha to present the already delayed S-30 and explain why the plan had not been completed by 1 July as stipulated. At its next meeting, perturbed at Vesenkha's inability to produce S-30, the RZ STO reaffirmed its commitment to making Vesenkha work toward achieving the Red Army's variant number 10—one based on maximal effort from industry.[61]

Still, until variant number 10 was complete, the Red Army had no alternative to Vesenkha's deeply flawed mobilization plans in the event of war. In September, Uborevich's deputy armaments director, Nikolai Efimov, tried to make the best of a bad situation by salvaging S-30 as a workable plan for spring 1931, but he found that it fell far short of the military's wartime needs. The production the MPU now projected of 18.7 million shells, 3,210 million bullets, and 1,080 76mm artillery pieces of all types, for example, compared unfavorably with the Red Army's wartime order of 50 million, 4,375 million, and 1,712, respectively. Efimov's mood was not helped by the fact that wartime production of rifles, shells, and field artillery was expected to come in significantly below that of 1916. Even the most rudimentary steps to rationalize production had not been taken: artillery plants had not specialized in particular types, shells produced in southern Russia had to travel to Moscow or Nizhny Novgorod to be armed, and chemical rounds produced in Leningrad had to be filled in Samara.[62]

The Revvoensovet, at the order of the RZ STO, explored in autumn 1930 ways of making S-30 a more serviceable plan or finding alternatives to it.[63] The results were disheartening. S-30's goals, let alone what it might achieve in practice, were significantly below military requests. Industry failed to meet those targets, so actual output under S-30 would be lower still. The latest projections showed that industry would produce, for example, only 77 percent of the 76mm guns the latest S-30 promised, and only 41 percent of the 3,054 small-caliber artillery pieces. Dependence on imported materials and machinery had grown, but even so, S-30 was supplied on paper with only 50 percent of the nonferrous metals it would require and a similar fraction of iron alloys, templates, and measuring implements. Even though capacity was in some cases quite high, that capacity was no better than the narrowest bottleneck at any point in the production stream.[64]

As a result of the "threatening situation" created by Vesenkha's mismanagement, the RZ STO ordered Vesenkha to complete S-30 by 1 February 1931 and to end the defense industry's dependence on imports. More importantly, the RZ STO took the fateful step in October 1930 of firmly endorsing the Red Army's variant number 10 as the basis for future mobilization planning, completing the move toward emphasizing the military's needs over industry's capacity to produce. The RZ STO conceded that Vesenkha would have some say in setting the precise details of variant number 10 and took into consideration Vesenkha's claim that variant number 10 would require 420 million rubles of investment.[65] This estimate proved low. Pavlunovskii met with Uborevich and Unshlikht in November to explore making variant number 10 the basis for economic war planning and found that the MPU now estimated that it would need 550 million rubles, not including expenditures on aviation, to meet it. Nitric acid output alone would have to triple from the current output of 60,000 tons to 185,000 to 190,000 tons.[66]

The strain required for Vesenkha to meet variant number 10 is evident from the briefest glance at its production targets. In July 1929, as part of its major defense decisions, the Politburo had set three- and five-year targets for wartime production of key military goods. S-30 was, at least in retrospect, seen as an intermediate step toward meeting the Politburo's three-year goal by the end of the 1930–1931 fiscal year. This is a fairly accurate characterization of S-30 when it is compared in general terms with the Politburo's July 1929 projections. Variant number 10, by contrast, was not only a significant advance beyond that three-year target set for 1930–1931, the third year of the Five-Year Plan, but in some cases it also substantially exceeded even the five-year targets set in 1929 for the end of the Five-Year Plan, particularly in tank production. Variant number 10 fell short of the Politburo's five-year targets most significantly in shells, but even that was partly by design. The Red Army Staff expected that growing tank strength and airpower would take over some of artillery's tactical roles, reducing the demand for shells (see table 16).[67]

The Red Army's decisive victory in getting the ambitious variant number 10 accepted as the basic plan for industrial mobilization in the event of war showed just how much the political atmosphere in the Soviet Union had changed. The fiscal restraint of 1927 and 1928 was rapidly fading, and the Red Army could anticipate a freer hand in dictating terms to Vesenkha. This victory, however, proved at least in part to be an empty one. As the next chapter discusses, Red Army officers found themselves frustrated for reasons they could not fully understand. The natural consequences of the Soviet economic system discouraged industrial managers from

Table 16. The Evolution of Industrial Mobilization Plans

Equipment	Plan S-30	"Corrected" Plan S-30	Politburo Three-Year Goal for 1930–1931	Variant Number 10 for Spring 1932	Politburo Five-Year Target for 1932–1933
Bullets (million)	3,000	2,887	5,000	5,500–5,725	6,000
Rifles	942,000	1,067,000		1,575,000	
Shells (million)	19–23.3		45	36.5–46	84.3
Machine guns	53,500	81,900	62,500	90,600–102,500	74,000
76mm artillery	1,075–2,100	1,156	2,100	1,400–2,225	2,064
122mm howitzer	520–760	600	760	1,880	1,289
152mm howitzer	190		190	800	500
107mm guns	200		200	300	260
Heavy artillery	138	197	138	300	228
Light artillery	1,201	2,725		7,840–8,700	
Tanks	1,000	1,239	1,055	2,500–20,000	1,500
Aircraft	4,596	4,596	4,360	7,098	6,865
Air motors	3,025	4,600	4,848	9,400–9,460	8,010

attempting innovative methods of production. Outward conformity to norms of managerial behavior imposed by fear of arrest or demotion was matched by an equally strong, hidden thirst to avoid or circumvent the burdens of preparing for war. The campaign against wreckers now displayed its most pernicious consequences. Industrial managers found that what they needed to do to keep their jobs—namely, meet the production plan at all costs—had little to do with the Red Army's preoccupation with successfully mobilizing or introducing new technology. The Red Army's high command had won copious mobilization plans from the RZ STO and Vesenkha, but they would do little good unless factory officials on the ground spent the time, money, and effort necessary to implement them.

7

Industrial Failure and Military Frustration

Over the two years between the Politburo's July 1929 defense decrees and the autumn 1931 Manchurian crisis, Soviet policy steadily moved toward higher military spending, more ambitious mobilization plans, and a greater role for the Red Army in determining economic policy. This shift, endorsed in the public pronouncements of Stalin and other Bolshevik leaders, manifested itself through the Politburo and the RZ STO's decrees, as well as in the endless meetings at which military and industrial representatives sat down to thrash out questions of investment and procurement. These conscious and intentional changes in policy were, however, supported and accelerated by more subtle systemic consequences of Soviet political and economic structures. Although not intended by anyone to speed rearmament, these structural features of the Soviet state and society produced precisely that result. This study has already argued that Stalinism's constant search for villains and scapegoats created innumerable opportunities for the Red Army to seize the initiative and push for more radical militarization of the Soviet economy. By 1930, moreover, a new setup for defense decision making removed moderating voices from debates over military spending. Voroshilov, Shaposhnikov, Tukhachevskii, Uborevich, and the rest of the Red Army's high command grew increasingly frustrated by Vesenkha's constant failures and evasions in defense policy. They had in Stalin understanding and supportive political leadership as they were driven to increasingly radical solutions to the problems of rearmament.

STALIN TAKES OVER

The continuing decline of the Bolshevik Right had profound implications for defense policy. As Stalin continued his humiliation and vilification of Bukharin, Rykov, Tomskii, and other rightists, Rykov's moderating influence on defense

policy was increasingly weakened, creating a vacuum that Stalin and his associates occupied. Stalin's initial victories over the Right in 1928 and 1929 had not
cost Rykov his chairmanship of either the defense cabinet (the RZ STO) or the
Council of People's Commissars (Sovnarkom). Still, Rykov stayed in office only
on Stalin's sufferance, and his high formal rank grew increasingly ridiculous in
comparison to his political impotence. In 1929, Stalin was already complaining
to his henchman Viacheslav Molotov about Rykov's continuing to preside at
Politburo meetings, asking "why do you allow such a comedy?"[1] Rykov lingered
on at the RZ STO, the lamest of lame ducks, even after Bukharin was expelled
from the Politburo in November 1929. Such tension could not continue for long.
By the end of 1930, the Stalinization of Soviet defense policy making would be
complete, and Stalin's personal domination of defense matters cemented in place.

Before Rykov's final ouster, measures had been in preparation for some time
to discard him and reorganize the management of the Soviet Union's defenses. In
September 1930, Stalin told Molotov that if Rykov stayed, limited as his power was,
this would produce "a break between soviet [state] and party leadership." As a result,
Stalin continued, Rykov was on his way out, and "you'll have to replace Rykov as
chair of Sovnarkom and the STO," with the chairmanship of the Soviet Union's
defense cabinet an unspoken corollary.[2] The necessary plans were in place no later
than mid-November 1930. At that time, when the RZ STO's new secretary, Nikolai
Kuibyshev, proposed reforms to make it more efficient, Voroshilov already knew
that the whole question would soon be decided. Kuibyshev suggested a preparatory
committee to ensure that all matters coming before the RZ STO had all the materials necessary for final decision, eliminating time-consuming and inefficient delays.
"I don't disagree," Voroshilov scribbled on Kuibyshev's proposal, but "we need to
wait until December. By that time the situation should clear up."[3]

Rykov's situation was cleared up by the Central Committee–Central Control
Commission's joint plenum of 17–21 December 1930, which appointed Molotov
to replace him as Sovnarkom chair. In conjunction with this, Molotov embarked
on a wholesale reorganization of the Soviet government. Rykov's RZ STO was
abolished and replaced by a new Defense Commission *(Komissiia oborony)*. This
Defense Commission, set up on 23 December 1930 by the Politburo and given
formal legal standing by a Sovnarkom proclamation the next day, was not merely
the RZ STO with rightists purged from its ranks. It was smaller and more streamlined and incorporated party, not just state, authority. The old RZ STO's functional
principle was maintained in part; four of the five original Defense Commission
members held seats by virtue of their important defense functions. Sergo Ordzhonikidze held a seat as chair of Vesenkha and later commissar of heavy industry.
He was joined by War Commissar Kliment Voroshilov, Gosplan chair Valerian
Kuibyshev, and new Sovnarkom chair Viacheslav Molotov. Those four offices
carried over from the RZ STO, but several people's commissariats lost their places
in the USSR's defense cabinet: Transportation, Finance, Trade, and the OGPU.[4]
In particular, the elimination of the people's commissar of finance from the Soviet

Union's defense cabinet marks a further step on the path to complete militarization. Such a step is a hallmark of total war, as it removes the most likely advocate of fiscal orthodoxy and restraint from the formation of policy. For the Soviet Union to take such an action in 1930 is a signal indication of the direction in which it was headed.[5] Unlike the old RZ STO and its predecessors, the Defense Commission was made up solely of faithful Stalinists. The addition of Lazar Kaganovich in June 1932 expanded the Defense Commission to six members and increased its identification with Stalin's inner circle.[6]

The most important member of the new Defense Commission was General Secretary Joseph Stalin, representing supreme party authority. For the first time, Stalin had a regular, statutory role in defense policy, rather than intervening through the Politburo to resolve disputes among his subordinates. When the RZ STO had run Soviet defense, Stalin and the Politburo had stepped in at key policy junctures or to make major personnel assignments. Still, Stalin was an outsider to the regular meetings that determined the important details of defense policy. Now he exercised control through the twice-monthly meetings of the Defense Commission, although he left the group's chairmanship to Molotov.

In his memoirs, G. K. Zhukov downplayed the significance of the Defense Commission, arguing that it "made preliminary studies and worked out the fundamental questions of principle on the construction of the armed forces and the development of the USSR's defense, passing them along to the Council of Labor and Defense [the STO] for examination and preparation in final legal form." He added that the Defense Commission and Revvoensovet had overlapping functions. This underestimates the Defense Commission's power. First of all, the Revvoensovet's mandate was limited to internal military matters. With Stalin's participation, the Defense Commission made all the most important policy decisions on national security, and the STO merely rubber-stamped decisions made higher up. Although the Defense Commission could issue orders in its own name, for purposes of secrecy, it would typically implement its decrees through other, more open bodies, such as the STO or Sovnarkom, or by the ex officio power of Defense Commission members such as Ordzhonikidze. For example, on 19 April 1932, the Defense Commission heard a report on plan fulfillment in the aircraft industry and acknowledged that work was on schedule, although quality-control problems needed to be addressed. A little less than a month later, the STO issued an identical decree taken almost verbatim from Defense Commission protocols. The only alterations made for greater precision in the decree's pronouncements.[7]

NEW MANAGEMENT IN SOVIET INDUSTRY

Stalin's new grip over defense policy was more effective than it otherwise would have been thanks to new, more competent management in Soviet heavy industry. Soviet rearmament received a substantial (though indirect) boost from the assault that Sergo Ordzhonikidze launched against Valerian Kuibyshev's (mis)management of Vesenkha in the summer of 1930. As head of Rabkrin, the Workers'-Peasants' Inspectorate, it was Ordzhonikidze's job to find impropriety, but the zeal with which he attacked Kuibyshev suggests that Ordzhonikidze had his eye on Kuibyshev's post. Speaking at the Sixteenth Party Congress in June, Ordzhonikidze lambasted Vesenkha (and, by implication, Kuibyshev) for allowing an immense nest of saboteurs to establish itself within Soviet industry. Ordzhonikidze mustered the confessions of imprisoned wreckers to implicate Vesenkha's management in lax practices at best and complicity in espionage at worst. Although Ordzhonikidze's report did not accuse Kuibyshev directly, the wreckers' confessions he produced named V. I. Mezhlauk and Iosif Kosior, Kuibyshev's two deputies, as prone to bad decisions and faulty use of technical specialists' counsel. Ordzhonikidze's attack was ironic justice: Kuibyshev had presided over the arrest and execution of innocent technicians and engineers, and now he was damned by the poor industrial performance that that campaign had produced.[8]

Kuibyshev spent the autumn of 1930 at Vesenkha waiting for the ax to fall. On 10 November 1930, the Politburo finally ordered him to surrender Vesenkha to Ordzhonikidze. Kuibyshev became deputy chair of Sovnarkom and chair of Gosplan. Gosplan's previous chair, Gleb Krzhizhanovskii, stepped down to run Gosplan's energy sector, ostensibly at his own request. Although Kuibyshev's Gosplan post was in principle not a demotion, he clearly had left Vesenkha under a cloud. He might have used Gosplan to take a central role in economic policy, but over the First Five-Year Plan, Gosplan had been steadily surrendering its influence over Soviet industrial development to Vesenkha.[9] Kuibyshev's personal inadequacies only hastened Gosplan's marginalization. He seems to have been an alcoholic, and Stalin's elite certainly found him unreliable. On one occasion when Stalin himself was away from Moscow, he was not pleased to hear that Molotov would be out of the capital for six weeks on vacation. "Is it really that difficult to understand," he wrote, "that you can't leave the Politburo and Sovnarkom *for long* in Kuibyshev's hands (he might start up drinking)."[10]

Kuibyshev was so lacking in managerial talent that Ordzhonikidze's takeover could certainly do nothing but good for the atmosphere within Vesenkha and the performance of Soviet industry. Without markets to resolve problems of resource allocation, the Soviet economy relied instead on intervention by bureaucratic authority. Ordzhonikidze's fiendish appetite for work and his ability to find and motivate capable subordinates allowed him to alleviate but not fully eliminate many of the chronic distribution problems the Soviet economy faced. Memoirs of Ordzhonikidze's term at Vesenkha and later at the People's Commissariat of Heavy Industry never fail to mention his prodigious capacity for working late into the night, calling factory directors personally to demand results or to order scarce construction materials shipped to a particularly vital project.[11] His enthusiasm was contagious; as one historian noted, Ordzhonikidze "owed much of his success as a Soviet leader to his ability to build morale and *esprit de corps* in institutions he headed."[12]

In addition to the simple advantage in competence that Soviet industry enjoyed under Ordzhonikidze as opposed to Kuibyshev, Ordzhonikidze also gradually toned down the campaign against bourgeois specialists. This took time; in late January and early February 1931, at an all-union conference of industrial managers, Ordzhonikidze delivered only a qualified endorsement of the work of bourgeois specialists. On 30 January, he told the delegates that "it would be wrong if we couldn't differentiate the honest specialists who work together with us from the good-for-nothings," but five days later he complained of "our wretched apparat . . . which contains to a significant degree an alien element. You know what a vile, traitorous role wrecking played in the life of our factories." This halfhearted approval of "honest" specialists gradually gave way to a more cooperative atmosphere.[13]

When Ordzhonikidze made his jump to Vesenkha, he brought along a cluster of his most trusted subordinates and protégés to staff important administrative slots in industry. Half of Vesenkha's sector heads in 1931 were former Rabkrin and Central Control Commission personnel, and eight of fifteen operations group directors moved with Ordzhonikidze from Rabkrin to Vesenkha. Of the eleven senior appointments Ordzhonikidze made upon taking office, eight were from Rabkrin and the Central Control Commission.[14] Even these figures underestimate the role of Rabkrin transferees in Vesenkha. They leave out Ivan Pavlunovskii, a former Cheka officer and director of Rabkrin's Military-Naval Inspectorate under Ordzhonikidze. Pavlunovskii took over military industry and stayed until the Great Purges. He had met and impressed Ordzhonikidze while serving as head of the Georgian GPU, and Ordzhonikidze brought him along when he moved to Rabkrin.[15]

Pavlunovskii's transfer from oversight over defense at Rabkrin's Military-Naval Inspectorate to a direct managerial role within military industry took place along with Ordzhonikidze's switch to Vesenkha at the end of 1930. In mid-July 1930, Postnikov and Uryvaev were removed from the MPU, the Mobilization-Planning Directorate, but it appears that Pavlunovskii and his associate, Martinovich, did not step in until November. In the interim, Ivan Smilga, the former Trotskyite,[16] took over the MPU. It appears that even before Ordzhonikidze's takeover of Vesenkha was imminent, Pavlunovskii was being considered for military industry. Although his career had been clearly linked to Ordzhonikidze's, it was Voroshilov who advanced his candidacy. Voroshilov may have been acting at Ordzhonikidze's suggestion or simply may have been impressed by Pavlunovskii's obvious skill at their common avocation: abusing and tormenting industrial managers. As director of Rabkrin's Military-Naval Inspectorate, Pavlunovskii had done much to win Voroshilov's approval. In a brief note to Stalin, Voroshilov suggested, "Let's put Pavlunovskii in Postnikov's place—it seems to me he'd be suitable." Stalin's dismissive reply—"I doubt he can handle it. It seems to me that he doesn't know industry"—suggests that Smilga, despite his Trotskyite past, was Stalin's preferred candidate.[17]

Ordzhonikidze's endorsement won out, and after Smilga's four months directing the MPU, Pavlunovskii was confirmed on 20 November as deputy chair of Vesenkha responsible for military industry. By January 1931, Martinovich, Pavlunovskii's former deputy at the Military-Naval Inspectorate, was running Vesenkha's renamed Mobilization-Planning Sector (MPS). The whole personnel shake-up took an ironic turn when Nikolai Kuibyshev ended his short stint as the RZ STO's secretary and replaced Pavlunovskii as head of Rabkrin's Military-Naval Inspectorate. His promotion came as a result of his older brother Valerian's dismissal from Vesenkha and the chain of personnel moves that it triggered.[18]

RED ARMY FRUSTRATION

While the twists and turns of Soviet high politics enabled constant growth in military orders, it was the everyday tensions between the Red Army and Soviet industry over peacetime production and war preparation that did the most to prepare the explosion in procurement that the Manchurian crisis would unleash. The rise in military orders for weapons and equipment, especially rapid in 1930 and 1931, had one major, unintended effect: a vicious circle of higher orders, larger production shortfalls, increasingly suspicious and demanding military officers, and still higher orders aimed at punishing industry. In the Red Army's view, the antiwrecking campaign in industry should have dramatically improved Vesenkha's performance, but quality and prompt delivery of military orders actually declined over time. It is quite obvious in retrospect that the arrest and execution of Vesenkha's most capable administrators and engineers disrupted production and made things worse, not better, for the Red Army. This, taken together with the rapidly growing demands on Vesenkha's military factories, produced both delays in delivery and a significant decline in quality. The Red Army's leadership certainly did not see the problem in this light; consequently, their increasing frustration would ultimately drive them toward more radical solutions to industry's problems.[19]

The newly created Armaments Directorate and its crusading director, Ieronim Uborevich, took up the Red Army's cause by pillorying industry in a comprehensive evaluation of quality control. Soon after his appointment in November 1929, Uborevich organized a coordinating meeting on 1 February 1930 to examine industrial performance over the 1928–1929 fiscal year and establish criteria for judging Vesenkha. First and foremost were production shortfalls. Second was quality of final production, measured by three indicators: the percentage of goods rejected outright as unacceptable *(brak),* goods below standards but still accepted by the military's inspectors, and goods accepted but later returned for repairs and correction. The final standard was cost-cutting in production. Further meetings established that the military fully intended to use unfilled orders *(nedodel)* as a tool to score points against industry. A 5 February meeting between military and industrial representatives showed sharp disagreements over what precisely constituted nonfulfillment of orders. For example, flare pistols had design changes instituted during production; could industry be held responsible for the resultant delays? The Red Army's Artillery Directorate insisted that the Degtiarev machine gun be considered behind schedule, since the Red Army had acquiesced only under duress to changes in production deadlines. Molodtsov of the GVPU, Vesenkha's Main Military-Industrial Directorate, held instead that the Artillery Directorate's agreement meant that the order could not be considered tardy. The Red Army's Armaments Directorate decided on a new system of reporting production delays that would allocate blame by dividing problems into four categories: (1) the producing trust was at fault; (2) industry was at fault, but not the trust placing the order (for example, as a result of not receiving necessary parts or raw materials); (3) the delay was beyond industry's control; (4) the military and industry were equally at fault.[20] Significantly, in the Armaments Directorate's scheme, there is no possibility that the Red Army could be held solely responsible for production delays.

The results of Uborevich's survey were disheartening. His report confirmed just what the Artillery Directorate's scheme for assigning blame suggested that it would find: 57.9 percent of all cases of nonfulfillment were the responsibility of the producing trust, and only 3.3 percent were entirely beyond industry's control. Blame was apportioned equally between the Red Army and industry in 33.2 percent of cases. Perhaps most disturbing for Uborevich was that nonfulfillment of production plans was growing in both absolute and relative terms, increasing from 8.1 percent to 11 percent of the total order from the 1927–1928 to the 1928–1929 fiscal year. To make matters even more dire, Uborevich found that nonfulfillment was in all cases worse in civilian industry, precisely the sector of the economy that the Red Army would rely on most heavily for ammunition production in the event of war. Quality problems were most apparent in new production, with 100 percent of the 37mm Hotchkiss tank guns spoiled in the forging process at the Motovilikhinskii machine-building factory. Even older, well-established types of production were not immune to serious defects: 19.8 percent of the Maxim machine guns accepted by the Red Army had to be returned for correction.[21]

The Revvoensovet could not let such drastic deterioration in quality and timeliness of production pass without protest. After purging wreckers and saboteurs from military industry, the Red Army expected that industrial performance would improve. When industrial performance in fact deteriorated, this did not trigger any reconsideration of the guilt of those purged; the Revvoensovet instead appealed to Vesenkha, the Politburo, and the Central Committee for redress. The situation was particularly alarming, in the Revvoensovet's view, since all indicators were getting worse, not better, with time.[22]

To make matters worse, Tukhachevskii, who had been banished from Moscow in 1928 to serve as commander of the Leningrad Military District, was stirring up trouble by constantly sending entreaties to military and political leaders in Moscow advocating radically increased military production. His 11 January 1930 memorandum argued that Soviet industry could attain yearly production of well over 100,000 tanks and aircraft. In March 1930, Tukhachevskii compared the Soviet

Union's economy to that of Germany in 1917, concluding that armaments production should be able to match that which Germany had achieved during World War I. That would mean wartime production, in Tukhachevskii's view, of 24,000 to 27,000 artillery pieces and over 100 million shells per year. In addition, the USSR should be able to manage, Tukhachevskii argued, 100,000 tanks and 122,500 aircraft in the first year of war. Stalin and Voroshilov (not without reason) dismissed these arguments as pure fantasy. They reprimanded Tukhachevskii for his temerity before the assembled high command of the Red Army and even banned him from discussing issues of defense production. Nevertheless, Tukhachevskii's suggestions planted the seed in the minds of his compatriots and friends, such as Shaposhnikov and Uborevich, that industry should be doing more for the Red Army than it had thus far done.[23]

Completion of military orders looked so bleak in spring 1930 that in March the RZ STO briefly considered putting some military factories—in particular, military aviation plants 26 and 29—on wartime standing, in effect mobilizing their workforce. The RZ STO backed away from such a drastic step, at least for the immediate future, instead ordering that some way be found to complete the production program without mobilization. Mikhail Uryvaev, along with the Commissariat of Foreign Trade, earned a "strict reprimand" from the RZ STO in April for "late delivery of specifications for imported machinery and equipment for military industry," for failing to follow orders and force the pace of defense imports, and for poor verification of the specifications for machinery that did get imported. As a result, even much of the imported machinery proved useless.[24]

Kuibyshev and Smilga could not simply let the military's complaints go unanswered. With revelations of wrecking in military industry a fresh and threatening memory, the leaders of Vesenkha and its MPU subsection, while conceding obvious shortcomings in defense work, defended their record and pointed at the Red Army's own contribution to slow production and poor quality. In a May 1930 reply to the RZ STO, the Revvoensovet, Rabkrin, and the People's Commissariat of Finance, Kuibyshev acknowledged a whole litany of sins blackening Vesenkha: poor quality, spoilage, slow mastery of new production, late delivery of supplies and materials, mismatched production of the components of complex production, untrained labor, and even the "excessive secrecy" earlier targeted by the antiwrecking campaign. Although Kuibyshev did not say this to the Politburo, the ills he described in military industry could as easily have been ascribed to the Soviet Union's entire industrial economy. Smilga, director of the MPU for only a few short months, told the Staff and the RZ STO the exact same thing. His list of factors explaining military industry's poor performance was so similar to Kuibyshev's list that he must have worked with Kuibyshev's report beside him.[25]

Although they acknowledged problems in the defense industry, Kuibyshev and Smilga did not wish to paint a picture of failure. First, they claimed that nonfulfillment for the 1929–1930 order had been cut to 5.6 percent by April 1930, making the problem less serious than Uborevich and the Armaments Directorate believed.

Introducing control bureaus in factories and individual shops had significantly reduced spoilage. Kuibyshev went on the offensive to shift the blame away from industry by accusing the military of chronically failing to settle on a firmly established, five-year order plan. As long as the Red Army refused to commit itself to a hard-and-fast schedule, preferring to retain the flexibility to respond to advances in technology and production capacity by altering its orders at will, Vesenkha could not prepare rationally for future needs. Furthermore, Kuibyshev charged, the Red Army persisted in changing both its order and designs already in production long after the year's manufacture had begun, requiring costly and time-consuming reorganization and retooling. The Red Army would irritatingly place orders without the models or designs necessary to produce them. Smilga, by contrast, had to concede that the picture was much brighter at military factories concentrating on defense orders than at the vast network of civilian factories with subsidiary military production. Artillery shells, for example, were decentralized at dozens of civilian plants, and there Smilga found that both manufacturing and quality control were significantly shakier. Spoilage reached 50 percent of production at the Dzerzhinskii factory and was in no case lower than 13 percent, a level achieved at Red Profintern.[26]

Over the summer of 1930, the Red Army's high command grew increasingly frustrated with industry's performance, despite Kuibyshev's and Smilga's attempts to explain away the problems. One episode concerning an artillery order was minor in its objective significance but clearly displayed the military's worsening irritation over industrial disputes. At the start of the 1929–1930 fiscal year, the Leningrad Machine-Building Trust was already 285 76mm regimental guns behind schedule. The Red Army wanted to set its 1929–1930 order at 635 pieces: 350 new guns, plus the 285 the factory owed it from the previous year. Vesenkha would only agree to 500: 215 new guns and the 285 the factory already owed. According to Kuibyshev, the Red Army's armaments director, Uborevich, had not objected to the smaller order in November 1929, granting Vesenkha an additional three months to produce the full order of 635. Responding on behalf of the Red Army, Unshlikht trumped Kuibyshev by invoking the RZ STO's 30 November 1929 decision requiring Vesenkha to complete the Red Army's orders "in full."[27]

Uborevich then appealed to the RZ STO in June 1930 for help in getting Vesenkha to complete the new order of 350 76mm guns, since Unshlikht's earlier letter and his own efforts had produced no results. Unshlikht, author of the Red Army's original dunning letter to Kuibyshev demanding full delivery, had in the meantime been transferred to military industry and now served as Kuibyshev's deputy for defense. In a striking turnaround, Unshlikht now denied that which he himself had demanded six months earlier, turning blame back on the Red Army. With a severe labor shortage, the Red Putilovets factory would be able to produce only 215, not 350, new artillery pieces. The fault lay not with the factory, however, but with Tukhachevskii, commander of the Leningrad Military District, who had failed to supply the factory with the 100 skilled machinists he had promised from the ranks of the Red Army.[28]

Uborevich was also disturbed by Vesenkha's preparation for wartime shell production. Posing a rhetorical question, he asked how production goals could be met under wartime conditions if industry could not even manage peacetime assignments. The Urals factory Parator, given a peacetime order of 55,000 fuses over eighteen months, managed to finish only 3,000. Its wartime assignment, however, was 1.9 million fuses. According to Uborevich, this was not an isolated case, but he had little to offer as a solution. He suggested only the usual Soviet litany of investigative commissions, greater vigilance and effort, expert meetings on boosting production, and greater Red Army influence over the defense industry.[29] Given the limited corrective measures at Uborevich's disposal, there was little hope of any further improvement.

The RZ STO became involved as well in August 1930 when, at the military's urging, it pronounced Vesenkha's research and development work with artillery "completely unsatisfactory." Concerned with modernizing the Red Army's old artillery park, the RZ STO wanted new types of artillery put into production more quickly. Ordering Vesenkha to plan the creation of additional design studios and workshops, it established special prize funds for design work, accelerated schedules for invention, and expanded the use of foreign technology. The RZ STO's increasing dissatisfaction with Vesenkha became even more evident when it weighed in decisively on Uborevich's and the Red Army's side in the ongoing dispute over the 1929–1930 artillery program. Ian Rudzutak's ruling on behalf of the RZ STO noted acidly that Vesenkha had never protested that the 1929–1930 artillery program was impossible to complete until August 1930— one month before the end of the fiscal year. On the vexed question of the 76mm artillery assignment, Rudzutak put all responsibility for resolving the dispute on Vesenkha.[30] Not only the Red Army but also the narrow circle of those who determined defense policy were losing patience with industry's continuing inability to meet its obligations.

In November 1930, Uborevich reopened the painful question of military industry's incapacity to produce quality goods on time, now with the support of the Armaments Directorate's technical staff. Reviewing the dynamics of the 1929–1930 fiscal year quarter by quarter, Uborevich found that the first quarter was dominated by wrecking. This wrecking, not excised by the secret police until December 1929, had involved "all of the most important types of artillery" and resulted in "the introduction of essential defects in prepared production," affecting bullets, machine guns, rifles, and artillery pieces. The second quarter was spent creating auditing commissions to uncover wrecking and correct any problems, resulting in improved quality in the third quarter. The "active participation" of military representatives, in Uborevich's view, sped the liquidation of wrecking. Despite these improvements, quality worsened considerably in the fourth quarter as a result of a push to complete the 1929–1930 production assignment and the dissolution of some auditing committees. An increasing proportion of production was returned to factories for repair.[31]

Going over wrecking cases, Uborevich saw a common denominator: use of substandard materials. As a result of tighter quality controls, especially over the metal that went into armaments, some improvement was already evident. For example, at one point, 40 percent of all machine guns had to be returned for retooling, and none precisely met specifications. By the time Uborevich reported, however, Vesenkha had improved its performance and introduced partially inter-changeable parts. Still, there was much Uborevich wanted to change. First, more precise specifications and tighter quality-control standards by the military's on-site inspectors, the *voenpredy,* would reduce returns for repair and correction. The Red Army could do that much to improve the situation, but real responsibility, in Uborevich's view, lay with industry. Directors and their workers did not pay sufficient attention to military orders, and as a result, production was poorly organized and slipshod. The consequences of wrecking were still not fully elimi-nated, and industrial trusts and associations had done little to standardize parts and materials. Workers were insufficiently trained, controls over pace and quality of production did not function, and factories did not do enough independent research and development, often lacking facilities for such work. Despite the elimination of wreckers, Uborevich concluded, there was still much to do. The Revvoensovet, disturbed by declining quality, fully endorsed Uborevich's con-clusions—once more, the Red Army saw industry's problems as a call for stricter discipline, not the inevitable result of just such draconian measures. The Rev-voensovet ordered Uborevich to formulate concrete proposals for delivery to Vesenkha.[32]

When Pavlunovskii and Martinovich took over military industry in the autumn of 1930, they began with a clean slate. Kuibyshev had suffered from the revelations of wrecking on his watch, and Smilga had had his opposition past to haunt him, but Pavlunovskii had Ordzhonikidze's backing and no skeletons in his closet. More to the point, industrial performance, at least in Pavlunovskii's view, was improving. In responding to military criticism of Vesenkha, Pavlunovskii asserted in January 1931 that the Red Army's orders for rifles, machine guns, artillery, and optical gear had all been satisfactorily filled. Even tank production—at least at the Bolshevik factory, if not at the Kharkov locomotive factory—was moving along nicely. When Pavlunovskii did concede problems, his explanation was stunning in its audacity, though quite obvious in retrospect. Turning to the continuing poor quality of shells, bombs, fuses, and explosives, Pavlunovskii simply argued that too large an order had come too quickly, that military demands were too great. Although that one factor could partly explain every delay, accident, and oversight in Soviet military industry, Pavlunovskii was one of the only industrial managers to advance such an argument. Since the real difficulty was trying to do too much too soon, rather than any real shortcoming in the organization or management of the defense industry, Pavlunovskii claimed that the situation was improving as factories slowly caught up with the Red Army's demands. During the special quarter, for example, order fulfillment had hit 85 percent.[33]

Despite Pavlunovskii's optimism, his honeymoon at military industry did not last long, and military criticism of Vesenkha soon resurfaced. Over the first half of 1931, production crises arose largely in newer types of production, but by late summer, the crisis grew more general. In July, the Red Army's new political director, Ian Gamarnik, found improvement in order completion, but there were glaring exceptions. In general, new or specialized production of any type fell far short of meeting the Red Army's expectations. Prototypes might be assembled relatively quickly by hand, but putting a particular design into mass production was much more complicated. Whereas standard-caliber artillery systems, in production since before World War I, were in decent shape, the state of newer, small-caliber artillery was "tense," and heavier artillery was hardly in production at all. Older firearms were leaving the factories on schedule, but tracers, chemical shells, and other specialized ammunition were not. The Revvoensovet explained that this was a result of poor cooperation among factories, slow acquisition of machinery and other materials, and poor mastery of production, rejecting Pavlunovskii's dangerous suggestion that the solution might be smaller military orders.[34] To the Red Army, Vesenkha's failings were the result of incompetent and inattentive management, not objective difficulties. Its high command could only draw the clear conclusion that industry should be capable of doing much more.

As the momentum of rearmament grew, Stalin and his Politburo rethought their objections to Mikhail Tukhachevskii's radicalism on the untapped potential of Soviet industry. Tukhachevskii replaced Uborevich as armaments director in June 1931. Despite Stalin's earlier ban on Tukhachevskii's discussing economic questions, Soviet policy had shifted far enough toward radical rearmament to allow Tukhachevskii's triumphant return to Moscow as the Red Army's supreme authority over industry.[35] He wasted no time in picking up where Uborevich had left off in attacking industry's poor performance. Echoing and extending Gamarnik's earlier complaints, Tukhachevskii reported to Molotov at the Defense Commission on a "threatening position" in July and August 1931, "characterized by worsening order fulfillment in an entire series of quite significant types of arms." In addition to Gamarnik's findings of poor coordination among factories and technical difficulties resulting from bad or nonexistent planning, Tukhachevskii found worse faults. He went beyond accusations of incompetence to accusations of active disregard for the importance of military orders, complaining that "fulfilling military orders is secondary to civil orders, which the press and social organizations follow and exert pressure for." Once again, though, Tukhachevskii had nothing to suggest other than some of that same pressure on Vesenkha to deal with defense orders.[36]

Tukhachevskii's and Gamarnik's protests did not go unanswered. In the wake of the Manchurian crisis, the STO formally gave its imprimatur to the military's interpretation of why industry could not produce sufficient arms. On 9 November, noting continuing problems with the Red Army's orders during 1931, it issued specific directives to resolve the problem and salvage the 1931 production program. Once again, however, the STO had no new solutions to offer. Whether the crisis arose in tanks or artillery, shells or cartridges, the STO could only order Vesenkha, the production associations, and individual factories to redouble their efforts. Directing the OGPU to investigate the theft of materials or creating another commission to verify quality control and the completion of contracts would have the same negligible effect on the actual difficulty confronting the defense industry: the Red Army wanted too much, too soon.[37]

The STO's remedial measures predictably resulted in no immediate results. Even after the Manchurian crisis, when the Red Army could clearly expect resources far beyond anything it had received in the past, Tukhachevskii still complained about military industry's poor showing. In January 1932, he reported that the Artillery Directorate had received less than three-quarters, 74 percent, of its 1931 order. This time, shortfalls affected even the simplest and best-established types of production: the Red Army got only 183,000 of 305,000 rifles it had ordered. Machine gun orders were in good shape, but artillery was a disaster. None of the new 37mm or 45mm tank guns had come in, along with only 80 of 250 152mm howitzers, and artillery factories had managed to carry out the modernization of only 350 of 963 older artillery pieces. The overall completion rate was a dismal 56 percent.[38]

Continuing problems hardly seem surprising, regardless of Vesenkha or Defense Commission efforts to resolve the situation. Directing scarce materials such as higher-quality steel to sectors in crisis (for example, small-caliber artillery shells) only sabotaged other production. Even directives from above on the allocation of materials were subverted by the constant struggle of factory directors to acquire materials for their own use regardless of overarching policy. Exhortation and intimidation both lost effectiveness with repetition, leaving the Red Army frustrated and willing to consider more drastic measures to ensure ample stocks of weaponry. When the Manchurian crisis presented an opportunity to put industry on something close to a full war footing, the Soviet military would be eager to seize that opportunity.

TESTING MOBILIZATION READINESS

As the Red Army's high command grew increasingly disgusted with Soviet industry's continuing inability to fill peacetime military orders promptly, the military's leadership also grew to doubt industry's ability to cope with wartime mobilization. In the case of peacetime orders and wartime mobilization alike, the causes of the Red Army's anxiety were not really within industry's control, and doubts reached new heights by the time of the Manchurian crisis. The Red Army's desire for more and better weaponry always remained greater than industry's ability to slake that thirst, so pique and irritation were the inevitable lot of the armaments director, whether Uborevich or Tukhachevskii. Similarly, the steps necessary to prepare fully for mobilization—stockpiling materials, machinery, designs, templates, and measuring instruments, or training factory workers in production techniques and skills they might never use—demanded enormous expenditures of time, money, and effort, three things the factory directors and Vesenkha's bureaucrats did not have to spare.

Red Army officers and military industrialists were driven to distraction by the task of merely determining how to measure and judge industry's preparation for war. They were even unsure what indicators could predict readiness for such an unpredictable and terribly disruptive event as war. This was no academic exercise—industry's preparedness was directly related to how much equipment the military would be forced to stockpile in peacetime, for the faster industry moved to full wartime production, the less equipment the Red Army would have to accumulate in advance. That is, the military would plan to mobilize its wartime army and expand it over the course of a few weeks from a cadre army of slightly over 600,000 men, together with territorial militias, to a fully mobilized force of nearly 100 divisions and over 3 million soldiers. All those soldiers had to be issued boots, uniforms, tents, cooking utensils, rifles, bullets, artillery pieces, shells, field telephones, and the vast agglomeration that makes up the equipment of modern war. It was one task to have all that equipment stockpiled and ready for the army at the outset of mobilization. It was another to maintain supply once fighting began.

From the first days of war, military equipment would be consumed in unimaginable quantities. Artillery pieces would be captured by the enemy, be destroyed by enemy fire, burst during firing, or simply break down from constant use. Soldiers would be killed, and their equipment might or might not be recovered to be used again. Regardless of the ordnance expended or lost at the front, new formations created during the war would also have to be fitted out with weapons and equipment. Ammunition requirements had grown steadily in the late nineteenth and early twentieth centuries—whereas in the 1870–1871 Franco-Prussian War the average Prussian field piece fired 200 rounds over five months, by 1914, the 1,000 rounds of ammunition per gun typical of Western armies were exhausted in six to eight weeks. By the end of World War I, Captain Harry S. Truman's artillery battery would fire 3,000 shells in four hours.[39] The Soviets studied the experience of World War I in great detail and constantly wrestled with the problem of ensuring that their armies would have boots to march in and rifles to shoot.

Based on data from World War I, corrected by newer visions of what the next war would be like, the Red Army carefully and painstakingly determined rates of loss for its equipment, varying by type. That is, a rifle carried by a foot soldier on an active part of the front could be expected to use a set amount of bullets each day. A rifle carried by a soldier in the rear or in a quiet sector of the front would use much less ammunition. The rifle itself was liable to undergo rough handling, and the soldier who carried it in an attack might not come back with his rifle, or might not come back at all. Light machine guns were easily carried forward in an attack and so were more likely to be lost or damaged. Medium and heavy machine guns, not so mobile and not so vulnerable to abuse, could be expected to last much longer. All this was expressed in percentages. For instance, the Staff's working assumption was that yearly loss rates for fighter aircraft in wartime would reach 300 percent, and for bombers and reconnaissance aircraft, 200 percent. The assumption for tank losses was 400 percent. As high as these rates might sound, they were in fact lower than those actually suffered by France and Britain during the First World War.[40]

From this, it could be calculated how much industry would have to produce to keep the field army in roughly the same state in which it started the war. If the Soviet army began the next war with 10,000 medium machine guns and projected a rate of loss of 100 percent, then over the first year of war, the military would require 10,000 more machine guns from existing stocks or factory production simply to keep pace, not counting the formation of new units. A further difficulty then arose: if it were quite clear how much industry would have to produce, and if Soviet industry had the theoretical capacity to meet all the military's demands in full, industry still would not be able to switch overnight to a war footing and full-scale military production. As Rykov told the Central Committee in November 1930, it could hardly take less than six months, and "the most important task for further preparing industrial mobilization is shortening the expansion time to liquidate this dangerous gap." Given unlimited resources, the Red Army might simply strive to have stockpiles large enough to last out any war, but Rykov felt that "it is particularly necessary to point out the impossibility of accumulating combat aircraft and tanks in peacetime, as a consequence of rapid technological development and rapid loss in wartime."[41] In addition to being prohibitively expensive, this practice would commit the Soviets to quickly obsolete models of weaponry. Since that option was impracticable, the Red Army had to know what to expect from industry. Five months of factory mobilization to full production meant smaller stockpiles and less expense; a year or more before full production meant a correspondingly higher burden on the army's budget. The Soviet army, like all armies of its day, had to balance the unlimited demands of industrialized warfare against the limited economic and political resources available. If the Red Army could figure out precisely how long industrial mobilization would take, its planning would be much more efficient.

The problem of predicting mobilization performance was hard enough at military factories, that is, plants that in peacetime largely produced military goods—the source, for example, of almost all the USSR's rifles and machine guns. Even under these relatively ideal circumstances of extensive experience with military production, it would still take several months after the outbreak of war to shift to fully mobilized function. Raw materials and parts would have to be gathered from suppliers while the railroads were otherwise occupied dispatching mobilized soldiers to the front. Millions of horses, trucks, and automobiles would be requisitioned in the first days of war, further complicating industry's task. The industrial workforce would have to be enlarged and additional shifts added when many of the men left for the front. Internal factory resources would have to be shifted from civilian to military production, which would mean rearranging the factory's internal space, retooling production processes, and retraining workers in new military production. The situation was worse at civil factories that produced military goods only in wartime. The Soviet Union's wartime production of shells, for example, would be dominated by civilian factories not previously oriented toward military production. In addition to problems of labor and raw materials common to all industry, these factories did not have skilled and experienced munitions workers and were often assigned wartime production they had *never* made before. Some factories were even instructed to switch production away from a fuse or shell they normally manufactured in peacetime to another fuse or shell for which they had no drawings, technical specifications, or trained workers.

Given the difficulties of industrial mobilization, it was vital for the army to know, first, precisely how long mobilization would take, and second, that it would take place as quickly as possible. The Red Army was thus fanatically interested in using any method to speed industrial mobilization and finding every bit of unseen production capacity to reduce the amount spent on mobilization stocks and save itself from the unhappy wartime experience of the tsarist army. Alan Milward characterized Soviet economic preparation for World War II as "jumbled and vacillating,"[42] but this was a result of the Great Purges that removed the most talented officers and administrators from the Red Army and Soviet industry. Until that point, Soviet thinking on the economic needs of war was quite sophisticated, partly as a result of the sad experience of World War I and a careful study of Western economies at war.

The disastrous defeats the tsarist army had experienced in 1915 resulted in part from a terrible shortage of armaments, especially shells. No one had expected the vast burdens that modern warfare would place on Russia's already inadequate production capacity. Russia's war ministry had no confidence in Russian industry's ability to produce modern war materials, but, ironically, it was the failure of British and American industry to meet Russian orders that made the shell shortage especially critical. As a result, stockpiles of arms and ammunition were soon drawn down or inadequate even for mobilization: at the end of 1914, Russia had 4.6 million rifles for 6.5 million soldiers. Norman Stone argued that "battles were not lost uniquely because of the shell-shortage, or even mainly because of it. . . . Certainly, shell was exaggerated as a feature of Russian defeats in the spring and summer of 1915." Furthermore, Britain and France had artillery superiority in the West equivalent to what Germany enjoyed in the East and still made no headway; the deciding factor was tactical skill, not ammunition.[43] Although Stone is undoubtedly correct that the Russian army had more problems than just a shortage of shells, this is beside the point for a discussion of interwar Soviet policy. Soviet officers, many of whom had served in 1915, certainly *believed* that the shell shortage had been crippling and insisted that the Soviet army not be put in a similar position. Unfortunately for the

Red Army, its interest in maximum speed of deployment, exhaustion of all possible production capacity, and the most economical development of industry ran directly counter to the interests of industrial bureaucrats and factory directors.

The military's preoccupation with the speed and effectiveness of industrial mobilization created a difficult problem of control.[44] How could the Red Army be certain that industry was prepared to meet the military's wartime demands when those in the best position to determine that—factory directors and other industrial managers—had better places to spend money than on preparing for mobilization? Directors had little incentive to expend scarce time, energy, and funds on training workers, buying machinery, and building stockpiles for wartime capacity that might never be used and had little bearing on whether they kept their jobs. Building housing for workers and accumulating slack capacity for ever-growing production assignments were much more immediate needs than providing for the peace of mind of Red Army Staff officers. This contradiction led to a series of measures by which the Red Army attempted to verify industry's preparedness, each of which proved that preparation was unsatisfactory and that industry could never master the switch from peace to war. As military influence over industrial policy increased and control mechanisms grew more and more elaborate but still could not guarantee acceptable levels of readiness, the alternative of simply keeping industry at or near a war footing all the time appeared increasingly attractive to the Red Army.

One of the first solutions to the problem of checking mobilization preparedness was assigning local factory agents to evaluate readiness. A December 1927 report on these "attached" observers found that of an estimated 600 industrial enterprises with mobilization assignments, seventy-four had attached agents, with twenty-eight reports submitted by the middle of December. Although Vesenkha and the Red Army held the work of these attached agents in high regard, there were some insoluble difficulties that made them at best a temporary means of evaluating war preparedness. They were best at checking stocks of equipment and raw materials. But because they were drawn from local personnel, they had an unfortunate tendency to go native and identify too closely with the institutions to which they were linked. In particular, they sympathized with the factory director on questions of cost-cutting and resource allocation, not with the distant military bureaucracy in Moscow. For example, whereas the Red Army planned on building cheap, temporary barracks housing for additional factory workers in wartime, attached observers advocated immediate increases in factories' housing budgets to house existing workers in peacetime. Vesenkha had to inform them that official policy was quite different. In general, these local observers, much like factory directors, pushed for more money, more machinery, and more attention. If the Red Army and Vesenkha were to guarantee mobilization readiness and keep their costs under control, they needed a different approach—one that was not so dependent on local agents susceptible to subversion by the people they were supposed to be supervising.[45]

The next solution, a typically Soviet one that avoided the dangers of localism, was to dispatch inspection commissions from Vesenkha itself to audit the mobilization readiness of the factories under its control. In February 1928, for example, a Vesenkha commission under Lukashev-Vadim from the Military-Industrial Section of Vesenkha's Chief Inspectorate produced a comprehensive report on the mobilization readiness of Leningrad factories. Both military factories such as Bolshevik and Mechanical Factory 7 and civil plants such as Red Dawn (formerly Erickson) and Kulakov (formerly Geisler) fell under the commission's jurisdiction. The inspectors looked at narrow issues of wartime production, such as stockpiles and the relationship of assignments to actual capacity, as well as broader concerns related to readiness, including transportation and evacuation schedules and defense against air and chemical attack—particularly important, given Leningrad's border location. Examining wartime production plans, the commission found a host of errors and oversights, a catalog of all that could go wrong with mobilization planning. The plans originally assigned to the factories (in mid-1926 for military factories, mid-1927 for civilian ones) had been intended only to reveal excess capacity, not to serve as actual operational plans. The effort required for paperwork alone brought other work to a standstill, as "factories are literally suffocated by the assembly of the various data." Bolshevik's assignment, originally issued on 22 May 1926, was changed on 26 August 1926, 27 May 1927, and 26 October 1927. Mechanical Factory 7 had received only three different plans but expected its fourth in the near future.[46]

Even worse than constant alterations in mobilization plans were the stubborn blunders and miscalculations those changes were ostensibly intended to eliminate. For example, the Morozov plant was assigned to deliver nearly 5,500 tons of particular types of powder and explosives that it had already taken out of production; resuming manufacture upon the outbreak of war would require a year and 1 million rubles. Factories routinely had spare capacity untapped by their assigned plans: Bolshevik's mobilization assignment included 3,000 pairs of binoculars, but even working only one shift a day, its yearly theoretical capacity was 4,800 pairs, and the factory was *already* producing 3,360 pairs a year. Even two years later, the same types of errors were uncovered: Factory 42 in Moscow had mobilization assignments for fuse and shell parts well below what it already produced in peacetime. This particular fault was abetted by factory managers' deliberately underestimating production capacity to make their lives easier. The Red Dawn plant, for example, estimated that in wartime it could produce only 3,012 field telephone components a month from an assignment of 5,133, but it was already producing 20,000 in peacetime. Assignments were poorly coordinated with factory stocks of plans and technical drawings, and different factories did not link their joint assignments. According to its mobilization assignment, in wartime, Bolshevik would produce trench periscope tubes for shipment to a factory that had no assignment to make finished periscopes.[47] Stockpiles looked no better. Three-quarters of what Factory 7 had accumulated was useless for wartime production. The

Avdeev factory had assembled a stockpile worth 48,369.33 rubles, but the need for the first year of war was over fifty times greater: 2,760,679.60 rubles. In short, Vesenkha's investigative commission found that no factory had sufficient stockpiles of scarce materials, in part because there was no set standard on what level of stockpiling would be sufficient.[48]

This situation was completely unacceptable to the examining commissioners. Attached to their final report was a truly impressive list of twenty-seven separate ways in which Leningrad plants and Vesenkha had prepared inadequately for mobilization. These ranged from slow distribution and confirmation of mobilization plans (number one) through excessive alterations in plans once set (number six) to factories' using mobilization assignments as means of getting additional cash and investment (number fifteen). The final policy recommendation boiled down to an appeal and a veiled threat to Vesenkha staff and factory management to take military work and war preparation more seriously.[49] Although this suggestion was not breathtaking in its originality, it led to two direct conclusions by the Red Army officers who read it. First and most obviously, industry had failed completely to prepare for mobilization. The second and more subtle conclusion was that the way in which the military checked and controlled industry's defense work was deeply flawed, and another method would have to be found.

Despite its artificiality, direct inspection remained an important method of verifying mobilization readiness. It was relatively inexpensive and nondisruptive, requiring only a few knowledgeable observers. The Red Army could draw on its *voenpredy,* quality-control inspectors attached to factories, to check preparedness and established its own inspection teams to match Vesenkha's. Perhaps responding to the disappointing results brought to light by Vesenkha's own inspectorate, later in 1928, Red Army Chief of Staff Boris Shaposhnikov turned to MPU director Postnikov to launch another inspection tour. To guarantee military predominance, Shaposhnikov wanted three of his military officers to accompany Postnikov's one representative. The factories Shaposhnikov suggested were not chosen to provide a random sample of Soviet factories; the list instead emphasized the most important military plants: Bolshevik, Red Putilovets, the Kazan powder and Samara fuse works, and the Kharkov locomotive factory.[50] Shaposhnikov was clearly no slouch at bureaucratic politics, but his understanding of military mobilization was naive, because the giant plants dedicated wholly or largely to military production were not the problem. The plants he mentioned were more likely to be prepared for war thanks to their constant military orders; it was the smaller factories producing military goods only in wartime that represented the greatest danger.

As late as 1931, when trial mobilizations seemed the new path to determining readiness, low-cost inspections continued to serve a valuable purpose. Voroshilov reported to Molotov on two separate large-scale inspections that showed, as usual, that industry was completely unready for war. The party committee of the Leningrad District had itself inspected ten factories, most of them not strictly military, and had found hidden capacity, maladroit distribution of mobilization assignments, and an untrained workforce. A special group from the Armaments Directorate was sent to a half dozen factories, evenly split between military and civilian, and found much the same thing.[51]

Over time, experience made it clear that trusts and factories could not be relied on to check their own mobilization readiness. Even when factory reports were combined with periodic inspections from the center and checks by local agents to verify compliance, factory directors found it in their interests to do little but to claim much, a fact that drove the Red Army Staff to distraction. In January 1930, the RZ STO tried to eliminate the worst abuses and regulate inspections by stipulating the exact makeup of inspection committees. Local industry would be inspected by representatives of local government, the local military command, and the responsible union republic people's commissariat. For all-union industry under Vesenkha, agents of both Vesenkha and the managing association would take responsibility.[52] In each case, the guiding principle was to have many different agencies represented to make willful concealment of problems as difficult as possible.

One problem was simply the suborning of visitors to the factories by enthusiastic hospitality, a phenomenon that undermined the reliability of both local inspectors and delegations from the center. In 1933, inveighing against a clearly long-standing practice, Pavlunovskii was horrified to find that

> at Factory #8 of the Artillery-Arsenal Association and at the Tula Armaments Factory a system was established of entertaining visiting representatives of the Association, the Commissariat of Heavy Industry, and the NKVM with meals, dinners, and drinking bouts on business trips, [creating] the danger that as a result the army might receive and [quality-control inspectors] might pass substandard production.

He accordingly ordered that no such events be permitted, that all separate facilities established for this purpose be eliminated, and that "the sale of spirits in factory cafeterias be stopped." Representatives visiting factories were henceforth to dine in the management and technical staff cafeterias. Ordzhonikidze echoed Pavlunovskii's outrage, declaring that "it has recently come to light that in several of military industry's factories the organization of banquets, parties, and dinners has been permitted at which not only over indulgence but all kinds of drunkenness and other disorders are allowed." He categorically ordered an end to all such "shameful behavior unbecoming workers of socialist industry." Party members were subject to expulsion for future offenses.[53]

As a result of inspection's obvious shortcomings, some new method of determining readiness had to be found. The traditional inspections of 1927 and 1928 gave way to more drastic measures. Postnikov met with Chief of Staff Shaposhnikov and his mobilization deputy, Efimov, in February 1929 to organize a new experiment. They agreed to conduct a mobilization drill of factories slated for wartime military production. As the current fiscal year was nearly half over, funds necessary to conduct the mobilization could not be assembled until the next budgetary year, but all agreed that some kind of trial run was absolutely necessary. Postnikov's MPU and the Staff would work out the final details for the drill, which was to include both civilian and military factories. The Revvoensovet approved this plan at the beginning of March, and work began on carrying out the mobilization.[54] That summer, the Politburo reaffirmed its commitment to this new method. In its important 15 July 1929 decree, the Politburo entrusted the RZ STO with periodic trial mobilizations.[55]

Nothing came of this, and the Revvoensovet grew increasingly frustrated with Postnikov's inactivity. Originally scheduled to report to the Revvoensovet on 23 November 1929, Postnikov postponed first once and then a second time on 13 December 1929, prompting the Revvoensovet to request RZ STO intervention to bring him into line. When Postnikov finally did speak, the military's high command was not happy with what he had to say. Its officers pronounced even the "obsolete, minimal, unsatisfactory" mobilization plan S as "completely unrealistic," for Soviet industry was not capable of producing what it promised. In the Red Army's view, Soviet industry had no mobilization plan worthy of the name, and the Revvoensovet requested "timely measures" from the RZ STO to correct the situation.[56]

The RZ STO obliged, and in a wide-ranging 15 January 1930 decree, it ordered Vesenkha to carry out a "testing and auditing" mobilization of some industrial enterprises. The next month, a year after the original decision to carry out such a drill, Vesenkha presented a plan for one to the RZ STO. This envisaged mobilizing three key enterprises (along with their suppliers): Verkhne-Turynskii to make shells, Separator to make explosives, and Sverdlov Factory 80 for chemical production. The three enterprises, with their twenty-two most important suppliers, were to continue the mobilization until they had produced one-twelfth of their basic wartime assignment. The RZ STO rejected this plan and told Vesenkha to expand it, increasing the number of participating enterprises to twenty with their most important suppliers. A central point of the drill was altered by redefining the term of the mobilization. Instead of mobilization over a fixed time span or mobilization until the full wartime production rate was reached, factories were to be mobilized until "output of the first models of production demanded from them by their mobilization assignment." This definition suggested that concern for economy took precedence over effective verification of mobilization readiness. The key to determining whether a factory was prepared for mobilization was not how long it took to produce a single shell or fuse, but how long it took to develop truly mass production. A single model could always be produced more or less by hand by skilled workers (in Soviet terms, by *kustarnyi* methods), but this had little relation to wartime conditions.[57]

The final plan was approved by the RZ STO on 10 March 1930. Over the year that had passed since the initial decision to run a trial mobilization, several changes had crept in. The RZ STO evidently believed that military factories producing munitions in peacetime could be assumed to be capable of mobilization without difficulty, and military factories were accordingly not included on the list of candidate factories. The list was dominated instead by large civilian factories scheduled to switch to fuses, shell casings, and finished shells in wartime. In addition to this core of a dozen factories, another forty to sixty were to mobilize "conditionally"; that is, to determine their own readiness for mobilization without actually mobilizing. How this improved on past efforts at self-regulation is unclear. Mobilized factories were to change over completely to wartime conditions and production assignments as soon as mobilization was announced, sometime in the fall of 1930.[58]

Next came meetings to settle procedures. On 29 March, representatives of Vesenkha's MPU met with trust and factory delegates to select factories and iron out problems. Some effort was put into devising a representative sample of plants, leaving out only those factories that produced significant amounts of war materiel in peacetime. The Machine-Building Associations of both the all-union Vesenkha and the Russian Republic's Vesenkha had several factories represented, as did the Steel Association. The Association of the Chemical Industry had five plants scheduled for mobilization, Ukraine's Vesenkha had another three. In all, twenty factories were to mobilize, and their most important suppliers were to mobilize the production they were to supply in wartime.[59]

The plan for the drill was duly passed to the Politburo, which approved most of it without reservation, although the RZ STO was instructed to delay the mobilization until at least September. The next day, the start date for the drill was set at 30 September.[60] Although military planning worked from the assumption that an attack on the Soviet Union would likely come in spring or summer, that period of relatively warm weather was construction season. In the constant race to catch up with the First Five-Year Plan, that time was far too valuable to be wasted on a drill mobilization. Once again, accuracy of measurement was sacrificed to economic exigency. Several problems of the original RZ STO formulation were corrected in working out the concrete plan. Recognizing the potential for information leaks, the MPU emphasized that all preparations were to be kept completely secret from participating factories until the precise moment came to announce mobilization. The list of thirty-two factories and suppliers was not chosen from the largest military plants but was skewed toward those items that the Russian government had conspicuously failed to produce in adequate amounts during World War I: artillery shells and their component shell casings, fuses, and explosive charges. The factories involved were to remain mobilized until they had produced one-twelfth of their one-year mobilization assignment (reinstating the earlier requirement) and carry on for at least one and a half months. Managers involved were also ordered to follow closely the effects of mobilization on the remaining civil production of their plants and on their sources of raw materials and intermediate goods.[61]

Over the summer of 1930, the date of the drill kept changing, and the list of factories was drastically cut in the interest of minimizing the disruption it would cause. In July, the RZ STO set the list of factories due for full mobilization as

Moscow Factory 42 (producing explosives), Slavsoda, Vysokogorsk mechanical factory (ammunition), and the First-of-May agricultural machinery plant (grenade components). Conditional mobilization, which the RZ STO had envisaged as a much larger group of plants carrying out only self-evaluations, was set for November and December. An MPU meeting set the drill's start date as 15 September 1930, with five days' notice for the associations and no advance notice for the factories themselves. Mobilization would last one or two months, varying with each factory. The MPU also added Moscow Kust, a consortium of seven smaller plants, to the mobilization list.[62]

By 20 September 1930, all was finally ready. The RZ STO set 22 September as the start date for Factory 42, Vysokogorsk, First-of-May, Slavsoda, and Moscow Kust. The Politburo approved the decision, and the drill began the next day.[63] The RZ STO notified Vesenkha on 21 September, and Vesenkha in turn fired off notification telegrams to the factories concerned at 6:00 P.M. that day, all of which were received within eighteen hours. Although notification went smoothly, Murphy's Law quickly took over, and matters swiftly deteriorated. Receipt of the ciphered telegrams was quick, but deciphering them sometimes took two days. Mobilization of the Dzerzhinskii factory took place four days after the entire management team had been fired, but expansion of production still seemed to run "very satisfactorily" initially. At other factories, the management, in Vesenkha's view, did not understand the concept of a "drill." One director announced to his factory that they were all in fact mobilizing for war. Another proclaimed that "world capital has declared war on the USSR." At the Slavsoda factory, foreign workers, unsure what to make of the drill, were "inert, inactive." That plant discharged all its workers liable to military service, instituted martial law, and invited the wives of its male workers to join its workforce. The First-of-May factory similarly told its draftees not to report for work. It was left to Vesenkha's local observers to explain that although the factory would be going on a war footing, there was in fact no war; two weeks after the start of mobilization, Smilga explained, "all of these mistakes (the martial law, dismissing the mobilized, inviting in workers' wives, and so on) are already corrected."[64] Factory management, despite Smilga's assessment, had in some ways a better grasp of the purpose of the drill than he did. Although it made little sense to proclaim global war to the factory's workforce, a real test of preparedness would indeed have to be run under wartime conditions of massive initial turnover in the workforce. Smilga sacrificed verisimilitude in the hope of producing better results.

When results came in, first as Smilga's ongoing reports and later as retrospective evaluations of limited successes and glaring failures, some conclusions were immediate and dramatic. Civilian factories could sooner or later come to terms with higher targets on items they normally produced for the military anyway, but introducing new lines of production proved excruciatingly difficult. The most immediate problem in introducing new goods was a lack of the necessary measuring implements: patterns, templates, gauges, calipers—everything Soviet machinists needed to ensure that the parts they made would fit as intended into the finished product. Although Soviet industry was already accustomed to wider tolerances than were typical in the West, there was a point at which no amount of hammering would make a fuse capable of triggering an explosive charge as intended. As a result of this and of workers who were not accustomed to making military goods, the proportion of output discarded as spoiled and unusable skyrocketed with the start of mobilization. Plan fulfillment, if that was in fact achieved, came basically from hidden capacity that factory directors had managed to conceal for just such an eventuality.[65]

Of all the factories involved in the drill, the Vysokogorsk factory probably delivered the best results. Mobilized for only fifty-two days, compared with well over two months for the other factories involved, the plant produced 10,045 of 10,400 107mm rounds and 1,398 of 1,860 122mm rounds in its assignment. Uborevich and the Armaments Directorate, however, could take absolutely no comfort from this as far as the general readiness of industry was concerned. For one, part of Vysokogorsk's assignment had been simply to produce as much as possible of the military goods included in its normal peacetime production; in another case, the plan had switched Vysokogorsk away from a type of shell already established in production.[66] Although Smilga accented the positive in his report on the factory, emphasizing the reduction in the time required to reach full war-time production, the Red Army could only have been disheartened to think that this was the best it could expect.[67]

Moscow's Factory 42 delivered an equally mixed performance. Early on, Smilga reported that manufacturing already established at the factory showed excellent results. The twenty-two-second fuse met its target of 180,000 units, and other assignments went almost as well. Ianson bitterly noted, however, that the wartime mobilization assignment was *lower* than what the factory normally produced in peacetime. With production lines *not* made in peacetime, the picture was much bleaker. For some types of fuses, the factory produced not a single fuse despite having orders in the thousands; other types were removed entirely from consideration six weeks into the drill, so poor were the initial results. Slavsoda's entire mobilization assignment was already in production in peacetime; the only requirement was to boost output. In all cases, however, the drill uncovered excess capacity, and the factory's management was characterized as allowing "criminal" inefficiency and disorder to such an extent that the trust's managers received an official reprimand.[68]

The only thing that saved the First-of-May agricultural machinery plant from having the worst performance of all the mobilized factories was that the Moscow Kust group did staggeringly badly. First-of-May, mobilized for two and a half months, produced just 8,436 of the 98,390 sets of hand grenade components it had been assigned. Final results were saved from being even worse by the establishment of something approaching mass production at the end of the mobilization period. At the start of the drill, First-of-May did not receive needed templates and measuring instruments from a Taganrog factory, resulting in large amounts of spoiled and useless production.[69]

Moscow Kust had the worst performance of all the plants included in the drill mobilization. Over seventy days of mobilization, despite having received earlier orders for a trial run, Moscow Kust made only 65 of the 35,000 5GT fuses[70] in its mobilization assignment. Ianson of the Red Army's Armaments Directorate found that, in addition to the problems common to all the mobilized factories, Moscow Kust suffered from factory leadership that tried to sabotage military production. Having a "passive relation to defense work," the directors "tended to use unsatisfactory production to show the unsuitability of their factories for military production."[71] The Russian Republic's Vesenkha was a bit more charitable, explaining poor performance as a result of shoddy preparation and disorganization, not active resistance. The chief factory of Moscow Kust had three directors during 1930, and the production machinery, tools, and raw materials supposed to be delivered before the start of the drill mobilization never arrived. The workforce was untrained and poorly allocated: of 2,664 workers obliged to serve in the military in wartime, 599 had received deferments for vital skills, but only 298 of those were used for military production.[72]

The Red Army, almost from the day the trial ended, accused Vesenkha of disorganization and obstructionism in presenting final results, demanding a full report by the first half of January 1931.[73] The military, once it had finally wheedled data from Vesenkha, wasted no time in assailing industry for poor performance. In addition to the standard charges of incompetence and disorganization, two representatives complained that the mobilization had not cast its net wide enough. Isaev and Sadlutskii, from the Armaments Directorate and its technical staff, felt compelled to point out that *no* enterprise among those mobilized had met its planned targets on time, an assertion that Voroshilov also included in a draft letter to Molotov. Other people's commissariats were not involved, making no effort to test their own readiness simultaneously with the industrial drill, and even the direct suppliers of the mobilized enterprises could not achieve wartime tempos.[74] Chief of Staff Egorov continued to bait Vesenkha in June 1931, nine months after the drill. Complaining that nothing had been learned from previous mistakes, he told Voroshilov that "Vesenkha has unfortunately not brought out the results of this trial mobilization, has not presented any report on it for the Defense Commission's examination, and in practice its mobilization work has not utilized the conclusions derived from the instructive trial mobilization."[75]

More fundamentally, the military felt that the mobilization drill exposed a basic misconception in mobilization plans: that civilian enterprises could begin production of military goods that they did not produce in peacetime without undue difficulty. In retrospect, this seems hardly shocking—Soviet industry during the First Five-Year Plan lacked everything needed for quick transitions. An ample stock of modern machine tools and, more importantly, the people to employ them were sorely lacking. Without effective managers, a large pool of engineers and technicians, and a high average level of skill among the workforce, industrial mobilization would take a great deal of time, more time than the military was willing to accept. The technical staff and the Armaments Directorate jointly concluded that "even cadre military factories . . . are not in a position to quickly meet the demands of the front." More seriously, *"factories which have not mastered production in peacetime are in no condition to fulfill the deployment schedule according to the mobilization plan."*[76] Egorov, almost certainly basing his opinion on this report, pointed to "weak mastery of the production process" as a primary cause of the industrial mobilization's failure, especially as mobilization assignments did not correspond to peacetime production. Some factories even switched from one type of shell to another upon the call to mobilize. Egorov concluded that Vesenkha and its rechristened Mobilization-Planning Sector needed to fundamentally rethink how they prepared for war.[77] Last, and possibly most maddening for Egorov, who had himself served briefly in military industry in the early years of expansion, was not that industry was mistaken in its conception of mobilization, but that it was doing nothing to correct the situation. "To a significant degree," Egorov wrote:

> this shortfall in industry's preparation for mobilization flows from the fact that the mobilization organs of the trusts, association, and finally of the Mobilization-Planning Sector of Vesenkha only lead in allocating mobilization assignments and assembling mobilization plans—almost no one does anything to carry out production-technical leadership with the factories.

The sole solution, in Egorov's view, was to have Soviet factories do the drill mobilization again in fall 1931 until they got it right.[78]

By August 1931, the Revvoensovet had heard enough and accepted Chief of Staff Egorov's recommendation to repeat the trial mobilization as soon as possible, preferably in the autumn.[79] This drill never took place, preempted instead by the Manchurian crisis. The underlying difficulty remained: factories were inherently unprepared for wartime production that was not included in their normal peacetime production demands. The problem was not resolved by improved assignments or better preparation. Instead, in a dangerous international environment, with political constraints on rapid military expansion removed, growing military dissatisfaction with both industry's yearly production and its preparation for war laid the groundwork for a radical alternative: putting the military economy on a level close to wartime mobilization even in peacetime. If the problem lay in switching from peace to war, why not keep the economy on a permanent war footing? The coming of the Manchurian crisis in fall 1931 created just such an opportunity. The Soviets chose the alternative of a militarized economy— a vastly increased production program that was not quite a full wartime mobilization, but very like it. Tank and aircraft production targets doubled and tripled literally overnight. Although it took the threat of war with Japan to trigger that change, all the conditions were in place by late 1931. Military officers had been driven to radical solutions to their problems, and a new and more effective generation of leadership in industry made it possible to implement such a solution. When a crisis finally arrived to make full mobilization feasible, the Red Army's high command was ready.

8

The Manchurian Crisis

From the Politburo decision of July 1929 through the end of 1931, the Soviet military budget grew steadily in accord with the new priority defense had assumed. All that time, as discussed earlier, pressures for still more radical increases in defense spending and arms procurement had been building within the Soviet system. One precipitating event, the Japanese invasion and conquest of Manchuria, catalyzed these twin forces for militarization into a massive mobilization of the defense industry and the production of vast amounts of military hardware. The Soviet defense economy went to a near-war footing, dramatically increasing its production targets for military equipment, especially tanks and aircraft. Although military industry proved incapable of expanding at the rate the Politburo and Defense Commission demanded, the resources thrown into military production managed to achieve a major acceleration in the manufacture of weaponry. Civilian factories turned to military production, disrupting the Soviet economy while furthering the military's dominance of economic policy. Soviet military production never dropped to more restrained levels after the Manchurian crisis, remaining at a plateau of half war, half peace that the Soviet economy would maintain until the final buildup leading into World War II.

On the night of 18 September 1931, a bomb mysteriously exploded along the tracks of the South Manchuria Railway near Mukden. The bombing triggered a carefully prepared plan for the rapid occupation of all of Manchuria by Japan's Kwantung Army. A cabal of officers had long plotted to provoke a crisis in Sino-Japanese relations and easily carried out their scheme against halfhearted and ineffective attempts from Tokyo to discipline them and bring the Kwantung Army under control. Although the civilian government in Japan had not given its approval to the Kwantung Army's adventurism, Moscow had no way of knowing this. Stalin and the Politburo could not be sure whether the occupation was a prelude to further moves against the USSR in the Far East, but they feared further Japanese aggression, and the event was at the very least a clear demonstration of the inability of Japanese civilian authority to control the military.[1]

Taken by surprise, the Soviet government desperately temporized in the immediate aftermath of the incident and tried to determine exactly what was going on in Manchuria before committing itself to a response. The day after fighting began, Deputy Commissar of Foreign Affairs Lev Karakhan[2] spoke with Japanese Ambassador Hirota Koki to determine Japan's intentions but learned less than he could have found from TASS wire-service reports. On 20 September, the Politburo gave its imprimatur to a waiting policy: it would make no decision until Karakhan and Commissar of Foreign Affairs Maksim Litvinov found out more from the Japanese. That would take time and proved more difficult than expected. Two days later, as instructed by the Politburo, Litvinov met with Hirota but could wheedle no more information out of him than Karakhan. In the meantime, Chinese Nationalists in Moscow were told that Moscow had come to no final decision on what it would do.[3]

Litvinov met Hirota again on 2 October, demanding an explanation for Japanese conduct and especially of alleged anti-Soviet subversion by White Russians under Japanese protection. Litvinov cuttingly pointed out to Hirota the vicious circle created by Japanese intervention: Hirota said that Japanese troops could not leave Manchuria until calm was restored, but in Litvinov's view, the very presence of troops preserved disorder. Litvinov warned that Soviet "public opinion" could not remain indifferent to Japanese troops so close to the Soviet border. Despite his harsh rhetoric, as Litvinov met with Hirota, the Politburo tried to control the situation by ordering TASS to deny rumors that Soviet troops had crossed the Manchurian border.[4]

The Politburo's caution was understandable. Japanese intervention in Manchuria threatened the Soviet Union where it was most vulnerable: in the thinly populated Far East, supplied only by thousands of miles of the Trans-Siberian Railway. Although the West was also taken aback by the Japanese invasion, the Soviet Union had the most to fear, and Soviet diplomats and communist parties abroad were quick to express their concern.[5] Soviet strategic planners must have had nightmares, recalling the uninspiring precedent of Russian performance in the Russo-Japanese War and the Japanese occupation of the Russian Far East during the civil war.

Stalin took the threat of a Japanese invasion of the Soviet Far East quite seriously, even if he did assume that several months might pass before hostilities began. Writing in late November to Voroshilov, who was temporarily out of Moscow, Stalin explained that "things with Japan are complicated, serious." He predicted that the Japanese intended to conquer all of China, not just Manchuria, and establish a puppet government. "More than that," he said, "it's not excluded and even probable that Japan will stretch out its hand to our Far East, and, possibly, to Mongolia." Although the Soviet Union had time to prepare, it would not be much. "It's possible that this winter, Japan won't try to trouble us. But next year it may make such an attempt." Japan could succeed "if we don't begin right now to organize serious preventative measures of a military and non-military character." Stalin assured Voroshilov that "the main thing now is preparing the defense of the Far East."[6] Stalin's attitude represented a consensus among party elites in Moscow. Litvinov told foreign diplomats that he expected imminent war with Japan. Reporting to the Central Executive Committee in late December, Molotov condemned the League of Nation's inaction on the Manchurian question and promised the assembled delegates that Soviet soldiers in the Far East would never let down their guard, for "we don't need others' land, but we will not yield a single inch of our own."[7]

Molotov's bravado aside, the sudden crisis and Japanese stonewalling seemed all the more disturbing since relations with Japan had been quite acceptable, if not friendly. Japan and the USSR had signed a treaty regularizing their relations in 1925 and maintained at least civil relations from that time forward. Economic ties quickly flourished: from 1925 to 1931, Soviet exports to Japan doubled, and Japanese exports to the USSR grew more than ten times (albeit from a much lower starting point). The thorny question of fishing rights, though a constant source of low-level friction, never seriously threatened to undermine Soviet-Japanese relations. In contrast to the USSR's rocky relations with China, few major difficulties arose with Japan. In 1929, Molotov could tell the Fifth Congress of Soviets that "not a single political conflict is recorded between the Soviet Union and Japan" since the 1925 treaty. In the run-up to the Manchurian crisis, according to David Dallin, "Soviet relations with Japan were at their best. Whatever disputes arose from time to time concerned purely economic matters which were always settled amicably and which did not becloud the Far Eastern sky." This made the Manchurian crisis more electrifying when it finally came.[8]

To make Soviet leaders even more apprehensive, before the crisis, Soviet intelligence had reported support within the Japanese military for war with the USSR. One March 1931 decrypted telegram from Yukio Kasahara, Japanese military attaché in Moscow, called it Japan's "unavoidable destiny to clash with the USSR sooner or later. . . . In short, I hope the authorities will make up their minds for a speedy war with the Soviet Union and initiate policies accordingly." Hirota himself remarked in another intercepted telegram that, "putting aside the question of whether or not Japan should make war against the Soviet Union, there is the need to take a strong policy vis-à-vis the Soviet Union, with the resolve to fight the USSR at any time necessary. The objective, however, should not be defense against Communism but, rather, the occupation of Eastern Siberia."[9]

Once the initial shock of the crisis had worn off, the Soviet Union reacted to it with a two-part strategy. The first strand, readily visible to the outside world, was diplomatic appeasement to find and remove any grounds for confrontation with Japan. As Thorne remarked, "Soviet policy was . . . to remain one of watchful determination to avoid being dragged into a fight at a time of domestic turmoil and a place of inadequate preparation." Jonathan Haslam characterized Russian policy in a similar way, noting that "the Russians had already embarked upon a seemingly endless series of concessions towards Japan, necessitated by economic and military weakness." This conciliatory line did not, however, preclude a second strand, secret but equally significant. The USSR embarked on an expansive defense buildup, a crash program of armaments production to prepare for the chance that a negotiated settlement with Japan would prove impossible. This second strand was so well hidden by the Soviet Union's public posture that contemporary opinion was shocked by the Soviets' "invincible restraint and impenetrable reserve," and French diplomats believed in the existence of a military and party faction that was humiliated by the prostrate position Soviet diplomacy had taken. William Strang reported to London that "in the present Far Eastern crisis [the Soviet leaders] have, in fact, hitherto shown an almost abject desire to keep out of trouble; so much so that they have been reproached by émigré Russian Social Democrats with being pusillanimous in their acquiescence in imperialist aggression."[10] Whatever foreign diplomats or émigrés believed, any high-placed Soviet officers or bureaucrats could hardly mistake the fevered military buildup taking place all around them.

Soviet diplomatic initiatives began with the offer of a nonaggression pact. When Yoshizawa Kenkichi passed through Moscow in December 1931 on his way to take up the post of Japanese foreign minister, Litvinov met him and pointed out the odd exception Japan represented: a state bordering on the USSR without a nonaggression pact or prospects of one. Yoshizawa refused to commit himself, and the initiative went nowhere. Yoshizawa told first Litvinov, then Aleksandr Troianovskii,[11] the USSR's ambassador to Japan, that he wished to see the development of good relations, but those words were never matched by deeds. Tension grew steadily. Through March 1932, Litvinov's and Troianovskii's numerous attempts at a nonaggression pact were rebuffed.[12] With the chances for diplomatic success slim, the Soviet Union's ruling elite extended those efforts with a program to boost military power.

This second, more bellicose side of Soviet policy itself had two parts. The long-term solution was rearmament, but the USSR's defenses in the Far East had to be bolstered without delay. On 13 January 1932, the Defense Commission strengthened the Special Red-Banner Far Eastern Army (OKDVA) with additional troops and equipment, along with further fortifications and bases in the Far East. Sovnarkom on 27 January 1932 ordered Rabkrin to investigate submarine manufacture, and by midsummer, the STO approved a dozen additional submarines for the Soviet Far East. Voroshilov, in a February order "not for publication and not for distribution in the Red Army," cautioned Bliukher, commander of the OKDVA, to beware of border violations. Any bands crossing the Soviet frontier were to be disarmed and interned, and if they resisted, destroyed. The Soviet Pacific Fleet came into existence on 21 April 1932. Although this fleet was slow to build up substantial strength, Soviet sources claimed that it surpassed other Soviet fleets in its professionalism and readiness.[13] In March, the Politburo and the Defense Commission sent seven tank battalions plus infantry escort tanks, armored trains, antiaircraft machine guns, and antitank guns to the Far East. Stalin himself took an interest in military equipment for the East: in response to plans to send six bombers, he told Voroshilov, "Six bombers for the Far East is nothing. We need to send no less than 50–60 TB-3s [four-engine heavy bombers]. And as soon as possible. Without this the defense of the Far East is only an empty phrase."[14]

Even the geography of industrial investment was altered by the immediate demands of defense. On 15 February 1932, the STO ordered the construction of two new aviation plants in Siberia. The first, planned for Lake Bolan'-Odzhal, near Komsomolsk-on-Amur, was to be able to produce 200 TB-3 bombers and other reconnaissance aircraft and repair up to 350 of the same type annually. The second, in Irkutsk, was to have a capacity of 500 R5 reconnaissance aircraft and matching repair potential. Still another factory, also in Irkutsk, would concentrate on the repair of tanks, tankettes, and tractors, handling 3,000 units per year. The STO ordered Gosplan and Narkomtiazhprom to give these projects highest priority in access to labor, capital, machinery, and scarce raw materials.[15]

Further economic adjustments followed soon after the new year with the Japanese rejection of a nonaggression pact. In January, the Politburo directed Molotov, Stalin, Ordzhonikidze, and two others to alter Vesenkha's capital investment priorities given the new situation in Siberia and the Far East. At the same time, plans were made for developing the eastern Siberian economy, again in the hope of upgrading the Soviet Union's defenses.[16] This was followed by special Politburo initiatives to make Siberia more economically self-sufficient. Most importantly, railway construction in the Far East, especially the double-tracking of the Trans-Siberian Railway, became a top priority. The Commissariat of Transportation established a new main directorate for Siberia and the Far East, and by September and October 1932, the Politburo demanded that railway construction and supply in the east be put in order. In August 1932, noting the "completely unsatisfactory" work on projects of "the most important defense significance" as a result of a "criminally negligent attitude on the part of the majority of people's commissariats and other central organs," Kuibyshev ordered all commissariats to assign one deputy commissar to investment and construction in the Far East.[17]

The regional crisis with Japan managed to provoke a general defense buildup, not simply local efforts to bolster Far Eastern defenses. As previous chapters have discussed, the Red Army's high command had long been impatient to reap the rewards of industrialization. Stalin's Politburo, now devoid of serious opposition to Stalin's general line, saw no reason to deny the Red Army the weaponry it desired, particularly when a specific and concrete threat to Soviet territory now presented itself. In contrast to immediate measures to protect the Far East, the Soviet Union's longer-term policy was a dramatic buildup in modern weaponry, especially tanks and planes, accelerating by several times the Soviet military's rearmament. Military production had already jumped significantly in 1931, and as a result, the original 1932 plans for the defense industry had been relatively conservative.[18] The original defense budget and procurement plans for 1932, including those drawn up in the summer of 1931 and even soon after the crisis, gave little hint of the approaching expansion. The Manchurian crisis began to change that.

The first response to the Japanese occupation of Manchuria did not initially, at least in late 1931, take the form of higher production targets; instead, the Defense Commission ensured that existing production was provided for and would be delivered in full and on time. In November 1931, the Defense Commission declared the Kharkov locomotive factory, the central plant for BT (Christie) tanks, a "super-shock" factory in its access to raw materials, transportation, and food. The OGPU was assigned to investigate the disappearance of vitally needed imported machinery. Rabkrin, checking war preparations, complained of the low priority civil industry gave both military orders and investment in military production. Rabkrin had two specific proposals to correct this: first, that factories and enterprises consider their production assignments complete only if their military obligations had been met in full, and second, that the premiums accruing to factory management for meeting deadlines early be applied only if all military obligations were finished ahead of schedule. Rabkrin also called for those violating these directives to be held to "strictest party responsibility."[19]

As the implications of the Japanese takeover of Manchuria sank in at the end of 1931 and the beginning of 1932, the Soviet government grew increasingly anxious and determined that its own security demanded rapid expansion of military production, not merely careful attention to existing programs. The first signs of increasing procurement came from a Defense Commission meeting on 7 December 1931. The order for military aircraft went to 3,505 planes; the previous year's production had been a little over 1,000. That was only the first step. Over the next few months, the most dramatic shift in military production would take place in the tank industry, but the 1932 defense budget, radically altered as a result of the crisis, also displayed the marks of hurried revision. Fiscal restraint became panicked expansion.

As was typical, assembling a 1932 defense budget had begun well behind schedule in mid-1931. The Red Army had promised a complete 1932 order in February 1931, but industrial managers in June 1931 were still using the lack of a military order as grounds to deny the military price cuts on continuing production—without time to plan ahead, there could be no cost reductions. Although there was still no industrial order, the Revvoensovet had at least approved the budget proposal that would determine its procurement order. On 14 June 1931, the Revvoensovet accepted the Staff's projected 1932 budget of 2,985 million rubles as the rough basis for its proposal to the Defense Commission. Until the Manchurian crisis altered everything, the military's final request would be for no more than 3,000 million to 3,025 million rubles, including an order for 3,600 tanks. Preparing final, precise figures for the Defense Commission was the Staff's responsibility.[20]

The Defense Commission felt unable to resolve the highly detailed military budget without further review and created a large and unwieldy special commission of seventeen members under Valerian Kuibyshev. Kuibyshev's commission trimmed the Red Army's order, but its final decision left many details unresolved. The budget Kuibyshev's group delivered specified only 3,613 aircraft and 6,000 motors, expressing the rest of the order in financial, not physical, terms (see the first column of table 17).[21] After minor adjustments, on 7 October 1931, the Revvoensovet grudgingly accepted Kuibyshev's verdict that its final procurement budget for 1932 would amount to 1,451 million rubles, just slightly under the figure reached on 6 September, "regardless of the fact that this plan is far from providing for the needs of the NKVM according to the planned and approved government plans for the armed forces' development." The Kuibyshev commission's final military budget was indeed significantly less than Tukhachevskii and Efimov at the Armaments Directorate would have wished to accept. Efimov calculated that for the budgetary items falling under his purview, Kuibyshev had approved only 627 million rubles of an original request for 777.8 million rubles, a cut of 19.4 percent.[22] As a condition for accepting a lower order, the Revvoensovet insisted that the Defense Commission force Vesenkha to live up to its obligations completely and accurately.[23] On 12 October, the Defense Commission approved the Kuibyshev commission's final recommendations with only a few minor alterations and later rounded it off to a total procurement of 1,500 million rubles.[24]

The initial 1932 budget that grew out of Kuibyshev's commission increased military spending largely in auxiliary services, that is, in "tail," not "teeth." For example, the Communications Directorate's order for 1932 grew (in nominal terms) from 1931's 26.226 million rubles to 70 million, a jump of 167 percent. The Artillery Directorate, by comparison, grew only 36 percent in nominal terms from 1931 to 1932, from 331.6 million to 450 million rubles. In physical terms, the Artillery Directorate had a similar limited increase from 1931 to 1932. Its rifle order, for example, increased by 39 percent, and artillery shells by 30 percent, while other orders fell. Demand for light machine guns decreased by 10 percent, and for medium-caliber (76mm to 152mm) artillery shells by 9 percent. In short, in autumn 1931, nothing in the preliminary order for 1932 suggested the explosion in production that would take place over 1932.[25]

But in the first few weeks of 1932, the military equipment order and procurement budget nearly doubled (see table 17).[26] The tank program saw the most drastic increases, but every sector of the Red Army's procurement increased sharply. The budget that Kuibyshev's commission had established in September 1931 (column 1) became with minor revisions the "basic budget" (column 2). "Additional spending" (column 3), above and beyond the basic budget and proportionally heaviest on tanks, represents the upsurge in procurement triggered by the Manchurian crisis. Total procurement spending nearly doubled, and the overall military budget, which also included pay and upkeep for soldiers and officers as well as military construction, grew by half.[27]

Table 17. Dynamics of 1932 Military Budget (million rubles)

Directorate	Kuibyshev's Commission 6 September 1931	"Basic Budget" for 1932	Additional Spending for 1932	Total Spending for 1932
Artillery	450	463.9	332.0	795.9
Air	243	260.0	128.6	388.6
Auto/Armor	220	212.1	270.2	482.3
Navy	210	220.6	161.5	382.3
Chemical	72	68.8	22.6	91.4
Communications	60	67.6	34.3	101.9
Engineering	42	30.0	13.8	43.8
Total technical	1,297	1,323	963	2,286
Equipment	125			
Medical/Vet/Map/Political	31			
Total procurement	1,453			
Total military budget		2,908.6		4,573.6

As the Red Army's budget burgeoned at the start of 1932, the Politburo allocated an additional 100 million rubles over already established investment for expanded defense production within civil industry. Military industry received another 118 million. A crash program of investment started at Izhevsk, one of the Soviet Union's two centers for rifle production. Expansion at Izhevsk was declared a "shock" project, with priority for both housing and transportation. With total investment of 50 million to 60 million rubles, the entire project was to be complete within six months and would take that long only if more machinery than expected had to be imported from outside the Soviet Union.[28]

As discussed earlier, in 1930, Tukhachevskii had proposed rapid and radical rearmament similar in spirit to what Soviet industry was now attempting, only to be banned from discussing economic issues for his pains. The post-Manchuria buildup in the military budget, defense procurement, and production was so monumental that it even drove Stalin to apologize to Tukhachevskii for his earlier condemnation of Tukhachevskii's ambitious military-industrial proposals. In stunning language, considering the unlikely source, Stalin told Tukhachevskii in May 1932 that "now, two years later, when some unclear questions have become more clear to me, I must recognize that my evaluation [of your proposals] was too sharp, and the conclusions of my letters were not in all things correct." Although Stalin still maintained that Tukhachevskii had asked for too much, he recognized that Tukhachevskii's proposals were closer to what the Soviet Union could and should achieve than Stalin had realized. "Don't curse me," Stalin concluded, "for the fact that I corrected the defects of my letters with some delay."[29] What had been justifiably seen as excessively radical and expensive was now official policy.

The Soviet Union was so close to a war footing that it made little sense to continue to draw an administrative line between peacetime military production and preparation for mobilization. The two functions were therefore brought together in a single organization. On 25 December 1931, the Central Committee had already ordered Vesenkha's reorganization by the removal of light, timber, and woodworking industries. Shortly thereafter, on 5 January 1932, Sovnarkom dissolved Vesenkha entirely and replaced it with the three new People's Commissariats of Heavy Industry (Narkomtiazhprom), Light Industry (Narkomlegprom), and Timber Industry (Narkomlesprom). Ordzhonikidze went from chair of Vesenkha to commissar of Narkomtiazhprom.[30] While Vesenkha fragmented, military industry reunited. On 7 February 1932, Ordzhonikidze formed a new Main Military-Mobilization Directorate (GVMU) as a subsection of Narkomtiazhprom under the leadership of his old protégé Pavlunovskii. As its name indicated, the new GVMU would plan wartime mobilization, but in addition, it would run the military-industrial trusts and supervise the work of some of the larger, more important defense plants directly, without any intermediary trust.[31] The old distinction between the VPU's running production and the MPU's handling war mobilization was gone. With the Soviet economy so close to war, maintaining the distinction was pointless.

Labor discipline tightened sharply at military factories, expanding the harsher standards already established in other sectors of the Soviet economy. As part of the earlier antiwrecking campaign, Sovnarkom had instituted stricter discipline in transportation. Violations of labor discipline could be punished by up to ten years imprisonment or, if committed with a "malicious, premeditated character," execution. On 23 December 1931, this stricter regime, intended to eliminate absenteeism, tardiness, and drunkenness, was expanded to military chemical and ammunition plants, as well as electrical stations and waterworks. Two months later, the Politburo approved a further expansion of that ruling to workers and administrators of the Artillery-Arsenal, Firearm–Machine Gun, and Aviation Trusts. This extension was crucial—instead of harsh discipline only for those working with inherently hazardous materials, such as explosives, all military workers fell under the more draconian standards, even though the goods they produced were hazardous to human life only when actually used.[32] In January, the Politburo also detailed special party organizers to invigorate party work at military factories, especially in aviation. These organizers, who would serve as secretaries of their plants' party committees, were responsible for quality-control campaigns. In addition, they would involve themselves as much as possible in manufacturing, screen out wreckers and class enemies, and check antiaircraft defenses and security procedures.[33]

Higher budgets, reorganized administration, and tighter discipline were means to an end: more weapons for the Red Army. Although all types of production increased, the focus of the Defense Commission and Soviet military and economic elites fell on tanks because of their inherent importance, but also because tanks' very novelty would make their mass production most difficult to implement. The T-18/MS-1 design had not proved especially successful, and in December 1929, Khalepskii and Pavlunovskii had produced a damning indictment for the Politburo of Vesenkha's tank design and manufacture. The Politburo, "in view of the weakness of our research and design strength . . . and the absence of tank designs answering the demands of modern war," ordered Vesenkha and the Red Army to send an authoritative commission abroad to purchase Western tank technology. As Voroshilov recalled the moment three years later, "the Politburo, and mainly Comrade Stalin, demanded from us: take all measures, spend the money, even large amounts of money, run people to all corners of Europe and America, but get models, plans, bring in people, do everything possible and impossible in order to set up tank production here."[34] Innokentii Khalepskii from the Motorization and Mechanization Directorate and Daniil Budniak from Vesenkha went abroad in early 1930 and brought back the three designs that would begin true mass production in the USSR: American designer Walter Christie's dual-drive tank, which would become the BT and contribute key elements to the later design of the T-34; a Vickers light tank, the Soviet T-26; and a Carden-Lloyd tankette, the T-27.[35]

Even though Soviet factories had barely managed the slow production of outdated models, Ordzhonikidze and Pavlunovskii were now supposed to introduce the mass production of the most modern types of tanks. The stark fact facing these two was that the new assignment was many times higher than the previous year's production. At the first Defense Commission meeting of the new year, on 10 January 1932, Stalin suggested a feasibility study on converting a civilian factory to full-scale production of BT (Christie) tanks and ensuring "maximum" provisions for a tank-building program. At the next meeting nine days later, feasibility became reality as the Defense Commission entrusted Ordzhonikidze, Tukhachevskii, Pavlunovskii, and Khalepskii with producing 10,000 tanks in 1932 (compared with production of around 2,000 in 1931) and systematically introducing tank production into tractor and automobile factories.[36]

Ordzhonikidze reported to the Defense Commission on this assignment's feasibility on 5 February 1932. If he had any doubts, the commission disregarded them and resolved that the 10,000-tank program was "absolutely not open to debate." Different models were assigned to different factories: the BT to the Kharkov locomotive factory, the T-26 to Bolshevik, and T-27 to Moscow Factory 2 of the All-Union Auto-Tractor Association. Armor was split among four factories: Izhorsk, Kulebaki, Vyksa, and Mariupol. The assembly of tank bodies went to Podolsk, Izhorsk, and Red Kotelshchik. Ordzhonikidze was directly responsible for the program's success and thus had the job of making more tanks than Soviet industry could hope to produce. Some of the needed shops were not even scheduled to be finished until May. Ordzhonikidze's attempt at a miracle began on 10 February 1932 with a Narkomtiazhprom order declaring his intention to produce 10,000 tanks, just as the Defense Commission had ordered. He split responsibility for the tank program among his deputies. Budniak, whose Artillery-Firearms

Association contained the Bolshevik factory, took T-26 production. Martinovich got the BT, and Pavlunovskii (the man technically responsible for all military industry) received the T-27 and general armor output.[37]

To bring as many resources to bear as possible, each tank's primary factory had specified feeder factories to provide it with required materials and parts. Bolshevik's tank section, newly separated as the Voroshilov factory, worked on its 3,000 T-26 tanks with the cooperation of Red Putilovets and Red October and received armored tank bodies from the Izhorsk works and parts from the Lepse, Karl Marx, and Liuberetskii factories. Cooperation was especially necessary since the Voroshilov factory could manage no more than about one-third of the total tank assignment on its own. In the end, at least twenty-six plants would be involved in producing the T-26 alone, but their precise capacity would not be known until February. The 2,000 BT medium tanks at the Kharkov locomotive factory were built with assistance from the Kharkov tractor factory and Moscow's Hammer and Sickle. Parts and armor came from Aviation Factory 1, Izhorsk, Mariupol, and Red Kotelshchik. The assignment for 5,000 T-27 tankettes was finally split between Moscow's Automobile Factory 2 and the Nizhny Novgorod automobile factory. Armored bodies came once again from Izhorsk, Kulebaki, and Vyksa, as well as from Podolsk Cracking. These assignments were not entirely divorced from the means to fulfill them, for Ordzhonikidze assigned 100 million rubles for new construction and financing.[38]

As Pavlunovskii and Ordzhonikidze built a Soviet tank industry from scratch, relations with Japan steadily worsened. Through February 1932, the Kwantung Army in Manchuria continued to press the management of the Soviet-controlled Chinese Eastern Railway for permission to transport its troops all the way up to the Soviet border and to take over railroad security. In response to delaying tactics by Soviet officials on the spot, Japanese officers threatened railway personnel, and Karakhan in Moscow had to permit Japanese troops to travel along the railroad. The Soviets made public their case against the Japanese on 4 March 1932 by publishing in *Izvestiia* the Japanese rejection of a nonaggression pact and the intercepted military cables arguing for war against the Soviet Union. Documents from "the highest military circles" argued that "on the question of whether Japan should start a war with the Soviet Union, I consider it necessary that Japan take the path of a hard policy in relation to the Soviet Union, being ready to start a war at any moment. The cardinal goal of such a war must be . . . the seizure of the Soviet Far East and Eastern Siberia." Another cable urged that "a Japanese-Soviet war, taking into account the state of Soviet armed forces and the position of foreign states, must be carried out as soon as possible" to seize territory up to Lake Baikal, and possibly further. *Izvestiia* suggested that Japan might ally with the Soviet army's traditional enemies, the Poles and the Romanians, and concluded that the situation required immediate improvements in Soviet defense.[39]

Some hope for avoiding war appeared on 18 March 1932 when Yamamoto Jotaro, president of the South Manchurian Railway, suggested to Troianovskii amalgamating his railroad with the Chinese Eastern. Selling the Chinese Eastern and removing a point of contention seemed to the Soviets a means of heading off confrontation. The Politburo sent Troianovskii instructions for talks with Yamamoto under the assumption that he was an unofficial agent of the Japanese government and interested in settling more than a mere commercial transaction. Troianovskii, stressing to the Japanese that he was speaking only privately, not as a representative of the Soviet government, was to tell Yamamoto that the USSR would make concessions in return for a nonaggression pact, either limited term or permanent, given a few conditions. The Soviet government would recognize the Manchurian government, sell the Chinese Eastern, and negotiate deals with the Japanese government on fishing rights, trade, and oil concessions. In return, the Soviets asked for an end to all support and arms for White Russian groups and to White Russian raids from Manchuria. On that basis, real negotiations could begin.[40]

This window of opportunity quickly closed. On 15 April, Troianovskii proposed unofficial talks to Yoshizawa on Soviet-Japanese relations, particularly the Chinese Eastern. In a display of good faith, the next day the Politburo approved new board members for the Chinese Eastern and allowed Japan to use the railway to exchange a division in Harbin for one from further south. This mood of reconciliation ended the next day when Yamamoto, claiming illness, canceled his meeting with Troianovskii. In response, the Politburo informed Troianovskii that it had learned of a Japanese military alliance with Poland and Romania and told him to make this known to the Japanese, while stressing that the Soviet Union would not be intimidated. Arranging a meeting was not to be his priority, for "if they don't want it, so much the worse for them." With reconciliation more distant than ever, the USSR explored the possibility of military cooperation with the United States to restrain Japan, but the military buildup continued apace.[41]

DEFENSE INDUSTRY IN CRISIS

As factories painfully expanded and retooled to meet the demands of rearmament in the spring of 1932, the mounting difficulties of keeping on schedule became apparent. Military and industrial authorities constantly stressed the production assignment's immutability, an excellent indication that it was in serious jeopardy. Ordzhonikidze regularly lambasted his subordinates and factory directors for insufficient zeal in speeding tank production. With few concrete suggestions, he resorted to exhortation to build tanks through force of will alone. In March, the Defense Commission reaffirmed its commitment to the "unconditional fulfillment" of the 2,000-tank BT program, and two weeks later, the Red Army's Motorization and Mechanization Directorate reiterated its own demand for 10,000 tanks. March and April did not offer enough time to prepare for mass production by the May

1932 target date. Lacking experience in making tanks, especially tank armor, Soviet industry was doomed to run far behind schedule.[42]

Individual factories slowly fell into line, displacing civilian lines and shifting to tanks. The Red Putilovets factory ended turbine production to produce 3,000 sets of running gears for T-26s, in addition to sending key technicians to assist other plants. A 156 million–ruble grant fueled new construction. The Defense Commission also expanded the immense Stalingrad tractor factory's tank capacity. On 25 May 1932, it ordered the organization of a production base at Stalingrad capable of delivering 12,000 T-26 light tanks and 6,000 sets of spare parts by the end of 1932, while directing Narkomtiazhprom to consider "converting the entire factory to the production of Carden-Lloyd tracked tractors with 50 horsepower motors." Tracked tractors offered the decided advantage over wheeled ones of easy conversion of production lines and conversion of the tractors themselves to military use. At the urging of the Defense Commission, the Politburo decided on 6 June to order 3 million rubles' worth of imported materials for tanks at the Stalingrad tractor factory, along with an additional 3 million for corresponding artillery systems at the New Sormovo plant.[43]

By the summer of 1932, however, the catastrophic state of tank manufacture was clear. The Defense Commission called Pavlunovskii to account, along with the directors of the tank-producing factories. The commission found "that fulfillment of the tank program goes completely unsatisfactorily, particularly with regard to production of armor and the BT (Christie) tank." Blaming the secondary factories assisting in BT production, the Defense Commission warned factory directors that "nonfulfillment of the program will be regarded as a violation of the most solemn directives of the government with all resulting consequences."[44]

While industrial managers grew increasingly frantic over the immense production assignments they received, there is some evidence that their superiors, Stalin and his compatriots in the Politburo and Defense Commission, saw the targets as an ideal to be strived for or a tool to goad administrators to maximum effort rather than a hard figure to be achieved. Stalin spoke in this spirit to Voroshilov once some of the obstacles had become clear. He noted with resignation that industry had not handled itself as it should, but "this is nothing! We'll put some pressure on and help them adapt. The whole point is to hold these certain branches of industry (mainly military) under constant control." After all, if the whole production program for tanks and planes could be filled "if not by all 100 percent but by 80–90 percent is that really so small?" Unshlikht, now at Gosplan, understood this—the need to show progress if not to fill the program completely. At an August meeting on the growing crisis in military production, he told the assembled administrators that they needed to "at least guarantee, if not 100 percent fulfillment of the program, that in any event it somehow gets close to that."[45]

Although industrial managers harbored doubts about the feasibility of their tasks, the officers of the Red Army showed no doubt and wasted no time in planning how to deploy and use the tanks they expected to receive. Working through the

Politburo, the Soviet military took steps intended to provide itself with the technically skilled soldiers and officers its new air and armored formations would demand. Even before the new year, the Politburo approved the Orgburo's proposal to mobilize 10,000 communists into military schools. On 6 February, less than a month after the Defense Commission had first decided on the new tank assignment, the Politburo ordered that 6,000 drivers and tractor operators be drafted into the Red Army to man the rapidly expanding tank units. Two months later, on 1 April, the Politburo mobilized 5,000 communists and Komsomols into flight schools for service in the air force.[46]

Two days after the Politburo ordered the conscription of tractor drivers, Tukhachevskii passed along suggestions to Khalepskii for organizing the new tank units. Given the embarrassment of riches Tukhachevskii expected by 1933, there was no need to worry about the proper place of tanks on the battlefield, whether in independent formations or interspersed with infantry. There would be tanks enough for both. He proposed twenty-five mechanized brigades, each with 208 tanks, as well as a 2,000–tank reserve under the high command's control. In addition, fifty rifle divisions would each be stiffened by a tank battalion, and those divisions' constituent infantry regiments would have a battalion of infantry escort tanks attached. Together with further reserve units, Tukhachevskii expected a total of 15,000 tanks in the Red Army in less than a year.[47]

Despite this optimism, Voroshilov was well informed of industry's growing crisis. Exasperated over slow economic progress in the Far East, Voroshilov complained to Ordzhonikidze that this vital part of the USSR's defense was not receiving due priority. The Red Army could not get information on work in eastern Siberia, nor could industrial representatives even discuss their own programs intelligently.[48] Voroshilov continued the Soviet tradition of personally visiting trouble spots to motivate administrators and workers, through inspiration or fear, to overcome whatever difficulties hindered the plan. He accompanied Ordzhonikidze's newly rehabilitated Trotskyite deputy Georgii Piatakov[49] on a junket to Stalingrad to investigate its troubled trio of industrial giants: Barrikady, Red October, and the tractor works. As a result of the disorder Voroshilov and Piatakov found, the Politburo rebuked Narkomtiazhprom for negligence but focused its discontent on the Red October metallurgical plant. Factory director Klipov was fired and replaced with Treidub, who brought with him a mandate to end disorder, rationalize production, and clean the factory. To create the necessary popular enthusiasm, *Pravda* was to keep a daily account of Red October's steel production.[50]

The Red Army also lobbied for increased use of foreign expertise in industrial mobilization to pull industry out of crisis. Turmoil in 1932, just like the supposed discovery of a vast conspiracy of wreckers and saboteurs, triggered military initiatives to employ more foreign technology and overcome production bottlenecks. At Voroshilov's urging, the Politburo authorized numerous trips abroad to study industrial mobilization; Red Army officers as well as industrial representatives went to gather information. Budniak received permission in March to spend two weeks abroad to buy military equipment. As late as December 1932, the Politburo sent another four Soviets to German military academies.[51] The Revvoensovet demanded that Soviet industry take advantage of German experience. It found that despite Efimov's efforts to publicize German accomplishments, 1932's poor results showed conclusively that industry had failed miserably on its own, and the Roevvoensovet formally asked the Defense Commission to hear Efimov's views on German methods. The chief obstacle to better mobilization, in the Revvoensovet's view, was that Soviet industry "was technically completely unprepared for mobilization as a consequence of the absence of an authoritative and technically competent organ directing this preparation," obliquely proposing a further increase in the Red Army's influence over industry.[52]

One of the first signs of stress in Soviet industry was increasing scarcity of the raw materials necessary for military production. Supplies were already under strain from the demands of the First Five-Year Plan, but they came under further pressure from the military buildup. The same materials required for industrial investment were also required for tank and aircraft production, producing critical shortages of nonferrous metals and high-quality steel and even of such inputs as machine tools and labor. Ordzhonikidze blamed dips in tank production on shortages and an inability to keep skilled workers at the bench, and he and Kuibyshev were forced into strict rationing of available metal.[53] As early as October 1931, Sovnarkom instituted new controls on the use of scarce stocks of raw materials. In September 1932, the Central Committee authorized Kuibyshev to release stocks of zinc, nickel, and scarce alloys to ease production bottlenecks at the Khar'kov and Stalingrad tractor factories—shortages of nickel had already disrupted the production of case-hardened tank armor. The Politburo decided on 16 September 1932 to institute yearly and quarterly plans of ferrous and nonferrous metal use, broken down in some cases to the level of individual enterprises. As part of this, Ordzhonikidze was invited to list sites whose supply would come under Politburo supervision, while Gosplan and Narkomtiazhprom were to cooperate on determining monthly usage levels.[54]

Even if the newly born tank industry had enjoyed ample supplies of raw materials, simple lack of knowledge of tank building would have crippled production. Splitting production among several different factories and frequent design changes made matters worse. Serial production of T-26 parts did not start until July. This was despite the T-26's simplicity compared with other models, even taking into account a design switch midway through production from two small side-by-side turrets to one turret mounting a 45mm gun. Still, the T-26 benefited from previous production at the Voroshilov factory, whose engineers could counsel cooperating plants. The Voroshilov factory hit nearly its full stride by July and had spare resources to assist other factories. By September, the Red October and Red Putilovets factories had also hit their key mark of 300 full complements of parts a month. Despite nagging problems with aluminum crankcase parts and a forced switch from iron to bronze clutch parts, matters did not look especially bad.[55]

So when Ordzhonikidze went before the Defense Commission in September to report on the T-26, he spoke with a curious mixture of triumph and surrender. With the help of Leningrad party authorities, labor turnover at the Voroshilov plant (40 percent over eight months) had been cut, technical production problems solved, and spoilage reduced below 15 percent. In sum, the obstacle to production was now supply, not technique: not enough aluminum for crankcases, and a 700,000-ruble shortfall in imported electrical equipment. Despite this generally positive picture, Ordzhonikidze asked the Defense Commission to reduce the T-26 program from 3,000 to 2,000 tanks. Ordzhonikidze was evidently angling for some slack in the production assignment, since Martinovich had reported to Ordzhonikidze's deputy Piatakov that "the T-26 tank program can undoubtedly be saved." Output was accelerating, and tank factories had achieved mass production.[56]

Although the T-26 faced continuing problems, matters were worse in the comparatively new production of the BT (Christie) medium tank and the T-27 (Carden-Lloyd) tankette. The complex BT required coordination among seven factories, and the primary factory, Kharkov locomotive, lacked personnel with tank experience, despite earlier failures to introduce tank production there. The expert technicians sent from the Voroshilov factory had never worked on a Christie design before. Kharkov used an American Liberty motor for the BT, but factory engineers hoped to adapt an M-17 instead, further slowing production. This scheme failed in the short term, so to cover the BT program, the Politburo ordered the import of 500 Liberty motors in January; then in March, it approved an STO decision to purchase 1,365 more, which was increased in June by 700.[57]

Manufacture of the T-27 tankette was disrupted by the transfer of armored body construction from the Izhorskii works to Podolsk Cracking. The situation was so dire at the primary factory, Moscow's Automobile 2, that the OGPU's Economic Directorate stepped in to investigate and found a plant that suffered from almost every problem a Soviet factory could endure. The factory had had three technical directors over a period of only six months and had not managed to fully automate production. Supply of raw materials and even electric power was unreliable. The factory had been denied financing for its capital projects, which were likewise behind schedule. Not surprisingly, it was unprepared for mobilization.[58]

Once production difficulties were ironed out, the lack of one component still proved an almost insuperable obstacle for all types of tanks: armor. This should not have been a surprise, for at the end of November 1931, Unshlikht had reported to Molotov on Vesenkha's alarming failure to abide by a 1 August 1931 Defense Commission order to prepare for wartime tank production. In particular, factories designated for armor production had not set up the needed capacity. The production of tank armor was not simply a matter of casting or shaping metal into the desired form; the metal, once shaped, had to be case-hardened. The Izhorsk and Kulebaki factories, both intended as centers for armor production, had not built special case-hardening ovens. The situation at Podolsk Cracking was quite similar, and the

Stalingrad tractor factory, intended as a wartime center for tankette production, had taken no actions to assimilate tankette and tractor manufacture.[59]

Armor production had not kept pace with the other components the Soviet factories manufactured, let alone with the Defense Commission's demands. Red Putilovets could produce 100 T-26 armored hulls monthly and transfer technicians to aid the Izhorskii works, but Izhorskii still could not establish daily output of fifteen armored hulls and thirty turrets. The case-hardened armor required imported alloys, and instituting a new method of producing armor without those alloys took time. That problem's resolution was followed by a severe shortage of nickel. The Izhorskii factory finally managed to push monthly production to 200 hulls by September, but the resulting armor was too heavy. The final weight of the T-26 was 17.5 percent above design: 9.4 tons instead of 8. Izhorskii technicians were forced to thin the armor from 15mm to 13mm to cut weight—hardly an ideal solution.[60] Armor was the biggest stumbling block for the BT medium tank as well: the Mariupol factory began the Christie's two-layer manganese steel armor only in August. The BT ended up nearly two tons heavier than its design weight. In addition to slowing the tank's maximum speed on treads from seventy-five to fifty-five kilometers per hour and increasing its fuel consumption, this overloaded the tank's suspension system. Tankette armor production was as bad. Ninety percent of the Kulebaki factory's turret armor was spoilage and unusable, and quality was only slightly better at Podolsk Cracking. July production of armored tankette bodies was still a fifth of what it should have been.[61]

In October 1932, Pavlunovskii again had to account for the poor state of tank production in order to salvage the 1932 program and ensure that 1933's program was both feasible and as ambitious as possible. Reporting to Voroshilov, Pavlunovskii stressed that the crawling pace of production grew out of the fact that the Soviet Union before 1932 simply "did not have a tank industry." This was little comfort to Voroshilov, as that fact was no secret. As Pavlunovskii explained, "we still have not completely managed to master the production of tanks on the scale assigned by the Government, especially with regard to malleable cast-iron, armor, thermal finishing of parts, and quality of assembly." According to the schedule, by October, 5,150 tanks should have been complete, and monthly output should have reached 1,365. Actual production was little better than a third of that: 1,365 tanks nominally complete, and 480 added each month. Even under Pavlunovskii's optimistic prediction that the production rate would double, the military could at best hope for only 4,200 tanks of its original order of 10,000. In his own defense, Pavlunovskii could only assert that despite falling short, he and his colleagues had indeed created a tank industry.[62]

The Defense Commission, unsatisfied by both meager results and Pavlunovskii's excuses but lacking effective tools to finish the impossible 10,000-tank program, formed yet another commission at the beginning of October. What this commission could attempt to do that had not been tried before was unclear; in the end, it merely set the program for the final quarter of 1932 and all of 1933. The

Defense Commission set the lower bound for 1933's program at 6,000 tanks plus any T-27s left over from 1932. In addition, three new types of tanks were to be put into production in 1933: the multiturreted T-35 heavy and T-28 medium tanks, as well as an improved amphibious tankette, the T-37.[63]

By mid-October, the Defense Commission had no choice but to admit defeat and give up hope that Soviet industry could come anywhere near its production targets for the year. The only way to win the game was to change the rules. Realizing that its goals were unattainable, and not wanting to have disastrous results on the books, the Defense Commission retroactively lowered its tank targets to something industry might reach by year's end: two-fifths of the original order. Instead of 5,000 T-27s, 3,000 T-26s, and 2,000 BTs, industry was now obligated to get 4,300 tanks through factory quality control: 2,100 T-27s, 1,600 T-26s, and 600 BTs. Even these modest goals assumed a vast improvement in industrial performance. Over half of each individual order was to be finished in the year's last quarter, and even by Soviet standards of storming, completing 1,200 T-27s, 925 T-26s, and 375 BTs in three months would be an extraordinary feat.[64]

To ensure that 1932 disasters were not repeated in 1933, the Defense Commission took a two-pronged approach: making the job easier, and improving the way it was done. First, it lowered 1933's target to 7,000 tanks, which, though still about 3,000 tanks over what Soviet industry would hit by the end of 1932, was 3,000 tanks lower than the original 1932 program. Production was stepped back slightly for BTs and T-26s and drastically for T-27s, which were to be phased out in favor of the new amphibious T-37 tankettes. Introducing three new models— the T-37, T-28, and T-35—would, however, present the same obstacles of new technology and processes that had so hamstrung industry in 1932.[65]

The Defense Commission also reformed the administration of the tank industry in October 1932. Soviet policy makers realized that lowering plan targets was a poor substitute for instituting actual measures to improve performance. With few managerial levers to employ, the Defense Commission drew from its limited toolbox increased centralization. Tank factories had been scattered among several trusts and associations, not all of which even fell under military industry. This structure, adding bureaucratic difficulties to the strains of a backbreaking production program, had to change. The Politburo liquidated the All-Union Auto-Tractor Association, which had controlled tankette production, and the Defense Commission centralized all tank production. Appointing K. A. Neiman to head a new tank-building trust directly under Narkomtiazhprom, the Defense Commission on 19 October gathered tank factories under unified authority to simplify the links among them. Called the Special Machine-Building Trust (Spetsmashtrest) to conceal its true nature, this tank-building group included the Kharkov locomotive factory, the Voroshilov and Red October plants from the All-Union Artillery-Arsenal Association, Moscow's Factory 2 of the All-Union Auto-Tractor Association, and (for a short time) the Izhorsk works. Red Putilovets, important to tank production, was removed from its home trust and placed directly under

Narkomtiazhprom jurisdiction.[66] By consolidating all tank factories in one trust, the Politburo and Defense Commission aimed to remove the barriers that had impeded cooperation.

To add to continuing woes in armor production, another crisis broke in December 1932. Tanks rolled off assembly lines with no guns to arm them, for the number of BT tanks produced had outstripped the number of guns to be mounted in them. This left the Red Army in the ridiculous predicament of possessing one of the best tanks in the world in its arsenal, but without weaponry. Tank guns could be scraped together for the first 260, but some other solution would have to be found for the remaining 340. As a stopgap measure, the Defense Commission ordered the Red Army and Narkomtiazhprom to cannibalize 340 older T-18 tanks, removing their 37mm Hotchkiss main guns for installation in the new BTs. The T-18s would instead be equipped with single machine guns. Even the 37mm gun would soon be obsolete; the 1933 production run of both BTs and T-26s was to be upgunned with a new 45mm cannon. As late as January 1933, 800 tanks lacked even turrets, and T-26s were armed only with machine guns.[67]

The 1932 final tally for tanks was hardly encouraging. The clearer the results, the darker the prognosis. Pavlunovskii reported on 2 January 1933 that of the reduced assignment of 4,300 tanks, 3,718 were assembled, 3,592 had been presented to military inspectors, but only 2,862 of an initial order of 10,000 had been handed over for delivery. Egorov found a similar situation in late January, but the true state of affairs was even bleaker than either one revealed. A draft report intended for Molotov found that 1932's grand total came to only 2,585 tanks—800 still had no turrets, and 290 lacked treads. Even completed T-26s carried only machine guns, because the three factories manufacturing turrets (Vorskii, Izhorsk, and Mariupol) had done almost nothing to convert to a turret mounting a 45mm gun.[68]

The Soviet military aviation industry faced almost as many problems as its tank industry. The 1932 crisis was perhaps less apparent if only because 1931 had already been a crisis. In 1930, aircraft production had gone relatively well, at least in retrospect, and the Red Army had received 1,359 aircraft from an order totaling 1,513. In 1931, however, the Red Army attempted to change its primary fighter from the I-3 to the I-5, its primary reconnaissance aircraft from the R-1 to the R-5, and its primary pilot trainer from the U-1 to the U-2, while more than doubling orders for its TB-1 heavy bomber. The result, not surprisingly, was that production fell by more than half, and only 584 of the 1,469 aircraft contracted for with industry (let alone the 1,935 the Red Army had wanted) were actually produced. As a result, the 1932 surge in defense production only added to the existing mess.[69] As mentioned earlier, the Defense Commission had set the military aircraft order at 3,505 on 7 December 1931. In early January, ambitious targets were set for aircraft production capacity, growing from an assumed capacity of 7,490 aircraft at the beginning of 1932 to 12,500 by 1933. The greatest increase would be in heavy bombers, with capacity set to grow by over 200 percent, from 640 to 2,000.[70]

Early results were mixed; in March, the production program was eased back to 3,421 aircraft, but in April, the Defense Commission noted with some satisfaction that first-quarter production was well ahead of schedule and that industry could change its priorities to emphasize quality control. By May, however, the picture looked less rosy. The Defense Commission stepped back its production assignment for 1933 to 3,000 units, aiming at a total air strength in the Red Air Force of 6,000 planes. Continuing quality-control problems made Soviet aircraft quite dangerous. The M-17 motor was liable to break down after five to ten hours of use, and Soviet pilots refused to fly. Surrender to the inevitable came earlier in aviation than in tanks. On 25 July 1932, the Defense Commission directed a commission under Nikolai Kuibyshev to consider delaying a substantial part of the aviation program until the next year.[71] By December 1932, the 1933 aviation order was set at a level quite similar to the previous year's, totaling 3,615 aircraft and 6,010 motors and cutting back on attempts to introduce new types of production.[72]

The most visible crisis came in tank production, but more traditional armaments managed little better in the deepening crisis within the defense industry. In August 1932, Martinovich reported to Piatakov on Stalingrad's Barrikady artillery plant. In June, nominal output was lower than the factory's payroll by 500,000 rubles, or 40 percent. Millions of rubles of machinery lay idle, and discipline was abysmal. The solution, in Martinovich's view, was pulling 300 skilled workers from other artillery plants such as Motovilikhinskii, Factory 8 in Khimki, or Bolshevik to get production going at Barrikady. Martinovich saw another problem at the Firearms Trust: poor management. He asked for new directors for the Firearms Trust and its factories. The Defense Sector of Gosplan reported to Molotov in August that the vast majority of military production was behind schedule, and manufacture of small and heavy artillery and shells was catastrophic.[73]

Not only did the 10,000-tank program directly increase the demand for small-caliber artillery pieces, a novel type of technology at Soviet plants, but its consumption of scarce supplies of high-quality steel and skilled labor took a toll on all Soviet armaments production. The Artillery Directorate had contracted for 2,995 small-caliber artillery pieces, but only 239, less than 10 percent, were delivered in 1932. Over two-thirds of the original order was for 45mm tank and antitank guns, but only eight passed military quality control. Of the overall order of 5,078 artillery pieces, only 1,232 passed muster and were handed over to the Artillery Directorate. The GVMU's Artillery Association did a similar calculation for only its plants, which showed similar results. Of 2,315 pieces ordered, 1,392 were in fact prepared, but only 631 measured up to required technical standards and were handed over to the Red Army. Not one single piece from an order of 164 assorted heavy and naval guns managed to pass quality control in 1932.[74]

RETURN TO SANITY

Seen in a different light, however, the picture was not entirely bleak. Bearing in mind Stalin's earlier remarks that exact fulfillment of the production program was not the most important thing, one could judge the Soviets' 1932 drive a success, in that it dramatically increased Soviet production at great expense and with the further cost of extending the militarization of the Soviet economy. The aggregate gross *(valovaia)* production totals of the tank-manufacturing Spetsmashtrest over 1932 amounted to 247.6 million rubles, still well under the drastically reduced production target of 263.8 million. That reduced target was itself less than half the original 1932 assignment of 556.4 million. Seen from this point of view, Spetsmashtrest's performance was disastrous. Conversely, 1932's actual production of 247.6 million rubles doubled 1931's total of 123.5 million. All of Spetsmashtrest's plants registered significant advances in output, with the Voroshilov factory and Factory 2 tripling previous totals.[75]

The Artillery-Arsenal Association's 1932 results displayed the same pattern: significant shortfalls from 1932 goals, but equally significant advances over 1931. The 1932 military production plan totaled 243.7 million rubles, reduced at the end of 1932 to 149.9 million. Actual military production amounted to only 119.2 million—well below plan, but still 73 percent greater than 1931's total. When the military program was combined with civil production and inter- and intrafactory orders, the picture was the same. An initial target of 478.1 million rubles was reduced to 348.7 million, a total almost exactly matched by actual production of 348.9 million. This was 68.3 percent higher than the previous year's production. Specifically, military production, examined across the range of defense production trusts, looked the same (see table 18).[76] Another source, including information on military aviation and a more detailed breakdown of the 1932 plan, tells the same story: orders were greater than industry could achieve, but desperate factory managers and industrial administrators managed to quickly increase production, even if not to the levels the Defense Commission demanded. This shows particularly

Table 18. Military Program of Soviet Defense Industry (million rubles, 1926–1927 prices)

Production Trust	1931 Actual Production	1932 Planned Production	1932 Actual Production	Percent Growth in Actual Production
Artillery-Arsenal	68.9	212.8	125.6	82.3
Firearms–Machine Gun	153.4	211.2	194.1	26.5
Cartridge-Fuse	111.5	252.8	163.8	46.9
Shell	42.2	105.2	81.4	92.9
Spetsmashtrest	57.3	191.4	174.6	204.7
Military-Chemical	57.1	89.1	67.8	18.7
Powder factories	46.7	102.7	48.2	3.2
Total	537.1	1,165.2	855.5	59.3

well the pattern of 1932: moderate initial targets that grew sharply in response to the Manchurian crisis but had to be lowered again once the true picture revealed itself (see table 19).[77]

This military buildup did not come without great costs in budgetary and human terms. The Soviet people and the Soviet economy felt the pressure the defense program inflicted on them from the outset. Collectivization's damage to agriculture and the resultant beginnings of mass famine in the countryside combined with overall economic chaos exacerbated by the rapid military buildup to make 1932 "Stalin's time of trouble." Discontent grew, not only among hungry peasants and urban workers faced with empty store shelves but among party elites as well. British and Italian diplomatic sources reported terrible strains in the Soviet metallurgical industry, rapid stockpiling of enough grain to feed the army for a year, and hunger and even famine. The British ambassador was told that in Leningrad, "there's no bread, no meat, no fats—nothing." Railways were among the first to feel the strain. Already stressed to the breaking point by the demands of industrialization, Soviet rails carried the weight of the iron and steel needed to build thousands of tanks and planes, as well as the troops and equipment sent to the Far East. A. A. Andreev took over as commissar of transport on 30 September 1931 in the atmosphere of intensifying crisis created by the Manchurian incident, and his purges and specialist-baiting only extended the chaos.[78]

The 1932 military buildup disrupted more than just military industry itself. Matters grew so desperate that industrial managers started to refuse military orders. Egorov was forced to report to Voroshilov on 31 August 1932 that he could not get Narkomtiazhprom to undertake the production of the tanks, planes, artillery pieces, and firearms necessary not only for timely completion of the military's expansion plans but also for its responsibility to defend the state.[79] Shortages of

Table 19. Gross Production of Soviet Defense Industry (million rubles, 1926–1927 prices)

Production Trust	1931 Actual Production	1932 Initial contr Figures	1932 Final Plan	1932 Corrected Plan	1932 Actual Production
Artillery-Arsenal	192.2	399.0	742.7	477.0	355.0
Firearms–Machine Gun	276.6	358.2	374.7	358.9	315.7
Bullet-Fuse	217.4	313.5	384.9	385.5	289.2
Shell	105.6	251.8	262.7	262.7	168.0
Aviation industry (main directorate)	156.3	353.0	438.2	438.2	350.5
Military-Chemical	151.8	361.0	303.0	303.0	
Powder	94.8		155.5	154.0	343.9?
Artificial fibers	44.4	—	115.0	116.5	
1st Chemical	8.0	10.3	12.8	12.8	
Spetsmashtrest	123.5	—	—	286.5	261.4

raw materials affected all Soviet industry, and those civilian plants supplying defense factories found their own plans and schedules thrown into disarray. As an example of how the defense program disrupted civil production, a Soviet history of the Kharkov tractor factory recounts how the new plant had achieved daily production of over 100 tractors by 25 April 1932, with more than 5,000 tractors produced from late 1931 through April 1932. This accomplishment earned the factory official congratulations from the Politburo, and workers and engineers received twenty-nine Orders of Lenin. The 1932 production target of 18,796 tractors should have been easily achieved. As the factory's management explained in a report on its work over 1932, however, a large, mysterious order from the nearby Kharkov locomotive factory (the primary factory for BT tanks) "demanded significant exertion from all the engineering-technical personnel and workers of the factory." As a result, tractor production for the rest of the year was significantly below projections, and the factory was forced to increase its payroll far over budget.[80] Stalingrad's Red October metallurgical plant, vital supplier of tank armor, managed to meet its 1931 obligations to produce high-quality steel, but 1932 was another story. The factory was running 30 percent behind schedule midway through the year and did not regain significant ground over the fall.[81]

The most terrible crisis the Soviet Union faced in 1932 and 1933 was the death of millions of peasants by starvation and disease. The historiography of the Soviet famine is far too complex to explore fully here, but explanations for this mass death by hunger have varied widely.[82] All explanations are, however, absolutely consistent with another exacerbating factor in the grain crisis of 1932–1933: the need to build up grain stocks for war with Japan, and the overloaded transportation network shipping troops east and hauling military production. Threats of war produced food hoarding, and part of a heavy grain requisition of March 1932 was earmarked for stockpiling in the event of war.[83]

At the end of the first quarter of 1932, well before the economic crisis was at its worst, Stalin and Molotov circulated a letter to party and state authorities from union republics down to the *krai* level to explain the need for their economic suffering. Referring to "the necessity of expanding construction for liberation from imports and for strengthening the defense readiness of the USSR," Stalin recognized the budgetary strains imposed by increasing outlays on "industry, transport, and defense." Stalin did not offer any prospect of immediate relief from the burdens defense imposed; he instead told his readers that local authorities had ruined the first quarter's financial plan and would have to reimpose fiscal discipline in the second quarter.[84]

Soviet leaders publicly conceded that the needs of Soviet defense hindered economic growth; in particular, they stressed the pernicious consequences of danger in the Far East, slowing completion of the First Five-Year Plan. Although this strategy may in part have been intended to shift blame for domestic mismanagement, the military buildup certainly did eat into resources available for investment. At the January 1933 Central Committee plenum, Stalin explicitly linked economic difficulties to the need to build the Soviet Union's defenses:

> It is true that we are 6 percent short of fulfilling the total program of the Five-Year Plan. But that is due to the fact that in view of the refusal of neighboring countries to sign pacts of non-aggression with us, and of the complications that arose in the Far East, we were hastily obliged, for the purpose of strengthening our defence, to switch a number of factories to the production of modern defensive measures. . . . But this was bound to affect adversely the fulfillment of the programme of output envisaged in the Five-Year Plan. It is beyond any doubt that, but for this incidental circumstance, we would almost certainly not only have fulfilled, but even overfulfilled the total production figures of the Five-Year Plan.[85]

At the plenum, Stalin conceded that the new Second Five-Year Plan could proceed at a more moderate pace than the First, for "we have already succeeded in raising the country's defense readiness to the necessary level."[86]

R. W. Davies argues that Stalin's blaming the failures of the First Five-Year Plan on the need to prepare for war "cannot . . . be taken seriously, nor should the abruptness of the shift to defense investment and production be exaggerated." Instead, Davies suggests, excessively ambitious economic targets in 1931 produced widespread shortages of labor and raw materials, along with profound economic crisis and falling production.[87] Although Davies is obviously correct that the USSR's excessively ambitious economic planning opened the way to crisis, the importance of the damage done by the crash military buildup should not be discounted. It is at the very least highly instructive that military production jumped so rapidly while production was actually falling in other key sectors of the Soviet economy. The sheer size of the military program and the way it exacerbated the Soviet economy's worst shortages in skilled labor and high-quality metallurgy indicate the profound damage the post-Manchuria military buildup did to the USSR.

Stalin was not alone in seeing the possibility of war with Japan as unleashing economic crisis. Molotov repeated Stalin's formulation of the reasons for the First Five-Year Plan's shortfalls, noting that a hostile international environment and the need to bulk up the USSR's defenses "forced the USSR to sacrifice several interests in the development of general industry with the switch of a series of enterprises to the production of contemporary means of defense."[88] Ordzhonikidze, people's commissar of heavy industry, also laid the blame for difficulties in the final year of the plan on Japanese aggression. Reiterating Stalin's words, Ordzhonikidze told the plenum:

> We could have fulfilled the Five-Year Plan by 100 percent, if the international situation in 1932 hadn't forced us to push the production of modern types of arms for the defense of our country, our fatherland, our Soviet socialist motherland. When the alarm sounded in the Far East at the end of 1931,

Comrade Stalin with all decisiveness set forth the problem, that problem which he repeatedly set forth: the weak and backward are always beaten. It is necessary to be strong and sturdy. For this we had to bring the country into a state of defense readiness, we had to arm our glorious Red Army in such away that it could counter any enemies. And we presented industry with a heavy-enough task: in the course of one year to do that which should require several years. In 1932 we were forced to mobilize our industry, casting aside civil production, to transfer industry to the production of modern tools of the country's defense.

As a result, despite the damage done to general development, Soviet military industry had become one of the economy's strongest branches.[89]

Sergei Kirov, reporting in Leningrad on this Central Committee plenum on the results of the First Five-Year Plan, made much the same point:

I already said at the beginning that we underfulfilled the Five-Year Plan for industrial production by a few percentage points. It should be said that we do not consider this a great harm, a great defect in our work. The fact is that over the last year and a half and especially in 1932 we were forced to carry out a great shift in the work of our machine-building factories to turn them towards the production of artillery and means of defense of our country. You know that on the dawn of the last year of the Five-Year Plan, the fourth year, around our Soviet Union storm clouds gathered very threateningly, mainly in the East. And then the Central Committee, at the initiative of Comrade Stalin, raised the question of the Five-Year Plan. Of course, the Five-Year Plan is the Five-Year Plan, consumer goods are consumer goods, light industry will have its turn, but we're going to sit by the sea and wait for nice weather. If we're going to sit and wait until someone tests to see how well-prepared the Soviet state is to defend our socialist project, and we don't take the measures as we need to meet any enemy, we might end up in a very difficult position.

As a result, "the relative nonfulfillment of our program . . . is wholly conditioned on the fact that we turned a significant share of our attention to defense production,"[90] and that sacrifice was worth making.

However necessary it seemed, the defense burden could not be borne indefinitely. As early as May 1932, there were already indications that the drive would be scaled back to more moderate levels. Voroshilov's May report to the Defense Commission on the 1933 military budget requested only 3,000 planes in 1933, down 500 from 1932, but kept tank procurement at 10,000. Real cuts in defense spending and production had to wait until the industrial shortfall's true extent had been clarified. In November 1932, the Defense Commission set up a commission of nearly twenty members to determine the military order for 1933, which produced a plan clearly bearing the stamp of the unpleasant experience of 1932. Aircraft production was to grow only slightly, from 3,505 to 3,615. Tank targets fell significantly, from 10,000 to 4,220.[91]

This new, lower order did not come from any improvement in relations between Japan and the Soviet Union. After dissembling for nearly a year, Uchida Kosai told Troianovskii secretly that the time was not right for a nonaggression pact. The Soviets, furious at being put off for so long and then rejected, published the relevant diplomatic correspondence over strenuous Japanese objections.[92] With little prospect of improvement on the diplomatic front, the reduction in the defense order came instead from a recognition that the pace sought in 1932 was not sustainable. Only a more moderate order, in keeping with what the production industry could manage without undue strain, would supply the Red Army with weaponry without bankrupting the Soviet economy.

Perhaps the best sign that Stalin and his Defense Commission realized that they had pushed too hard and too fast is something that did not happen. The terrible shortfall in Soviet industry led to no purges. Ordzhonikidze's grasp on Narkomtiazhprom remained firm. Pavlunovskii, Martinovich, Budniak, and Piatakov all kept their jobs until they perished during the Great Purges. The key figures within military industry stayed in place, and there was no new wave of persecution of bourgeois specialists or failed managers.[93] Stalin realized that he had pushed too hard, but whereas there was no reason to strive to achieve more than industry had been able to do, there was also no real reason to retreat substantially from what had already been achieved. The level of armaments production and industrial mobilization provoked by the Manchurian crisis would remain steady until the final rush to prepare for the Second World War. An army of planners and bureaucrats now coordinated a network of military and civilian factories supplying everything the Red Army might desire. The militarization of the Soviet Union was essentially complete and would endure through World War II and, ultimately, until the final collapse of the Soviet Union.

Conclusion

The new year in 1933 did not just mean that Soviet military industry would turn its energies to a new and more moderate production program. January 1933 also marked the end of the First Five-Year Plan, which was proclaimed completed ahead of schedule after four years and three months. This provoked a flurry of retrospective examinations of Stalin's triumphs. Despite the dramatic failures of the military buildup in 1932, planners in the Red Army and Narkomtiazhprom were forced by the end of the Five-Year Plan to take a longer-term view back at their own performance. They were impressed with what they found.

The comparison between Soviet defenses in 1933 and their feeble state in the mid-1920s is truly striking and is not solely a creation of Stalinist agitprop. Concentrating on issues of mobilization, one review prepared on 12 October 1932 stated that there had never really been a five-year plan for defense. Since the First Five-Year Plan had never been matched by a specific defense plan, it was quite difficult to measure precisely the extent to which the Soviet defense industry had reached its goals. Even so, there was cause for satisfaction. Focusing its attentions on mobilization variant number 10, the report found that a kind of stability had been achieved in what the Red Army expected from industry. Moreover, mobilization variant number 10 "delivers a decisive blow for qualitative change in the Red Army's structure." Whereas older weapons such as firearms and field artillery remained relatively stable, variant number 10 modernized the Red Army through rapid growth in howitzers, small-caliber artillery, and especially tanks.[1]

Despite continuing difficulties in the production of artillery shells, the Red Army had matched foreign armies in the state of its communications, optical gear, and other technically advanced equipment and could no longer be described as backward. All those achievements could be traced to the accomplishments of the First Five-Year Plan and the inseparable unity between industrializing the Soviet economy and building Soviet defenses:

210

The growth process explained above in the quantitative and military-technical level of the NKVM's order is an expression and consequence of the general industrial growth of the USSR, and of the successes achieved on the socialist construction front. These successes created the material base for the growth of the Red Army. The NKVM order generally created a demand, and the preconditions for satisfying it were created by the very course of socialist construction.

The weaknesses of Soviet defense had come from backwardness; the USSR's current strength proved the extent of Soviet achievements.[2]

Another retrospective report found that the First Five-Year Plan "brought about stormy growth in the combat and military-technical base of the Red Army." Put together on 31 October 1932 from materials prepared by N. L. Shpektorov, this report concentrated on manufacturing over mobilization. It found that over the course of the First Five-Year Plan, as a result of over 1,600 million rubles of investment in military industry, with another 400 million rubles in defense production of civil industry, entirely new types of weapons had been put into production: light machine guns, small-caliber and heavy artillery, and tanks. The production capacity for old systems had skyrocketed, with machine gun capacity growing by nine times and artillery by twelve to thirteen times. "On the basis of these successes," the report concluded, "the Red Army has moved into the same rank of the most powerful armies of the capitalist countries by the structure and technical level of its arms."[3]

Conversely, it was questionable, the report found, whether industry would be able to meet the mobilization commitments it had assumed. Both ferrous and nonferrous metallurgy were insufficient for wartime needs, and the chemical industry was too reliant on foreign technology and produced inadequate quantities of key raw materials. Waste was everywhere: shell manufacture used twice as much metal per shell as British factories. Despite efforts to involve civil industry more deeply in military production, the USSR was still too reliant on military factories. Important construction projects were half complete, tying up vital capital and creating bottlenecks and disproportions in the supply of components for complex systems. Military production in civil industry and capital investment remained in desperate need of improvement. The overall conclusion was clear: the Red Army, despite its successes, required still more capital for military industry.[4]

Yet another look at the results of capital investment repeated the celebration of newly instituted production. Rifle capacity had doubled, bullet capacity had quadrupled, and shell capacity was five times greater than at the start of the Five-Year Plan. Tanks, military aircraft, and poison gas had become major industries in their own right, despite starting from negligible beginnings. Antitank guns were produced where none had existed before.[5] Improvements were qualitative as well as quantitative. The T-26 and BT tanks produced in 1932 and 1933 were far superior to the T-18/MS-1—not just in the number produced, but in their battlefield effectiveness as well. The Red Army of 1933 looked much different from the Red Army that began the First Five-Year Plan.[6]

Although Frunze was long dead by the completion of the First Five-Year Plan, his vision of a militarized Soviet society lived and flourished. By the end of 1932, the militarization of the Soviet economy was firmly established. The military sector took up a strong and growing portion of the Soviet economy, and the Red Army was the key beneficiary. By the end of 1932, the combined employment of military industry's production trusts and military factories directly under the GVMU's authority had grown to 310,000. This figure is extremely conservative, for it does not include workers in civil factories who produced armaments and equipment for the Red Army. It likewise neglects employment in the Soviet aviation industry, which was almost entirely dominated by military production.[7] From perhaps 3 percent of industrial employment in 1928, the defense industry's share of a growing pool had grown, in R. W. Davies's calculation, to 5.3 percent in 1930 and 7.1 percent in 1932. Military production also rose as a share of net industrial production from 2.6 percent in 1930 to 5.7 percent in 1932. Davies also estimated that the proportion of the state budget spent on defense grew from 4 percent in 1929–1930 to perhaps as much as 9 percent in 1932.[8] This may be too low. A document on defense spending in the First Five-Year Plan suggests that total defense spending after adding investment, defense spending within civil administration, and other items to the Red Army's budget reached 6,422.9 million rubles in 1932, nearly 17 percent of 1932's 38,000 million–ruble budget.[9]

Figures do not reveal an equally significant aspect of the militarization of the Soviet society: the increasing importance of military considerations, and of actual military personnel, in making economic policy. This book has detailed industrial managers' decaying ability to resist more arduous demands from the Red Army. The network of mobilization cells and constant attention to preparing all industry for war provided the means by which the Red Army's high command could exert steady pressure to achieve its end. By the end of 1932, the military's place at the center of the Soviet economy was secure. At the very top of the Soviet administrative hierarchy, regular meetings of Stalin's Defense Commission ensured that economic planning was closely linked to military needs.

As the Second Five-Year Plan unfolded, Stalin was confident in the USSR's military might. At the 1934 Seventeenth Congress of the Communist party (the "Congress of Victors"), to a man, the party's highest authorities hailed the results of the First Five-Year Plan in building the Soviet Union's defense potential. Molotov, opening the congress on 29 January 1934, told the delegates:

> Now our country has such a powerful industry, armed with such technology and such machinery, that it can in the future build everything in the quantities necessary for the technical rearmament of all branches of the national

economy—industry itself, agriculture, and transport—and for the strengthening of the country's defense potential.

Stalin echoed this more subtly in discussing the capitalist world's preparations for war against the USSR. While the Soviet Union continued its struggle for peace, it prepared for the eventuality of war, and "it cannot be said that the USSR's exertions in this sphere have had no success." As a result of the "growth of the strength and power of the USSR," foreign states, in particular Poland, had been forced into friendlier relations with the USSR.[10]

Ordzhonikidze, recounting for the delegates the triumphs of Soviet industry over the first years of industrialization, opened his speech by explaining that the party had solved three key problems simultaneously through Stalin's revolution: creating an industrial infrastructure, reorganizing agriculture on a socialist base, and "strengthening the defense of the country." The unprecedented expansion of Soviet industry had "determined the resolution of the country's defense problem." Although he declined to give the congress any specifics on the defense industry, Ordzhonikidze did tell the delegates that great progress had been made since 1930.[11] Even the losers of the factional struggles of the 1920s were called out to proclaim the growing military might of the Soviet Union. Bukharin told the congress that the Bolshevik leadership had done two things to reduce the threat of war: first, careful diplomacy had averted war, and second, the party had "with great pressure, with great exertions, conducted and constructed a *military defense,* introducing a base of heavy industry. That industry's development was called for not only by our internal situation, but also our *external* situation."[12]

The successes that Stalin hailed and the high levels of military production that the Manchurian crisis provoked had a darker side as well. Once the USSR had reached the plateau of mass production achieved in the wake of the crisis in the Far East, it never stepped back. Military factories continued to produce weapons at the same high level, and the pace accelerated even more with the approach of World War II. Figures for military production through the 1930s vary widely and make precise judgments difficult, especially as qualitative improvements in design continued all the time. Still, it seems evident that there was no drop-off in military production after 1932. Mark Harrison and R. W. Davies's survey of military production during the Second Five-Year Plan, 1933–1937, found a more stable environment than the turmoil and rapid advances of the First Five-Year Plan. Even a slight dip in production in 1935 represented only a temporary disruption, caused by a shift to still more intensive production, in an otherwise steady advance. Aircraft procurement fell as individual aircraft designs grew more complex and expensive, but tank production remained at an elevated level, and artillery purchases increased. By the late 1930s, as general war approached, military production pushed forward even further from an already high level (see table 20).[13]

Table 20. Production of Key Military Goods during the 1930s

Year	Military Aircraft	Tanks	Machine Guns	Artillery Pieces
1931	860–1,489	740	40,900–48,860	1,911–2,500
1932	1,734–2,483	3,038–3,040	45,000–63,357	1,206–2,574
1933	2,952–3,670	3,509	32,600–32,700	4,368–4,638
1934	3,109–3,962	3,565	29,200	4,123
1935	1,612–2,124	3,055	29,600–31,800	4,383
1936	2,688–3,478	4,803–4,804	21,900–31,100	4,347–5,235
1937	4,435–5,823	1,559	42,300–74,657	5,443–5,473
1938	5,469–7,380	2,271	77,100–112,010	7,126–12,867

Despite the satisfaction Stalin expressed with the militarized economy he had created, it is highly questionable whether this served the best interests of the Soviet state. Leaving aside the millions of deaths caused by Stalin's criminal agricultural policy and the appalling living conditions endured by those who built socialism for him, his military-industrial revolution had pernicious consequences for the Soviet people and the Soviet state. This does not refer merely to the economic stagnation of the Brezhnev era; some of the USSR's terrible losses in World War II can be blamed on Stalin's military buildup. This study has assumed throughout that Stalin's revolution from above is worthy of study in itself; now, it is appropriate to examine some of its implications for later Soviet history.

The debate on the necessity of the militarization of the Soviet Union and the debate over industrialization turn on the question of World War II. Put simply, could the Soviet Union have beaten Hitler without the immense sacrifices of industrialization and militarization over the prewar five-year plans? It is easy to find Soviets who lived through Stalinism and see the issue exactly as Marshal Zhukov does in his memoirs:

> The peoples of the world generally realize that before all else it was Soviet soldiers and Soviet weapons that saved Europe from the plague of fascism, that the destruction of Hitler's Germany is the greatest historical achievement of the Soviet nation. I think that the foundation for this was already laid in those years when the Soviet people at the call of the party took up the industrialization of the country.[14]

In other words, the sacrifices of Stalin's industrialization were justified by the subsequent need to use Soviet industry to destroy Hitler's Third Reich.

This line of argument is given more weight by some Western scholars who have claimed that Hitler's war against the Soviet Union was lost by the winter of 1941–1942. Klaus Reinhardt asserts that "Hitler's plans and Germany's chances of successfully prosecuting the war had failed by October 1941, or at the latest by the start of the Russian counter-offensive outside Moscow in December 1941." By 31 January 1942, the Germans had suffered nearly 1 million casualties, producing terrible manpower shortages. By the same date, 4,241 tanks and self-propelled guns had been destroyed, meaning that "by 30 March 1942 the 16 panzer divisions were left with only 140 operational panzers." Earl Ziemke and Magna Bauer concur that the battle of Moscow "terminated Germany's bid for world power," and thereafter, Hitler could only hope to stave off defeat, not struggle to victory.[15] If this argument is correct and Germany had no hope of victory by the end of 1941, Stalin deserves some credit. Despite the terror that destroyed the Red Army's best officers on the eve of the war and led Soviet villagers to greet the invading *Wehrmacht* with bread and salt, it was the tanks and planes that Stalin built in the interwar years that blunted the German attack and stopped fascism. Are we then to follow the verdict of Jerry Hough that the industrialization drive was, in military terms, "spectacularly successful"?[16]

The question of whether the Soviet Union might have been better prepared for World War II by following a different economic path has been most carefully examined by Holland Hunter and Janusz Szyrmer. Hunter's earlier work gave a rather prominent role to the pernicious effects of defense expenditure on the Soviet economy during the 1930s. Specifically, he argued that "rearmament . . . cut sharply into household consumption after the first few years and at the end of the 1930s cut sharply into civilian fixed capital formation as well."[17] A detailed model of the Soviet economy from 1928 to 1940 led him to change his mind. He and Szyrmer concluded that collectivization was the single most damaging of Stalin's economic policies. By not making that one policy choice, regardless of military spending or levels of domestic consumption, Soviet capital stock at the outbreak of World War II would have been about 30 percent higher than it in fact was. By contrast, as the counterfactual argument runs, if Stalin had maintained his actual policies of keeping consumption low and collectivizing agriculture but had slowed the growth of military spending, the benefit to the Soviet economy would have been a mere 5 percent. In this examination, the lesson seems clear. The real issue appears to have been collectivization; military spending apparently had only a marginal impact on the performance of the Soviet economy.[18]

But the case is not closed. Hunter and Szyrmer's data on defense spending rely on published sources and hence significantly underestimate the defense burden. For example, their figures show defense spending in 1932 at the height of the Manchurian crisis as 1,296 million rubles, or a mere 4.3 percent of the state budget.[19] Davies, by contrast, found that the Red Army's budget for 1932 was 4,308 million rubles and that procurement of equipment and weaponry *alone* came to 2,197 million rubles. As mentioned earlier, archival sources suggest that the total defense budget for 1932 amounted to 6,422.9 million rubles, nearly five times greater than the amount Hunter and Szyrmer used in their calculations.[20] In short, Hunter and Szyrmer naturally concluded Stalin that could have found few savings from cutting military expenditures, because their data portrayed military spending as far lower than it actually was. Their conclusion that Stalin could have done more for the Soviet people by forgoing collectivization than by any other step is certainly correct, but the possibilities offered by reduced defense spending should not be overlooked. Rubles spent on military procurement were not investment, in that they provided no future benefits to the Soviet economy. Even the possible benefits of technological spin-offs from defense spending were minimized in the Soviet Union by the pervasive secrecy that blocked the diffusion of innovations purchased from the West or developed at home. If that funding had been directed to productive investment, the Soviet economy would have been that much stronger when the time came to prepare for war with Nazi Germany.

High levels of military spending through the 1930s had an important unintended result beyond the general damage they did to the Soviet economy. In a sense, the Soviet Union rearmed for World War II six or seven years too early. By producing so much ordnance during the early and mid-1930s, the Soviet Union began the Great Fatherland War burdened with tens of thousands of obsolete tanks and planes. The total German tank stock in September 1939 at the outbreak of war was 3,200 tanks, less than the Soviet Union produced in a year. As of May 1940, the Soviet army had 20,074 tanks: 69 T-35s; 470 T-28s; 7,300 BTs; 7,985 T-26s; 1,027 T-26 flamethrowing tanks; and 3,223 assorted T-37, T-38, and T-40 tankettes. All those tanks were to a greater or lesser degree obsolete, with armor too thin and guns of too small a caliber to match the demands of World War II. The Soviets possesed tank designs of truly stunning superiority in comparison to the tanks of other powers, but during 1940 and the first half of 1941, only 639 KV-1 heavy tanks and 1,215 T-34 medium tanks entered the Soviet army. The huge fleet of obsolete tanks choking the Soviet army in the earlier days of the war would only consume valuable fuel, ammunition, and trained crews.[21] Stockpiling weapons such as rifles and machine guns that improved slowly in design carried no risk; building thousands of tanks and planes guaranteed that scarce resources went to technology that would quickly be out of date.

For both economic development and military effectiveness, the correct policy would have de-emphasized current production, turning instead toward building capacity and improving design and technology. Such an alternative, however, ran against the very essence of Stalinism, which was to recognize no compromises or trade-offs. Military planners never truly saw the need to decide between devoting resources to expanding production capacity and increasing current production. Stalin himself, along with his closest associates, saw no need to slow the growth of the Red Army for the sake of the overall economy. By granting the Red Army a powerful voice in policy, while radicalizing Soviet society to such an extent that moderation became criminal, Stalin ensured that the Soviet defense economy would grow unchecked. The military-industrial revolution, aimed at providing security for the Soviet Union, instead nearly destroyed it in the opening days of the clash with Nazi Germany. By the 1980s, the rigid and inflexible economy this revolution bequeathed to the Soviet people ultimately undermined the Soviet state itself, destroying that which it was meant to defend.

Appendix 1

Soviet Defense Budgets

	Published Defense Budget	Davies: NKVM Budget	Stone: NKVM Budget	Total Defense Budget	Overall State Budget
1922–1923	230.9				1,460.0
1923–1924	402.3		248.2		2,317.6
1924–1925	443.8		405		2,969.5
1925–1926	638.0		602.5		4,050.9
1926–1927	633.8		700		5,334.6
1927–1928	774.6		743		6,465.0
1928–1929	879.8	850	850	1,211.3	8,240.9
1929–1930	1,046.0	1,046	995	1,685.7	12,335.0
Special quarter	433.7			690.0	5,038.2
1931	1,288.4	1,790	1,810	2,976.2	25,097.0
1932	1,296.2	4,308	4,574	6,422.9	37,995.1
1933	1,420.7	4,738	4,733		42,080.6
1934	5,019.1				5,444.7
1935	8,185.8				73,571.7
1936	14,882.7				92,480.2
1937	17,481.0				106,238.3

Million rubles, current prices.
The figures I found for the NKVM budget are not precisely the same as those Davies found, but they are quite close. Their divergence from Soviet published figures is relatively small through 1930 but increases quickly thereafter.
Note that the total defense budget was *not* limited to spending on the NKVM, the Red Army. Other defense expenditures added an amount roughly equivalent to one-third of the Red Army budget. These figures, it must be stressed, are nominal and not adjusted for inflation.

Sources:
Published Defense Budget: R. W. Davies, *Emergence of the Soviet Budgetary System* (Cambridge, 1958) 83.
Davies NKVM Budget: R. W. Davies, "Soviet Military Expenditure and the Armaments Industry, 1929–1933," *EAS* 45 (1993): 593.
Stone NKVM Budget: Drawn from budgetary allotments covered in the text.
Total Defense Budget: Briefing paper on financing of defense work from 1928–1929 to 1932 (million rubles): RGVA f. 4, op. 14, d. 1051, l. 2. Cost basis unspecified, but probably current year. The subfigures for the NKVM budget matched neither Davies's nor mine: for 1928–1929, 890 million rubles; 1929–1930, 1,075.8 million; special quarter, 441.4 million; 1931, 1,830 million; 1932, 3,970 million.
Overall State Budget: Davies, *Emergence of the Soviet Budgetary System,* 83, 296.

Appendix 2

Military Industry during the First Five-Year Plan

Borodin (GVMU) Report on Military Industry, 1926–1927 through 1932

	Gross Production Nonaviation	Gross Production Aviation	Capital Investment	Labor Force Nonaviation	Labor Force Aviation
1926–1927	181.9	—	—	69,023	5,094
1927–1928	290.2	32.4	78.1	75,109	6,824
1928–1929	379.9	46.2	114.6	80,462	7,944
1929–1930	574.7	90.1	170.7	110,381	12,466
Special quarter	222.4	34.3	67.1	146,101	20,437
1930	687.2	83.3	—	123,681	15,139
1931	1,137.9	156.3	433.6	193,390	36,419
1932	1,622.7	345.6	739.9	—	—

Valovaia (gross) production, million rubles, 1926–1927 prices. Aggregate production of military-industrial trusts. These figures do *not* include much tank production or defense production of civil factories. This chart also includes a production figure for the nonexistent 1930 fiscal year—evidently an interpolation calculated from the last three quarters of the 1929–1930 fiscal year and the special quarter. Capital investment figures do not specify cost basis and do include housing. January? 1933: RGAE f. 7279, op. 41, d. 12, ll. 55–76, 100–110. "Labor force" includes only blue-collar workers and apprentices, not white-collar, technical, or service workers. Also excluded are workers in the tank industry and defense workers in civil industry. Other sources suggest that the non-blue-collar workers not included amounted to 30 to 35 percent of the total labor force.

A similar Gosplan source gives figures that, unlike those above, include Spetsmashtrest, the tank-building trust. The correspondence between the two sets is close if not exact (see the second table).

Basic Indicators of Fulfillment of the Five-Year Plan of Military Industry

	Gross Production Civil and Military	Gross Production Military	Gross Production Aviation	Labor Force Nonaviation	Labor Force Aviation
1927–1928	302.5	145.3	35.1	88,195	6,589
1928–1929	410.0	184.2	48.6	99,177	8,787
1929–1930	613.4	243.9	74.6	133,067	11,771
1930	733.4	315.3	86.5	155,565	14,501
1931	1,207.7	564.5	164.6	219,336	36,269
1932	1,733.1	874.4	350.5	263,524	58,175

Valovaia (gross) production, million rubles, 1926–1927 prices. Aggregate production of military trusts, including Spetsmashtrest. Nonaviation figures from report of 14 July 1933: RGAE f. 4372, op. 91, d. 1198, ll. 84–86; aviation figures from ibid., ll. 84–86.

The first two columns do *not* include aviation. Aviation includes single line item from gross production, with breakdown between military and civil production unspecified. Aviation at this period was, however, overwhelmingly military in nature.

"Labor force" includes only blue-collar workers and apprentices, not white-collar, technical, or service workers. Also excluded are defense workers in civil industry. Other sources suggest that the non-blue-collar workers not included amounted to 30 to 35 percent of the total labor force.

Appendix 3

Abbreviations and Terms

ARCHIVAL CITATIONS

f.	*fond,* collection
op.	*opis',* subgroup within a collection; also, a catalog of such a group
d.	*delo,* file
l., ll.	*list, listy,* leaf or page, pages
ob.	*obratnaia,* obverse

ARCHIVES

GARF	*Gosudarstvennyi arkhiv Rossiiskoi Federatsii,* State Archive of the Russian Federation
RGAE	*Rossiiskii gosudarstvennyi arkhiv ekonomiki,* Russian State Archive of the Economy
RGVA	*Rossiiskii gosudarstvennyi voennyi arkhiv,* Russian State Military Archive
RTsKhIDNI	*Rossiiskii tsentr khraneniia i izucheniia dokumentov noveishei istorii,* Russian Center for the Preservation and Study of Documents of Contemporary History

JOURNALS

AHR	*American Historical Review*
EAS	*Europe-Asia Studies* (formerly *Soviet Studies*)

EcHR	*Economic History Review*
NNI	*Novaia i noveishaia istoriia*
OI	*Otechestvennaia istoriia*
PoC	*Problems of Communism*
RR	*Russian Review*
SR	*Slavic Review*
SS	*Soviet Studies*
VI	*Voprosy istorii*
ViR	*Voina i revoliutsiia*
ViT	*Voina i tekhnika*
VIZh	*Voenno-istoricheskii zhurnal*

GROUPS AND ORGANIZATIONS

GPU, OGPU	(Ob"edinennoe) Glavnoe politicheskoe upravlenie, (Unified) Main Political Directorate. Secret police.
GUAP	Glavnoe upravlenie aviatsionnoi promyshlennosti, Main Directorate of the Aviation Industry.
GVMU	Glavnoe voenno-mobilizatsionnoe upravlenie, Main Military-Mobilization Directorate. Created in 1932 to run peacetime military production as well as war planning and mobilization.
GVPU	See VPU.
Ispolkom	Ispol'nitel'nyi komitet. Executive Committee.
KO	Komissiia oborony, Defense Commission. Soviet defense cabinet from the end of 1930.
MMK, MMZ	Mezhduvedomstvennyi mobilizatsionnyi komitet, zasedanie, Interinstitutional Mobilization Committee, Session.
MPU	Mobilizatsionno-planovoe upravlenie Vesenkha, Mobilization-Planning Directorate. Ran war planning and mobilization for Vesenkha.
Narkomtiazhprom	People's Commissariat of Heavy Industry.
NK	Narodnyi komissar, Narodnyi komissariat, People's Commissariat. The rough equivalent of a ministry (in

	the British system) or a cabinet-level department (in the American system).
NKFin	Narodnyi komissariat finansov, People's Commissariat of Finance.
NKRKI	Narodnyi komissariat raboche-krest'ianskoi inspektsii; see Rabkrin.
NKTP	Narodnyi komissariat tiazheloi promyshlennosti; see Narkomtiazhprom.
NKVM	Narodnyi komissariat po voennym i morskim delam, People's Commissariat for Military and Naval Affairs. The Soviet ministry of defense.
OGPU	See GPU.
Rabkrin	Raboche-krest'ianskaia inspektsiia, Workers'-Peasants' Inspectorate.
Revvoensovet	Revoliutsionnyi voennyi sovet, Revolutionary Military Council. Supreme collective decision-making body of the Red Army, 1918–1934.
RKKA	Raboche-krest'ianskaia Krasnaia Armiia, Workers' and Peasants' Red Army. Official name of the Red Army.
RZ	rasporiaditel'noe zasedanie, executive session; or rasshi-rennoe zasedanie, expanded session.
RZ STO	Executive Session of Council of Labor and Defense. Soviet defense cabinet from 1927 to 1930.
SNK	Sovnarkom sovet narodnykh komissarov, Council of People's Commissars. Nominal government of the Soviet Union, functioning as a cabinet of ministers.
Spetsmashtrest	Special Machine-Building Trust. Founded in 1932 to run tank production.
STO	Sovet truda i oborony, Council of Labor and Defense. Sub-committee of Sovnarkom nominally responsible for defense but in fact usually handling economic policy instead.
UMM	Upravlenie motorizatsii i mekhanizatsii, Motorization and Mechanization Directorate of the Red Army.
VAO	Gosudarstvennyi vsesoiuznoe ob"edinenie aviatsionnoi promyshlennosti, State All-Union Association of the Aviation Industry.
Vesenkha	VSNKh, or Vysshii sovet narodnogo khoziaistva, Supreme Council of the National Economy. Served as Soviet Ministry of Industry until the creation of Narkomtiazhprom.

VMF	Voenno-morskoi flot, navy.
VO	Voennyi okrug, military district.
Voenprom	Proizvodstvennoe ob"edinenie voennoi promyshlennosti, Production Association of Military Industry.
VPU, GVPU	(Glavnoe) Voenno-promyshlennoe upravlenie, (Main) Military-Industrial Directorate. Administered production trusts and factories of military industry.
VVS	Voenno-vozdushnye sily, air force.

Appendix 4

Biographical Directory

Avanesov, Varlaam Aleksandrovich (Martirosov, Suren Karpovich; Suren Kara-metovich Martirosian). (1884–1930). Social Democrat from 1903, Bolshevik from 1914. From 1925, member of presidium of Vesenkha. Request to leave military industry approved by the Politburo 2 December 1926.

Bogdanov, Petr Alekseevich (1882–1939). From 1919 to 1925, head of the Council (later Main Directorate) of Military Industry under Vesenkha. From 1920, also chair of the Main Directorate of Metal Industry under Vesenkha. From 1921 to 1925, also chair of Russian Republic Vesenkha. Also chair of KVZ, the Committee for Military Orders. February 1926, named chair of Ispolkom of the North Caucasus Krai. December 1929, named to head Amtorg; also unofficial Soviet representative to the United States.

Efimov, Nikolai Alekseevich (1897–1937). From 1925, chief of Red Army's II (Organization-Mobilization) Directorate. Later (as of late 1931) Red Army's deputy director of armaments and head of the Main Artillery Directorate.

Egorov, Aleksandr Il'ich (1883–1939). Red Army representative in Military-Industrial Directorate, 1926–1927? Chief of staff, 1931–1937.

Frunze, Mikhail Vasil'evich (1885–1925). People's commissar for military and naval affairs, 1925.

Khalepskii, Innokentii Andreevich (1893–1938). Director of the Military-Technical Administration of the RKKA, 1924–1929. Head of Red Army's Motorization and Mechanization Directorate from November 1929.

Krzhizhanovskii, Gleb Maksimilianovich (1872–1959). Chair of Gosplan until 1930.

Kuibyshev, Nikolai Vladimirovich (1893–1938). Secretary of RZ STO from October–November 1930; director of Rabkrin's Military-Naval Inspectorate from November 1930.

Kuibyshev, Valerian Vladimirovich (1888–1935). People's commissar of the Workers'-Peasants' Inspectorate–Central Control Commission from 1923 to 1926. Chair of Vesenkha from 1926 to 1930. Member of Politburo from 1927. Chair of Gosplan and deputy chair of Sovnarkom/STO from 1930.

Mekhonoshin, Konstantin Aleksandrovich (1889–1938). From 1928, deputy director of the Defense Sector of Gosplan. Chair of Gosplan's Defense Sector from March–April 1929.

Molotov (Skriabin), Viacheslav Mikhailovich (1890–1986). From 1930 to 1941, chair of Sovnarkom and Defense Commission. Candidate member of Politburo from 1921 to 1926; full member from 1926 to 1957.

Ordzhonikidze, Sergo (Grigorii Konstantinovich) (1886–1937). Following service in Transcaucasia, chair of Rabkrin and Central Control Committee from 1926 to 1930. Made chair of Vesenkha in November 1930; upon breakup of Vesenkha in 1932, made people's commissar of heavy industry. Member of Central Committee, 1921–1926; candidate member of Politburo, 1926–1930; full member of Politburo, 1930–1937.

Pavlunovskii, Ivan Petrovich (1888 or 1889–1940). From c. 1919 to 1926, in Cheka in Siberia, then plenipotentiary representative of the OGPU in Transcaucasia from 1926 to 1928. From 1928 to 1930, director of Military-Naval Inspectorate of Rabkrin. Deputy chair of Vesenkha from November 1930, and director of Main Military-Mobilization Directorate from 1932. Candidate member of Central Committee from 1934.

Postnikov, Aleksandr Mikhailovich (1886–1937). Director of Vesenkha's Mobilization-Planning Directorate from April 1927 until July 1930. As of July 1930, deputy people's commissar of transportation.

Rykov, Aleksei Ivanovich (1881–1938). Bolshevik from 1903. Member of Politburo from 1919 (1923?) to 1930. From 1924 to 1930, chair of Sovnarkom, from 1926 to 1930, chair of the STO, and from 1927 to 1930, chair of the RZ STO. Removed as chair of Sovnarkom on 19 December 1930; in the same month, removed from the Politburo. From 1931 to 1936, people's commissar of posts and telegraphs.

Shaposhnikov, Boris Mikhailovich (1882–1945). Colonel in tsarist general staff. Party member from 1930. From 1925 to 1927 and 1935 to 1937, commander of Leningrad Military District. From 1927 to 1928, commander of Moscow Military District. Red Army chief of staff from 1928 to 1931. In May 1931, transferred to command the Volga Military District. From 1932 to 1935, director of the Frunze Academy. After May 1937, again director of the general staff through 1940.

Smilga, Ivar Tenisovich (1892–1937 or 1938?). Bolshevik from 1907. Civil war veteran, and deputy director of Gosplan from 1923 to 1926. Expelled from party in 1927 for Trotskyite activities. Returned to party and made deputy director of Mobilization-Planning Directorate in February 1930. Director of Mobilization-Planning Directorate from July 1930 until autumn 1930? Moved in 1932 to deputy chair of Central Asian Gosplan.

Stalin, Joseph Vissarionovich (1879–1953). Member of Central Committee from January 1912. Participant in revolution and civil war as member of Revvoensovet and on southern, southwestern, and western fronts. Member of Central Committee from March 1918. General secretary of the party from 1922.

Tolokontsev, Aleksandr Fedorovich (1889–1937). From August–September 1926, acting director of VPU. From December 1926 to March 1929, director of VPU. From November 1929 to August 1930, chair of Association of General Machine-Building; chief of Heavy Machine-Building from August 1930.

Tukhachevskii, Mikhail Nikolaevich (1893–1937). From July 1924, Red Army's deputy chief of staff; from November 1925 to May 1928, Red Army's chief of staff. From May 1928 to June 1931, commander of Leningrad Military District. From 19 June 1931, deputy people's commissar for military and naval affairs, director of armaments.

Uborevich, Ieronim Petrovich (1896–1937). From 1930 to 1931, deputy chair of Revvoensovet and Red Army's director of armaments. From 1931 to 1937, commander of the Belorussian Military District. Candidate member of the Politburo from 1930 to 1937.

Unshlikht, Iosif Stanislavovich (1879–1938). From 1925, candidate member of the Politburo. After service in Cheka, deputy chair of Revvoensovet from February 1925. Released from the Red Army on 30 May 1930 and transferred to Vesenkha as Kuibyshev's deputy for defense matters. December 1930, appointed deputy chair of Gosplan, responsible for defense matters. From 1933 to 1935, chief of Main Directorate of the Civil Air Fleet.

Uryvaev, Mikhail Georgievich. Director of VPU/GVPU, March 1929 to July? 1930. Removed as director of GVPU by July 1930 Politburo decision and temporarily made deputy director of Mobilization-Planning Directorate. Chair of Aviation Association, July 1930 to March 1931.

Ventsov, Semen I. Chief of Red Army's Staff II (Organization-Mobilization Directorate) until 1925. Secretary of RZ STO until 30 March 1928.

Vladimirskii, Mikhail Fedorovich (1874–1951). Chair of Defense Sector of Gosplan, 1926? to 1928?

Voroshilov, Kliment Efremovich (1881–1969). Central Committee member from 1921; Politburo member from 1926 to 1952. People's commissar for military and naval affairs from November 1925 to June 1934; people's commissar of defense from 1934 to 1940.

Appendix 5

Archival Sources

Working with Russian archival documents proved much less complex than working with Russian archives. The nature of this study, which explores an often contentious relationship between the Soviet military and civil institutions, ensures that almost all events are covered from a variety of disputing points of view. This allows for valuable cross-checking and greatly reduces the danger of systematic falsehoods. After all, the Red Army would have been delighted to catch industrial managers inflating their production figures. To illustrate the extent of this cross-checking, one remarkable document (RGAE f. 7297, op. 38, d. 170, ll. 116–18) traces the whereabouts of every single one of the 4,315 new artillery pieces produced in 1933, balancing the number produced by industry with the number received by the army and internal security troops.

Furthermore, the priority of military security meant that the attention of the Soviet state's watchdog bodies was disproportionately directed toward the military and military industry. Rabkrin's Military-Naval Inspectorate regularly audited military industry to find bottlenecks, inefficiencies, and subterfuges. The secret police also paid close attention to defense production through its Economic Administration. Although these documents are much more difficult for historians to see, their very existence attests to the checks on official duplicity in internal correspondence. In short, the unreliability of Soviet archival documents is not beyond control.

The Russian archives that hold these documents, however, are in a terrible state of flux. Dedicated archivists work for miserly or nonexistent pay without clear guidelines on archival access. Numerous documents I examined for this study changed status from classified to declassified or vice versa over the time I was doing my research in Moscow. I was also told that a specific archival collection, extensively cited by another scholar, simply did not exist. My producing the book and pointing out the footnotes proved fruitless.

The collections I did manage to access and found most useful are described briefly below.

Russian State Military Archive (Rossiiskii gosudarstvennyi voennyi arkhiv, or RGVA). This archive's holdings cover the history of the Soviet military from 1917 through 1941. The most valuable materials for this work were found in:

f. 4	Revvoensovet
f. 7	Staff
f. 33987, 33988, and 33989	Secretariats of the People's Commissar for Military and Naval Affairs and his first and second deputies.

I also found some useful materials in the following, although the collections were not quite so rich:

f. 31811	Motorization and Mechanization Directorate
f. 33991	Armaments Directorate

Russian State Archive of the Economy (Rossiiskii gosudarstvennyi arkhiv ekonomiki, or RGAE). Records of central economic administrative bodies and production trusts are housed in this archive, which shares its space with GARF (see below). In contrast to RGVA, where defense materials are naturally the archive's reason for being, at RGAE, military matters are generally held in separate *opisi* within the collections of civil institutions. The most helpful materials at RGAE came from:

f. 2097	defense-related economic materials from the early 1920s
f. 3429	Vesenkha
f. 4372	Gosplan
f. 7297	Narkomtiazhprom

State Archive of the Russian Federation (Gosudarstvennyi arkhiv Rossiiskoi Federatsii, or GARF). For the Soviet period, this archive holds the records of central state institutions not specifically either military or economic in nature. This limited its overall relevance to this work, with some exceptions.

f. 374	Workers'-Peasants' Inspectorate. The most important documents of the Military-Naval Inspectorate are clearly stored elsewhere. Its open collections held almost nothing of interest.
f. 5446	Sovnarkom/STO. This *fond* as a whole offered little, with the surprising exception of *opis'* 55, the personal collection of Aleksei Rykov.

Russian Center for the Preservation and Study of Documents of Contemporary History (Rossiiskii tsentr khraneniia i izucheniia dokumentov noveishei istorii, or RTsKhIDNI). The former party archive, this collection contained in general two types of relevant materials.

The Central Committee collection (f. 17) contains the Politburo protocols (op. 3 and 162), which are quite terse but can be a valuable source. They include only decisions made, without record of debates or the materials on which the decisions were based. When combined with materials from other archives, these records are invaluable for establishing the chronology of policy.

Other sources fall into the larger category of personal collections of Bolshevik leaders. Although these collections contain a great deal of material of marginal value, there are some quite important documents, especially in the Ordzhonikidze and Dzerzhinskii files.

f. 74	Voroshilov
f. 76	Dzerzhinskii
f. 85	Ordzhonikidze
f. 325	Trotsky
f. 374	Vladimirskii

The Stalin, Molotov, and Frunze collections have little to offer.

Notes

INTRODUCTION

1. On Russian and Soviet military industry before World War I, see Peter Gatrell, *Government, Industry, and Rearmament in Russia, 1900–1914: The Last Argument of Tsarism* (Cambridge: Cambridge University Press, 1994), and Joseph Bradley, *Guns for the Tsar: American Technology and the Small Arms Industry in Nineteenth-Century Russia* (De Kalb, Ill.: Northern Illinois University Press, 1990). For World War I and the Russian civil war, see the quite good early survey by A. M. Volpe, "Voennaia promyshlennost' v grazhdanskoi voine," in *Grazhdanskaia voina, 1918–1921* (Moscow: Voennyi Vestnik, 1928), 371–97. See also Peter Gatrell and Mark Harrison, "The Russian and Soviet Economies in Two World Wars: A Comparative View," *EcHR* 46 (1993): 425–52; D. A. Kovalenko, *Oboronnaia promyshlennost' Sovetskoi Rossii v 1918–1920gg* (Moscow: Nauka, 1970); Silvana Malle, *The Economic Organization of War Communism, 1918–1921* (Cambridge: Cambridge University Press, 1985), 466–94.

2. Aspects of these issues have been touched on in other works, most notably Dmitri Fedotoff-White, *The Growth of the Red Army* (Princeton, N.J.: Princeton University Press, 1944), and John Erickson, *The Soviet High Command* (New York: St. Martin's, 1962). More recently, the opening of the Soviet archives has made possible more extensive research into the Soviet defense economy, much of it focusing on Mikhail Tukhachevskii. See R. W. Davies, "Soviet Military Expenditure and the Armaments Industry, 1929–33: A Reconsideration," *EAS* 45 (1993): 577–608; Lennart Samuelson's study of mobilization planning and defense industry, *Soviet Defence Industry Planning: Tukhachevskii and Military-Industrial Mobilisation* (Stockholm: Stockholm School of Economics, 1996); Nikolai Simonov, *Voenno-Promyshlennyi kompleks SSSR v 1920–1950–e gody* (Moscow: Rosspen, 1996); and Sally Stoecker's examination of military innovation, *Forging Stalin's Army: Marshal Tukhachevskii and the Politics of Military Innovation* (Boulder Colo.: Westview, 1998).

3. V. I. Lenin, "Report on War and Peace," quoted in Robert Tucker, ed., *The Lenin Anthology* (New York: Norton, 1975), 542; V. I. Lenin, *Polnoe sobranie sochinenii,* 5th ed. (Moscow: Politizdat, 1958–1965), vol. 36, ll.116–17.

4. Lenin to IX Congress of RKP(b), 5 April 1920, in *Polnoe sobranie sochinenii,* vol. 40, ll.283–84; "'Left-Wing' Communism" quoted in Tucker, *Lenin Anthology,* 550–51; "Communism and the East: Theses on the National and Colonial Questions," 5 June 1920, in ibid., 621; "Soviet Economic Development and World Revolution," May 1921, in ibid., 635–36.

5. *VKP(b) v rezoliutsiiakh i resheniiakh s"ezdov, konferentsii i plenumov TsK* (Moscow: Partizdat, 1936), 27, 29. The resolution was careful to point out that its position on the ultimate need for socialist revolution in other states did not coincide with Trotsky's.

6. Ibid., 47, 49–50.

7. Robert Tucker, *Stalin in Power: The Revolution from Above, 1928–1941* (New York: Norton, 1990), 46, 48–49. On fear of war in Bolshevik policy in general, see Manfred v. Boetticher, *Industrialisierungspolitik und Verteidigungskonzeption der UdSSR 1926–1930* (Düsseldorf: Droste, 1979).

8. Trotsky, *The Real Situation in Russia,* 140, quoted in E. H. Carr and R. W. Davies, *Foundations of a Planned Economy* (London: Macmillan, 1969–1976), vol. 3, bk. 1, 11.

9. Richard Pipes, *Russia under the Bolshevik Regime* (New York: 1994), 167; M. V. Frunze, "Edinaia voennaia doktrina i Krasnaia armiia," in *Izbrannye proizvedeniia* (Moscow: Voenizdat, 1940), 31–32.

10. *Izvestiia,* 23 February 1930, reprinted in V. V. Kuibyshev, *Izbrannye proizvedeniia* (Moscow: Politizdat, 1958), 163–65.

11. *Pis'ma I. V. Stalina V. M. Molotovu, 1925–1936gg* (Moscow: Rossiia Molodaia, 1995), doc. 62, 209.

12. David Shearer, *Industry, State and Society in Stalin's Russia* (Ithaca: N.Y.: Cornell University Press, 1996), 95, 106–7, makes a similar point that Rabkrin, the Workers'-Peasants' Inspectorate dedicated to ferreting out inefficiency and mismanagement, often created the chaos it was meant to eliminate.

13. Janos Kornai, *Economics of Shortage* (Amsterdam: North Holland, 1980), 27–28, 191–95.

14. On Rabkrin's peculiar role as inspector–general to the Soviet state, see E. A. Rees, *State Control in Soviet Russia: The Rise and Fall of the Workers' and Peasants' Inspectorate* (London: Macmillan, 1987); Shearer, *Industry, State and Society;* and two works by S. N. Ikonnikov, *Organizatsiia i deiatel'nost' RKI v 1920–1925gg* (Moscow: Akademiia Nauk, 1960), and *Sozdanie i deiatel'nost' ob"edinennykh organov TsKK-RKI v 1923–1934gg* (Moscow: Nauka, 1971).

15. Gabriel Gorodetsky, *The Precarious Truce: Anglo-Soviet Relations, 1924–1927* (Cambridge: Cambridge University Press, 1977), 232–33, makes a useful distinction between the Soviets' chronic "constant fear of war" at some indeterminate future date and a contrasting "war scare" of immediate danger.

16. Harold Lasswell's seminal "The Garrison State," *American Journal of Sociology* 47 (1941): 455–68, describes the garrison state as a one-party state obsessed with propaganda and the symbolic manipulation of its population, imposing a universal work obligation, flattening income distributions, and depending "upon war scares as a means of maintaining popular willingness to forgo immediate consumption," but then declares that no such states actually exist. Alfred Vagts's *A History of Militarism,* rev. ed. (New York: Meridian, 1959), 451, finds that before the outbreak of World War II, militarism was in decline everywhere, a conclusion difficult to reconcile with a careful look at the Soviet Union. Even Brian Bond's masterful *War and Society in Europe, 1870–1970*

(Leicester: Leicester University Press, 1983), 157–58, omits Stalin in its discussion of Hitler and Mussolini as "civilian militarists" or "militarists in mufti."

17. Mark Von Hagen, *Soldiers in the Proletarian Dictatorship: The Red Army and the Soviet Socialist State, 1917–1930* (Ithaca, N.Y.: Cornell University Press, 1990), 7.

18. Gillis draws a distinction between militarism—traditionalist rule by military officers or the domination of military values in society—and militarization—the more modern organization of society for violence. Most authorities, including Volker Berghahn, use the terms more or less interchangeably. In citing other authors' work, I use their terminology, but in general I adopt Gillis's distinction. See John R. Gillis, "Introduction," in *The Militarization of the Western World,* ed. John R. Gillis (New Brunswick, N.J.: Rutgers University Press, 1989), 1–2.

19. Herbert Spencer, *Principles of Sociology* (New York: Appleton,1906), vol. 2, sec. 547–61, 568–602; Otto Hintze, "Military Organization and the Organization of the State," in *The Historical Essays of Otto Hintze,* ed. Felix Gilbert (Oxford: Oxford University Press, 1975), 180–215. Bond (*War and Society,* 65) shares to some degree this emphasis on conscription and universal service, calling it "the most important instrument of militarization."

20. Bond, *War and Society,* 58.

21. H. C. Engelbrecht and F. C. Hanighen, *Merchants of Death: A Study of the International Armaments Industry* (New York: Dodd Mead, 1934); William McNeill, *The Pursuit of Power: Technology, Armed Force, and Society since A.D. 1000* (Chicago: University of Chicago Press, 1982), chap. 8, esp. 270, 274, 276.

22. Gillis, "Introduction," 1–2; Michael Geyer, "The Militarization of Europe, 1914–1945," in Gillis, *Militarization of the Western World,* 65, 70. See also Patrick M. Regan, *Organizing Societies for War: The Process and Consequences of Societal Militarization* (Westport, Conn.: Praeger, 1994), 4–5.

23. For militarism as a phenomenon of culture and values, see Bond, *War and Society,* 63, and Michael Howard, *War in European History* (Oxford: Oxford University Press, 1976), 109–10.

24. On this issue I follow William Odom's model of shared values between Soviet military and civil elites as presented in "The Party-Military Connection: A Critique," in *Civil-Military Relations in Communist Systems,* ed. Dale Herspring and Ivan Volgyes (Boulder, Colo.: Westview, 1978). Alternative interpretations of Soviet civil-military relations include Roman Kolkowicz's model of constant conflict between a professional military and an ideological party in *The Soviet Military and the Communist Party* (Princeton, N.J.: Princeton University Press, 1967) and Timothy Colton's of a military bribed by payoffs from the civilian leadership in *Commissars, Commanders, and Civilian Authority* (Cambridge, Mass.: Harvard University Press, 1979). For a summary of the issues involved, see Dale Herspring, *Russian Civil-Military Relations* (Bloomington, Ind.: Indiana University Press, 1996). Thomas M. Nichols, *The Sacred Cause: Civil-Military Conflict over Soviet National Security, 1917–1992* (Ithaca, N.Y.: Cornell University Press, 1993), writing on the post-Stalin period, sees constant conflict between an ideological military and a pragmatic party. On civil-military consensus, see also Stoecker, *Forging Stalin's Army,* 33–34.

25. Geyer, "Militarization of Europe," 94, makes precisely the opposite argument, denying that technology produced European militarization and emphasizing instead the role of civil society. Again, any explanation based on civil society does not work in the Soviet case.

26. See Thomas Owen's insightful discussion of "Military-Autocratic Rule and Corporate Capitalism in the Era of the Great Reforms," paper delivered at the American Association for the Advancement of Slavic Studies conference, November 16, 1996.

27. George Yaney, *The Urge to Mobilize: Agrarian Reform in Russia, 1861–1930* (Urbana: University of Illinois Press, 1982); there are intriguing parallels between the militarization of the Soviet Union and the projects of "authoritarian high modernism" described in James C. Scott's *Seeing Like a State* (New Haven, Conn.: Yale University Press, 1998).

28. Roger R. Reese, "Red Army Opposition to Forced Collectivization, 1929–1930: The Army Wavers," *SR* 55 (1996): 45. For discussion of the issue of collectivization and army resistance, see Von Hagen, *Soldiers in the Proletarian Dictatorship*, 319, Jonathan Haslam, *Soviet Foreign Policy, 1930–33* (London: Macmillan, 1983), 121–22; Stoecker, *Forging Stalin's Army*, 14.

29. Stephen Cohen, *Bukharin and the Bolshevik Revolution* (Oxford: Oxford University Press, 1973), 315; 60–106, esp. 82–83; 215. For a full discussion, see chapter 4. On the Right's lack of military service during the civil war, see also Von Hagen, *Soldiers in the Proletarian Dictatorship*, 335.

1. LAYING THE FOUNDATIONS OF REARMAMENT

1. The best short summary is Alec Nove, *An Economic History of the USSR,* rev. ed. (London: Penguin, 1989), 37–108.

2. On this process, see Charles Maier, *Recasting Bourgeois Europe: Stabilization in France, Germany and Italy in the Decade after World War I* (Princeton, N.J.: Princeton University Press, 1975).

3. Jon Jacobson, *When the Soviet Union Entered World Politics* (Berkeley: University of California Press, 1994), 36–37, 133–34. The literature on early Soviet foreign relations is voluminous; Jacobson's is an able, recent synthesis.

4. Stephen Cohen, *Bukharin and the Bolshevik Revolution* (Oxford: Oxford University Press, 1980), 147–48, 186–88. See also Robert Tucker, *Stalin as Revolutionary* (New York: Norton, 1973), 368–77; Robert Tucker, *Stalin in Power* (New York: Norton, 1990), 45–50; Isaac Deutscher, *Stalin: A Political Biography,* 2d ed. (New York: Oxford University Press, 1966), 281–93.

5. R. Craig Nation, *Black Earth, Red Star: A History of Soviet Security Policy* (Ithaca, N.Y.: Cornell University Press, 1992), 64–65.

6. I. V. Stalin, *Sochineniia* (Moscow: Politizdat, 1946–1949), vol. 6, 374–75, from the 1925 preface to *Na putiakh k Oktiabriu.*

7. Resolution of Fourteenth Party Congress, 18–31 December 1925: *VKP(b) v rezoliutsiiakh i resheniiakh s"ezdov, konferentsii i plenumov TsK* (Moscow: Partizdat, 1936), pt. 2, 48–49.

8. Teddy Uldricks, *Diplomacy and Ideology: The Origins of Soviet Foreign Relations, 1917–1930* (London: SAGE, 1979), 69.

9. On this, see Tucker, *Stalin as Revolutionary,* 292–394; Leonard Schapiro, *The Communist Party of the Soviet Union* (New York: Random House, 1960), 271–312; and Isaac Deutscher, *Trotsky: The Prophet Unarmed, 1921–1929* (London: Oxford University Press, 1959).

10. In contrast to most areas of Soviet military history, there is a sizable historiography on the Frunze reforms. The key Soviet source is I. B. Berkhin, *Voennaia reforma v SSSR* (Moscow: Voenizdat, 1958). For the Soviet view in brief, see S. A. Tyushkevich, *Soviet Armed Forces: History of Their Organizational Development* (Washington, D.C.: U.S. Air Force, 1980) 147–80 (English translation and publication by the U.S. Air Force of *Sovetskie vooruzhennye sily* [Moscow: Voenizdat, 1978]). See also Dmitrii Fedotoff-White, *Growth of the Red Army* (Princeton, N.J.: Princeton University Press, 1944), 199–276; John Erickson, *The Soviet High Command* (New York: St. Martin's, 1962); E. H. Carr, *Socialism in One Country* (New York: MacMillan, 1958–1964), vol. 2, 394–406; Melvin Hulse, "Soviet Military Doctrine, 'Militarization' of Industry, and the First Two Five-Year Plans: Developing the Military-Economic Mobilization" (Ph.D diss., Georgetown University, 1990), 126–56. Isaac Deutscher's otherwise definitive biography of Trotsky pays little attention to this matter (*Trotsky: The Prophet Unarmed*, 134–35, 162). Dmitrii Volkogonov, despite his military background, also largely ignores Trotsky's ouster in *Trotsky: The Eternal Revolutionary* (New York: Free Press, 1996), 258–59, 268.

11. M. Frunze, "Front i tyl v voine budushchego," in P. Karatygin, *Obshchie osnovy mobilizatsii promyshlennosti dlia nuzhd voiny* (Moscow: Voennyi Vestnik, 1925). Frunze's essay has been reprinted in numerous collections and appeared roughly simultaneously with Karatygin's book in the collection *Na novykh putiakh* (Moscow: Voennyi Vestnik, 1925). During the 1920s, Karatygin seems to have worked as a military economist. He most likely became acquainted with Frunze when they served together in Central Asia during the civil war. See also M. A. Gareev, *M. V. Frunze: Military Theorist* (Washington, D.C.: Pergamon, 1988); Hulse, "Soviet Military Doctrine," 84–125; James J. Schneider, *The Structure of Strategic Revolution: Total War and the Roots of the Soviet Warfare State* (Novato, Calif.: Presidio, 1994), 104–28.

12. Mikhail Frunze, "Edinaia voennaia doktrina i Krasnaia armiia," in *Izbrannye proizvedeniia* (Moscow: Voenizdat, 1940), 27; Frunze, "Front i tyl," 71–72.

13. Frunze, "Front i tyl," 72–77; on the superiority of socialism for military planning, see also Gareev, *Frunze*, 112–13.

14. Karatygin, *Obshchie osnovy*, 17, 20.

15. Ibid., 21, 30–31. By industries of dual application, Karatygin has in mind industries such as chemicals and metalworking. Technologies of dual application could include standardization of parts, tractors suitable for agricultural work or hauling artillery, or other such adaptations.

16. Ibid., 32–35, 77. For remarks on the contemporary Soviet bent for rationalization and the "scientific organization of labor," see Richard Stites, *Revolutionary Dreams* (Oxford: Oxford University Press, 1989), 144–64; Mark Beissinger, *Scientific Management, Socialist Discipline, and Soviet Power* (London: Tauris, 1988), 19–90. On the comparable German phenomenon, see J. Ronald Shearer, "Talking about Efficiency: Politics and the Industrial Rationalization Movement in the Weimar Republic," *Central European History* 28, no. 4 (1995): 483–506.

17. Frunze's theories reflect numerous earlier influences, including Colmar von der Goltz, *Das Volk in Waffen* (Berlin: 1883), and the concrete example of Ludendorff's management of the German war economy. Friedrich Meinecke traces a "modern technological-militarist spirit" as far back as Friedrich Wilhelm's Prussian state in *The German Catastrophe* (Cambridge, Mass.: Harvard University Press, 1950), 39–40.

18. Michael Geyer, "The Militarization of Europe," in *Militarization of the Western World,* ed. John Gillis (New Brunswick, N.J.: Rutgers University Press, 1989) 70.

19. On Tukhachevskii's *Future War,* see Sally Stoecker, *Forging Stalin's Army* (Boulder, Colo.: Westview, 1998), 148–49; Lennart Samuelson, *Soviet Defence Industry Planning* (Stockholm: Stockholm School of Economics, 1996) 46–52; Aleksandr Svechin, *Strategy* (Minneapolis: Eastview, 1992), 91, 170–71 (translation and reprint of *Strategiia,* 2d ed. [Moscow: Voennyi Vestnik, 1927]). On Svechin, see Schneider, *The Structure of Strategic Revolution,* 36–61.

20. A. M. Vol'pe, "Voennaia promyshlennost' v grazhdanskoi voine," in *Grazhdanskaia voina* (Moscow: Voennyi Vestnik, 1928), 395; B. M. Shaposhnikov, excerpt from *Mozg armii* (Moscow: Voennyi Vestnik, 1927–1929), included in *Vospominaniia* (Moscow: Voenizdat, 1974), 450; Michael Checinski, "The Economics of Defence in the USSR," *Survey* 29 (1985): 62–63. Unfortunately, Checinski does not discuss Karatygin's work.

21. See Erickson, *Soviet High Command,* 172–73, 328. The Revoliutsionnyi voennyi sovet SSSR (typically abbreviated Revvoensovet, or RVS) was a council of approximately a dozen senior officers of the Red Army responsible for determining major policy. Although the people's commissar of military and naval affairs also served as chair of the Revvoensovet, his authority was not absolute. This group seems to have served as a *collective* decision-making body.

22. On the development of the Politburo, see John Lowenhardt, James R. Ozinga, and Erik Van Ree, *The Rise and Fall of the Soviet Politburo* (New York: St. Martin's, 1992), esp. 11–25.

23. Central Committee protocols #55, pt. 18, 2 April 1925: RTsKhIDNI f. 17, op. 3, d. 495, l. 5; #56, pt. 35, 9 April 1925: ibid., d. 496, l. 6; #65, pt. 64, 4 June 1925: ibid., d. 505, l. 13; #71, pt. 7, 16 July 1925: RTsKhIDNI f. 17, op. 3, d. 511, l. 3. On Rykov, see Samuel A. Oppenheim, "Aleksei Ivanovich Rykov (1881–1938): A Political Biography" (diss., Indiana University, 1972), and Dmitrii Shelestov, *Vremia Alekseia Rykova* (Moscow: Progress, 1990).

24. Politburo protocol #70, pt. 13, in response to proposal of Central Committee plenum, 14 February 1924: RTsKhIDNI f. 17, op. 3, d. 418, l. 4; Revvoensovet protocol #195, 18 February 1924: GARF f. 5446, op. 55, d. 517, l. 31. On the Soviet budget in general, see R. W. Davies, *The Development of the Soviet Budgetary System* (Cambridge: Cambridge University Press, 1958).

25. Frunze to Rykov and Stalin, 10 July 1924: GARF f. 5446, op. 55, d. 515, ll. 1–2; Tyushkevich, *Soviet Armed Forces,* 150.

26. Revvoensovet decision, 17 August 1924: RTsKhIDNI f. 325, op. 1, d. 132, ll. 1–2; Carr, *Socialism in One Country,* vol. 1, 335–36, 458–59. Carr puts this interim military budget at 380 million rubles out of a total state budget of 2,100 million rubles. On the decline in grain exports, see M. R. Dohan, "Foreign Trade," in *From Tsarism to the New Economic Policy,* ed. R. W. Davies (Ithaca, N.Y.: Cornell University Press, 1991), 95, 99.

27. Stenogram of Central Committee plenum, 17–20 January 1925: RTsKhIDNI f. 17, op. 2, d. 165, ll. 48–55; Stalin's speech also appears in Stalin, *Sochineniia,* vol. 7, 11–14. See also Erickson, *Soviet High Command,* 209–10; Carr, *Socialism in One Country,* vol. 1, 460. After the plenum, continuing growth in tax revenue meant that the overall budget grew to 2,876 million rubles by June 1925.

28. Politburo protocol #93, pt. 3, 3? November 1925: RTsKhIDNI f. 17, op. 162, d. 2, l. 202. The numbering of meetings here seems to be out of order. On the 1925–1926 budget and economy in general, see Carr, *Socialism in One Country,* vol. 1, 464–69, and Davies, *From Tsarism,* 95, 99, 221. My conclusion that there were no serious debates over the 1925–1926 budget is, of course, tentative; I cannot prove a negative. However, I came across no evidence of a budget dispute for that fiscal year.

29. Frunze's death has led to speculation about whether he was the victim of medical murder. See the accusations in Leon Trotsky, *Stalin: An Appraisal of the Man and His Influence* (New York: Harper and Bros., 1941), 418; Boris Bazhanov, *Bazhanov and the Damnation of Stalin* (Athens: Ohio University Press, 1990), 99–101; and Erickson, *Soviet High Command,* 199. The most recent evidence is in V. D. Topolianskii, "Gibel' Frunze," *VI* 6 (1993): 93–106.

30. On Voroshilov, there are two Soviet biographies of limited worth: V. S. Akshinskii, *Kliment Efremovich Voroshilov: Biograficheskii ocherk* (Moscow: Politizdat, 1968), and Vladislav Kardashov, *Voroshilov* (Moscow: Molodaia Gvardiia, 1976). For less complimentary appraisals, see Erickson, S*oviet High Command,* 200–1, and Dmitri Volkogonov, "Voroshilov," in *Stalin's Generals,* ed. Harold Shukman (New York: Grove, 1993), 313–26.

31. Bruce Menning's current work on Soviet war plans in the interwar period amply demonstrates this focus on Poland and Romania. See also Jacobson, *When the Soviet Union Entered World Politics,* 152–53, and Samuelson, *Soviet Defence Industry Planning,* 106–7. For comparison, see Carr, *Socialism in One Country,* vol. 3, 439; and Anna M. Cienciala and Titus Komarnicki, *From Versailles to Locarno: Keys to Polish Foreign Policy, 1919–1925* (Lawrence: University Press of Kansas, 1984), 288, who suggest that Moscow was not concerned by Polish designs on a pact with Romania and the Baltics but only wished to pressure Germany. Jan Karski, *The Great Powers and Poland, 1919–1945: From Versailles to Yalta* (New York: University Press of America, 1985), 125, makes a similar argument that the Soviets intended to use Poland as a bargaining chip in relations with Germany. On Soviet war planning in general, see Samuelson, *Soviet Defence Industry Planning,* 39–52.

32. Protocol #14 of Rykov's Commission, 29 July 1926: RGVA f. 4, op. 1, d. 321, l. 307. See also Tukhachevskii's report on the defense of the USSR, August 1926: RGVA f. 33988, op. 2, d. 671, ll. 1–2, 4, 8.

33. Ibid.; see also August report, RGVA f. 33988, op. 2, d. 671, ll. 139–40. Tukhachevskii did not make explicit the parallels between his thinking and prewar German strategy, but he did compliment the Schlieffen plan's aim at denying France the time and space to fully mobilize in "Voprosy sovremennoi strategii," in Tukhachevskii, *Izbrannye proizvedeniia* (Moscow: Voenizdat, 1964), vol. 1, 254–55. The USSR, in Tukhachevskii's formulation, would compensate for its technical backwardness by preparing to strike quickly. Tukhachevskii's logic seems quite close to an argument Yoakhim Vatsetis made on the need for the USSR to compensate for technical backwardness with quick victory. See Checinski, "Economics of Defence," 63.

34. Protocol #14 of Rykov's Commission, ll. 306, 308; see August report, ll. 38–39, on poor prospects of production. See also Svechin, *Strategy,* especially commentary by Jacob Kipp, "General-Major A. A. Svechin and Modern Warfare: Military History and Military Theory," 23–56.

35. See report of commission under Chutskaev (Rabkrin), early September 1926: RGVA f. 4, op. 1, d. 321, ll. 362–72, esp. ll. 369–70; undated budget briefing paper enclosed with preceding, ibid., l. 374.

36. Ibid., ll. 370, 374.

37. Chutskaev (Rabkrin) to Stalin, 8 November 1926: RGVA f. 4, op. 1, d. 321, l. 327; Politburo protocol #67, pt. 3, 11 November 1926: RTsKhIDNI f. 17, op. 3, d. 601, l. 3. This military budget was published in fairly accurate form. See Davies, *From Tsarism*, 8, 304.

38. Nikolai Simonov, *Voenno-promyshlennyi kompleks SSSR* (Moscow: Rosspen, 1996), 65, citing GARF f. 8418, op. 16, d. 3, ll. 334–35.

39. Sovnarkom meeting #192, pt. 2.1/v, 7 January 1927: RGVA f. 4, op. 17, d. 6, l. 330; stenogram of Central Committee plenum, 7–12 February 1927: RTsKhIDNI f. 17, op. 2, d. 259, l. 24; see also Red Army protest against 700 million–ruble budget, 25 February 1927: RGVA f. 33988, op. 3, d. 81, l. 184.

40. Despite this fall from grace, Bogdanov's career would gain new life when he became chair of Amtorg, the Soviet government's company for trade with the United States.

41. Briefing paper on history of military industry, undated [early 1929?]: RGVA f. 33987, op. 3, d. 131, l. 246; Bogdanov to Dzerzhinskii, Rykov, Stalin, Frunze, Lepse, 16 June 1925: RTsKhIDNI f. 76, op. 2, d. 182, ll. 76–77; Politburo protocol, pt. 14, 25 June 1925: RTsKhIDNI f. 17, op. 3, d. 508, l. 4.

42. Bogdanov became chair of the North Caucasus Executive Committee. Politburo protocols #73, pt. 25; #90, pt. 17; #91, pt. 8; #94, pt. 23 and app. 2; 30 July, 12 November, 19 November, and 10 December 1925: RTsKhIDNI f. 17, op. 3, d. 513, l. 6; ibid., d. 530, l. 7; ibid., d. 531, l. 5; ibid., d. 534, l. 7. In a testimony to Mikoian's astonishing political longevity, he spoke at a memorial ceremony for the rehabilitated Bogdanov on 12 December 1972. See Mikoian's interview with Bogdanov's sons: RGAE f. 9590, op. 1, d. 94, ll. 26–32, and Mikoian's speech: ibid., d. 93, 93a.

43. Bogdanov to same addressees as resignation letter (see note 41), 16 June 1925: GARF f. 5446, op. 55, d. 747, ll. 39–41. On layoffs required by monetary reform, see Simonov, *Voenno-promyshlennyi kompleks,* 56.

44. The Committee for Military Orders in Russian is Komitet po voennym zakazam, or KVZ. The Committee for De- and Mobilization is Komitet De- i Mobilizatsii promyshlennosti, or KDM. See K. G. Maksimov (chair of KDM and KVZ) to Rabkrin, 1 December 1925: GARF f. 5446, op. 55, d. 747, ll. 51–64.

45. See Frunze's recapitulation of Vesenkha's position in letter to Dzerzhinskii, date uncertain: RGVA f. 7, op. 11, d. 214, l. 41.

46. Dzerzhinskii to Rykov's Commission, 31 July? 1925: RTsKhIDNI f. 76, op. 2, d. 182, l. 82; Dzerzhinskii to Defense [Rykov's] Commission, 12 August 1925: ibid., l. 86.

47. Dzerzhinskii to KO, 12 August 1925: RTsKhIDNI f. 76, op. 2, d. 182, l. 86.

48. Dzerzhinskii's thinking as expressed in staff briefing paper, August 1925: RGVA f. 7, op. 11, d. 214, ll. 49–49ob.

49. Dzerzhinskii and Maksimov draft decision, date uncertain: ibid., ll. 37–40.

50. Ibid., ll. 41–42.

51. Staff briefing paper on organization of military industry, August 1925: RGVA f. 7, op. 11, d. 214, l. 50.

52. See, for example, the draft of an administrative scheme emphasizing the need for centralization, mid-1925: RGVA f. 7, op. 11, d. 214, ll. 29–30.

53. Politburo protocol, #90, pt. 5, 12 November 1925: RTsKhIDNI f. 17, op. 3, d. 530, l. 4; see also #92, pt. 14, 21 November 1925 [protocol dated to 26 November]: RTsKhIDNI f. 17, op. 3, d. 532, l. 5. Konstantin Maksimov, who had served as interim administrator after Bogdanov, was given other work upon Avanesov's appointment.

54. For the details of Avanesov's life, see V. A. Avanesov, *Stat'i, doklady, materialy* (Yerevan: Aiastan, 1985), esp. 3–8. Almost nothing is included on Avanesov's work with military industry.

55. K. G. Maksimov (Vesenkha) report to Rabkrin on VPU, 1 December 1925: GARF f. 5446, op. 55, d. 747, ll. 63–64. See also Hulse, "Soviet Military Doctrine," 213–14. The VPU's full name was Voenno-promyshlennoe upravlenie; Voenprom was an abbreviation for Proizvodstvennoe ob"edinenie voennoi promyshlennosti.

56. Maksimov report, ibid., ll. 58–62.

57. Report on employment in military industry as of 1 May 1926: RTsKhIDNI f. 76, op. 2, d. 182, ll. 194–95. See also the closely comparable figures (at least for overall groupings) included in the report "On the State of Military Industry," 3 July 1926: ibid., l. 190. For production breakdowns, see report from Revvoensovet representative in Vesenkha on the state of Voenprom over the first half of the 1925–1926 fiscal year, 17 June 1926, RGVA f. 33987, op. 3, d. 131, ll. 2ob-3.

58. Report from Revvoensovet representative in Vesenkha on the state of Voenprom over the first half of the 1925–1926 fiscal year, 17 June 1926: RGVA f. 33987, op. 3, d. 131, l. 1. These figures do not include intrafactory orders of 11,197,307 rubles, which would increase the total production program to 157,054,621 rubles. The year-on-year increase is slightly problematic. Due to inadequate information, the document priced military equipment in 1925–1926 prices, whereas civilian production was priced in terms of the current year. This should not alter the basic thrust of the figures.

59. Avanesov report on his term in military industry, 3 February 1927: RGVA f. 33987, op. 3, d. 131, ll. 110, 118; Avanesov report to Defense Commission/Rykov's Commission, 5 July 1926: RTsKhIDNI f. 76, op. 2, d. 182, l. 198.

60. Protocol of meeting under Dzerzhinskii, late June 1926: RTsKhIDNI f. 76, op. 2, d. 182, l. 230. Uglanov was also present. See also Tamarin and Mikhailov theses on military industry, 23 October 1926: RGVA f. 33987, op. 3, d. 131, l. 42.

61. Protocol of meeting under Dzerzhinskii, late June 1926: RTsKhIDNI f. 76, op. 2, d. 182, l. 230; see also Avanesov's later account of this meeting in his retrospective report on his term in military industry, 3 February 1927: RGVA f. 33987, op. 3, d. 131, ll. 118–19, and preparatory material for Rykov's Commission, 3 July 1926: RTsKhIDNI f. 76, op. 2, d. 182, ll. 176 ff. The oversight commission of more than a dozen members was to include Voroshilov, Avanesov, Dzerzhinskii, and Unshlikht.

62. Excerpt from Protocol #13 of Rykov's Commission, 5 July 1926: RTsKhIDNI f. 76, op. 2, d. 182, l. 175; Avanesov's report, 5 July 1926: ibid., ll. 198–208; ibid., l. 230; preparatory materials for meeting, 3 July 1926: RTsKhIDNI f. 76, op. 2, d. 182, ll. 176 ff. See also Tamarin and Mikhailov's account of the Dzerzhinskii meeting and its results, October 1926: RGVA f. 33987, op. 3, d. 131, ll. 47–48.

63. Avanesov report for Defense Commission/Rykov's Commission meeting, 5 July 1926: RTsKhIDNI f. 76, op. 2, d. 182, ll. 201–2.

64. Avanesov report to Defense Commission/Rykov's Commission, 5 July 1926: RTsKhIDNI f. 76, op. 2, d. 182, ll. 203–4; see also Tamarin and Mikhailov's comments on bad record keeping, 23 October 1926: RGVA f. 33987, op. 3, d. 131, l. 42; Tamarin to Voroshilov, 6 July 1926: RGVA f. 33987, op. 3, d. 131, l. 7.

65. Order 116 of GVPU, 25 October 1926: RGVA f. 4, op. 1, d. 269, ll. 154–56; Tolokontsev to Stalin, Rykov, Voroshilov, Kuibyshev, 30 October/1 November 1926: GARF f. 5446, op. 55, d. 1062, l. 4.

66. Tolokontsev to Stalin, Rykov, Voroshilov, Kuibyshev, Ordzhonikidze, 4 December 1926: RTsKhIDNI f. 85, op. 27, d. 390, l. 1.

67. Excerpt from Rykov's Commission Protocol #13, pt. 3, 5 July 1926: RTsKhIDNI f. 76, op. 2, d. 182, l. 175. This reorganization of military industry as the result of fiscal crisis contradicts Simonov's assertion that Voenprom's split was a sign of economic recovery (*Voenno-promyshlennyi kompleks,* 57).

68. Excerpt from Rykov's Commission Protocol #13, pt. 3, 5 July 1926: RTsKhIDNI f. 76, op. 2, d. 182, l. 175; Dzerzhinskii circular, 6 July 1926: ibid., l. 97. Although the trusts began acting as separate agents soon after Dzerzhinskii's order, the official dissolution of Voenprom into component trusts did not come until 15 December 1926. See the directory for RGAE f. 2097, op. 5.

69. Report on Voenprom by NKVM representative in Vesenkha, 17 June 1926: RGVA f. 33987, op. 3, d. 131, l. 6.

70. Egorov to Tolokontsev and Unshlikht, 21 September 1926: RGVA f. 4, op. 1, d. 386, l. 3; RGAE, f. 2097, op. 5: opis' directory.

71. On Rudzutak, see G. A. Trukan, *Ian Rudzutak* (Moscow: Gospolitizdat, 1963). On Kuibyshev, see *Valerian Vladimirovich Kuibyshev* (Moscow: Politizdat, 1966); *Valerian Vladimirovich Kuibyshev—biografiia* (Moscow: Politizdat, 1988); and M. I. Vladimirov, "Partiinaia, gosudarstvennaia i voenno-organizatorskaia deiatel'nost' V. V. Kuibysheva (1921–1935)" (diss., Frunze Academy, 1990). The literature on Ordzhonikidze is extensive, including I. Dubinskii-Mukhadze, *Ordzhonikidze* (Moscow: Molodaia Gvardiia, 1963); *Grigorii Konstantinovich Ordzhonikidze: Biografiia* (Moscow: Politizdat, 1986); and most recently Oleg Khlevniuk, *Stalin i Ordzhonikidze: Konflikty v Politburo v 30-e gody* (Moscow: Rossiia Molodaia, 1993).

72. Christopher Andrew and Oleg Gordievsky, *KGB: The Inside Story* (New York: HarperCollins, 1990), 107–8. Intriguingly, Avanesov is just one example of a common early Bolshevik type—the fanatically disciplined party organizer wasting his health from overwork and dying young. Consider Sverdlov, Dzerzhinskii, and Lenin himself.

73. Order #101 of the VPU of Vesenkha (Tolokontsev), 27 September 1926: RGAE f. 2097, op. 5, d. 582, l. 4.

74. Tamarin and Mikhailov's theses, 23 October 1926: RGVA f. 33987, op. 3, d. 131, ll. 42, 46. With regard to output per unit of capital, though they may have entertained the possibility, Tamarin and Mikhailov do not seem to have suggested that military production was underpriced, thanks to the Red Army's status as a sole customer with political clout.

75. Ibid., ll. 44–45.

76. Ibid., l. 43; stenogram of Tolokontsev's report to Revvoensovet, 5 March 1927: RGVA f. 4, op. 1, d. 320, l. 12.

77. Tolokontsev report to Politburo, 2 December 1926: RGVA f. 33987, op. 3, d. 131, ll. 101–4.

78. Revvoensovet decree in response to Tolokontsev's report, 16 March 1927: RGVA f. 4, op. 18, d. 11, ll. 201–5.

79. Tukhachevskii to Unshlikht, 27 January 1927: RGVA f. 4, op. 1, d. 318, ll. 27–28. For this and subsequent discussions of the five-year plan of orders, see the various versions, which differ only in minor detail: order plan: 12 February 1927: RGVA f. 4, op. 1, d. 320, ll. 84–88; enclosure in 11 April report on "orientation order": RGVA f. 7, op. 10, d. 1275, ll. 2–5; Garf report on five-year order plan, 15 February 1927: RGVA f. 4, op. 1, d. 318, ll. 37 ff.; Efimov report on long-range order plan, 27 May 1927: RGVA f. 4, op. 1, d. 455, ll. 104–8. The Supply Directorate increased the staff's five-year total from 674 million to 687 million rubles, chiefly through an increase in the rifle order from 1 million to 1.1 million and in the bullet order from 1,750 million to 1,950 million.

80. See the December 1926 orders to industry: RGVA f. 4, op. 18, d. 11, ll. 118 ff. This order includes, just as in the 1926–1927 section of the five-year order plan, 200,000 rifles, 1,200 Maxim machine guns, 1,750 Maxim-Tokarev machine guns, 16,000 Nagant revolvers, 12 1902 model 76mm guns, 200 122mm howitzers, and so forth. There are minor differences resulting from cost and accounting differences, but this 1926–1927 order is clearly fundamentally the same as the 1926–1927 section of the long-range plan.

81. Garf report on military orders to industry for 1926–1927, March 1927: RGVA f. 33987, op. 3, d. 131, l. 168.

82. RZ STO protocol #3, pt. 2, 28 May 1927: RGVA f. 33988, op. 3, d. 89, ll. 81–81ob; also ibid., f. 4, op. 17, d. 61, ll. 18–19; Dybenko and Lukin report on 1926–1927 orders, 4 June 1927: RGVA f. 33989, op. 1, d. 28, ll. 2–9.

83. See 18 November 1926 VPU report by Egorov (deputy director), Grigor'ev (director of Section for Mobilization of Industry), and Rusaev (director of Mobilization-Planning Subsection): RGVA f. 4, op. 1, d. 319, ll. 8–9; also Iagoda report on VPU, 29 November 1926: RGVA f. 33987, op. 3, d. 131, l. 74. For the particulars of industrial mobilization plans, see Simonov, Voenno-promyshlennyi kompleks, 115–16.

84. See "basic principles" endorsed by Dzerzhinskii on 19 March 1926 enclosed in a communiqué of 15 November 1926: RGVA f. 4, op. 1, d. 319, ll. 61–67.

85. See Tukhachevskii's comments in a report for the 3 July 1926 meeting with Dzerzhinskii: RTsKhIDNI f. 76, op. 2, d. 182, ll. 158–59.

86. Ibid., ll. 67–69. See also a methodological document explaining the creation of a mobilization plan and presented to Avanesov 29 June 1926: RTsKhIDNI f. 76, op. 2, d. 182, ll. 141–42.

87. "Methodology of Construction of Mobilization Plan of Industry," 29 June 1926: RTsKhIDNI f. 76, op. 2, d. 182, ll. 139–41. This is quite similar in style and content to the document circulated by Avanesov to the members of Rykov's Commission on 3 July 1926: ibid., ll. 144–55.

88. "Methodology of Construction of Mobilization Plan for Industry," 29 June 1926: RTsKhIDNI f. 76, op. 2, d. 182, ll. 140–140ob. On the distinction between plans A and R, see also the discussion in Egorov's (VPU) report on mobilization readiness, 18 November 1926: RGVA f. 4, op. 1, d. 319, ll. 10–10ob. The code letters A and R likely signify "actual" (aktual'nyi) and "reserve" (rezervnyi). Simonov, Voenno-promyshlennyi kompleks, 70, incorrectly characterizes the later mobilization plan S-30 as the USSR's first industrial mobilization plan.

89. Compare Tukhachevskii report on defense of USSR, August 1926: RGVA f. 33988, op. 2, d. 671, ll. 37–38, with report on work of RZ STO over eight months, April? 1928: RGVA f. 4, op. 1, d. 473, ll. 52 ff.

90. "Methodology of Construction," 29 June 1926: RTsKhIDNI f. 76, op. 2, d. 182, ll. 140ob-41; Efimov report on long-range order plan and war-year order, 27 May 1927: RGVA f. 4, op. 1, d. 455, ll. 104–8.

91. Tukhachevskii report for 3 July 1926 meeting with Dzerzhinskii: RTsKhIDNI f. 76, op. 2, d. 182, ll. 157–63.

92. Chutskaev report on mobilization readiness of Red Army, September 1926: RGVA f. 4, op. 1, d. 321, ll. 362–72; attached chart comparing Red Army's needs with stockpiles: ibid., l. 373.

93. Egorov, Grigor'ev (director of Section for Mobilization of Industry), and Rusaev (director of Mobilization-Planning Subsection) on state of mobilization work in industry, 18 November 1926: RGVA f. 4, op. 1, d. 319, ll. 9–18, 20, 23ob.

94. Ibid., ll. 45–46.

95. Draft protest, RVS protocol #16, pt. 1, 29 January 1929; final version RVS protocol #22, pt. 2, 5 March 1927: RGVA f. 4, op. 1, d. 319, l. 5; also ibid., op. 18, d. 11, ll. 156–58, 193, 197–98.

96. Ibid., ll. 159–60, 198–99.

97. Ibid., ll. 160–61, 199–200.

98. RZ STO protocol #1, pt. 2, 7 May 1927: RGVA f. 4, op. 17, d. 61, l. 2. In Russian, Mobilizatsionno-planovoe upravlenie, or MPU.

99. RZ STO protocol #3, pt. 3, 28 May 1927: RGVA f. 4, op. 17, d. 61, ll. 20–21, also ibid., f. 33988, op. 3, d. 89, l. 83.

100. RZ STO protocol #4, pt. 4, 11 June 1927: RGVA f. 4, op. 17, d. 61, l. 29. On the internal structure of the MPU and its Planning, Production-Technical, and Design and Scientific Research Sectors, see Shpektorov report on MPU, 17 May 1930: RGAE f. 3429, op. 16, d. 105, ll. 13–25.

2. RUMORS OF WAR

1. The end of NEP has generated voluminous scholarship. One strand argues that NEP was sustainable but was deliberately destroyed by Stalin. See Robert Tucker, *Stalin in Power* (New York: Norton, 1990), and "Stalinism as Revolution from Above," in *Stalinism: Essays in Historical Interpretation,* ed. Robert Tucker (New York: Norton, 1971); Stephen Cohen, *Bukharin and the Bolshevik Revolution* (Oxford: Oxford University Press, 1980). Mark Harrison, in "Why Did NEP Fail?" in *Soviet Industrialisation and Soviet Maturity,* ed. K. Smith (London: Routledge, 1986), 8–22, argues that the NEP was a sustainable economic policy but could not have achieved industrial growth on the scale of the First Five-Year Plan. An alternative interpretation sees strains in NEP society that made it unstable in the long term. See, for example, Alec Nove, *An Economic History of the Soviet Union* (London: Penguin, 1989), 139–41; Lewis Siegelbaum, *Soviet State and Society between Revolutions, 1919–1929* (Cambridge: Cambridge University Press, 1992), 165–229; Moshe Lewin, *Russian Peasants and Soviet Power* (London: Allen & Unwin, 1968); David Shearer, *Industry, State, and Society in Stalin's Russia, 1926–1934* (Ithaca, N.Y.: Cornell University Press, 1996).

2. For Tukhachevskii's specific argument that collectivization would turn peasants into proletarians, see David R. Stone, "Tukhachevskii in Leningrad: Military Politics and Exile, 1928-31," *EAS* 48 (1996): 1377-78.

3. On the war scare, see John P. Sontag, "The Soviet War Scare of 1926-27," *Russian Review* 34 (1975): 66-77; Alfred Meyer, "The War Scare of 1927," *Soviet Union/Union Sovietique* 5 (1979): 1-25; Jon Jacobson, *When the Soviet Union Entered World Politics* (Berkeley: University of California Press, 1994), 206-32.

4. Louis Fischer, *Russia's Road from Peace to War: Soviet Foreign Relations, 1917-1941* (New York: Harper & Row, 1969), 172.

5. Sheila Fitzpatrick, "The Foreign Threat during the First Five-Year Plan," *Soviet Union/Union Sovietique* 5 (1978): 30-31; Meyer, "War Scare," 2; Joseph Stalin, "Zametki na sovremennye temy," 28 July 1927, in *Sochineniia* (Moscow: Politizdat, 1946-), vol. 9, 330; John Erickson, *The Soviet High Command* (New York: St. Martin's, 1962), 284-85.

6. N. S. Simonov, "'Krepit' oboronu strany sovetov': 'Voennaia trevoga' 1927 goda," *OI* 3 (1996): 155-61.

7. E. H. Carr and R. W. Davies, *Foundations of a Planned Economy* (London: Macmillan, 1969-1976), vol. 3, bk. 1, 76-80; Sontag, "Soviet War Scare," 67-68.

8. Stalin, *Sochineniia*, vol. 8, 262-64.

9. On the collaboration, see Hans Gatzke, "Russo-German Collaboration During the Weimar Republic," *AHR* 63 (1958): 565-97; Iu. L. D'iakov and T. S. Busheva, eds., *Fashistskii mech kovalsia v SSSR* (Moscow: Sov. Rossiia, 1992); Manfred Zeidler, *Reichswehr und Rote Armee, 1920-1933: Wege und Stationen einer ungewöhnlichen Zusammenarbeit* (Munich: Oldenbourg, 1993).

10. Stalin, *Sochineniia*, vol. 9, 170; Meyer, "War Scare," 4-6.

11. David J. Dallin, *The Rise of Russia in Asia* (New Haven, Conn.: Yale University Press, 1949), 224-34; Xenia Joukoff Eudin and Robert C. North, *Soviet Russia and the East, 1920-1927* (Stanford, Calif.: Stanford University Press, 1957), 299, 304, 364-68.

12. Louis Fischer, *The Soviets in World Affairs* (Princeton, N.J.: Princeton University Press, 1951), vol. 2, 680-93.

13. Referring to Voikov as "ambassador" is a slight misnomer. Voikov's official title was *polpred*, short for "plenipotentiary representative." Fischer, *Soviets in World Affairs*, vol. 2, 724-25; Politburo protocol, 7 June 1927: RTsKhIDNI f. 17, op. 3, d. 638, l. 1; Stalin, *Sochineniia*, vol. 9, 321-22. On the rather ineffective mass mobilization campaign, see Kenneth D. Slepyan, "The Limits of Mobilization: Party, State, and the 1927 Civil Defense Campaign," *EAS* 45 (1993): 851-68. Also, I. Spirigonov, "Nedeli i dekada oborony," *VIZh* 7 (1970): 107-9.

14. See meeting protocols of the Postoiannoe mobilizatsionnoe soveshchanie, RGAE f. 3429, op. 16, d. 3, passim. In particular, note meeting 1, 16 June 1927, ll. 150-52, and meeting 6, 8 July 1927, ll. 135-36, which changed the name of the group to the jawbreaking Meeting of the Standing Conference under the Presidium of Vesenkha for Mobilization and Military-Industrial Questions.

15. Kliment Voroshilov, speech of 13 December 1927, in *Stat'i i rechi* (Moscow: Partizdat, 1937), 196. Compare subpoint 4 of RZ STO protocol #5, pt. 1, 25 June 1927: RGAE f. 3429, op. 16, d. 6, l. 127; on the previous existence of Gosplan's military commission, see, for example, Revvoensovet protocol #176, pt. 9, October 1923: RGVA f. 33988, op. 2, d. 497, l. 61.

16. RZ STO protocol #2, pt. 2, 14 May 1927: RGVA f. 33988, op. 3, d. 89, l. 87; ex-

cerpt from RZ STO protocol #5, pt. 1, 25 June 1927: RGAE f. 3429, op. 16, d. 6, l. 127, and decree, ibid., ll. 128–30. On Tukhachevskii's campaign to be head of Gosplan, see Politburo protocols of 9 June, 23 June, 30 June, and 7 July 1927: RTsKhIDNI f. 17, op 3, d. 638, l. 4; d. 640, l. 4; d. 642, l. 4; d. 643, l. 6. See also Lennart Samuelson, *Soviet Defence Industry Planning* (Stockholm: Stockholm School of Economics, 1996), 69–71. Gosplan order 112a, 11 July 1927: RGVA f. 4, op. 1, d. 456, l. 25; Directorate of Affairs to Ventsov (secretary RZ STO), 22 July 1927: ibid., l. 27; for the order to send twelve to fifteen officers to Gosplan, see RZ STO protocol #5, pt. 1, 25 June 1927: RGAE f. 3429, op. 16, d. 6, l. 127.

17. Vladimirskii, unlike the vast majority of the Old Bolsheviks, survived the purges of the late 1930s and died a natural death. His life is thus relatively well documented in standard Soviet reference works. Mekhonoshin was purged, but there is a glasnost biography of him: V. A. Obozhda, *Konstantin Mekhonoshin: Sud'ba i vremia* (Moscow: Politizdat, 1991). See also the short essay by L. N. Seliverstova in *Revvoensovet Respubliki* (Moscow: Politizdat, 1991), 242–55.

18. Kliment Voroshilov, speech of 13 December 1927, in *Stat'i i rechi*, 196. See also Dmitrii Fedotoff-White, *Growth of the Red Army* (Princeton, N.J.: Princeton University Press, 1944), 279. STO is the abbreviation for Sovet truda i oborony.

19. On 18 April 1924, Frunze told the military academy, "The STO, by the character of its work, completely neglected the second half of its name and was transformed from the Council of Labor and Defense into the Council of Labor" ("O reorganizatsii voennogo apparata," *Sobranie sochinenii* [Moscow: 1929], vol. 2, 28).

20. In Russian, the Executive Session of the Council for Labor and Defense is Rasporiaditel'noe zasedanie Soveta truda i oborony, or RZ STO. Politburo protocol #78, pt. 4, 13 January 1927: RTsKhIDNI f. 17, op. 162, d. 4, l. 42; see stenograms of the plenum in RTsKhIDNI f. 17, op. 2, d. 259 and 276. For the special treatment of Voroshilov's and Litvinov's reports, see RTsKhIDNI f. 17, op. 2, d. 276, pt. 3, l. 53.

21. The name "Defense Commission" had first belonged to an earlier group exercising similar functions that had subsequently lapsed into nonactivity and would later be applied to a reworked and Stalinized defense cabinet. Protocol of Politburo meeting of 24 February 1927 and attached materials: RTsKhIDNI f. 17, op. 3, d. 621, ll. 6, 11. Samuelson, *Soviet Defence Industry Planning*, 60–61, claims that the Defense Commission and the RZ STO were distinct groups existing simultaneously, but this seems to me incorrect.

22. RZ STO meeting #1, point 1: RGVA f. 33988, op. 3, d. 89, l. 94; STO meeting, 13 May 1927, pt. 9: RGVA f. 4, op. 1, d. 617, l. 60; Politburo protocol, pt. 4: RTsKhIDNI f. 17, op. 162, d. 5, l. 60. As RZ STO deputy chair, Voroshilov had the technical right to lead meetings in Rykov's absence but appears not to have done so. For a retrospective report on the first year of the RZ STO, see Ventsov to Rykov and Voroshilov, 16 December 1927: RGVA f. 4, op. 1, d. 617, ll. 5–6, and April? 1928 report on work of RZ STO, 1 July 1927 to 1 March 1928: ibid., d. 473, ll. 64–74.

23. "Evaluation of the International and Military Position of the USSR at the Beginning of 1927," from RGVA f. 33987, op. 3, d. 128, ll. 24, 26, as cited in Samuelson, *Soviet Defence Industry Planning*, 54–55.

24. Valerian Kuibyshev speech, 8 June 1927, in *Pravda,* 10 June 1927, 5.

25. Compare Sally Stoecker's argument in *Forging Stalin's Army: Marshal Tukhachevskii and the Politics of Military Innovation* (Boulder, Colo: Westview, 1998), 45–48, that the war scare gave the military new opportunities to lobby for increased funding.

26. Excerpt from STO meeting #280, pt. 15, 5 October 1926: RGVA f. 4, op. 1, d. 318, l. 1; briefing paper prepared by NKVM Directorate of Affairs, early 1927: RGVA f. 33988, op. 3, d. 81, ll. 211–12; Vesenkha to NKVM, 10 December 1926: RGVA f. 4, op. 1, d. 318, l. 16; Tukhachevskii to Unshlikht, 27 January 1927: ibid., ll. 27–28.

27. Rukhimovich and Budnevich to STO, 5 April 1927: RGAE f. 4372, op. 91, d. 35, l. 53.

28. Ibid., ll. 24–40; here and later, see also briefing paper on Vesenkha's plan with identical investment figures prepared for 28 May 1927 RZ STO meeting: RGVA f. 4, op. 1, d. 455, ll. 109–22.

29. Rukhimovich and Budnevich to STO, l. 22; see also briefing paper based on Vesenkha report prepared for RZ STO meeting of 28 May 1927: RGVA f. 4, op. 1, d. 455, ll. 109–10.

30. Ventsov to Unshlikht and Vladimirskii, 17 May 1927: RGVA f. 4, op. 1, d. 455, l. 140; Gosplan memorandum, 28 May 1927: ibid., ll. 106–7; Unshlikht memorandum, 26–27 May 1927: ibid., l. 95. Compare staff report, 27 May 1927: ibid., ll. 89–94; also, related briefing paper: ibid., ll. 109–22.

31. RZ STO protocol #3, pts. 1, 2, and 3, 28 May 1927: RGVA f. 4, op. 17, d. 61, ll. 18–21; also available in RGVA f. 4, op. 2, d. 253, l. 1, and RGAE f. 4372, op. 91, d. 35, l. 66.

32. Postnikov and Grigor'ev, "Basic Initial Data for Assembly of the Military Variant of Industrial Control Figures for 1927/8 and for the Introduction of Correctives into the Five-Year Development Plan for Industry," 16 June 1927: RGAE f. 4372, op. 91, d. 64, ll. 101–2, 110, 149.

33. Kuibyshev (Vesenkha) to STO on long-range plan for military industry, 29 August 1927: RGAE f. 4372, op. 91, d. 35, ll. 87–149.

34. Tukhachevskii report, 1 September 1927: RGVA f. 4, op. 1, d. 318, ll. 71–72; see also Staff briefing paper, September 1927: RGAE f. 4372, op. 91, d. 64, ll. 28–40.

35. Budget briefing paper on 1926–1927 and 1927–1928 defense budgets, late spring 1928?: RGVA f. 4, op. 1, d. 473, l. 31.

36. Standing Mobilization Conference, protocol #11, pts. 1 and 2, 3 August 1927: RGAE f. 3429, op. 16, d. 3, ll. 120–21. The machine-building investment program, described as being directed specifically at military production, came to 29 million rubles; the overall investment program for the chemical industry amounted to 79.7 million rubles, of which at least 4.19 million was for military production. In July, the conference had declined even to discuss Kuibyshev's five-year plan for lack of preparation. Protocol #5, pt. 3, 4 July 1927: ibid., ll. 138–39.

37. See Standing Mobilization Conference meeting protocol, pt. 1, 15 November 1927: ibid., ll. 103–4.

38. RZ STO protocol #1, pt. 3, 7 May 1927: RGVA f. 4, op. 17, d. 61, l. 2; RZ STO meeting #3, pt. 1, 28 May 1927: RGVA f. 4, op. 2, d. 253, l. 1, also RGAE f. 4372, op. 91, d. 35, l. 66.

39. Tukhachevskii report on defense of USSR, August 1926: RGVA f. 33988, op. 2, d. 671, l. 58; Tukhachevskii's theses on the four-year plan, 10 May 1927: f. 4, op. 1, d. 561, ll. 7–16. On Tukhachevskii's vision, see A. Ryzhakov, "K voprosu o stroitel'stve bronetankovykh voisk Krasnoi armii v 30–e gody," *VIZh* 8 (1968): 105. On old technology, see report from Revvoensovet representative in Vesenkha on Voenprom over the first half

of the 1925–1926 fiscal year, 17 June 1926: RGVA f. 33987, op. 3, d. 131, l. 1ob. Also, N. Efimov, "Evoliutsiia sistemy vooruzheniia," *ViR* 10 (1928): 43.

40. Tukhachevskii's theses on the four-year plan: RGVA f. 4, op. 1, d. 561, l. 7; note the continued predominance of cavalry and the absence of tanks in Tukhachevskii's thinking.

41. RGVA f. 4, op. 1, d. 561, ll. 7 ff., esp. 15.

42. Excerpt from Revvoensovet protocol of 11 May 1927, pt. 1: RGVA f. 4, op. 1, d. 561, l. 5; the subcommission included Unshlikht, Tukhachevskii, Kamenev, Postnikov (!), Muralov, and Dybenko. Excerpt from Revvoensovet protocol of 22 June 1927, pt. 1: ibid., l. 6.

43. RZ STO protocol of 25 June 1927, pt. 2: RGVA f. 4, op. 17, d. 61, l. 38; RZ STO protocol of 9 July 1927, pt. 1: ibid., l. 45.

44. See RZ STO preparatory materials from 16 June 1927: RGVA f. 4, op. 1, d. 321, ll. 208–12.

45. Excerpt of Revvoensovet meeting of 19 July 1927, pt. 4: RGVA f. 4, op. 1, d. 562, l. 62; attached Revvoensovet decree: ibid., ll. 63 ff.

46. Excerpt from protocol of RZ STO meeting of 28 May 1927, pt. 1: RGVA f. 4, op. 2, d. 253, l. 1.

47. Excerpt from protocol of Revvoensovet of 5 August 1927, pt. 2: ibid., l. 3.

48. Report by Garf and Lukin, 7 August 1927: ibid., l. 4.

49. Unshlikht to Chief of Naval Directorate, 26 September 1927: ibid., l. 5.

50. Ventsov to Unshlikht, 17 November 1927: ibid., l. 6.

51. Kamenev to STO, 28 November 1927: RGVA f. 4, op. 2, d. 253, l. 7; Ventsov to Unshlikht, 24 January 1928: ibid., l. 8.

52. Shaposhnikov briefing paper on Gosplan control figures for first period of war, 19 May 1928: RGVA f. 4, op. 3, d. 3055, ll. 1–1ob. Shaposhnikov replaced Tukhachevskii as Chief of Staff in May 1928; see Stone, "Tukhachevskii in Leningrad," 1371–72.

53. RZ STO #11, pt. 3, 5 November 1927: RGVA f. 4, op. 17, d. 61, l. 120; RZ STO decision, 19 November 1927: ibid., ll. 166–67.

54. RZ STO protocol #14, pt. 1, 6 February 1928: RGVA f. 4, op. 17, d. 61, l. 194.

55. Standing Mobilization Conference #20, pt. 1, 28 March 1928: RGAE f. 3429, op. 16, d. 3, ll. 68–69; decision of Presidium of Vesenkha, 19 April 1928: ibid., d. 61, ll. 3–11.

56. The Soviet distinction was normally between group A, or heavy industry, and group B, or light industry. In these documents, military industry was always added to group A but was not a part of group A.

57. On MPU's control figures for first period of war, see decision of Presidium of Vesenkha, 19 April 1928: RGAE f. 3429, op. 16, d. 61, ll. 3–11; also compare 21 April 1928 Gosplan report: RGVA f. 4, op. 3, d. 3055, l. 61; and Shaposhnikov's 19 May 1928 summary: ibid., ll. 2ob-3.

58. Aleksandr Svechin's *Strategy* (Moscow: 1927; reprint and trans., Minneapolis: Eastview, 1992), 124, 126, displays a similar concern for minimizing disturbance of the civilian economy.

59. Decision of Presidium of Vesenkha, 19 April 1928: RGAE f. 3429, op. 16, d. 61, ll. 3–11.

60. Gosplan report on control figures for first period of war, 21 April 1928: RGVA f. 4, op. 3, d. 3055, ll. 25 ff., esp. 35, 42, 61, 97.

61. Shaposhnikov's briefing paper on control figures for first period of war, 19 May 1928: RGVA f. 4, op. 3, d. 3055, ll. 1ob-2.

62. Ibid., ll. 2–3ob.

63. RZ STO protocol #18, pt. 1, 21 May 1928: RGVA f. 4, op. 17, d. 61, l. 289.

64. Bulletin of GVPU for first half of 1926–1927, RGVA f. 33988, op. 2, d. 676, ll. 8–10.

65. RZ STO protocol #3, pts. 1 and 2, 28 May 1927: RGVA f. 4, op. 1, d. 318, l. 57; also RGAE f. 4372, op. 91, d. 35, l. 66; RGVA f. 33988, op. 3, d. 89, l. 81.

66. RZ STO decision, 25 June 1927: RGVA f. 4, op. 17, d. 61, l. 43; RZ STO protocol #16, pt. 2, 26 March 1928: RGVA f. 4, op. 1, d. 423, l. 128; RZ STO decision, 23 August 1928: RGVA f. 4, op. 17, d. 61, ll. 382–83.

67. Martinovich report for Ordzhonikidze, 7 December 1928: RTsKhIDNI f. 85, op. 27, d. 394, ll. 1–3.

68. Staff report, late 1930: RGVA f. 7, op. 10, d. 1390, l. 1; Gosplan report on results of First Five-Year Plan, 18 October 1932: RGAE f. 4372, op. 91, d. 312, l. 22.

69. Protocol #8 of Standing Mobilization Conference, 13 July 1927: RGAE f. 3429, op. 16, d. 3, ll. 129–30.

70. Decision of Standing Mobilization Conference, 19 May 1928: RGAE f. 3429, op. 16, d. 3, ll. 61–63.

71. Standing Mobilization Conference protocol #10, pt. 1, 26 July 1927: RGAE f. 3429, op. 16, d. 3, ll. 125–26; for the split among trusts (Military-Chemical, 23.85 million; Artillery-Arsenal, 17.2 million; Cartridge-Fuse, 14.1 million; Firearm–Machine Gun, 13.1 million; Military-Acid, 4.75 million), see VPU investment breakdown [26 August 1927?]: RGAE f. 4372, op. 91, d. 35, ll. 80–86. On the 1926–1927 figure, see VPU investment chart, 26 August 1927: ibid., l. 74.

72. RZ STO protocol #9, pt. 4, 2 September 1927: RGVA f. 4, op. 1, d. 318, l. 80.

73. Briefing paper for RZ STO meeting of 8 October 1927: RGVA f. 4, op. 1, d. 321, l. 195; RZ STO protocol #10, pt. 6, 8 October 1927: RGVA f. 4, op. 17, d. 61, l. 104.

74. RZ STO #9, pt. 1, 9 July 1927: RGVA f. 4, op. 17, d. 61, l. 38; Revvoensovet protocol #40, pt. 2, 14 September 1927: RGVA f. 4, op. 18, d. 11, l. 353.

75. Finance briefing memorandum, 1 October 1927: RGVA f. 4, op. 1, d. 617, ll. 11–12; RZ STO meeting #10, pt. 1, 8 October 1927: RGVA f. 4, op. 17, d. 61, l. 97.

76. Voroshilov to Stalin, 12 October 1927: RGVA f. 4, op. 1, d. 473, ll. 12–14.

77. Briefing memorandum, December 1927: RGVA f. 4, op. 1, d. 321, ll. 69–70; RZ STO protocol #12, pt. 1, 27 December 1927: RGVA f. 4, op. 17, d. 61, l. 136.

78. See charts of budgetary expenditure for 1927–1928 and 1928–1929, 27 July 1928 and 16 December 1928: RGVA f. 4, op. 18, d. 13, ll. 269, 363.

3. THE HUNT FOR INTERNAL ENEMIES

1. On the Shakhty affair, see Kendall Bailes, *Technology and Society under Lenin and Stalin* (Princeton, N.J.: Princeton University Press, 1978), chap. 3, and E. H. Carr and R. W. Davies, *Foundations of a Planned Economy* (New York: Macmillan, 1969), vol. 1, 584–90.

2. Gleb Krzhizhanovskii, "Vreditel'stvo—kak ono est'," *Pravda,* 13 February 1930, 2–3; Unshlikht circular letter to the chairs of numerous *ob"edineniia* (associations),

15 November 1930: RGAE f. 3429, op. 16, d. 110, l. 77. This letter was largely taken from the 20 August 1930 report of Messing from the OGPU on the long-standing presence of wreckers in military industry: ibid., l. 48.

3. Sheila Fitzpatrick, "The Foreign Threat during the First Five-Year Plan," *Soviet Union/Union Sovetique* 5 (1978): 28. Bailes, *Technology and Society,* 95–96 is similarly puzzled.

4. On war danger, see Robert Tucker, *Stalin in Power* (New York: Norton, 1990), 76–80, 98–101, and Roy Medvedev, *Let History Judge* (New York: Knopf, 1971), 125.

5. On the Bolshevik Right, see Fitzpatrick, "Foreign Threat," 29; also Stephen Cohen, *Bukharin and the Bolshevik Revolution* (Oxford: Oxford University Press, 1980), 281–83; Nicholas Lampert, *The Technical Intelligentsia and the Soviet State: A Study of Soviet Managers and Technicians, 1928–1935* (London: Macmillan, 1979), 44.

6. On engineer resistance to industrialization, see Bailes, *Technology and Society,* chaps. 3 and 4, esp. 96–97, 120–21 (quote at 97); Hiroaki Kuromiya, *Stalin's Industrial Revolution* (New York: Cambridge University Press, 1988), chaps. 2 and 3 (quote at 35); see also Loren Graham, *Ghost of the Executed Engineer* (Cambridge, Mass.: Harvard University Press, 1993); R. W. Davies, *The Soviet Economy in Turmoil, 1929–1930* (London: Macmillan, 1989), 110–25, esp. 112; Carr and Davies, *Foundations of a Planned Economy,* vol. 1, pt. 2, 574, 578, 580–81; Lampert, *Technical Intelligentsia,* 48–50; Jeremy Azrael, *Managerial Power and Soviet Politics* (Cambridge, Mass.: Harvard University Press, 1966), 57.

7. Bailes, *Technology and Society,* 70.

8. Gleb Krzhizhanovskii, "Vreditel'stvo—kak ono est'," *Pravda,* 13 February 1930, 2–3.

9. See chapter 1, note 61.

10. Kulik to Revvoensovet, 14 November 1926: RGVA f. 33988, op. 3, d. 131, ll. 61–64.

11. Petition to Stalin, Ordzhonikidze, Voroshilov, 14 November 1926: RTsKhIDNI f. 85, op. 27, d. 165, ll. 8–13.

12. Iagoda briefing paper, 29 November 1926: RGVA f. 33987, op. 3, d. 131, ll. 74–79.

13. 11 October 1927 statement: RGVA f. 33988, op. 3, d. 112, ll. 117–19.

14. Messing (OGPU representative in Leningrad) and Peterson (deputy director of special section of OGPU) report on tank production, 18 October 1927: ibid., l. 104. The Russian word here, *vrednyi,* shares the same root as the term for wrecking, *vreditel'stvo.*

15. Lakhinskii to Tukhachevskii, 20 February 1928: RGVA f. 7, op. 10, d. 1334, ll. 17–26; Lakhinskii letter, 30 April 1928: RGVA f. 33987, op. 3, d. 131, ll. 250–54.

16. I. F. Sharskov report to Voroshilov, 28 March 1928: REVA f. 33987, op. 3, d. 131, l. 243–43ob; protocol of RKI-TsKK commission investigating military industry, 3 June 1929: RGVA f. 4, op. 14, d. 92, l. 2.

17. Sharskov report, 28 March 1928, ll. 244–46.

18. Lakhinskii letter, 18 July 1928: RGVA f. 33987, op. 3, d. 131, ll. 260–65.

19. Tolokontsev's circular letter, Rykov's copy, 27 April 1929: GARF f. 5446, op. 55, d. 1843, ll. 5–10.

20. Ibid., ll. 5, 7. The switch from VPU to GVPU was a minor one from Voenno-Promyshlennoe Upravlenie to Glavnoe Voenno-Promyshlennoe Upravlenie—Military-Industrial Directorate to Main Military-Industrial Directorate.

21. Central Control Commission protocol #38, pt. 1, 12 August 1929, found in Politburo protocol: RTsKhIDNI f. 17, op. 3, d. 753, l. 10.

22. Ibid., l. 11.

23. Ordzhonikidze decision, 18 November 1929: RTsKhIDNI f. 613, op. 1, d. 81, ll. 117–18.

24. Central Committee protocol 89, pt. 37, and protocol 105, pt. 22. RTsKhIDNI f. 17, op. 162, d. 7, ll. 97–99, 188, 192. V. A. Viktorov, *Bez grifa "sekretno"* (Moscow: Iurid. Lit., 1990), 152–53, reports that the case against these men was initiated as a result of Stalin's pronouncements in early 1929. Although the actual trial may have begun then, the investigations and arrests began long before. Two of the four, Dymman and Vysochanskii, were the highest-ranking noncommunists in the trusts organized in 1926.

25. Politburo decision of 15 July 1929: GARF f. 5446, op. 55, d. 1966, l. 24.

26. Central Control Commission protocol, 19 July 1929: RTsKhIDNI f. 613, op. 1, d. 80, l. 50; Politburo decision of 15 July 1929: GARF f. 5446, op. 55, d. 1966, ll. 21–24.

27. Joseph Berliner, *Factory and Manager in the USSR* (Cambridge, Mass.: Harvard University Press, 1957), 75 ff. Berliner's book is an exhaustive catalog of the subterfuges and tactics Soviet managers used to make their way successfully through the Soviet system. On hoarding, see also Janos Kornai, *Economics of Shortage* (Amsterdam: North Holland, 1980), 100–4, and in general, David Granick, *Management of the Industrial Firm in the USSR* (New York: Columbia University Press, 1954).

28. Protocol #7 of auditing commission, 14 June 1929: RGVA f. 33988, op. 3, d. 124, l. 9.

29. Iagoda (deputy chair of OGPU) and Molochnikov (assistant to director of Economic Directorate of OGPU) to Voroshilov, Unshlikht, and Ordzhonikidze, 15 October 1929: RGVA f. 33988, op. 3, d. 124, l. 51.

30. Confessions of Skvortsov, B. I. Kanevskii, and B. Ia. Uspenskii: ibid., ll. 52–54, 56–57.

31. Prokof'ev report to Rykov, 25 December 1929: GARF f. 5446, op. 55, d. 2059, ll. 155, 166–67; Politburo protocol #114, pt. 3, 20 January 1930: RTsKhIDNI f. 17, op. 162, d. 8, ll. 49 ff.

32. Prokof'ev report to Rykov, 25 December 1929: GARF f. 5446, op. 55, d. 2059, ll. 155, 164; Makarovskii's statement, 16 November 1929: ibid., ll. 150–54, 161–62.

33. Ibid., ll. 156–60.

34. Krzhizhanovskii, "Vreditel'stvo—kak ono est'," *Pravda,* 13 February 1930, 2–3; Kozlovskii at Factory 15 meeting, 6 April 1930: RGAE f. 3429, op. 16, d. 113, l. 81; report on wrecking at Barrikady, 26 March 1930: ibid., d. 111, l. 409 (a wrecker was clearly placed in charge of numbering the pages of this file); ibid., d. 113, l. 87.

35. Politburo decision on military industry, 15 July 1929: GARF f. 5446, op. 55, d. 1966, ll. 21–22.

36. See 1930? report on wrecking in mobilization plans: RGAE f. 3429, op. 16, d. 110, ll. 41–46; on Shlisselburg, see report of 23 May 1930: ibid., d. 113, l. 87.

37. Politburo protocol #118, pt. 4, 25 February 1930: GARF f. 5446, op. 55, d. 1966, ll. 12–19; also RTsKhIDNI f. 17, op. 162, d. 8, ll. 81, 85–91.

38. Ketura report, 28 April 1930: RGAE f. 3429, op. 16, d. 113, ll. 50–53.

39. Gai (OGPU) to Shpektorov, 27 May 1930: RGAE f. 3429, op. 16, d. 111, l. 130; undated OGPU report on purge of GVPU enclosed in above 27 May letter: ibid., l. 129.

40. Ibid., ll. 128–29ob.

41. Ibid., ll. 127–28ob.

42. Uborevich order 39/7, 6 March 1930: RGAE f. 3429, op. 16, d. 110, l. 25; circular of 7 March 1930: RGVA f. 33991, op. 1, d. 20, ll. 6–7.

43. Uborevich's report, 6 June 1930, forwarded to Unshlikht 10 June 1930: RGAE f. 3429, op. 16, d. 110, ll. 82–104.

44. 23 August 1930: RGAE f. 3429, op. 16, d. 111, ll. 253–56; Smilga (director of MPU) order 235, 16 October 1930: ibid., d. 110, l. 57.

45. The Russian *kontrol'* is not equivalent to *control* in English. The Russian term means oversight, auditing, or verification, as opposed to active command in the English meaning.

46. Order 716 of VSNKh/NKVM/VTsSPS, 14 May 1929, referred to in STO decision of 14 March 1930: RGAE f. 3429, op. 16, d. 77, l. 116; Politburo decision on military industry, 15 July 1929: GARF f. 5446, op. 55, d. 1966, ll. 20, 24.

47. RZ STO decision of 14 March 1930: RGAE f. 3429, op. 16, d. 77, l. 116; meeting protocol on Factory 15, 6 April 1930: ibid., d. 113, l. 79.

48. Voroshilov to Pavlunovskii, 13 March 1930: RTsKhIDNI f. 85, op. 27, d. 86, l. 1; Smilga report on defense industry over first half of 1929–1930, 28 May 1930: RGVA f. 7, op. 10, d. 1415, ll. 37 ff.; Muklevich cited in R. W. Davies, "Soviet Defence Industries," in *Economy and Society in Russia and the Soviet Union,* ed. Linda Edmonson and Peter Waldron (New York: St. Martin's, 1992), 250; Unshlikht circular, 15 November 1930: RGAE f. 3429, op. 16, d. 110, l. 77.

49. Central Committee protocol 113, pt. 11, 15 January 1930: RTsKhIDNI f. 17, op. 162, d. 8, l. 40; Politburo decision of 25 February 1930: GARF f. 5446, op. 55, d. 1966, ll. 12–18; Rakhmanin report to Shpektorov commission, 5 November 1930: RGAE f. 3429, op. 16, d. 75, l. 110.

50. Politburo protocol #36, pt. 2, 2 August 1928: RTsKhIDNI f. 17, op. 162, d. 6, l. 118. On the retreat in general, see Lampert, *Technical Intelligentsia,* 56–59.

51. Budniak to Voroshilov, 20 February 1928: RTsKhIDNI f. 85, op. 27, d. 78, l. 4.

52. Sergo Ordzhonikidze, *Izbrannye stat'i i rechi* (Moscow: Politizdat, 1939), 252. For Ordzhonikidze's criticisms of Kuibyshev's management of Vesenkha, see Sheila Fitzpatrick, "Ordzhonikidze's Takeover of Vesenkha: A Case Study in Soviet Bureaucratic Politics," *SS* 37 (1985): 161. On Ordzhonikidze's role in easing persecution of bourgeois specialists once at Vesenkha, see also Oleg Khlevniuk, *In Stalin's Shadow: The Career of "Sergo" Ordzhonikidze* (Armonk, N.Y.: Sharpe, 1995), 44–50, who argues that Stalin played a key role in moderating earlier policies.

53. Uryvaev report on personnel policy, May? 1929: RGVA f. 4, op. 14, d. 92, ll. 43–44; report of Shlisselburg Liquidation Commission, 23 May 1930: RGAE f. 3429, op. 16, d. 113, l. 87; Vesenkha and OGPU order #139, 15 May 1930: ibid., d. 110, l. 63.

54. Politburo protocol #32, pt. 26/31, 10 April 1931: RTsKhIDNI f. 17, op. 162, d. 10, l. 7; Politburo protocol #63, pt. 14, 20 September 1931: ibid., d. 11, l. 11; Voroshilov to Ordzhonikidze 27 June [1932?]: RTsKhIDNI f. 85, op. 27, d. 89, l. 1.

55 Kosarev report, April? 1931: RTsKhIDNI f. 17, op. 120, d. 54, ll. 1–5.

56. Ibid.

57. Mark Beissinger, *Scientific Management, Socialist Discipline, and Soviet Power* (London: Tauris, 1988), 129–30.

4. THE SHIFT TOWARD RADICAL REARMAMENT

1. Excerpt from RZ STO protocol #15, pt. 6, 20 February 1928: RGVA f. 33988, op. 3, d. 89, l. 23; Revvoensovet protocol #29, pt. 1, 29 February 1928: RGVA f. 4, op. 18, d. 13, l. 88; Postnikov to Unshlikht, 26 March 1928: RGVA f. 4, op. 1, d. 662, l. 40; excerpt from RZ STO protocol #16, pt. 1, 26 March 1928: RGAE f. 3429, op. 16, d. 6, l. 45.

2. RZ STO protocol, 23 April 1928: RGVA f. 4, op. 17, d. 16, ll. 250–51; list of commission members, 30 April 1928: RGVA f. 7, op. 10, d. 1310, l. 1. See also the comment in Lennart Samuelson, *Soviet Defence Industry Planning* (Stockholm: Stockholm School of Economics, 1996), 105–6. On the generally low priority for naval spending, see Sally Stoecker, *Forging Stalin's Army* (Boulder, Colo.: Westview, 1998), 63.

3. David R. Stone, "Tukhachevskii in Leningrad: Military Politics and Exile, 1928–31," *EAS* 48 (1996): 1369–75.

4. Meeting protocol, 27 April 1928: RGVA f. 7, op. 10, d. 1310, ll. 2 ff.; also Tukhachevskii report to Revvoensovet, protocol #20, 27 April 1928: RGVA f. 4, op. 1, d. 761, ll. 169 ff.; plan of work for commission: RGVA f. 7, op. 10, d. 1310, ll. 6–7.

5. Efimov report, April? 1928: RGVA f. 7, op. 10, d. 1310, ll. 12–15; commission protocol #1, 30 April 1928: ibid., l. 73.

6. Efimov report to commission, April? 1928: ibid., l. 14; commission protocol #1, 30 April 1928: ibid., l. 73; "Short Report of Voroshilov's Governmental Commission to the RZ STO on the Five-Year Plan of Construction of the RKKA and Draft Decision" [July 1930], ibid., l. 189.

7. Voroshilov's commission, protocol #3, 14 May 1928: RGVA f. 7, op. 10, d. 1319, ll. 78–79; draft report of commission [May? 1928]: ibid., ll. 88 ff.; "Short Report . . . on Mobilization Order" of commission and draft decision [July 1928]: ibid., l. 173, 177; "Short Report" on five-year plan [July 1928]: ibid., l. 180.

8. Protocols #3, #4, and #6 of Voroshilov's commission, 14, 16, and 25 May 1928: RGVA f. 7, op. 10, d. 1319, ll. 76–79, 80–83, 85–86; "Short Report . . . on Mobilization Order," July 1928: ibid., ll. 168–70, 173, 178; "Short Report . . . on Five-Year Plan," July? 1928: ibid., l. 182. The three-year tank order for T-12s, T-18s, and Lilliputs breaks down as 55, 450, and 450; the five-year order breaks down as 110, 650, and 740.

9. "Short Report . . . on Mobilization Order," July 1928: ibid., ll. 161–79; "Short Report . . . on Five-Year Plan," July? 1928: ibid., ll. 180–91, esp. 181, 186–87.

10. Ibid., ll. 187–91.

11. RZ STO protocol #20, pt. 1, 30 July 1928: RGVA f. 4, op. 17, d. 61, ll. 312–13. A. Ryzhakov, "K voprosu o stroitel'stve bronetankovykh voisk," *VIZh* 8 (1968): 105, claims that on this day the RZ STO gave its overall approval. It should be noted that the actual decision refers the matter to Rudzutak, Voroshilov, and Kuibyshev for major modifications, and the RZ STO declined to commit to five-year projections.

12. RZ STO decision, 23 August 1928: RGVA f. 4, op. 17, d. 61, ll. 379–80.

13. Ibid., ll. 380–82.

14. On the 1928 debate over the level of investment, see E. H. Carr and R. W. Davies, *Foundations of a Planned Economy* (London: Macmillan, 1969), vol. 1, bk. 1, 312–32.

15. See, for example, April? 1928 Efimov report on five-year plan of armed forces: RGVA f. 7, op. 10, d. 1310, l. 14; plan of work on 1928–1929 budget, undated: RGVA f. 4, op. 18, d. 13, l. 169.

16. "Polozhenie on Financial-Planning Commission," undated: RGVA f. 4, op. 18, d. 13, ll. 170–71. Besides its chair, Unshlikht, the deputy people's commissar, the other members of this temporary body were the deputy chief of staff, director of supply, head of the Main Directorate (handling administrative matters and paperwork), deputy director of the Political Directorate, deputy commanders of the navy and air force, and head of the Financial-Planning Directorate. See protocols for meetings of 6, 9, and 20 June and 14–16 July 1928: RGVA f. 4, op. 18, d. 13, ll. 272–76, 282, 292–94.

17. Summary of budgetary figures, 27 July 1928: RGVA f. 4, op. 18, d. 13, l. 269. In this budget, purchases of equipment and industrial goods would amount to just over 30 percent of the total.

18. RZ STO #21, pt. 1, 13 August 1928: RGVA f. 4, op. 17, d. 61, l. 359; also report to Voroshilov, 23 October [1928], RTsKhIDNI f. 74, op. 2, d. 95, ll. 140–140ob; Politburo protocol #39, pt. 16, 25 August 1928: RTsKhIDNI f. 17, op. 3, d. 701, l. 3. See also Carr and Davies, *Foundations of a Planned Economy,* vol. 1, bk. 1, 312–32; Stephen Cohen, *Bukharin and the Bolshevik Revolution* (Oxford: Oxford University Press, 1980), 295–96.

19. Appoga to Voroshilov, 23 October [1928]: RTsKhIDNI f. 74, op. 2, d. 95, l. 140 and ob.; Lizdin (deputy secretary RZ STO) briefing paper, 6 November 1928: ibid., d. 101, ll. 81–83; Ordzhonikidze to Voroshilov, 28 October 1928: ibid., d. 43, l. 39; RZ STO #25, pt. 2, 22 October 1928: RGVA f. 4, op. 17, d. 61, ll. 442–43.

20. Appoga to Voroshilov, 23 October [1928]: RTsKhIDNI f. 74, op. 2, d. 95, ll. 140–140ob; Litunovskii to Voroshilov, 10 and 16 November 1928: RTsKhIDNI f. 74, op. 2, d. 101, ll. 84–86ob, 87.

21. Ordzhonikidze to Voroshilov, 28 October 1928: RTsKhIDNI f. 74, op. 2, d. 43, l. 39.

22. Voroshilov (personal letter) to Ordzhonikidze, 9 November 1928: RTsKhIDNI f. 85, op. 27, d. 81, ll. 2–3. Note that the "you" in this excerpt is *vy*. Voroshilov probably had in mind the collective "you" cutting the Red Army's budget, not Ordzhonikidze in particular, with whom he used *ty*.

23. Unshlikht's speech to TsK plenum, 20 November 1928. Unshlikht later reconstructed this for Stalin's reference: RGVA f. 33988, op. 3, d. 148, ll. 30–33.

24. RZ STO #26, pt. 1, and #27, pt. 3, 3 and 17 December 1928: RGVA f. 4, op. 17, d. 61, l. 448. See also Carr and Davies, *Foundations of a Planned Economy,* vol. 1, bk. 1, 312–32; Cohen, *Bukharin and the Bolshevik Revolution,* 296–300.

25. On the final struggle with the Right, see Robert Tucker, *Stalin as Revolutionary* (New York: Norton, 1973), 407–20, and Cohen, *Bukharin and the Bolshevik Revolution,* 306–12. Roger Reese, "Red Army Opposition to Forced Collectivization, 1929–1930," *SR* 55 (1996): 44–45, wonders why the Red Army and Bukharin did not unite.

26. See Budnevich (GVPU) to Postnikov (MPU), 30 July 1928: RGAE f. 3429, op. 16, d. 47, l. 32.

27. Postnikov and Shpektorov (MPU) to GVPU, 8? August 1928: ibid., ll. 33–34.

28. Kuibyshev and Postnikov to Voroshilov and Mekhonoshin, 16 August 1928: RGAE f. 3429, op. 16, d. 21, ll. 40–41ob. For a further take on this 1,843.2 million–ruble plan, see the table in the appendix to the plan with the 1,843 million–ruble investment plan (albeit with numerous arithmetical errors) broken down by production type and industrial trust (ibid., l. 27).

29. Ibid., ll. 35–37ob.

30. Ibid., ll. 31–35.

31. Tolokontsev to Postnikov and Kuibyshev, 12 October [November?] 1928: RGAE f. 3429, op. 16, d. 47, ll. 3–4; Tolokontsev to NKVM, 14 December 1928: ibid., l. 6; Postnikov to Tolokontsev, 20 December 1928: ibid., l. 8; Postnikov to Tolokontsev, 16 February 1929: ibid., l. 9; Standing Mobilization Conference protocol #9, pt. 1, 19 March 1929: ibid., d. 14, l. 96; Postnikov to Tolokontsev, 21 March 1929: ibid., d. 47, l. 11.

32. Standing Mobilization Conference, protocol #9, pt. 1, 19 March 1929: ibid. See also Postnikov to Mekhonoshin, 20 March 1929: RGAE f. 3429, op. 16, d. 22, l. 4.

33. Standing Mobilization Conference protocol #9, pt. 1, 19 March 1929: RGAE f. 3429, op. 16, d. 14, l. 96. See also reference in Postnikov to Mekhonoshin, 20 March 1929: ibid., d. 22, l. 4.

34. On Postnikov's (director of the MPU) warning, see decree of 24 July 1928: RGVA f. 7, op. 10, d. 1284, l. 439, identifying the new plan as number 10. A Standing Mobilization Conference protocol of 5 October 1928 and Shpektorov's (acting director of the MPU) report of 12 October both cover ongoing work on mobilization plan S: RGAE f. 3429, op. 16, d. 3, l. 35, and d. 22, ll. 18–24. Another 30 October meeting of the Standing Commission on 30 October, however, refers again to plan 10: ibid., d. 14, ll. 121–22. For plan S's production targets, see Kuibyshev and Shpektorov report to RZ STO, 16 September 1929: RGVA f. 4, op. 1, d. 1036, ll. 8–20, esp. 9. Compare chapter 1.

35. For the RZ STO decree of 24 December 1928, see protocol #28, pt. 12: RGAE f. 3429, op. 16, d. 6, ll. 179–82; staff reaction of January? 1929 to plan S: RGVA f. 7, op. 10, d. 996, ll. 1–5.

36. Voroshilov decree, 2 February 1929: RGVA f. 4, op. 18, d. 15, ll. 43–48.

37. RZ STO decree, 6 March 1929: RGAE f. 3429, op. 16, d. 6, ll. 120–24; RZ STO protocol #33, pt. 1, 13 May 1929: RGVA f. 4, op. 17, d. 62, ll. 148–49; RZ STO decree, 31 May 1929: RGAE f. 3429, op. 16, d. 6, ll. 67–68.

38. RZ STO decision, 4 September 1928: RGAE f. 3429, op. 16, d. 6, ll. 218–19; Standing Mobilization Conference #1, pt. 2, 30 October 1928: ibid., d. 14, ll. 121–22.

39. RZ STO protocol #26, pt. 2, 3 December 1928: RGAE f. 3429, op. 16, d. 6, l. 193.

40. RZ STO protocol #27, pt. 2, 17 December 1928: RGAE f. 3429, op. 16, d. 6, l. 168; also RZ STO decision, 20 December 1928: RGVA f. 4, op. 17, d. 62, ll. 9–11.

41. RZ STO decision, 26 March 1929: RGAE f. 3429, op. 16, d. 61, l. 113; RZ STO #32, pt. 2, 16 April 1929: RGAE f. 3429, op. 16, d. 6, l. 107.

42. Rabkrin report on miscalculation of production capacity, 7 July 1928: RGVA f. 33988, op. 3, d. 100, l. 63.

43. Lakhinskii to Ordzhonikidze and Voroshilov, 18 July 1928: RGVA f. 33987, op. 3, d. 131, ll. 260–61.

44. Rabkrin report on production capacity, 6–7 July 1928: RGVA f. 4, op. 1, d. 686, ll. 7–9; also RGVA f. 33988, op. 3, d. 100, ll. 61–63; Aleksandr Svechin, *Strategy* (Moscow: Voennyi Vestnik, 1927; English trans., Minneapolis: Eastview, 1992), 127.

45. Staff briefing paper on Rabkrin report, June–July 1929: RGVA f. 4, op. 1, d. 686, ll. 2–5; staff addendum to Rabkrin report, 2 July 1928: RGVA f. 33988, op. 3, d. 100, ll. 72–76.

46. Ibid.

47. Voroshilov to Stalin, 31 December 1928: RTsKhIDNI f. 74, op. 2, d. 39, l. 19.

48. On this general tendency, see Z., "Sovremennaia artilleriia i modernizatsiia," *ViT*

4 (1929): 9–14, and N. Efimov, "Evoliutsiia sistemy vooruzheniia," *ViR* 10 (1928): 26; also Gerhard Weinberg, *A World at Arms: A Global History of World War II* (Cambridge: Cambridge University Press, 1994), 536–37.

49. Revvoensovet protocol #6, pt. 2, 23 January 1929: RGVA f. 4, op. 18, d. 15, ll. 32–35. The 122mm howitzer and 107mm field gun were often measured in *lin*, for *liniia*, a unit of measure equivalent to 2.54 millimeters or one-tenth of an inch. Thus, those pieces were often referred to as the 48-*lin* howitzer and 42-*lin* field gun. Also, 152mm was often expressed as 6 *diuimov*, a *diuim* being equivalent to an inch.

50. Z., "Sovremennaia artilleriia," 11.

51. Revvoensovet protocol #12, 13 February 1929: RGVA f. 4, op. 18, d. 15, l. 77; Revvoensovet protocol #25, pt. 4, 22 May 1929: ibid., l. 164.

52. Revvoensovet protocol #2, pt. 1, 23 January 1930: RGVA f. 4, op. 18, d. 19. l. 17; Revvoensovet protocol #10, pt. 2, 2 June 1930: ibid., ll. 169–72.

53. Revvoensovet decision, 27 July 1931: ibid., d. 21, ll. 70–73.

54. Efimov to Revvoensovet, March 1933: RGVA f. 4, op. 14, d. 958, ll. 79–80ob.

55. Revvoensovet protocol #32, pt. 9, 8 June 1927: RGVA f. 4, op. 18, d. 11, l. 272. The Degtiarev would eventually serve as the Red Air Force's standard turret machine gun but was unsuitable for being mounted to fire through the aircraft's propeller. A modified Maxim gun, under the name PV-1, was used instead.

56. "Ruchnye pulemety," *Tekhnika i vooruzhenie* 6 (1971): 12.

57. Postnikov to Voroshilov, 12 June 1928: RGVA f. 33987, op. 3, d. 131, l. 258. The Kovrovskii plant was also known as Instrument Factory 2.

58. Revvoensovet protocol #10, 6 February 1929: RGVA f. 4, op. 18, d. 15, ll. 60–61. On issues of interchangeable parts, see also Joseph Bradley, *Guns for the Tsar* (De Kalb: Northern Illinois University Press, 1990), 29–33, 89–90.

59. Revvoensovet protocol #30, pt. 10, 31 July 1929: RGVA f. 4, op. 18, d. 15, l. 208; RZ STO protocol #38, pt. 5, 9 September 1929: RGAE f. 3429, op. 16, d. 6, l. 16; RZ STO protocol #42, pt. 3, 30 November 1929: RGVA f. 4, op. 1, d. 1159, l. 19.

60. Revvoensovet protocol #37, pt. 12, 8 August 1927: RGVA f. 4, op. 18, d. 11, l. 326.

61. Protocol #1 of Financial-Planning Commission of NKVM, 6 June 1928: RGVA f. 4, op. 18, d. 13, l. 272; Shaposhnikov report on order fulfillment, 5–7 January 1929: RGVA f. 4, op. 2, d. 513, l. 7.

62. Revvoensovet protocol #5, pt. 6, 16 January 1929: RGVA f. 4, op. 2, d. 513, l. 1; meeting protocol, 17 January 1929: ibid., ll. 3–6.

63. Kulik (Artillery Directorate) briefing paper, 13 August 1929: RGVA f. 33991, op. 1, d. 44, l. 2.

64. RZ STO protocol #42, pt. 3, 30 November 1929: RGVA f. 4, op. 1, d. 1159, l. 19; RZ STO protocol #44, pt. 4, 30 January 1930: RGAE f. 3429, op. 16, d. 77, l. 80a; RZ STO decision, 5 February 1930: ibid., l. 82.

65. A. Mostovenko, *Tanki* (Moscow: Voenizdat, 1955), 75–77; Khalepskii and Poliakov short history of tank production, 25 November 1929: RGVA f. 31811, op. 1, d. 1, ll. 11–12; *Istoriia tankovykh voisk Sovetskoi armii* (Moscow: Akademiia im. Kalinovskogo, 1975), 72; *Oruzhie pobedy: Oboronnaia promyshlennost' SSSR v gody voiny* (Moscow: Mashinostroenie, 1987), 190.

66. Iagoda and Prokof'ev (OGPU) report to Ordzhonikidze, 31 January 1928: RGVA f. 33987, op. 3, d. 131, l. 228.

67. Protocol of meeting under Glavmet, 11 May 1928: RGVA f. 4, op. 1, d. 662, ll. 7–10; Unshlikht's report on the state of tank production attributes substantially these figures to the specification of a governmental commission of 30 April 1928: RGVA f. 4, op. 14, d. 92, l. 116.

68. Inventory of tanks in Red Army, 22 October 1928: RGVA f. 33988, op. 1, d. 622, l. 203; Berzin to Voroshilov on cooperation with Reichswehr, 24 December 1928: RGVA f. 33987, op. 3, d. 295, l. 80. For this last reference, I am grateful for Mary Habeck's assistance.

5. 1929 AND THE CREATION OF THE FIRST FIVE-YEAR PLAN

1. *Narodnoe khoziaistvo SSSR za 70 let* (Moscow: Finansy i Statistika, 1987), 41.

2. Alec Nove, *An Economic History of the Soviet Union* (London: Penguin, 1989), 183, 217; *Narodnoe khoziaistvo,* 161, 163–64.

3. Naum Jasny, *Soviet Industrialization, 1928–1952* (Chicago: University of Chicago Press, 1961), viii. This argument is much older than Jasny; Paul Haensel in 1930 pointed to "crushing taxation" as the source of Soviet investment capital in *The Economic Policy of Soviet Russia* (London: P. S. King, 1930), 83. On Preobrazhenskii, see Stephen Cohen, *Bukharin and the Bolshevik Revolution* (Oxford: Oxford University Press, 1980), 160 ff.; Nove, *Economic History,* 115–16.

4. On the terrible damage collectivization did to Soviet agriculture and thereby to the economy as a whole, see Holland Hunter and Janusz M. Szyrmer, *Faulty Foundations: Soviet Economic Policies, 1928–1940* (Princeton, N.J.: Princeton University Press, 1992). For a nuanced discussion of whether agriculture drained resources from the Soviet economy, see James Millar, Alec Nove, and Jerry Hough, "A Debate on Collectivization," *PoC* 4 (1976): 49–62. James Millar's article "Mass Collectivization and the Contribution of Soviet Agriculture to the First Five-Year Plan," *SR* 33 (1974): 750–66, based on the work of the Soviet scholar A. A. Barsov, concludes that agriculture was a drain on the Soviet economy after collectivization. See also Millar's "Soviet Rapid Development and the Agricultural Surplus Hypothesis," *SS* 22 (1970): 77–93, and Alec Nove's critical comment, *SS* 22 (1971): 394–401.

5. Robert C. Allen's work in progress argues that agriculture was not, in fact, a drain on the Stalinist economy and that mobilizing rural labor into the urban workforce, along with concentrating investment in capital goods, was sufficient for economic growth during the First and Second Five-Year Plans (paper delivered to Yale University Economics Department, 3 October 1996).

6. V. B. Drobizhev, *Industrializatsiia i izmeneniia v sotsial'noi strukture sovetskogo obshchestva* (Moscow: Nauka, 1970), 4–5. See also Sheila Fitzpatrick, "The Great Departure: Rural-Urban Migration in the Soviet Union, 1929–33," and Stephen Kotkin, "Peopling Magnitostroi: The Politics of Demography," both in *Social Dimensions of Soviet Industrialization,* ed. William Rosenberg and Lewis Siegelbaum (Bloomington: Indiana University Press, 1993), 15–40, 63–104; Gail Lapidus, *Women in Soviet Society: Equality, Development, and Social Change* (Berkeley: University of California Press, 1978), 95 ff., 164–66; *Narodnoe khoziaistvo,* 414–45; Norton T. Dodge, *Women in the Soviet Economy* (Baltimore: 1966).

7. A. Erlich, *The Soviet Industrialization Debate* (Cambridge, Mass.: Harvard University Press, 1967), 165; Holland Hunter, "The Overambitious First Soviet Five-Year

Plan," *SR* 32 (1973): 237; Moshe Lewin, "The Disappearance of Planning in the Plan," *SR* 32 (1973): 272.

8. Robert Tucker, *Stalin as Revolutionary* (New York: Norton, 1973), 93–94. See also Mark Von Hagen, *Soldiers in the Proletarian Dictatorship* (Ithaca, N.Y.: Cornell University Press, 1991), 334–35.

9. Jasny, *Soviet Industrialization*, 4; Lewis Siegelbaum, *Soviet State and Society between Revolutions, 1919–1929* (Cambridge: Cambridge University Press, 1992), 165–80, esp. 174–76.

10. Adam Ulam, *Expansion and Coexistence*, 2d ed. (New York: Praeger, 1974), 181–82; Erlich, *Soviet Industrialization Debate*, 51, 37 (quoting Preobrazhenskii's speech to the Communist Academy in *Vestnik Kommunisticheskoi akademii* 16 [1926]: 231), 167–68.

11. See, for example, Aleksinskii (NKVM Directorate of Affairs) on five-year plan, 12 July 1927: RGVA f. 4, op. 1, d. 562, ll. 24–25. Nonferrous metals—zinc, copper, aluminum, tin, lead, and others—were vital for the production of key alloys as well as ammunition and aircraft. See also Sheila Fitzpatrick, *The Russian Revolution, 1917–1932* (Oxford: Oxford University Press, 1982), 131.

12. Pugachev (staff) position paper on five-year plan [October–November 1927?]: RGAE f. 4372, op. 91, d. 75, ll. 150–151ob.

13. Hunter, "The Overambitious Five-Year Plan," 237, 254–56; I. Stalin, "Ob industrializatsii strany i o pravom uklone v VKP(b)," in *Sochineniia* (Moscow: Politizdat, 1946–), vol. 12, 246–48.

14. David M. Glantz, *The Military Strategy of the Soviet Union: A History* (London: Frank Cass, 1992), 29–30; Richard Pipes, *Russia under the Bolshevik Regime* (New York: Knopf, 1993), 276.

15. V. I. Lenin, *Polnoe sobranie sochinenii* (Moscow: Politizdat, 1958–1965), vol. 45, 287.

16. For a discussion of the factors pushing the USSR toward autarkic policies, one that I think underestimates the deliberate nature of the Soviet push, see Michael R. Dohan, "The Economic Origins of Soviet Autarky, 1927/8–1934," *SR* 35 (1976): 603–35. See also E. H. Carr and R. W. Davies, *Foundations of a Planned Economy* (London: Macmillan 1969), vol. 1, pt. 1, 402–3.

17. Carr and Davies, *Foundations of a Planned Economy*, vol. 1, pt. 1, 295.

18. Von Hagen, *Soldiers in the Proletarian Dictatorship*, 334.

19. Staff reaction to Gosplan five-year plan [early July 1927?]: RGVA f. 4, op. 1, d. 562, l. 29; V. A. Bazanov, "Printsipy postroeniia perspektivnykh planov," *Planovoe khoziaistvo* (February 1928): 49, quoted in Erlich, *Soviet Industrialization Debate*, 68; *Istoriia Velikoi Otechestvennoi voiny* (Moscow: Voenizdat, 1961), vol. 1, 64–65.

20. Carr and Davies, *Foundations of a Planned Economy*, vol. 1, pt. 2, 843–61; Z. K. Zvezdin, *Ot plana GOELRO k planu pervoi piatiletki* (Moscow: Nauka, 1979), 173–94.

21. This document uses a three-part grouping of industries instead of the more familiar division into group A industry producing means of production and group B industry producing goods for mass consumption. In this scheme, group I, "basic *[osnovnoi]* capital," and group II, "turnover *[oborotnyi]* capital," are equivalent to group A. The distinction seems to be between instruments of production (say, machine tools) and raw materials (fuel and metals). Group III, goods for mass consumption, is equivalent to group B. See RGVA f. 4, op. 1, d. 562, ll. 49 ff.

22. Undated [June-July 1927] NKVM reaction to Gosplan draft: ibid., ll. 23–24, 40–41.

23. Ibid., ll. 22, 30–31.

24. The source is a 12 July 1927 briefing paper: RGVA f. 4, op. 1, d. 562, l. 23, and NKVM reaction to Gosplan draft: ibid., ll. 36–37. The column "Red Army: Total Defense" includes outlays for the OGPU and other miscellaneous defense expenditures in addition to the Red Army budget. The column "Red Army: Red Army Budget" is made up of expenditures on personnel, construction, and other matters, but roughly half was taken up by procurement of supplies and equipment. This last column does not include "natural" supplies (food and other provisions) but only "technical" supplies (weapons and other equipment).

25. 12 July 1927 briefing paper: ibid., l. 23; NKVM conclusion, ibid., ll. 33–35.

26. NKVM conclusion: ibid., ll. 37–38; Aleksinskii briefing paper, 12 July 1927: ibid., l. 24.

27. Resolution of IV Congress of Soviets, 18–26 April 1927, in *Vserossiiskie s"ezdy sovetov, II-X s"ezdy* (Moscow: Institut Sovetskogo stroitel'stva i prava, 1935), 389, 391.

28. Revvoensovet protocol #35, pt. 3, 19 July 1927: RGVA f. 4, op. 18, d. 11, l. 292.

29. Carr and Davies, *Foundations of a Planned Economy*, 862–64; Zvezdin, *Ot GOELRO*, 198–99.

30. Carr and Davies, *Foundations of a Planned Economy*, 864–70; also Zvezdin, *Ot GOELRO*, 188–89, 195–200. For an illustration of the steady growth in plan targets over time, see the table in Carr and Davies, 981–82.

31. L. S. Rogachevskaia, "Kak sostavlialsia plan pervoi piatiletki," *VI* 8 (1993): 149; Carr and Davies, *Foundations of a Planned Economy*, 872–73; Zvezdin, *Ot GOELRO*, 202–12; Krzhizhanovskii speech, 12 December 1927, in *XV s"ezd Vsesoiuznoi kommunisticheskoi partii (b): Stenograficheskii otchet* (Moscow: Gosizdat, 1928), 794–95; *VKP(b) v rezoliutsiiakh i resheniiakh s"ezdov, konferentsii i plenumov TsK* (Moscow: Partizdat, 1936), 243.

32. Vladimirskii (Defense Sector of Gosplan) to Postnikov (MPU), 1 November 1927: RGAE f. 4372, op. 91, d. 64, l. 151.

33. Krzhizhanovskii speech, 12 December 1927, 790; *VKP(b) v rezoliutsiiakh*, pt. 2, 240.

34. In addition to a stenographic record of the congress, Voroshilov's remarks were reprinted in Kliment Voroshilov, *Stat'i i rechi* (Moscow: Partizdat, 1937), 188 ff. See especially 13 December 1927, "Question of defense and the Five Year Plan," 196, 199; emphasis Voroshilov's.

35. On military industry, see ibid., 205 ff.; on remaining industry, see 199–205.

36. Carr and Davies, *Foundations of a Planned Economy*, 873, 876; Zvezdin, *Ot GOELRO*, 212–13.

37. RZ STO #15, pt. 6, 20 February 1928: RGVA f. 33988, op. 3, d. 89, l. 23; see also protocol 21 of the Standing Mobilization Conference, 19 April 1928: RGAE f. 3429, op. 16, d. 3, ll. 64–67.

38. See N. D. Kondrat'ev, *Osoboe mnenie* (Moscow: Nauka, 1993), biographical afterword, vol. 2, 530–31; Carr and Davies, *Foundations of a Planned Economy*, 858–61 (citing *Planovoe khoziaistvo* 4 [1927]: 31, 33), 878–79.

39. Cohen, *Bukharin*, 289–91; Carr and Davies, *Foundations of a Planned Economy*, 768, 314–15; *VKP(b) v rezoliutsiiakh*, 284–89.

40. Carr and Davies, *Foundations of a Planned Economy*, 879–80.

41. Cohen, *Bukharin*, 295–96.

42. Ibid., 296–301.

43. Rogachevskaia, "Kak sostavlialsia," 150; Zvezdin, *Ot GOELRO*, 232–33; Carr and Davies, *Foundations of a Planned Economy*, 881–83, 888–92.

44. RZ STO protocol #20, pt. 1, 30 July 1928: RGVA f. 4, op. 17, d. 61, ll. 312–13; RZ STO protocol #29, pt. 2, 4 February 1929: RGAE f. 3429, op. 16, d. 6, l. 32; also RGVA f. 4, op. 1, d. 921, l. 53.

45. Gosplan (deputy chair of Defense Sector Mekhonoshin) to Vesenkha, 16 February 1929: RGAE f. 3429, op. 16, d. 22, l. 4.

46. Standing Mobilization Conference protocol and decision #9, pt. 1, 19 March 1929: RGAE, f. 3429, op. 16, d. 14, l. 96; also Postnikov (MPU) and Kott (II Section MPU) to Defense Sector of Gosplan, 20 March 1929: ibid., d. 22, l. 4.

47. Transcript of Sovnarkom/STO meeting, March–April 1929: RGVA f. 4, op. 3, d. 3208, ll. 72ob-73.

48. Nickel, like cobalt, is technically a ferrous metal, close to iron in its properties, but its relative scarcity made the Soviets place it in the category of nonferrous metals.

49. Shaposhnikov (staff) report on Five-Year Plan, 30 March 1929: RGVA f. 4, op. 14, d. 91, ll. 1, 4ob-5; Mekhonoshin (deputy chair of Gosplan) to Voroshilov on military aspects of Five-Year Plan, 5 April 1929: ibid., ll. 18–19; RZ STO decree, 13 June 1929: RGAE f. 3429, op. 16, d. 6, ll. 90–95.

50. Shaposhnikov report, l. 5ob; also, Mekhonoshin to Voroshilov, ibid., ll. 17ob, 24, 28.

51. Mekhonoshin to Voroshilov, ibid., ll. 29–30.

52. R. W. Davies, "Soviet Defence Industries during the First Five-Year Plan," in *Economy and Society in Russia and the Soviet Union, 1860–1930,* ed. Linda Edmondson and Peter Waldron (New York: St. Martin's, 1992), 246; *16–aia konferentsiia VKP(b): Stenograficheskii otchet* (Moscow: Politizdat, 1962), 49; Carr and Davies, *Foundations of a Planned Economy*, 888–92.

53. RZ STO protocol #31, pt. 1, 8 April 1929: RGAE f. 3429, op. 16, d. 6, l. 69; RZ STO protocol #32, pt. 1, 16 April 1929: ibid., l. 108.

54. Lennart Samuelson, *Soviet Defence Industry Planning* (Stockholm: Stockholm School of Economics, 1996), 142–44.

55. Two- to three-year targets decreed 4 February 1929 from 30 July 1928 RZ STO assignment: RGVA f. 4, op. 17, d. 61, ll. 312–13; targets for end of Five-Year Plan decreed by RZ STO, 27 May 1929: RGVA f. 4, op. 17, d. 62, ll. 188–89.

56. See *KPSS o vooruzhennykh silakh Sovetskogo Soiuza: Sbornik dokumentov* (Moscow: Voenizdat, 1958), 318–21, for an expurgated version of "O sostoianii oborony SSSR." Apparently, "O voennoi promyshlennosti" was never published. *50 let vooruzhennykh sil SSSR* (Moscow:Voenizdat, 1968), 196, calls the Politburo's decision the basis for the first military five-year plan, "which determined the basic directions of the armed forces' development," ignoring the fact that the document itself refers to the just-completed 1924–1929 military five-year plan and another 1928 military five-year plan. A. Ryzhakov, "K voprosu o stroitel'stve bronetankovykh voisk Krasnoi Armii v 30–e gody," *VIZh* 8 (1968): 106, discusses this decree but misdates it as 15 June 1929 and says that its purpose was to redo the military's five-year plan. See also the discussion in Samuelson, *Soviet Defence Industry Planning,* 145–49.

57. Politburo decision "On the State of Defense," 15 July 1929: GARF f. 5446, op. 55, d. 1966, ll. 38, 40 ff.

58. Ibid., l. 43.

59. Ibid., l. 39. The issue of foreign technology and the Soviet military is beyond the scope of this study, but Soviet reliance on foreign technical aid and licensed technology was immense. The vaunted collaboration with Weimar Germany was only a small part of Soviet purchases abroad. For an introduction, see A. C. Sutton, *Western Technology and Soviet Economic Development, 1917–1930* (Stanford, Calif.: Hoover, 1968), and on the specific case of tanks, see chapter 8.

60. Politburo decision "On the State of Defense," l. 37.

61. On the Tolmachevskii opposition, see Steven J. Main, "The Red Army and the Soviet Military and Political Leadership in the Late 1920s: The Case of the 'Inner-Army Opposition of 1928,'" *EAS* 47 (1995): 337–55.

62. Politburo decision "On the State of Defense," ll. 35–36, 40.

63. RZ STO #36, pt. 1, 26 June 1929: RGAE f. 3429, op. 16, d. 6, l. 56.

64. Politburo decree "On Military Industry," 15 July 1929: GARF f. 5446, op. 55, d. 1966, l. 27.

65. Ibid., ll. 26–27.

66. Ibid., ll. 23–24.

67. Ibid., l. 23.

68. Ibid., ll. 20–22.

69. Ibid., l. 32.

70. R. W. Davies, *The Soviet Economy in Turmoil* (London: Macmillan, 1989), 187 ff., 195, 197–99; Rogachevskaia, "Kak sostavlialsia," 151. See also R. W. Davies, "The Management of Soviet Industry, 1928–41," in Rosenberg and Siegelbaum, *Social Dimensions of Soviet Industrialization,* 110, emphasizing Ordzhonikidze's and Rabkrin's role in pushing higher plan targets. David Shearer, *Industry, State, and Society in Stalin's Russia, 1926–1934* (Ithaca, N.Y.: Cornell University Press, 1996), also points to Rabkrin as a key force for centralization and radicalization in economic policy. In my opinion, this is not inconsistent with a Politburo mandate for higher targets in defense-related industry.

71. Revvoensovet protocol #29, pt. 1, 17–18 July 1929: RGVA f. 4, op. 18, d. 15, l. 190.

72. On Kork, see "Avgust Ivanovich Kork," *VIZh* 7 (1962): 125–26; *VIZh* 7 (1967): 124–28. After service as commander of the Moscow military district, he became commander of the Frunze Military Academy in 1935. He was killed in the Great Purges.

73. Kork to NKVM, 15 July 1929: RGVA f. 4, op. 1, d. 1009, ll. 1–2; additional Kork reform proposal, 13 November 1929: ibid., l. 6.

74. Kork to NKVM, 15 July 1929: ibid., ll. 1–2.

75. See draft decree, 31 October 1929: RGVA f. 4, op. 1, d. 1021, ll. 7–8; actual decision creating the Motorization and Mechanization Directorate *(Upravlenie motorizatsii i mekhanizatsii),* Revvoensovet protocol #35, pt. 2, 3 November 1929: RGVA f. 4, op. 18, d. 15, l. 243. See also UMM charter, 22 November 1929: RGVA f. 31811, op. 1, d. 14, ll. 10–11. I am grateful to Mary Habeck for these references.

76. Kork's report, 13 November 1929: RGVA f. 4, op. 1, d. 1009, l. 3.

77. Appendix to 13 November 1929 report: ibid., l. 6.

78. V. Danilov, "Sovershenstvovanie tsentral'nykh organov voennogo rukovodstva v 1929–1939gg," *VIZh* 6 (1982): 77.

79. See Molotov to Ordzhonikidze on Pavlunovskii's findings, 25 November 1929: RTsKhIDNI f. 85, op. 27, d. 93, l. 1; Pavlunovskii report on Artillery Directorate, 17 December 1929: RGVA f. 33991, op. 1, d. 20, ll. 80–92; Politburo's reaction to Pavlunovskii report, Politburo protocol #113, pt. 11, 15 January 1930: RTsKhIDNI f. 17, op. 162, d. 8, l. 40. Dybenko was a revolutionary hero and the lover of Bolshevik feminist Aleksandra Kollontai. On him, see A. F. Aksenov, "Revoliutsionnye i voenno-organizatsionnye deiatel'nosti P. E. Dybenko" (diss., Humanitarian Academy of the Armed Forces, 1992).

80. Revvoensovet protocol #36, pt. 2, 18 November 1929: RGVA f. 4, op. 18, d. 15, ll. 248–49; Politburo protocol #106, pt. 33, 25 November 1929: RTsKhIDNI f. 17, op. 3, d. 766, l. 6.

81. On Uborevich, see V. I. Savost'ianov and P. Ia. Egorov, *Komandarm pervogo ranga* (Moscow: Politizdat, 1966), *Komandarm Uborevich: Vospominaniia druzei i soratnikov* (Moscow: Voenizdat, 1964), and *Geroi grazhdanskoi voiny* (Moscow: Molodaia Gvardiia, 1963).

82. On Tukhachevskii's appointment as armaments director, see David R. Stone, "Tukhachevskii in Leningrad: Military Politics and Exile, 1928–1931," *EAS* 48 (1996): 1381–82.

83. Evgenii Vorob'ev, "Smotrite priamo v glaza," *Literaturnaia gazeta* 27 (1987): 12; G. K. Zhukov, *Vospominaniia i razmyshleniia* (Moscow: Novosti, 1992), vol. 1, 208.

84. Vesenkha order 119?ss, 28 October 1929: RGAE f. 3429, op. 16, d. 23, ll. 1–3.

85. Ibid., ll. 3–5; for additional working groups, see ibid., d. 24, ll. 7–10, and Standing Mobilization Conference order of 21 November 1929: ibid., d. 23, l. 9.

86. Voroshilov to Uborevich and Shaposhnikov, 7 March 1930: RGVA f. 4, op. 1, d. 1164, l. 3; Uborevich to Voroshilov, 22 March 1930: ibid., l. 6.

87. Revvoensovet protocol #25 on 1929–1930 budget, 29 May 1929: RGVA f. 4, op. 18, d. 15, ll. 175–76.

88. See RZ STO protocols #40, pt. 3, and #41, pt. 1: RGVA f. 4, op. 17, d. 62, ll. 299–300, 313–14.

89. RZ STO decision on defense measures budget for 1929–1930, 11 December 1929: RGVA f. 4, op. 17, d. 62, ll. 358–63; R. W. Davies, "Soviet Military Expenditure," 593.

90. RZ STO decision, 11 December 1929: RGVA f. 4, op. 17, d. 62, l. 360.

91. See, in particular, Tucker, *Stalin as Revolutionary,* 462–87, esp. 477–81; also Robert Tucker, *Stalin in Power* (New York: Norton, 1990), 128–29, and Isaac Deutscher, *Stalin* (New York: Oxford University Press, 1966), 317.

6. THE RED ARMY CONSOLIDATES ITS VICTORY

1. See Jonathan Haslam, *Soviet Foreign Policy: The Impact of the Depression* (London: Macmillan, 1983), esp. 1–9; R. Craig Nation, *Black Earth, Red Star* (Ithaca, N.Y.: Cornell University Press, 1992), 68–69; Adam Ulam, *Expansion and Coexistence,* 2d ed. (New York: Praeger, 1974), 188–89.

2. Konstantin Mekhonoshin, *Izvestiia,* 16 June 1930, and Ventsov and Petukhov, *Izvestiia,* 26 June 1930, quoted in R. W. Davies, *The Soviet Economy in Turmoil, 1929–1930* (London: Macmillan, 1989), 448–49.

3. *VKP(b) v rezoliutsiiakh i resheniiakh s"ezdov, konferentsii i plenumov TsK* (Moscow: Partizdat, 1936), 399–400; emphasis in original.

4. On the concepts of organized capitalism and the stabilization of capitalism, see Jon Jacobson, *When the Soviet Union Entered World Politics* (Berkeley: University of California Press, 1994), 142–47, and Stephen Cohen, *Bukharin and the Bolshevik Revolution* (Oxford: Oxford University Press, 1980), 28–35; *VKP(b) v rezoliutsiiakh,* 399, 414.

5. *VKP(b) v rezoliutsiiakh,* 414–15, 400.

6. Alec Nove, *An Economic History of the Soviet Union,* 2d ed. (London: Penguin, 1989), 204; Davies, *Soviet Economy in Turmoil,* 241–42; David Shearer, *Industry, State, and Society in Stalin's Russia* (Ithaca, N.Y.: Cornell University Press, 1996), 112–20, 167 ff., 205; Savitskii briefing paper on industrial organization, February 1930?: RGVA f. 4, op. 1, d. 1234, l. 9. The 5 December 1929 Central Committee decision has been published in several places, including *Direktivy KPSS i sovetskogo pravitel'stva po khoziaistvennym voprosam* (Moscow: Politizdat, 1957), vol. 2, 126–33, and V. Z. Drobyzhev et al., eds., *Upravlenie narodnym khoziaistvom SSSR, 1917–1940gg* (Moscow: Ekonomika, 1968), 171–80.

7. Sharskov and Rakhmanin to Vesenkha Working Commission, 2 December 1929: RGAE f. 3429, op. 16, d. 38, l. 12.

8. Kuibyshev to Central Committee, 27 December 1929: RGVA f. 33987, op. 3, d. 331, ll. 35–37.

9. Ibid., ll. 37–39ob.

10. Krzhizhanovskii and Mekhonoshin to Rykov, 3 January 1930: RGVA f. 7, op. 10, d. 959, ll. 14–15.

11. Politburo decision of 15 January 1930: GARF f. 5446, op. 55, d. 1966, ll. 6–9; RZ STO decision of 21 January 1930: RGAE f. 3429, op. 16, d. 77, ll. 63–68, also ll. 194–99.

12. Politburo protocol #115, pt. 6, 25 January 1930: RTsKhIDNI f. 17, op. 3, d. 774, l. 2; RZ STO decision, 30 January 1930: RGVA f. 4, op. 1, d. 1210, l. 20; also RGAE f. 3429, op. 16, d. 77, l. 80; Politburo protocol #116, pt. 7, 5 February 1930: RTsKhIDNI f. 17, op. 3, d. 775, l. 3; RGVA f. 4, op. 1, d. 1226, l. 7. See also Nikolai Simonov, *Voenno-promyshlennyi kompleks SSSR* (Moscow: Rosspen, 1996), 39.

13. Vesenkha briefing paper of 30 March? 1930: RGVA f. 4, op. 1, d. 1210, l. 134. In Russian, the associations were Orudiino-oruzheino-pulemetnoe ob"edinenie and Patronno-trubochno-vzryvatel'noe ob"edinenie, known more familiarly as Patrubvzryv.

14. Shaposhnikov to Voroshilov, 26 December 1929: RGVA f. 33987, op. 2, d. 280, ll. 7–8, cited in Lennart Samuelson, *Soviet Defence Industry Planning* (Stockholm: Stockholm School of Economics, 1996), 162.

15. Uborevich to Voroshilov, 13 March 1930: RGVA f. 7, op. 10, d. 1103, l. 14; RZ STO protocol #48, pt. 11, 31 March 1930: RGVA f. 4, op. 1, d. 1226, l. 10, and RGAE f. 3429, op. 16, d. 77, l. 133.

16. Politburo protocol #122, pt. 31a, 5 April 1930: RTsKhIDNI f. 17, op. 3, d. 781, l. 7.

17. On Smilga, see Politburo protocol #113, pt. 1, 15 January 1930: GARF f. 5446, op. 55, d. 1966, l. 10; Politburo protocol #116, pt. 6, 5 February 1930: RTsKhIDNI f. 17, op. 3, d. 775, l. 3. On Unshlikht, see Politburo protocol #128, pt. 28, 15 June 1930 [decision of 30 May 1930]: RTsKhIDNI f. 17, op. 3, d. 787, l. 8; see also P. A. Golub, "Zhizn'-podvig," *Voprosy istorii KPSS* 7 (1964): 84–88, and Davies, *Soviet Economy in Turmoil,* 417, 448.

18. Voroshilov to Stalin, July 1930: RGVA f. 4, op. 19, d. 10, l. 359. VAO is an abbreviation for Vsesoiuznoe aviatsionnoe ob"edinenie, but the official name often appeared as Vsesoiuznoe ob"edinenie aviatsionnoi promyshlennosti. The distinction is, to be sure, rather academic.

19. Politburo protocol #2, pt. 44, 25 July 1930 [decision from 20 July]: RTsKhIDNI f. 17, op. 3, d. 790, l. 10; Sovnarkom decision #42, 28 July 1930: RGAE f. 3429, op. 16, d. 77, l. 189.

20. "On the Transfer of VAO from VSNKh to NKVM," Revvoensovet protocol #19, pt. 2, 3 September 1930: RGVA f. 4, op. 18, d. 19, ll. 337–38, 343.

21. Revvoensovet protocol #9, 15 February 1931: RGVA f. 4, op. 18, d. 20, l. 89; Politburo protocol #26, pt. 66/68, 15 February 1931: RTsKhIDNI f. 17, op. 3, d. 813, l. 18.

22. A. Gromakov, "Deiatel'nost' Kommunisticheskoi partii po razvitiiu oboronnoi promyshlennosti (1921–1925gg.)," VIZh 10 (1975): 87, citing RTsKhIDNI f. 19 [17?], op. 3, d. 202, l. 189.

23. Stephen Kotkin, "Peopling Magnitostroi," in Social Dimensions of Soviet Industrialization, ed. William Rosenberg and Lewis Siegelbaum (Bloomington: Indiana University Press, 1993), 65.

24. A. S. Belin, "Uchastie voinskikh chastei v sozdanii predpriiatii tiazheloi promy-shlennosti na Urale," Ural i oborona sovetskoi strany (Sverdlovsk: UGO im Gor'kogo, 1968), 236–45.

25. List of personnel, 6 December 1929: RTsKhIDNI f. 17, op. 85, d. 125, ll. 5–6; N. Kuibyshev to GVPU, 27 March 1930, and list of personnel: ibid., ll. 11, 26.

26. Khalepskii and Bokis to multiple addressees, 4 September/31 August 1930: RGVA f. 31811, op. 1, d. 135, l. 5 and passim. On the Ural party committee, see Belin, "Uchastie voinskikh chastei," 240.

27. Special Administration of Diesel Trust to UMM, 5 November 1930: RGVA f. 31811, op. 1, d. 135, l. 124.

28. Ivanov to UMM, 13 October 1930: ibid., l. 10; Bokis to Ivanov, 16 October 1930: ibid., l. 11.

29. See, for example, ibid., ll. 24, 33.

30. Unshlikht (Vesenkha) to STO, copy to Uborevich (armaments director), 7 August 1930: RGVA f. 4, op. 1, d. 1249, l. 75.

31. RZ STO decision, 1 March 1930: RGVA f. 4, op. 17, d. 63, l. 90; Revvoensovet protocol #10, pt. 5, 2 June 1930: RGVA f. 4, op. 18, d. 19, l. 173.

32. RZ STO protocol #52, pt. 1, 20 June 1930: RGVA f. 4, op. 1, d. 1249, l. 46, also RGAE f. 3429, op. 16, d. 77, l. 183.

33. Compare commission protocol, 28 July 1930: RGAE f. 3429, op. 16, d. 78, ll. 82–83, and Uborevich report, 31 July 1930: RGVA f. 33988, op. 3, d. 154, l. 56ob.

34. Uborevich report, 31 July 1930: RGVA f. 33988, op. 3, d. 154, l. 56ob; Uborevich circular letter, 30 July 1930: RGVA f. 33988, op. 3, d. 154, ll. 36–37.

35. RZ STO protocol #54, pt. 2, 30 July 1930: RGAE f. 3429, op. 16, d. 78, l. 5b; also RGVA f. 4, op. 1, d. 1249, l. 68.

36. Uborevich report, 31 July 1930: RGVA f. 33988, op. 3, d. 154, l. 56ob. Uborevich here mistakenly refers to the RZ STO's 30 July decision as the Politburo's 30 July decision. RZ STO protocol #55, pt. 1, 10 August 1930: RGVA f. 4, op. 17, d. 63, ll. 255–56.

37. Uborevich report, 31 July 1930: RGVA f. 33988, op. 3, d. 154, ll. 52–56; Smilga

(MPU) to Uborevich, 13 August 1930: RGVA f. 7, op. 10, d. 1103, l. 221; Revvoensovet protocol, #17, pt. 18, 13 August 1930: RGVA f. 4, op. 18, d. 19, ll. 301–2; Politburo protocol #8, pt. 56/56, 15 September 1930: RTsKhIDNI f. 17, op. 162, d. 9, l. 32.

38. On the summer 1930 crisis, see Davies, *Soviet Economy in Turmoil,* 346–77, 430–34, esp. 351–52.

39. See Politburo protocol #8, pt. 56/56, 15 September 1930: RTsKhIDNI f. 17, op. 162, d. 9, l. 32, in which the Politburo approves an RZ STO procurement budget for 1930–1931. On surprise, see Davies, *Soviet Economy in Turmoil,* 404–6.

40. Politburo decision of 20 September 1930: RTsKhIDNI f. 17, op. 3, d. 798, ll. 21 ff., 26–27; see also Davies, *Soviet Economy in Turmoil,* 404–5.

41. RZ STO decisions of 20 and 28 September 1930: RGAE f. 3429, op. 16, d. 78, ll. 56, 68.

42. Efimov to Uborevich and Smilga 29–30 September 1930: RGVA f. 4, op. 1, d. 1336, l. 24.

43. RZ STO protocol #56, pt. 1, 30 September 1930: RGVA f. 4, op. 17, d. 63, l. 288; RZ STO protocol #57, pt. 1, 1 October 1930: ibid., ll. 302 ff.; Revvoensovet protocol #21, pt. 19, 1–2 October 1930: RGVA f. 4, op. 18, d. 19, l. 361.

44. Vesenkha order 194ss of 2 October 1930: RGVA f. 4, op. 1, d. 1375, ll. 60–61.

45. RZ STO commission, 3 October 1930: RGVA f. 4, op. 1, d. 1202, l. 40; RZ STO decision, 5 October 1930: RGVA f. 4, op. 17, d. 63, ll. 313–14.

46. RZ STO decision, 11 December 1930: RGAE f. 3429, op. 16, d. 78, l. 104; STO decision #138, 27 December 1930: ibid., l. 113.

47. Revvoensovet protocol #24, pt. 2, 26 October 1930: RGVA f. 4, op. 18, d. 19, l. 404; RZ STO protocol #59, pt. 3, 26 October 1930: RGVA f. 4, op. 1, d. 1249, l. 80.

48. Unshlikht to RZ STO, 11 November 1930: RGVA f. 4, op. 1, d. 1249, ll. 81 ff.

49. Politburo protocol #16, pt. 1/11, 25 November 1930: RTsKhIDNI f. 17, op. 162, d. 9, ll. 77–79; chart comparing orders, 26 November 1930?: RGVA f. 33988, op. 3, d. 154, l. 19. On the 1931 order completing the Red Army's requirements for deployment, see protocol of Voroshilov's commission on military orders, 29 November 1930, included as appendix to Politburo protocol #17, pt. 19/27, 5 December 1930 [decision of 30 November 1930]: RTsKhIDNI f. 17, op. 162, d. 9, ll. 88–89. This refers to the total order plan as 883 million rubles, not 890 million.

50. Grin'ko report to Politburo on draft budget, 12 December 1930: RTsKhIDNI f. 85, op. 28, d. 37, ll. 6–7. Compare R. W. Davies, "Soviet Military Expenditure and the Armaments Industry," *EAS* 45 (1993): 593, table 2, which has the defense budget as 1790 million rubles and military orders as 845 million.

51. Postnikov and Kott (MPU) on mobilization plan S, 14 December 1929: RGVA f. 4, op. 1, d. 1036, ll. 2–7.

52. Ibid., esp. ll. 6–7, and accompanying "basic indicators" for S-30.

53. Reaction [probably by staff] to MPU report on S-30, 21 December 1929: RGVA f. 7, op. 10, d. 807, ll. 13–15.

54. Revvoensovet protocol, #41, pt. 1, 23 December 1929: RGVA f. 4, op. 18, d. 15, l. 295.

55. Pavlunovskii to Ordzhonikidze, Voroshilov, Stalin, Kuibyshev, and others, 29 December 1929: RTsKhIDNI f. 85, op. 27, d. 187, ll. 1–3.

56. Ibid., ll. 4–10.

57. RZ STO protocol #43, pt. 1, 30 December 1929: RGVA f. 4, op. 17, d. 62,

l. 352; Krzhizhanovskii and Mekhonoshin (Gosplan) to Rykov, 3 January 1930: RGVA f. 7, op. 10, d. 959, ll. 14 ff.

58. See minutes of meetings of Shaposhnikov's commission, 3, 4, and 6 January 1930: RGVA f. 7, op. 10, d. 959, ll. 1–5. On counting wartime production from the outbreak of hostilities, see meeting 1, pt. II.

59. Politburo protocol #113, pt. 1, 15 January 1930: GARF f. 5446, op. 55, d. 1966, ll. 5–10; RZ STO decision of 21 January 1930: RGAE f. 3429, op. 16, d. 77, ll. 63–68; also ll. 194–99.

60. Shaposhnikov report, 2 March 1930: RGVA f. 7, op. 10, d. 1434, l. 1; draft letter of Shaposhnikov and Ventsov (director of II Directorate of Staff) to MPU, 21 March 1930: RGVA f. 7, op. 10, d. 959, l. 16; Shaposhnikov and Ventsov report on mobilization plans, 11 July 1930: RGVA f. 4, op. 1, d. 1321, l. 2ob.

61. RZ STO decision, 10 March 1930: RGAE f. 3429, op. 16, d. 77, l. 98; RZ STO protocol #53, pt. 19, 20 July 1930: ibid., l. 193; RZ STO protocol #54, pt. 1, 30 July 1930: RGVA f. 4, op. 17, d. 63, ll. 242–43.

62. Efimov to Uborevich, 13 September 1930: RGVA f. 4, op. 1, d. 1434, ll. 7–12.

63. See 7 October 1930 meeting of Voroshilov with deputies, ibid., l. 2; RZ STO protocol #58, pt. 1, 10 October 1930: RGAE f. 3429, op. 16, d. 78, l. 72; Uborevich to Voroshilov, 11 October 1930: RGVA f. 4, op. 1, d. 1434, l. 1.

64. RZ STO protocol on S-30, 26 October 1930: RGVA f. 4, op. 1, d. 1210, ll. 176–78.

65. Ibid.; also RZ STO protocol #59, pt. 2, 26 October 1930: RGAE f. 3429, op. 16, d. 78, l. 120.

66. Meeting protocol before 12 November 1930: RGAE f. 3429, op. 16, d. 109, ll. 107–21, esp. 121.

67. The mobilization plans are compiled from various sources, including an untitled comparison of S-30, corrected S-30, and variant number 10, undated: RGVA f. 33988, op. 3, d. 182, l. 131; variant number 10, in appendix to Politburo protocol #17, pt. 19/27, 30 November 1930: RTsKhIDNI f. 17, op. 162, d. 9, l. 91; S-30, corrected S-30 (listed as S-30, May 1931), and variant number 10 in a retrospective examination of the First Five-Year Plan and defense, 12 October 1932: RGVA f. 4, op. 14, d. 1051, ll. 30, 32, also RGAE f. 4372, op. 91, d. 834, ll. 12–18; Politburo goals, S-30, and the initial military version of variant number 10, in Rykov report to Central Committee on defense, 30 November 1930: RGVA f. 33988, op. 3, d. 148, ll. 1–6. On shell usage, S-30, and variant number 10, see staff report "On the Construction of the Armed Forces," November? 1930: RGVA f. 7, op. 10, d. 1067, ll. 48ob-49. The constant changes in these plans make definite figures difficult to determine. Compare, for example, the generally similar (but different in detail) chart of mobilization plans in Samuelson, *Soviet Defence Industry Planning,* 153. Simonov also presents closely corresponding figures for S-30, the Politburo targets for 1930–1931 and 1932–1933, and mobilization variant number 10. He refers to this last (it seems to me incorrectly) as a variant of S-30 (see *Voenno-promyshlennyi kompleks,* 69–70).

7. INDUSTRIAL FAILURE AND MILITARY FRUSTRATION

1. Stalin to Molotov, 30 September 1929, in *Pis'ma I. V. Stalina V. M. Molotovu* (Moscow: Rossiia Molodaia, 1995), doc. 50, 166–67.

2. Stalin to Molotov, 22 September 1930, in ibid., doc. 68, 222–24.

3. Nikolai Kuibyshev (1893–1938), the younger brother of Stalin's associate Valerian Kuibyshev, was briefly the secretary of the RZ STO before becoming head of Rabkrin's Military-Naval Inspectorate. Kuibyshev to Voroshilov and Rudzutak, 13 November 1930: RTsKhIDNI f. 74, op. 2, d. 100, l. 200; Kuibyshev to Voroshilov, 13 November 1930: ibid., l. 201. On N. Kuibyshev, see Protasov, "Iskliuchit' iz spiskov," *Voennyi vestnik* 9 (1990): 83–87.

4. On Rykov's dismissal, see *Stalinskoe Politbiuro v 30–e gody* (Moscow: Airo-XX, 1995), doc. 92, 107–12. Politburo decision, 23 December 1930, protocol 21, pt. 7/36: ibid., doc. 14, 30–31 (see also doc. 17); corresponding Sovnarkom decision 126s, 24 December 1930: RGVA f. 4, op. 17, d. 64, l. 112.

5. For the nonrole of finance ministries in total war, see Martin Van Creveld, *The Transformation of War* (New York: Free Press, 1991), 47.

6. RGVA f. 4, op. 17, d. 76, l. 95; also Politburo protocol #103, pt. 53/7, 8 June 1932 [decision of 5 June 1932]: RTsKhIDNI f. 17, op. 162, d. 12, l. 175.

7. G. K. Zhukov, *Vospominaniia i razmyshleniia* (Moscow: Novosti, 1992), vol. 1, 177; compare Defense Commission protocol, RGVA f. 4, op. 17, d. 76, l. 55, with STO decree 538/177ss, ibid., l. 420.

8. Sheila Fitzpatrick, "Ordzhonikidze's Takeover of Vesenkha: A Case Study in Soviet Bureaucratic Politics," *SS* 37 (1985): 160–62.

9. See R. W. Davies and O. Khlevniuk, "Gosplan," in *Decision-making in the Stalinist Command Economy, 1932–1937,* ed. E. A. Rees (New York: St. Martin's, 1997), 35, and "Conclusion," ibid., 265.

10. List of important dates in Kuibyshev's life: RTsKhIDNI f. 79, op. 1, d. 27, l. 2; Central Committee protocol, 10 November 1930: RTsKhIDNI f. 17, op. 3, d. 804, l. 9; *Valerian Vladimirovich Kuibyshev: Biografiia* (Moscow: Politizdat, 1988), 277. Stalin to Molotov, 1 September [1933], in *Pis'ma Stalina Molotovu,* doc. 78, 247; see also Feliks Chuev, *Sto sorok besed s Molotovym* (Moscow: Terra, 1991), 197, and R. W. Davies, *The Soviet Economy in Turmoil* (London: Macmillan, 1989), 415–18.

11. For samples of this sort of testimony, see those collected in *O Sergo Ordzhonikidze* (Moscow: Politizdat, 1981), or A. F. Khavin, *U rulia industrii* (Moscow: Politizdat, 1968). Diane Koenker, "Factory Tales: Narratives of Industrial Relations in the Transfer to NEP," *RR* 55 (1996): 384–412, notes the prevalence of these images in descriptions of "good" Soviet managers. Katerina Clark, *The Soviet Novel: History as Ritual* (Chicago: University of Chicago Press, 1981), 61–62, 71–73, traces this line of Soviet hagiography back to the death of Iakov Sverdlov (1885–1919), who did yeoman's work running the Bolsheviks' secretariat after the Revolution.

12. Fitzpatrick, "Ordzhonikidze's Takeover," 165; see also Kendall Bailes, *Technology and Society under Lenin and Stalin* (Princeton, N.J.: Princeton University Press, 1978), 144–46.

13. See Ordzhonikidze's speeches in *Stat'i i rechi* (Moscow: Institut Marksizma-leninizma, 1957), 280, 286; also Bailes, *Technology and Society,* 146–56; Fitzpatrick, "Ordzhonikidze's Takeover," 164–65.

14. Fitzpatrick, "Ordzhonikidze's Takeover," 163.

15. Amy Knight, *Beria: Stalin's First Lieutenant* (Princeton: N.J.: Princeton University Press, 1993), 38.

16. Isaac Deutscher, *Trotsky: The Prophet Unarmed* (London: Oxford University

Press, 1959), 339, identifies Smilga as a follower of Zinov'ev. See also A. P. Nenarokov, "I. T. Smilga," in *Revvoensovet Respubliki* (Moscow: Politizdat, 1991), 349–59.

17. Undated note [July 1930?] from Voroshilov to Stalin with reply: RTsKhIDNI f. 74, op. 2, d. 39, l. 60.

18. Central Committee protocol 16, pt. 16/29, 20 November 1930: RTsKhIDNI f. 17, op. 3, d. 805, l. 8; RZ STO decision, 25 November 1930: RGAE f. 3429, op. 16, d. 78, l. 100. On Martinovich, see, for example, Pavlunovskii and Martinovich's joint report: RGVA f. 4, op. 14, d. 180, ll. 4–6.

19. For some figures on production shortfalls from 1929 through 1933, see Nikolai Simonov, *Voenno-promyshlennyi kompleks SSSR* (Moscow: Rosspen, 1996), 84.

20. Meeting protocol, 1 February 1930: RGVA f. 33991, op. 1, d. 6, l. 18; meeting protocol, 5 February 1930: ibid., ll. 21–22.

21. Production and quality control report, March? 1930: ibid., ll. 28–30.

22. Revvoensovet protocol #5, pt. 12, 23 March 1930: RGVA f. 4, op. 18, d. 19, l. 85; excerpt from Standing Commission of Revvoensovet, 20 April 1930: RGVA f. 4, op. 1, d. 1249, l. 1.

23. Tukhachevskii circular letter, 8 March 1930: RGVA f. 33988, op. 2, d. 693, ll. 70–82; David Stone, "Tukhachevskii in Leningrad," *EAS* 48 (1996): 1376–81.

24. RZ STO protocol #48, pts. 6 and 8, 31 March 1930: RGAE f. 3429, op. 16, d. 77, ll. 125–26. On Uryvaev, see RZ STO protocol #49, pt. 1, 30 April 1930: RGVA f. 4, op. 17, d. 63, ll. 142–44. Uryvaev was on his way out of military industry at this point; the decision refers to him as the "former" director of the GVPU, but he was not formally replaced until July.

25. Kuibyshev circular letter, 9 May 1930: RGAE f. 3429, op. 16, d. 115, l. 571; Smilga (MPU) report to Shaposhnikov (staff) and Appoga (RZ STO), 28 May 1930: RGVA f. 7, op. 10, d. 1415, ll. 36–36ob.

26. Kuibyshev, circular letter, 9 May 1930; Smilga report to Shaposhnikov and Appoga, 28 May 1930, ll. 36–38ob.

27. Kuibyshev (Vesenkha) to Voroshilov and Uborevich (NKVM), 17 January 1930: RGVA f. 4, op. 1, d. 1159, l. 32; Unshlikht (NKVM) to Kuibyshev, 6 February 1930: ibid., l. 29; RZ STO protocol #42, pt. 3, 30 November 1929: ibid., l. 19.

28. Uborevich to RZ STO, 5 June 1930: RGVA f. 4, op. 1, d. 1249, l. 27; Unshlikht to STO, copy to Uborevich, 7 August 1930: ibid., ll. 75–75ob.

29. Uborevich to director MPU, 8 August 1930: RGVA f. 4, op. 1, d. 1375, l. 49.

30. RZ STO protocol #55, pt. 2, 10 August 1930: RGAE f. 3429, op. 16, d. 78, l. 52; Rudzutak (RZ STO) to Uborevich and Unshlikht, 12 August 1930: RGVA f. 4, op. 1, d. 1249, l. 74. Ian Rudzutak (1887–1938) was at this time deputy chair of the RZ STO.

31. Uborevich (Armaments Directorate) and Ianson (director of technical staff of Armaments Directorate) to Revvoensovet, 22 November 1930: RGVA f. 4, op. 1, d. 1369, ll. 1–2ob.

32. Ibid., ll. 3 ff.; excerpt from Revvoensovet protocol, 17 December 1930: RGVA f. 4, op. 1, d. 1369, l. 18.

33. Pavlunovskii (deputy chair of Vesenkha) and Martinovich (director of MPS) to Voroshilov, Stalin, and Molotov, 20 January 1931: RGVA f. 4, op. 14, d. 180, ll. 4–8.

34. Revvoensovet decision, 27 July 1931: RGVA f. 4, op. 18, d. 21, ll. 70–73. Pavlunovskii to Ordzhonikidze, 3 June 1933: RGAE f. 7297, op. 38, d. 170, ll. 12–28, cited in Simonov, *Voenno-promyshlennyi kompleks,* 87.

35. Stone, "Tukhachevskii in Leningrad," 1381–83.
36. Tukhachevskii to Molotov, September? 1931: RGVA f. 4, op. 14, d. 328, ll. 2–4.
37. STO decision 229ss, 9 November 1931: RGVA f. 4, op. 17, d. 64, l. 290.
38. Tukhachevskii report, 9? January 1932: RGVA f. 4, op. 14, d. 603, l. 33.
39. Martin Van Creveld, *Technology and War from 2000 B.C. to the Present* (New York: Free Press, 1989), 175; Martin Gilbert, *The First World War: A Complete History* (New York: Henry Holt, 1994), 465.
40. Efimov (staff) report on aviation, 30 April 1928: RGVA f. 7, op. 10, d. 1310, ll. 23–24; Ventsov (staff) report on tank production, 7 January 1930: ibid., d. 1124, l. 8. Compare meeting protocol under Uborevich, 2 January 1931: ibid., d. 1037, l. 92ob, which anticipates slightly lower levels of "irretrievable" losses for aircraft in wartime and, incidentally, expects 75 percent yearly losses at Soviet flight schools in peacetime.
41. Rykov to Central Committee, 30 November 1930: RGVA f. 33988, op. 3, d. 148, ll. 5–6.
42. Alan S. Milward, *War, Economy, and Society, 1939–1945* (Berkeley: University of California Press, 1977), 44–46.
43. Richard Pipes, *The Russian Revolution* (New York: Knopf, 1990), 206; Norman Stone, *The Eastern Front, 1914–1917* (London: Scribner's, 1975), 144–64. For a discussion of military industry during World War I, see also Simonov, *Voenno-promyshlennyi kompleks*, 50–55.
44. On the problem of control in the USSR, see E. A. Rees, *State Control in Soviet Russia* (London: Macmillan, 1987), chap. 1.
45. Postnikov? on attached agents at factories with mobilization assignments, 27 December 1927: RGVA f. 4, op. 1, d. 321, ll. 47–55.
46. Vesenkha commission report on mobilization readiness of Leningrad factories, February 1928: RGVA f. 7, op. 10, d. 1284, ll. 261–93.
47. Ibid., ll. 264–69; on identical later problems at Factory 42, see Ianson to Uborevich, undated [late 1930–early 1931]: RGVA f. 4, op. 1, d. 1252, l. 33.
48. Commission report, February 1928: RGVA f. 7, op. 10, d. 1284, ll. 276ob-78.
49. Ibid., ll. 288 ff.
50. Shaposhnikov to Postnikov on mobilization, 23 July 1928: ibid., l. 421.
51. Voroshilov to Molotov on difficulties of mobilization, 8 March? 1931: RGVA f. 4, op. 1, d. 1252, ll. 30–31.
52. RZ STO decision, 6 January 1930: RGAE f. 3429, op. 16, d. 77, ll. 56–58.
53. Circular from Pavlunovskii to factory directors, 25 May 1933: RGAE f. 7297, op. 41, d. 52, l. 41; Narkomtiazhprom order 68s (Ordzhonikidze), 29 May 1933: RGAE f. 7297, op. 38, d. 38, l. 18.
54. Excerpt from Revvoensovet meeting #10, pt. 3, 6 February 1929: RGVA f. 4, op. 1, d. 1074, l. 1; meeting protocol, February 1929: ibid., l. 3; Revvoensovet meeting, 6 March 1929, pt. 4: ibid., l. 5.
55. Politburo decision, 15 July 1929: GARF f. 5446, op. 55, d. 1966, l. 43.
56. Revvoensovet protocols #37, pt. 2, #39, pt. 2, and #41, pt. 1, 23 November, 13 December, and 23 December 1929: RGVA f. 4, op. 18, d. 15, ll. 252, 260, 295.
57. RZ STO meeting, 21 February 1930, pt. 2: RGVA f. 4, op. 17, d. 63, ll. 52–53; preparatory materials for this meeting: RGVA f. 4, op. 1, d. 1210, l. 62.
58. RZ STO decision, 10 March 1930: RGAE f. 3429, op. 16, d. 77, ll. 103–5.
59. 29 March 1930 meeting protocol: RGAE f. 3429, op. 16, d. 81, ll. 221–22.

60. Politburo protocol of 15 March 1930: RTsKhIDNI f. 17, op. 162, d. 8, l. 111; RZ STO decision of 16 March 1930: RGAE f. 3429, op. 16, d. 78, l. 118.

61. Various planning documents from March 1930: RGVA f. 7, op. 10, d. 1103, ll. 75–78, 80–81.

62. RZ STO protocol #53, pt. 1, 20 July 1930: RGVA f. 4, op. 17, d. 63, ll. 222–23; MPU meeting under Smilga and Shpektorov, 12 August 1930: RGAE f. 3429, op. 16, d. 103, l. 58.

63. RZ STO decision, 20 September 1930: RGVA f. 4, op. 17, d. 63, ll. 294–94ob; Politburo protocol #10, pt. 24/32, 20 September 1930 [protocol dated 25 September]: RTsKhIDNI f. 17, op. 162, d. 9, l. 39.

64. Smilga's report to the RZ STO, 3 October 1930: RGVA f. 7, op. 10, d. 1603, ll. 1–4.

65. Egorov to NKVM, 1 June 1931: RGVA f. 4, op. 14, d. 279, ll. 1–2.

66. Ianson to Uborevich, undated: RGVA f. 4, op. 1, d. 1252, l. 33; Smilga to RZ STO, 3 October 1930: RGVA f. 7, op. 10, d. 1603, l. 3; Egorov to NKVM, 1 June 1931: RGVA f. 4, op. 14, d. 279, l. 1.

67. Smilga to RZ STO, 1 November 1930: RGVA f. 7, op. 10, d. 1603, ll. 5–7.

68. Smilga to RZ STO, 3 October 1930: ibid., l. 2; Smilga to RZ STO, 1 November 1930: ibid., ll. 5ob-6; Ianson to Uborevich, undated: RGVA f. 4, op. 1, d. 1252, l. 33.

69. Smilga to RZ STO, 3 October 1930, l. 3; Ianson to Uborevich, undated: RGVA f. 4, op. 1, d. 1252, ll. 33–34.

70. The name of the fuse in the original document reads "UGT," but the *U* here in all likelihood represents the roman numeral five, by analogy with the 3GT and 4GT fuses discussed in I. I. Vernidub, *Na peredovoi linii tyla* (Moscow: TsNIINTIKPK, 1994), 93.

71. Ianson to Uborevich on results of drill mobilization of 1930, undated: RGVA f. 4, op. 1, d. 1252, ll. 32–34.

72. Vesenkha RSFSR to Sovnarkom RSFSR, February 1931: RGVA f. 7, op. 10, d. 1603, l. 9.

73. II Directorate of Staff to Directorate of Affairs, 28 December 1930: RGVA f. 4, op. 1, d. 1455, l. 6.

74. Isaev (Armaments Directorate) and Sadlutskii (technical staff) report on drill mobilization, 8 April 1931: RGVA f. 33988, op. 3, d. 182, ll. 84–99; Voroshilov to Molotov, 8 March? 1931: RGVA f. 4, op. 1, d. 1252, ll. 30–31.

75. Egorov report to NKVM on drill mobilization, 1 June 1931: RGVA f. 4, op. 14, d. 279, l. 1.

76. Isaev and Sadlutskii report, 8 April 1931, ll. 84–85; emphasis in original.

77. Egorov report, 1 June 1931, ll. 1–1ob.

78. Ibid., ll. 1–2.

79. Revvoensovet protocol #29, pt. 2, 13 August 1931: RGVA f. 4, op. 18, d. 21, l. 81.

8. THE MANCHURIAN CRISIS

1. Takehiko Yoshihashi, *Conspiracy at Mukden: The Rise of the Japanese Military* (New Haven, Conn.: Yale University Press, 1963); George Alexander Lensen, *The Damned Inheritance: The Soviet Union and the Manchurian Crises, 1924–1935* (Tallahassee, Fla.: Diplomatic Press, 1974), 181 ff.

2. On Lev Karakhan (1889–1937), see V. V. Sokolov, *Na boevykh postakh diplomaticheskogo fronta* (Moscow: Politizdat, 1983).

3. On the initial Soviet reactions, see Lensen, *Damned Inheritance*, 181 ff., and Jonathan Haslam, *Soviet Foreign Policy, 1930–1933* (London: Macmillan, 1983), 74; Karakhan memorandum of conversation with Hirota, 19 September 1931: *Dokumenty vneshnei politiki SSSR* (hereafter *DVP SSSR*) 1931, vol. 14, doc. 269, 529–30; Politburo protocols #63, pt. 6, and #64, pt. 32/2, 20 and 22 September 1931: ibid., ll. 9, 13; Litvinov memorandum of conversation with Hirota, 22 September 1931: ibid., doc. 271, 531–33.

4. Litvinov memorandum of conversation with Hirota, 2 October 1931: *DVP SSSR* 1931, vol. 14, doc. 288, 559–61; Lensen, *Damned Inheritance*, 188–90; Haslam, *Soviet Foreign Policy*, 77; Politburo protocol #67, pt. 25/3, 2 October 1931: RTsKhIDNI f. 17, op. 162, d. 11, l. 21.

5. Christopher Thorne, *The Limits of Foreign Policy: The West, the League, and the Far Eastern Crisis of 1931–1933* (London: Hamilton, 1972), 276.

6. Stalin to Voroshilov, 27 November 1931: RTsKhIDNI f. 74, op. 2, d. 38, ll. 52–53.

7. Haslam, *Soviet Foreign Policy*, 80, 84–93; Molotov speech to Central Ispolkom, 22 December 1931: *DVP SSSR* 1931, vol. 14, doc. 385, 725–28.

8. David J. Dallin, *The Rise of Russia in Asia* (New Haven, Conn.: Yale University Press, 1949), 244–48; David J. Dallin, *Soviet Russia and the Far East* (New Haven, Conn.: Yale University Press, 1948), 4–5. See also Max Beloff, *Foreign Policy of Soviet Russia, 1929–1941* (London: Oxford University Press, 1947), 76–77, and L. N. Kudashev, "Iz istorii bor'by sovetskogo gosudarstva za razvitie dobrososedskikh otnoshenii s Iaponiei (1925–1936gg)," *Istoriia SSSR* 5 (1960): 24–36.

9. Quoted in Christopher Andrew and Oleg Gordievsky, *KGB: The Inside Story* (New York: HarperCollins, 1990), 178–80.

10. Thorne, *Limits of Foreign Policy*, 133; Haslam, *Soviet Foreign Policy*, 81; on France, see Beloff, *Foreign Policy of Soviet Russia*, 77–78; Strang to Simon, 23 April 1932: *British Documents on Foreign Affairs* (Frederick, Md.: University Publications of America, 1984–1986), vol. 16, doc. 57, p. 74. John Erickson, *The Soviet High Command, 1918–41* (New York: St. Martin's, 1962), 335, and Isaac Deutscher, *Stalin: A Political Biography* (New York: Oxford University Press, 1966), 333; also see the comment in Deutscher on the Soviet Union's "passivity" in the face of Japanese provocation. Akira Iriye, *Origins of the Second World War in Asia and the Pacific* (New York: Longman, 1987), 13, pronounces the Soviet government "satisfied" with Japanese assurances in the early days of the crisis.

11. Aleksandr Antonovich Troianovskii (1882–1955) served as ambassador to Japan from 1927 to 1933.

12. Memorandum of conversation, Litvinov and Yoshizawa, 31 December 1931: *DVP SSSR* 1931, vol. 14, doc. 401, 746–48; Sokolov, *Na boevykh postakh*, 157; Haslam, *Soviet Foreign Policy*, 80; Lensen, *Damned Inheritance*, 337–41.

13. S. Isaev, "Meropriiatie KPSS po ukrepleniiu dal'nevostochnykh rubezhei v 1931–1941," *VIZh* 9 (1981): 64–69; Revvoensovet order #30, 28 February 1932: RTsKhIDNI f. 74, op. 2, d. 88, ll. 9–10; S. Zakharov, "Krasnoznamennomu Tikhookeanskomu flotu— 50 let," *VIZh* 4 (1982): 93–96; V. Dmitriev, "Stroitel'stvo sovetskogo podvodnogo flota v mezhvoennyi period," *VIZh* 10 (1974): 82–83.

14. Politburo protocol #90, pt. 71/35, 3 March 1932: RTsKhIDNI f. 17, op. 162, d. 11, ll. 196–97; Stalin to Voroshilov, 30 July 1932: RTsKhIDNI f. 74, op. 2, d. 38, l. 78.

15. STO decision 89/44 of 15 February 1932: RGAE f. 7297, op. 38, d. 3, l. 88. For other defense measures taken in the Far East, see Sally Stoecker, *Forging Stalin's Army* (Boulder, Colo.: Westview, 1998), 70 ff.

16. Politburo protocol, #82 pts. 32 and 87/49, 8 January 1932: RTsKhIDNI f. 17, op. 3, d. 867, ll. 10, 20.

17. Haslam, *Soviet Foreign Policy,* 83; E. A. Rees, *Stalinism and Soviet Rail Transport, 1928–1941* (New York: St. Martin's, 1995), 63–64; STO (Kuibyshev) decision 1072/323ss, 29 August 1932: RGAE f. 4372, op. 91, d. 1000, ll. 69–74.

18. R. W. Davies, *Crisis and Progress in the Soviet Economy* (London: Macmillan, 1996), 111–15.

19. Excerpt from Defense Commission meeting, 12 November 1931: RGAE f. 3429, op. 16, d. 198, l. 68; TsKK-RKI resolution, 14 January 1932: RGAE f. 7297, op. 41, d. 9, ll. 5–6.

20. Meeting protocol, 5 June 1932: RGAE f. 3429, op. 16, d. 172, ll. 91–92; Revvoensovet protocol, 14 June 1931: RGVA f. 4, op. 18, d. 20, ll. 315–16. The precise breakdown of the tank order was 1,500 Vickers light tanks, 600 Christie fast tanks, and 1,500 tankettes.

21. Defense Commission protocol #12, 1 August 1931: RGVA f. 4, op. 17, d. 64, l. 59; protocols of Kuibyshev's commission, 15 August and 6 September 1931: RGVA f. 4, op. 14, d. 417, ll. 29, 31 ff.

22. Efimov report to NKVM, October 1931: RGVA f. 33988, op. 3, d. 209, ll. 189–211. Efimov's calculations cover artillery (including firearms and ammunition), chemical, engineering, and communications equipment. See also Efimov to Voroshilov on 1932 order, 5 October 1931: RGVA f. 4, op. 14, d. 329, ll. 1–24.

23. Revvoensovet protocol #32, pt. 1, 7 October 1931: RGVA f. 4, op. 14, d. 329, l. 25, also ibid., op. 18, d. 21, l. 135.

24. Defense Commission protocol #13, pt. 2, 12 October 1931: RGVA f. 4, op. 17, d. 64, l. 67. This decision stipulated that the 1932 program would include 3,000 tanks and 6,000 aircraft engines. See also Defense Commission decision, 9 November 1931: ibid., l. 71.

25. See Efimov's order report comparing 1932 and 1931 Artillery Directorate orders in physical and financial terms, October 1931: RGVA f. 33988, op. 3, d. 209, ll. 189–211.

26. Table 17, column 1, comes from protocols of Kuibyshev's commission, 15 August and 6 September 1931: RGVA f. 4, op. 417, ll. 29, 31 ff. Columns 2–4 are from Egorov letter to Voroshilov on 1932 and 1933 budgets, 23 May 1932: RGVA f. 4, op. 14, d. 603, l. 31.

27. I could not locate a single decree ordering the additional spending. Instead, the documents I found order an increase in the production of specific items or represent after-the-fact aggregate spending totals.

28. Politburo protocols #83, pt. 1, 14 January 1932; #85, pt. 4, 23 January 1932; and #87, pt. 8, 8 February 1932: RTsKhIDNI f. 17, op. 3, d. 868, l. 1; d. 869, l. 2; and d. 871, l. 3.

29. Stalin to Tukhachevskii, copy to Voroshilov, 7 May 1932: RTsKhIDNI f. 74, op. 2, d. 38, ll. 56–57.

30. V. Z. Drobyzhev, *Glavnyi shtab sotsialisticheskoi promyshlennosti* (Moscow: Mysl', 1966) 171–72; see also Don K. Rowney, "The Scope, Authority, and Personnel of

the New Industrial Commissariats in Historical Context," in *Social Dimensions of Soviet Industrialization*, ed. William Rosenberg and Lewis Siegelbaum (Bloomington: Indiana University Press, 1993), 134–36; Davies, *Crisis and Progress*, 204–9.

31. RGAE f. 7297, op. 41, introduction to *opis'* directory; R. W. Davies, *Soviet Economy in Turmoil, 1929–1930* (London: Macmillan, 1989), 241, 243. See also F. G. Seiranian, *Nadezhneishii voennyi rabotnik: Ocherk o voenno-organizatorskoi deiatel'nosti G. K. Ordzhonikidze* (Moscow: Voenizdat, 1989), 138. The GVMU would survive until 1936, when it was split into two main directorates—for military industry and ammunition. See N. S. Simonov, *Voenno-promyshlennyi kompleks SSSR* (Moscow: Rosspen, 1996), 39.

32. Rees, *Stalinism and Rail Transport*, 44; Politburo protocol #89, pt. 80/48, 23 February 1932: RTsKhIDNI f. 17, op. 3, d. 873, ll. 14, 34.

33. Politburo protocol #83, pt. 17/10, 12 January 1932: RTsKhIDNI f. 17, op. 3, d. 868, l. 7.

34. Politburo protocol #108, pt. 11, 5 December 1929: RTsKhIDNI f. 17, op. 162, d. 8, ll. 13, 18–19; see also draft decision with note on acceptance by Politburo without alteration: RGVA f. 31811, op. 1, d. 1, ll. 52–53. For Voroshilov's comments, see the stenogram of the January 1933 TsK/TsKK plenum: RTsKhIDNI f. 17, op. 2, d. 514, pt. 1, l. 125.

35. A. C. Sutton, *Western Technology and Soviet Economic Development, 1930–1945* (Stanford, Calif.: Hoover Institution Press, 1971), 240–42. On tanks, Sutton should be used with care: many of the details are inaccurate. See also George F. Hofmann, "Doctrine, Tank Technology, and Execution: I. A. Khalepskii and the Red Army's Fulfillment of Deep Offensive Operations," *Journal of Slavic Military Studies* 9 (1996): 283–334, and Stoecker, *Forging Stalin's Army*, 115–28.

36. Defense Commission protocols #1 and #2, 10 and 19 January 1932: RGVA f. 4, op. 17, d. 76, l. 10. The 10,000-tank order broke down as 2,000 BT (Christie) tanks, 3,000 T-26 (Vickers) tanks, and 5,000 T-27 (Carden-Lloyd) tankettes.

37. Defense Commission protocol #3, 5 February 1932: RGVA f. 4, op. 17, d. 76, l. 21; Narkomtiazhprom order # 27ss, 10 February 1932: RGAE f. 7297, op. 38, d. 4, ll. 265–69.

38. Martinovich to Piatakov, 10 August 1932: RGAE f. 7297, op. 41, d. 25, l. 41; see also production chart on T-26: ibid., l. 53; Narkomtiazhprom order #27ss, 10 February 1932: RGAE f. 7297, op. 38, d. 4, ll. 265–69.

39. Lensen, *Damned Inheritance*, 204–6; "Sovetskii Soiuz i Iaponiia," *Izvestiia*, 4 March 1932, 1.

40. Lensen, *Damned Inheritance*, 225–26; Politburo protocol #94, pt. 32/22, and app. 1, 26 March 1932: RTsKhIDNI f. 17, op. 162, d. 12, ll. 36, 68.

41. Lensen, *Damned Inheritance*, 225; Politburo protocol #96, pt. 17g, 16 April 1932: RTsKhIDNI f. 17, op. 162, d. 12, l. 94; Politburo protocol #97, pt. 24/1, 17 April 1932: ibid., ll. 107–8. On the American card, see Stalin's remarks to this effect to Voroshilov, 12 June 1932: RTsKhIDNI f. 74, op. 2, d. 38, l. 66.

42. On Ordzhonikidze's style, see his directives of 17 March 1932 and Narkomtiazhprom order #86s, 13 April 1932: RGAE f. 7297, op. 38, d. 5, ll. 94–95, 102–3. Defense Commission protocol, 19 March 1932: RGVA f. 4, op. 17, d. 76, l. 47; protocol of meeting under Davydov, deputy director of Technical Directorate of Motorization and Mechanization Directorate, 9 April 1932: RGVA f. 4, op. 14, d. 586, l. 32. Pavlunovskii report to Voroshilov, October 1932: RGAE f. 7297, op. 41, d. 25, l. 51.

43. On Putilovets, see R. W. Davies "Soviet Defence Industries," in *Economy and Society in Russia and the Soviet Union, 1860–1930*, ed. Linda Edmondson and Peter Waldron, (New York: St. Martin's, 1992), 264. Defense Commission protocol #14, 25 May 1932: RGVA f. 4, op. 17, d. 76, l. 68. The Soviet army expected to use tracked tractors on a large scale for hauling artillery in wartime. Politburo protocol #103, pt. 73/27, decision of 6 June 1932: RTsKhIDNI f. 17, op. 162, d. 12, l. 175; also available in *Stalinskoe Politburo v 30–e gody* (Moscow: Airo-XX, 1995), doc. 36, 56.

44. Defense Commission protocol, 22 June 1932: RGVA f. 4, op. 17, d. 76, l. 79.

45. Stalin to Voroshilov, 24 June 1932: RTsKhIDNI f. 74, op. 2, d. 38, l. 72; stenogram of Unshlikht meeting, 10 August 1932: RGAE f. 4372, op. 91, d. 1050, l. 161. Wilhelmine Germany provides another example of impossible production targets as a motivational tool, but in this case for a state actually at war. See William McNeill, *The Pursuit of Power* (Chicago: University of Chicago Press, 1982), 338.

46. Politburo protocol #78, pt. 63/35, 1 December 1931: RTsKhIDNI f. 17, op. 162, d. 11, l. 74; Politburo protocol #87, pt. 55/18, 8 February 1932: ibid., l. 175; Politburo protocol #94, pt. 76/46, 1 April 1932: ibid., d. 12, l. 39.

47. Tukhachevskii to Khalepskii, 8 February 1932: RGVA f. 33988, op. 3, d. 227, l. 18. His mechanized brigades would have 120 T-26s, 38 BTs, and 50 T-27s; tank battalions attached to divisions would include 10 T-26s and 10 T-27s. Regimental tank battalions would have 10 T-18s and 10 T-27s. The 15,000 total number of tanks would be made up of 5,000 T-26s, 6,000 T-27s, 3,000 BTs, and 1,000 T-18s.

48. Voroshilov to Ordzhonikidze, 28 June 1932: RGAE f. 7297, op. 38, d. 3, l. 29.

49. On G. L. Piatakov, see Andrea Graziosi, "G. L. Piatakov (1890–1937): A Mirror of Soviet History," *Harvard Ukrainian Studies* 16 (1992): 102–66.

50. Politburo protocols, #115 and #116: RTsKhIDNI f. 17, op. 3, d. 899, l. 3, and d. 900, l. 37; see also A. Erlikh and V. Solov'ev, "Stal' dlia traktorov i avtomobilei," *Pravda*, 18 July 1932, 2, on problems at Red October.

51. Politburo protocol #88, decisions of 10 and 16 February 1932: RTsKhIDNI f. 17, op. 162, d. 11, ll. 180, 183; protocol #91, decision of 8 March 1932: ibid., d. 12, l. 4; Politburo protocol # 126, pt. 48/20, 16 December 1932 [decision of 15 December]: ibid., d. 14, l. 39. The four sent were I. N. Dubovii, V. M. Primakov, M. K. Levandovskii, and S. M. Uritskii.

52. Revvoensovet decision, 22 July 1932: RGVA f. 4, op. 14, d. 512, l. 175.

53. Ordzhonikidze report to Defense Commission on production of T-26, 21 September 1932: RGAE f. 7297, op. 41, d. 25, ll. 56–57, 61.

54. On Sovnarkom, see Davies, *Crisis and Progress*, 115. Central Committee protocol #114, pt. 29, 1 September 1932: RTsKhIDNI f. 17, op. 162, d. 13, l. 84; Politburo protocol #116, pt. 30, decision of 16 September 1932, in *Stalinskoe Politburo*, doc. 23, 39.

55. Martinovich report to Piatakov, 10 August 1932: RGAE f. 7297, op. 41, d. 25, ll. 41–42; Ordzhonikidze on tank production, 21 September 1932: ibid., ll. 62–63; Pavlunovskii to Voroshilov, report on tank production, October 1932: ibid., ll. 49–50.

56. Ordzhonikidze's report to Defense Commission, 21 September 1932: RGAE f. 7297, op. 41, d. 25, ll. 54–57; Martinovich to Piatakov, 10 August 1932: ibid., l. 41; Graziosi, "G. L. Piatakov," argues that Piatakov was the power behind the throne in Soviet industry and responsible for Ordzhonikidze's successes. Although Piatakov's experience

in industry and finance was certainly greater than Ordzhonikidze's, one of Ordzhonikidze's assets seems to have been a talent for leadership and motivation.

57. Pavlunovskii to Voroshilov, report on tank production, October 1932: RGAE f. 7297, op. 41, d. 25, ll. 48–52; also ibid., d. 8, ll. 97–101; Politburo protocols #83, pt. 24/17, 14 January 1932, #92, pt. 79/48, 16 March 1932, and #105, pt. 106/48, 23 June 1932: RTsKhIDNI f. 17, op. 162, d. 11, l. 122, and d. 12, ll. 10, 196. The Liberty motor, although intended for use in aircraft, could also be adapted for tanks with some loss of efficiency.

58. Gai (Economic Directorate of OGPU) to Martinovich (GVMU) on #2 VATO, 10 August 1932: RGAE f. 7297, op. 41, d. 25, l. 47.

59. Unshlikht to Molotov, 27 November 1931: RGAE f. 4372, op. 91, d. 953, l. 4. Case-hardening was a process by which carbon and nitrogen atoms were introduced to the steel's surface at high temperatures, hardening the surface and making it more impact resistant while the interior remained softer and more ductile, improving its armor performance dramatically. As one Soviet source described the process used at Red October on tractor parts, the parts to be case-hardened were covered with a mixture of carbon (charcoal) and carbonates (soda or potash), then heated to a temperature of 600 to 900 degrees Celsius for two and a half hours (N. A. Mokienko, *Pervenets industrializatsii: Stalingradskii traktornyi zavod* [Moscow: Gos. Nauk.-Tekh. Izdat., 1931], 49).

60. Ordzhonikidze to Defense Commission, 21 September 1932: RGAE f. 7297, op. 41, d. 25, ll. 61–62; Pavlunovskii to Voroshilov, report on tank production, October 1932: ibid., ll. 49–50.

61. Piatakov to Molotov, 8 August 1932: RGAE f. 7297, op. 41, d. 9, ll. 43–44; also October report, ibid., d. 8, l. 99; Pavlunovskii to Voroshilov, report on tank production, October 1932: ibid., d. 25, ll. 48–52; Gai to Ordzhonikidze on Podol'sk Cracking, 10 August 1932: ibid., l. 46.

62. Pavlunovskii to Voroshilov, "Report on Fulfillment of Program for Tanks as of 1 October 1932," early October 1932: ibid., ll. 48–52.

63. Defense Commission protocol #21, 4 October 1932: RGVA f. 4, op. 17, d. 76, l. 140.

64. Defense Commission protocol #22, pt. 1, 19 October 1932: ibid., l. 144.

65. Defense Commission protocol #22, pt. 1, 19 October 1932: ibid. The precise order was for 100 T-36s *(sic)*, 300 T-28s, 1,500 BTs, 2,500 T-26s, 2,000 T-37s, and 600 T-27s, for a total of 7,000. See also N. Kuibyshev (Rabkrin) to Molotov and Voroshilov, 13 February 1933: RGVA f. 4, op. 14, d. 717, ll. 16–17.

66. See Defense Commission protocol #22, pt. 1, 19 October 1932: RGVA f. 4, op. 17, d. 76, ll. 144–45; also Politburo protocol: RTsKhIDNI f. 17, op. 3, d. 903, l. 2; Defense Commission decision, 15 November 1932: RGVA f. 4, op. 17, d. 76, l. 158. Even the list of factories in Spetsmashtrest was intended to be secret; see NKTP order 243s, 11 December 1932: RGAE f. 7297, op. 38, d. 5, l. 246.

67. Defense Commission protocol #24, 4 December 1932: RGVA f. 4, op. 17, d. 76, l. 169; draft report "Fulfillment of the Defense Commission–Confirmed Tank Program for 1932" from Voroshilov to Molotov, January 1933: RGVA f. 4, op. 14, d. 717, ll. 9–10.

68. Pavlunovskii to Voroshilov, 2 January 1933: RGVA f. 4, op. 14, d. 717, ll. 11–12. The final breakdown of delivered tanks was 1,031 T-26s, 396 BTs, and 1,435 tankettes. See also Egorov's report, 26 January 1933: ibid., d. 896, l. 7. Draft report from Voroshilov to Molotov on fulfillment of tank program over 1932, January 1933: ibid., d. 717, ll. 9–

10. The breakdown of tanks delivered to the Red Army came to 911 T-26s, 239 BTs, and 1,435 T-27s.

69. Consistent figures on aircraft orders and production are particularly difficult to come by. These figures are drawn from a 22 January 1934 report on aircraft production from 1930–1933: RGVA f. 4, op. 14, d. 1027, ll. 13–17. Compare the slightly different 19 January 1931 report on 1930 production: ibid., d. 391, l. 6. *Samoletostroenie v SSSR (1917–1945)* (Moscow: TsAGI, 1992), vol. 1, 432–35, gives much higher production figures, probably by including planes ordered but not actually built in their target years, as well as planes produced but not accepted by military quality control.

70. STO decision 8ss, 11 January 1932: RGVA d. 4, op. 17, d. 76, l. 200.

71. Defense Commission protocol #16, 7 December 1931: RGVA f. 4, op. 17, d. 64, l. 78; STO decision #157/64ss, 2 March 1932: ibid., d. 76, l. 256; Defense Commission protocols #12, 19 April 1932, #14, 25 May 1932, and #18, 25 July 1932: ibid., d. 76, ll. 55, 70, and 95. On quality control, see Botner to Molotov, 21 August 1932: RGAE f. 4372, op. 91, d. 1050, ll. 182–84.

72. STO decision 1528/435ss, 5 December 1932: RGVA f. 33988, op. 3, d. 231, l. 31.

73. Martinovich to Piatakov, August 1932: RGAE f. 7297, op. 41, d. 9, ll. 121–23; Martinovich to Belov (Cadres Sector of Central Committee), September? 1932: ibid., ll. 65–66; Botner (Defense Sector of Gosplan) to Molotov, 21 August 1932: RGAE f. 4372, op. 91, d. 1050, ll. 179–85.

74. Briefing paper on artillery production over 1932: RGAE f. 7297, op. 38, d. 170, l. 115; Pavlunovskii to Ordzhonikidze on state of artillery production, May? 1933: ibid., l. 21; also ibid., op. 41, d. 8, l. 95.

75. 1932 retrospective report, Spetsmashtrest: RGAE f. 7297, op. 41, d. 21, l. 188. Spetsmashtrest did not exist at the beginning of 1932, so its retrospective performance was determined by aggregating the performance of its individual constituent factories. These totals, being based on monetary figures and not on physical units, present some difficulties of interpretation, but the overall pattern is clear.

76. Table 18 represents gross production of military production, not civil or interfactory orders. These particular figures are aggregated from separate figures for old and new types of production (27 August 1933 report on 1932 results: RGAE f. 4372, op. 91, d. 1198, ll. 177–89). Note the respectable performance of tank-manufacturing Spetsmashtrest in comparison to its planning production, indicating that the targets used are reduced ones, not the targets at their peak 10,000-tank level.

77. 1932 retrospective report, Artillery-Arsenal Association: RGAE f. 7297, op. 41, d. 21, ll. 32–34. Table 19 represents gross production of military, civil, and interfactory orders. The "final plan" is the production schedule agreed on at the beginning of 1931; the "corrected plan" represents the lower targets conceded to industry at the end of 1932. Columns 1–4 come from report on plan fulfillment, 1 January 1933: RGAE f. 4372, op. 91, d. 1050, l. 6. Column 5 comes from retrospective chart of military production, 14 July 1933: RGAE f. 4372, op. 91, d. 1198, ll. 42, 84–86.

78. Robert Tucker, *Stalin in Power* (New York: Norton, 1990), 204–22; Haslam, *Soviet Foreign Policy,* 84; Rees, *Stalinism and Rail Transport,* 40–56, 63–64. On food in Leningrad, see Lesley A. Rimmel, "Another Kind of Fear: The Kirov Murder and the End of Bread Rationing in Leningrad," *SR* 56 (1997): 481–99.

79. Egorov to Voroshilov, 31 August 1932: RGVA f. 4, op. 14, d. 660, ll. 1–3.

80. *Ocherk istorii Khar'kovskogo traktornogo zavoda im. Ordzhonikidze, 1931–1961* (Khar'kov: Khar'kovskoe Kn. Izdat., 1962), 36; Politburo protocols #98, pt. 38/14, and #100, pt. 3, 4 and 16 May 1932: RTsKhIDNI f. 17, op. 3, d. 882 and 884, ll. 1, 18; *Istoriia Khar'kovskogo traktornogo zavoda im. Ordzhonikidze: Sbornik dokumentov i materialov* (Khar'kov: Khar'kovskoe Kn. Izdat., 1960), vol. 1, doc. 86, 173–77.

81. *Opyt peredovogo zavoda* (Stalingrad: Kraev. Gos. Izdat., 1934), 22–23.

82. Orest Subtelny, *Ukraine: A History,* 2d ed. (Toronto: University of Toronto Press, 1994), 416. The historiography of the famine is extensive and highly polarized. For arguments attributing the famine to incompetence, climate, and design, respectively, see W. E. D. Allen, *The Ukraine: A History* (New York: Russell and Russell, 1940 [1963]), 329; Mark B. Tauger, "The 1932 Harvest and the Famine of 1933," *SR* 50 (1991): 70–89; and Robert Conquest, *The Harvest of Sorrow: Soviet Collectivization and the Terror-Famine* (London: Hutchinson, 1986).

83. Dana G. Darymple, "The Soviet Famine of 1932–1934," *SS* 15 (1964): 273.

84. Stalin and Molotov circular letter, 31 March 1932: RGAE f. 7297, op. 41, d. 33, ll. 23–24.

85. Stalin to Central Committee and Central Control Commission plenum, 7 January 1933, in *Sochineniia* (Moscow: Politizdat, 1946–1949), vol. 13, 182–83.

86. Stalin's address to the Central Committee plenum, 7 January 1933: RTsKhIDNI f. 17, op. 2, d. 514, pt. 1, l. 9.

87. Davies, "Soviet Defence Industries," 266; Davies argues this point at great length in *Crisis and Progress;* see esp. 176.

88. Molotov to Central Committee plenum, 8 January 1933: RTsKhIDNI f. 17, op. 2, d. 514, pt. 1, l. 27.

89. Ordzhonikidze speech to plenum, 10 January 1933: RTsKhIDNI f. 17, op. 2, d. 514, pt. 1, l. 107.

90. Sergei Kirov, 17 January 1933 speech to Leningrad party active, in *Izbrannye stat'i i rechi, 1918–1934* (Moscow: Politizdat, 1944), 202–3. I am grateful to Julian Cooper for this reference.

91. Defense Commission protocol #14, 25 May 1932: RGVA f. 4, op. 17, d. 76, l. 70; Defense Commission protocol #23, 14 November 1932: ibid., l. 150; STO decision 1528/435ss, 5 December 1932: RGVA f. 33988, op. 3, d. 231, l. 31.

92. Lensen, *Damned Inheritance,* 344–50.

93. Compare the nonpurge of 1932–1933 with Roberta Manning's description of the Great Purges as a partial result of economic crisis ("The Soviet Economic Crisis of 1936–1940 and the Great Purges," in *Stalinist Terror: New Perspectives,* ed. J. Arch Getty and Roberta Manning [New York: Cambridge University Press, 1993], 116–41). Oleg Khlevniuk, *1937–i: Stalin, NKVD i sovetskoe obshchestvo* (Moscow: Respublika, 1992) suggests that Stalin in 1937 imagined that the conspiracy against him dated back to this period: 1932–1933.

CONCLUSION

1. "Results of Industry's Defense Preparations in the Period of the First Five-Year Plan," 12 October 1932: RGVA f. 4, op. 14, d. 1051, ll. 15 ff.; also found in RGAE f. 4372, op. 91, d. 1268, ll. 90 ff.

2. Ibid., ll. 17–21ob.

3. "Theses of Report on Results of Defense Preparation of Industry in the First Five-Year Plan," 31 October 1932: RGVA f. 4, op. 14, d. 1051, ll. 10–11; also found at RGAE f. 4372, op. 91, d. 1268, ll. 105–9.

4. Ibid., ll. 10–14.

5. Botner report on capital investment in military industry over the First Five-Year Plan, 4 January 1933: RGVA f. 4, op. 14, d. 1051, l. 5.

6. Note on quality of arms produced over First Five-Year Plan, 14 January 1933: RGAE f. 7297, op. 38, d. 170, ll. 1–5.

7. Calculated from trust and factory reports on operations in 1932 included in RGAE f. 7297, op. 41, d. 29.

8. R. W. Davies, "Soviet Military Expenditure and the Armaments Industry," *EAS* 45 (1993), 600–602.

9. Report on First Five-Year Plan, RGVA f. 4, op. 14, d. 1051, l. 2; see also this book's appendix 1.

10. *XVII s"ezd Vsesoiuznoi kommunisticheskoi partii (b): Stenograficheskii otchet* (Moscow: Partizdat, 1934), 5, 8, 13.

11. Ordzhonikidze, in ibid., 167, 178.

12. Bukharin, in ibid., 127.

13. See Mark Harrison and R. W. Davies, "The Soviet Military-Economic Effort during the Second Five-Year Plan (1933–1937)," *EAS* 49, no. 3 (1997): 369–406, esp. 371, 375, 386. Table 20 figures complied from ibid.; *Samoletostroenie v SSSR (1917–1945)* (Moscow: TsAGI, 1992), 432–35; Julian Cooper, *Defence Production and the Soviet Economy, 1929–1941* (Birmingham: CREES, 1976); *Istoriia vtoroi mirovoi voiny* (Moscow: Voenizdat, 1973), vol. 1, 214, and vol. 2, 191; Mark Harrison, *Soviet Planning in Peace and War, 1938–45* (Cambridge: Cambridge University Press, 1985), 8; archival document on fulfillment of military orders in 1931 and 1932: RGAE f. 7297, op. 41, d. 29, ll. 1–6; and N. S. Simonov, *Voenno-promyshlennyi kompleks SSSR* (Moscow: Rosspen, 1996) 84, 91–92, 112.

14. G. K. Zhukov, *Vospominaniia i razmyshleniia,* corr. ed. (Moscow: Novosti, 1992), vol. 1, 179.

15. Klaus Reinhardt, *Moscow: The Turning Point: The Failure of Hitler's Strategy in the Winter of 1941–42* (Oxford: Berg, 1992), x, 367–68; Earl F. Ziemke and Magna E. Bauer, *Moscow to Stalingrad: Decision in the East* (Washington, D.C.: Center for Military History, 1987), 514.

16. Jerry Hough and Merle Fainsod, *How the Soviet Union Is Governed* (Cambridge, Mass.: Harvard University Press, 1982), 155.

17. Holland Hunter, "The New Tasks of Soviet Planning in the Thirties," in *Marxism, Central Planning, and the Soviet Economy,* ed. Padma Desai (Cambridge, Mass.: MIT Press, 1983), 194.

18. Holland Hunter and Janusz Szyrmer, *Faulty Foundations: Soviet Economic Policies, 1928–1940* (Princeton, N.J.: Princeton University Press, 1992), 231–54, esp. 248.

19. Ibid., 138.

20. Davies, "Soviet Military Expenditure," 593–94; appendix 1.

21. I. M. Sukhomlin, *Stroitel'stvo bronetankovykh voisk i razvitie teorii ikh primeneniia v predvoennye gody* (Moscow: Voen. Pol. Ak., 1976), 11–13; Walter Dunn, *The Soviet Economy and the Red Army, 1930–1945* (Westport, Conn.: Praeger, 1995), 21; see also William McNeill, *The Pursuit of Power* (Chicago: University of Chicago Press, 1982), 350–51.

Index

Transportation, People's Commissariat of,
    32, 77, 99, 115, 158, 188, 205
Trans-Siberian Railway, 185, 188
Treidub, 197
Tret'iakov, P., 74
Troianovskii, Aleksandr, 187, 195, 209
Trotsky, Leon, 4, 14–16, 27, 47, 95
Tsiurupa, Aleksandr, 48
Tukhachevskii, Mikhail, 4, 18, 39, 48–50,
    52–54, 69, 107, 111, 145, 157, 165,
    226
  as Armaments Director, 131–32, 168–
    70, 190–91, 193, 197
  1928 transfer to Leningrad Military
    District, 86–87
  on preventive war and 1926–27 budget,
    22–24
  radical rearmament proposals, 163–64,
    192
Tula Cartridge Factory, 30
Tula Firearms Works, 29, 31, 52, 74–75,
    101, 140, 176
  Scientific-Technical Bureau, 74
Turkey, 28

Uborevich, Ieronim, 78, 103, 226
  as Armaments Director, 131–33, 140–
    41, 146, 148, 154, 162–68, 170,
    180
  background, 131–32
Uchida, Kosai, 209
Uglanov, Nikolai, 120
Ukraine, 16, 178
UMM. See Motorization and
    Mechanization Directorate
United Kingdom, 10–11, 46, 93–94, 172,
    187
United States, 10–11, 21, 72, 81, 172,
    193
Unshlikht, Iosif, 30–31, 51, 55–56, 65,
    74, 78, 80, 86, 91, 93–94, 104–5,
    107, 123, 141, 143, 145, 148–49,
    154, 165, 196, 199, 226
Urals, 113, 143, 166
Uryvaev, Mikhail, 71, 82, 104–5, 141,
    145, 161, 164, 227
Uspenskii, Boris, 74

Venetskii, 141
Ventsov, Semen I., 27, 49–50, 55, 135,
    152, 227
Verkhne-Turynskii Factory, 177
Vesenkha (VSNKh, Supreme Council of
    the National Economy), 4, 6, 20, 32–
    33, 38, 45, 47–49, 59–62, 86, 90,
    99–101, 103, 105, 107, 123, 125,
    128, 145, 148–58, 160–70, 188, 190,
    192–93, 199, 222
  and drafting of First Five-Year Plan,
    115, 118–21
  Dzerzhinskii on place of defense in,
    26–29
  Main Economic Directorate, 26–27
  military criticism of, 40–42
  mobilization readiness of, 173–79,
    181–82
  plan for military industry, 49–53, 95–
    99, 132–33
  Presidium, 58, 71, 140–41
  reforms of, 137–41, 192
  on Soviet economy at war, 55–59
  Standing Planning Conference, 120
  takeover by Ordzhonikidze, 159–61
  wrecking in, 73–74, 76–83
Vickers, 193
Vladimirskii, Mikhail, 48–49, 87, 227
Voenprom, 24–25, 29–33, 37, 68, 127
Voikov, P., 46
Voroshilov, Kliment, 20, 28, 31–32, 34,
    54, 60, 97–98, 100–102, 104, 133–
    34, 140–41, 157–58, 161, 164, 175,
    181, 185–88, 193, 197, 200–201,
    205, 208, 227
  and budget disputes, 22, 62, 91, 93–95,
    145–47
  on First Five-Year Plan, 111, 118–19,
    122–23
  as People's Commissar for Military and
    Naval Affairs, 21
  and Red Army's five-year plan, 86– 90
  and reorganization of Red Army, 128–
    31
  and Right Opposition, 7, 11, 93–95
  on war scare and defense policy, 47–49
  and wrecking, 68, 70, 74, 80, 83